M000290056

Zion's Final Destiny

ZION'S FINAL DESTINY

The Development of the
Book of Isaiah

A REASSESSMENT OF ISAIAH 36–39

Christopher R. Seitz

FORTRESS PRESS　　　　MINNEAPOLIS

ZION'S FINAL DESTINY
The Development of the Book of Isaiah

Copyright © 1991 Augsburg Fortress. All rights reserved. Except for brief quotations in critical articles or reviews, no part of this book may be reproduced in any manner without prior written permission from the publisher. Write to: Permissions, Augsburg Fortress, 426 S. Fifth St., Box 1209, Minneapolis, MN 55440.

Scripture quotations, unless otherwise noted, are from the New Revised Standard Version of the Bible, copyright © 1989 by the Division of Christian Education of the National Council of the Churches of Christ in the United States of America.

Cover design by Jim Gerhard
Interior design by Jim Gerhard

Library of Congress Cataloging-in-Publication Data

Seitz, Christopher R.
    Zion's final destiny : the development of the Book of Isaiah : a
reassessment of Isaiah 36–39 / Christopher R. Seitz
        p.   cm.
    Includes bibliographical references and indexes.
    ISBN 0-8006-2504-8 (alk. paper)
    1. Bible. O.T. Isaiah—Criticism, Redaction. 2. Bible. O.T.
Isaiah XXXVI–XXXIX—Criticism, interpretation, etc. I. Title.
BS1515.2.S46   1991
224'.1066—dc20   91-33994
                                                                CIP

The paper used in this publication meets the minimum requirements of American National Standard for Information Sciences—Permanence of Paper for Printed Library Materials, ANSI Z329.48–1984.

Manufactured in the U.S.A.   AF 1-2504

95   94   93   92   91   1   2   3   4   5   6   7   8   9   10

To Honored Teachers

Brevard S. Childs
Klaus Baltzer

and

In Memory of
John A. Hollar

C O N T E N T S

Preface   ix

Abbreviations   xi

1. **Two Independent Isaiahs**   1

    The Centennial of Duhm's Isaiah   1

      Historical vs. Editorial Independence in the Book of Isaiah

      The Emerging Identity of Second Isaiah, Prophet and Book

      Summary

    Isaiah in the Modern Period: The Uneven Duhm Legacy   14

      The Book of Isaiah as Three Independent Books

      Redactional Approaches: Type A

      Redactional Approaches: Type B

    Beyond Duhm: Second Isaiah within the Book of Isaiah   30

    Summary and Proposal   33

2. **"Former Things"—The Scope and Rationale of Proto-Isaiah**   37

    Isa 36–39: The Nature of the Problem   37

    The Puzzle of Isaiah's Growth   39

    Prospective   45

3. **No Escape for a Blasphemer (Isaiah 36–37)**   47

    Introduction   47

    The Priority of Kings   48

    The Status of 2 Kgs 18:14–16—Annals Notice or
    Editorial Supplement?   51

    Account A and the Annals of Sennacherib   61

    Isa 36–37 ("Account B"): A Unified Narrative?   66

    King Hezekiah's Foreign Alliances (Isa 36–37, 38)   72

    King Hezekiah's Foreign Alliances (Isa 1–35˚)   75

    The Literary Integrity of "Account B"   81

The Prayer of Hezekiah (Isa 37:14–20 // 2 Kgs 19:14–19)
Further Additions in Isa 37:21–38 (2 Kgs 19:20–37)
Conclusions
Matters of Function, Date, and Provenance   96
The Hezekiah-Isaiah Narratives: Conclusions   116

4. **The Destiny of Zion (701 and 587 B.C.E.)**   **119**
The Puzzle of Isaiah's Growth Reconsidered   119
The Correlation of 701 and 587 Events   123
Alternative Correlation (701 and 587)   127
Method: Hardmeier's Narrative Analysis   135
A Question of Context: Account A Reconsidered   141
Conclusions: The Destiny of Zion (701 and 587)   146

5. **Zion-King: Death Sentence Diverted (Isaiah 38)**   **149**
Preliminary Matters: Isa 38 in Its Literary Context   149
Hezekiah's Idealization   153
Isa 38: Analysis   162
Divergence
Isa 38:21–22
The Psalm of Hezekiah (38:9–20)
Tradition-History: An Alternative Reconstruction   172
A Sick City   176
Final Remarks: 2 Kgs 20:12–19 and Isa 39:1–8   182

**Conclusion: The Hezekiah-Isaiah Narratives and
the Growth of the Book of Isaiah**   **193**
Retrospect   193
Implications: First Isaiah   195
Implications: Second Isaiah   196
Return to the Divine Council
Appeal to Former Things
Zion's Final Destiny
Exilic Provenance?
Second Isaiah as Prophecy
Conclusion   208
Bibliography   209
Scripture Index   217
Author Index   226

P R E F A C E

My interest in Zion's destiny began from the side of Second Isaiah. In an intriguing essay Ronald Clements pursued a suggestion that was implicit in other works and had always fascinated me, namely, that chapters 40–55 of Isaiah were composed in relationship to developing Isaiah traditions. But this begged the question of the scope and form of those traditions. Under what circumstances were they composed? It would be difficult to pursue an analysis of Second Isaiah's relationship to First Isaiah without knowing what the latter term truly meant.

This in turn raised another question, one posed by Peter Ackroyd in an essay on the presentation of Isa 1–12: Why did the Isaiah traditions grow so extensively in the first place? Why was the message of an eighth-century prophet extended so dramatically into later periods, thereby giving rise to the present sixty-six-chapter book?

This book focuses on these two questions. In wondering about the conclusion to First Isaiah chapters, I naturally considered the present final chapters (Isa 36–39). Unfortunately, however, virtually all work on this section of Isaiah (until the more recent period) had been undertaken in the context of 2 Kgs 18:13—20:19, within a set framework of quite specific historical and literary-critical questions concerning what happened in 701 B.C.E. Even when this discussion was shifted to the Isaiah context and made to address the sorts of questions just raised, most of the traditional historical and literary-critical presuppositions were brought over whole-cloth, or in only slightly modified form.

In this fresh examination of Isa 36–39 new conclusions are reached about the status of King Hezekiah in the Book of Isaiah and the place of royal theology within First Isaiah traditions. I have tried to account for the growth of Isaiah traditions under the broad rubric of concern over the destiny of Zion. Zion's deliverance in 701 ironically created certain theological problems that the extension of the Isaiah tradition has sought to probe and resolve. The thesis pursued here is that the Book of Isaiah grew out of a concern to understand and then adumbrate Zion's final destiny. In the final chapter I make provisional observations about the question that originally intrigued me, namely, how First Isaiah traditions, and especially traditions found in Isaiah 36–39, have affected the composition of Second Isaiah.

Readers should note that I have supplied translations for the passages in German and French not available in English. I have, however, left many technical terms in the original language, using quotation marks to indicate when I am giving direct quotes. Italics have been reserved to designate technical terms that are not direct quotes.

This book is dedicated to my teachers Brevard Childs and Klaus Baltzer in gratitude for all I have learned from them. Childs's essay on Isaiah and the Assyrian crisis remains a model of exegetical method and careful analysis after nearly a quarter of a century. Ironically, much of Childs's own later work on canon has had a decided influence on the sorts of questions and modifications I have proposed here, vis-à-vis his original work. With an enthusiasm that is his trademark, Klaus Baltzer introduced me to the critical study of Second Isaiah. From him I believe I learned what "tradition" truly means. He has been a friend and gracious host over the last ten years.

Finally, were he still alive, I could not find the words to thank John Hollar. John taught me much about writing during my years in Philadelphia, and I remain in his debt. His encouragement was crucial in my decision to pursue this project. Whenever I see an editor's marks I have the suspicion that John is visiting me with his now silent signature; sometimes there even seems to be a faint whiff of cigar smoke. May God grant him eternal rest and peace.

Corrine L. Patton prepared the bibliography and indexes in a timely and thorough fashion and helped with proofreading at several stages. I want to thank her for jumping into the breach when it was difficult for me to get "hands on" access to the typescript, being abroad on leave. Finally, I would be remiss if I did not mention the help of Marshall Johnson and his fine staff at Fortress Press. At every point along the way his professionalism and attention to detail was most appreciated.

Christopher R. Seitz

ABBREVIATIONS

AB	Anchor Bible
AnBib	Analecta biblica
ANET	J.B. Pritchard (ed.), *Ancient Near Eastern Texts*
AOAT	Alter Orient und Altes Testament
AS	Annals of Sennacherib
ASTO	*Annual of the Swedish Theological Institute*
ATD	Das Alte Testament Deutsch
B.Bat.	*Baba Batra*
BEvT	Beiträge zur evangelischen Theologie
BETL	Bibliotheca ephemeridum theologicarum lovaniensium
BHK	R. Kittel, *Biblia hebraica*
BHS	*Biblia hebraica stuttgartensia*
Bib	Biblica
BKAT	Biblischer Kommentar: Altes Testament
BWANT	Beiträge zur Wissenschaft vom Alten und Neuen Testament
BZAW	Beihefte zur *Zeitschrift für die alttestamentliche Wissenschaft*
DtrH	Deturonomistic History
FB	Forschung zur Bibel
FRLANT	Forschungen zur Religion und Literatur des Alten und Neuen Testaments
HKAT	Handkommentar zum Alten Testament
IEJ	*Israel Exploration Journal*
Int	*Interpretation*
IOS	*Israel Oriental Society*
JBL	*Journal of Biblical Literature*
JCS	*Jouranl of Cuneiform Studies*

JNES	*Journal of Near Eastern Studies*
JSOT	*Journal for the Study of the Old Testament*
JSOTSup	Journal for the Study of the Old Testament—Supplement Series
JTS	*Journal of Theological Studies*
LXX	Septuagint
MT	Masoretic Text
NCB	New Century Bible
NEB	New English Bible
NorTT	*Norsk Teologisk Tidssgrift*
OBT	Overtures to Biblical Theology
OTL	Old Testament Library
OTS	*Oudtestamentische Studien*
RSV	Revised Standard Version of the Bible
SBS	Stuttgarter Bibelstudien
SBT	Studies in Biblical Theology
SEÅ	*Svensk exegetisk årsbok*
SJT	*Scottish Journal of Theology*
TynBul	*Tyndale Bulletin*
TZ	*Theologische Zeitschrift*
VT	*Vetus Testamentum*
VTSup	Vetus Testamentum, Supplement
WBC	Word Biblical Commentary
WMANT	Wissenschaftliche Monographien zum Alten und Neuen Testament
WUNT	Wissenschaftliche Untersuchungen zum Neuen Testament
ZAW	*Zeitschrift Für die alttestamentliche Wissenschaft*
ZDPV	*Zeitschrift des deutschen Palästina-Vereins*
ZTK	*Zeitschrift für Theologie und Kirche*

CHAPTER ONE

Two Independent Isaiahs

THE CENTENNIAL OF DUHM'S ISAIAH
Historical vs. Editorial Independence in the Book of Isaiah

Nearly a century ago Bernhard Duhm published what has come to be regarded as an "epoch-making" commentary on the Book of Isaiah.[1] Seen within the critical climate of its day, the most original thesis proposed in the commentary involved the last eleven chapters (56–66). These chapters Duhm attributed to a single prophetic hand, whom he named Trito-Isaiah, thus (1) separating them from Deutero-Isaiah chapters (40–55) on literary grounds; (2) positing for them a socio-historical location far removed from Deutero-Isaiah, in the period of Nehemiah; and (3) describing the theological proclivities of Trito-Isaiah in terms sharply distinct from his exilic predecessor ("a *Theokratiker* of purest ilk," p. 390).

As can happen when greater specification is proposed, one effect of Duhm's thesis regarding Trito-Isaiah was the production of a much sharper profile for Deutero-Isaiah, in every respect (literary, historical, biographical, sociological, theological). So one can concede that the attribution to Duhm of the now regnant Three-Isaiah hypothesis is not mistaken.

Nevertheless, while a certain simplicity and logic marked Duhm's treatment of Parts Two and Three (chaps. 40–66), the complexity of Part One (chaps. 1–39)—historical, literary, editorial—was by no means lost on him. In this respect, neither Duhm's assessment of the First Isaiah problem nor his own contribution to it could be termed innovative, measured against his work in 40–66. As had others before him, Duhm recognized that levels of text within chapters 1–39 carried one well beyond the period of Deutero- and even Trito-Isaiah, and forced one to consider the editorial history of First Isaiah chapters in the broader context of Second and Third Isaiah chapters—or,

---

1. *Das Buch Jesaia* (HKAT 3.1; Göttingen: Vandenhoeck & Ruprecht, 1892).

what one might refer to in the present climate of Isaiah research: a consideration of the reciprocal relationships[2] among the three Isaiah sections within the
final form of the canonical Book of Isaiah.

Here one confronts an irony. Duhm is rightly credited with spawning a
method of approach to the Book of Isaiah whose single most important consequence has been the treatment of Isaiah as three independent "books." Yet
Duhm did not himself feel free to treat Isaiah as three independent books
without first providing some account of how the whole Book of Isaiah took
shape. Admittedly, the times demanded such an accounting, as did the format
constraints under which Duhm worked in the HKAT series, which obliged the
author of one Isaiah to treat (what would shortly become) three. Nevertheless,
it is not clear to this author that Duhm would have been fully content with the
direction Isaiah studies eventually took in respect of the independence issue,
even when the course of that direction was largely set by him. At a minimum,
it must be emphasized that the treatment of First Isaiah for Duhm involved
broader questions regarding the editorial history of the entire Isaiah collection. This is true even as Duhm argued for a relatively independent process of
editorial growth for chapters 1–39 over against chapters 40–66. This argument for editorial independence did not drop down from the sky, but
depended on a prior explanation of the relationship of chapters 40–66 to what
preceded.

It is at the question of editorial—not historical—independence that one
should pause and read Duhm again, especially in the present climate of Isaiah
research. No one disputes the historical distance of chapters 40–66 from what
precedes, a portion of which certainly preserves the eighth-century preaching
of Isaiah of Jerusalem. Evidence internal to chapters 40–66 (the mention of
Cyrus; the post-587 perspective) is incontrovertible on these (historical)
grounds. Duhm did not have to press this issue, as within scholarly circles of
his day the historical distance was all but conceded, and had been since the
late eighteenth century (Döderlein; Eichhorn; Gesenius). But how was one to
account for the editorial factors that brought historically distant material into
literary relationship?

Here Duhm argued from two different directions, from the First Isaiah

---

2. This is the English phrase used in R. Rendtorff's *The Old Testament: An Introduction*
(Philadelphia: Fortress, 1986) 190; see also "Zur Komposition des Buches Jesaja," *VT* 34 (1984)
295–320; and now "Jesaja 6 im Rahmen der Komposition des Jesajabuches" in *The Book of
Isaiah* (J. Vermeylen, ed.; BETL 81; Leuven: University Press, 1989) 73–82, where the expression
Wechselbeziehung frequently appears. In a most recent collection of essays on the Book of
Isaiah, O.H. Steck speaks of *Querverbindungen* and *gesamtjesajanischen Interrelationen*
("Tritojesaja im Jesajabuch," in *The Book of Isaiah*, 361–406). For the broader literature on this
question, see also R. Clements, "Beyond Tradition-History: Deutero-Isaianic Development of
First Isaiah's Themes," *JSOT* 31 (1985) 97, who speaks of "the truly intrinsic connection of
content between the various blocks of material" (97). Also C. Seitz, "Isaiah 1–66: Making Sense of
the Whole," in *Reading and Preaching the Book of Isaiah* (Philadelphia: Fortress, 1988) 105–26.

collection forward to Isa 40–66, and from the Second and Third Isaiah chapters back to First Isaiah. The first direction of the argument is far better known, and the legacy of Duhm on this matter extends unquestionably to the present period. Duhm argued for a similarity of final editorial structure between First Isaiah and the other two major prophetic collections, Jeremiah and Ezekiel.[3] As he saw it, all three began with indigenous oracles of judgment, moved to oracles against the nations, and ended with oracles of salvation, or eschatological oracles—thus exhibiting a loose organizational structure.[4] The pattern is reasonably clear in Ezekiel; it requires LXX Jeremiah (and some explanation for the third section);[5] it would function in Isaiah with the subdivisions 1–12, 13–23, 24–35 (again, sections 1 and 3 seem to be mixed internally).

The final key argument for the independence of First Isaiah from Second and Third Isaiah depended on Duhm's assessment of Isa 36–39. Duhm argued that the original home of this material was in Kings (2 Kgs 18:13—20:19).[6] It was brought over into First Isaiah to serve as a conclusion (*Abschliessung*) to this "book" (1–35 + 36–39), on analogy with the bringing over of Jer 52 (originally located in Kings according to Duhm) to serve as the historical conclusion to the Book of Jeremiah.[7] In sum, First Isaiah was a closed collection like the books of Jeremiah (LXX) and Ezekiel in final literary form.

---

3. O.H. Steck, *Bereitete Heimkehr: Jesaja 35 als redactionelle Brücke zwischen dem Ersten und dem Zweiten Jesaja* (SBS 121; Stuttgart: Katholisches Bibelwerk, 1985) 57–58; O. Kaiser, *Einleitung in das Alte Testament* (5th ed.; Gütersloh: Gütersloher Verlagshaus Gerd Mohn, 1984) 248; H. Barth, *Die Jesaja-Worte in der Josiazeit* (WMANT 48; Neukirchen-Vluyn: Neukirchener, 1977) 298; P.-M. Bogaert, "L'organisation des grands receuils prophétiques," *The Book of Isaiah*, 147–53; J. Vermeylen, "L'unité du livre d'Isaïe," *The Book of Isaiah*, 34. I will discuss these works in detail in chapter 2.

4. "Die dritte Gruppe c. 24–35 ist wesentliche eschatologischen Characters" (*Jesaia*, viii). Duhm credited Ezekiel with the invention of this tripartite schema.

5. See the correct remarks of R. Smend, *Die Entstehung des Alten Testaments* (Stuttgart: Kohlhammer, 1978) 157; also especially, P. Ackroyd, "Isaiah I-XII: Presentation of a Prophet," *VTSup* 29 (1978) 19–21; O. Steck, *Heimkehr*, 57–59; and C. Seitz, "The Prophet Moses and the Canonical Shape of Jeremiah," *ZAW* 101 (1989) 18–27.

6. A theory going back to Gesenius (*Commentar über den Jesaia* [Leipzig: Friedr. Christ. Wilh. Vogel, 1821] 2.932–36) and challenged most recently by K.A.D. Smelik, "Distortion of Old Testament Prophecy: The Purpose of Isaiah xxxvi and xxxvii," *OTS* 24 (1989) 70–93. See also my treatment in the forthcoming *AB* Dictionary article, "Isaiah (First)." These chapters must be the subject of an independent treatment below, so important is their interpretation on the question of Isaiah's fuller redactional development.

7. The basic priority of 2 Kgs 18–20 over Isa 36–39 is maintained in modified form by most modern scholars. For a discussion, see B.S. Childs, *Isaiah and the Assyrian Crisis* (SBT 3; Naperville, Illinois: Alec R. Allenson, 1967) and R. Clements, *Isaiah and the Deliverance of Jerusalem* (JSOTSup 13; Sheffield: JSOT Press, 1980). Compare the study of K.A.D. Smelik. For a different interpretation of the function of Isa 36–39 within the Book of Isaiah, see P. Ackroyd, "An Interpretation of the Babylonian Exile," *SJT* 27 (1974) 328–52, and "Isaiah 36–39: Structure and Function," in *Von Kanaan bis Kerala, Festschrift für Prof. Mag. Dr. Dr. J.P.M. van der Ploeg, O.P. zur Vollendung des siebzigsten Lebensjahres am 4. Juli 1979* (W.C. Delsman, J.T. Nelis, J.R.T.M. Peters, eds.; AOAT 211; Neukirchen-Vluyn: Neukirchener, 1982) 3–21. On the relationship between Jer 52 and 2 Kgs 25, see C. Seitz, *Theology in Conflict: Reactions to the Exile in the Book of Jeremiah* (BZAW 176; Berlin: Walter de Gruyter, 1989) 164–200.

This was true even as sections of First Isaiah postdated Second and Third Isaiah *by a considerable degree.*

It is on this last score that one might feel Duhm's flank to be most exposed. How is it that Second and Third Isaiah collections, relatively unified compositions whose final form was not accomplished prior to the fourth century, came to be attached to an altogether independent First Isaiah collection whose own literary stabilization did not come about until much later, well into the second century B.C.E.? Would one not have expected more "cross-fertilization" among First, Second, and Third Isaiah sections, thus calling into question the rigid independence claimed by Duhm for the First Isaiah book? The only possible answer was that chapters 40–66 were kept wholly independent until chapters 1–39 themselves achieved final form; that is, these two major sections of the book remained isolated from each other and were not joined until the dawn of the Common Era. This is the answer Duhm gave, by arguing back from chapters 40–66 to the Book of First Isaiah.

Duhm viewed this form of argument for the independence of First Isaiah from other Isaiahs as based upon "external evidence," in order to differentiate it from internal, largely literary/historical judgments.[8] Another way to describe this in the present redaction-critical climate would be to term it "editorial" or "compositional" argumentation, since it had to do finally with the external moves that brought about the editorial consolidation of the Book of Isaiah.[9] As we have seen, it was necessary for Duhm to establish that Second and Third Isaiah sections (joined prior to First Isaiah's stabilization) were so independent of First Isaiah that the latter could continue to develop several centuries beyond the former, with no evidence of (1) additions by a common hand to both collections, or (2) editorial efforts at coordinating the Three Isaiahs (actually, 1–39 and 40–66) into a sixty-six chapter, editorially coherent whole. Duhm had to establish that chapters 40–66 circulated for a considerable period of time completely outside the orbit of (the still evolving) First Isaiah. It would not do to simply theorize this independence or speculate about it as a *desideratum.* Here Duhm richly deserves his acclaim as a thorough, consistent critic.

Duhm noted that when the Chronicler—in the third century by his estimate—wanted to cite the prophet responsible for promising that Cyrus would rebuild the temple, he spoke of the "word of the LORD by the mouth of Jeremiah" (2 Chr 36:12; Ez 1:1) when, according to Duhm, he should have referred to Deutero-Isaiah, or more precritically, to Isaiah. That this is a

---

8. That is, findings based upon "fortuitous notices in other writings" (*Jesaia,* vi).
9. As we shall see, Duhm's use of external evidence strikes one now as crude, measured against present redactional argumentation; nevertheless, his goal was to determine how the Book of Isaiah reached final canonical form, and the observation of external sources (Sirach; 2 Maccabees; Chronicles) was one way to get at the problem.

critical observation open to debate is beside the point. The more pressing question is whether or not this form of argument was *indispensable* for establishing the independence of chapters 40–66 from what preceded. On the basis of this external evidence from the Chronicler, Duhm concludes "that this section did not yet belong to the Book of Isaiah" (vii), thus resulting in chapters 40–66 being (wrongly) attributed to Jeremiah.[10]

Duhm uses evidence from this same source (Chronicles) to argue that First Isaiah was still in flux at this time, since material from Isa 36–39 is cited by the Chronicler as deriving from Kings, not Isaiah (2 Chr 32:32); in Duhm's view, the Chronicler finds his relationship to Samuel/Kings *lästig*, and therefore he would have cited Isaiah, had the option been open to him.[11] Moreover, since additions continued to be made in Isa 36–39 beyond the time of the redactor who placed these chapters as a conclusion to 1–35°, it cannot be determined if at this time he "already possessed the first 39 chapters in their entirety" (vii). Even the evidence of Sirach (early second century) cannot tell us anything conclusively about the state of First Isaiah with respect to the sections 24–27 and 33–35, which Duhm argues postdate even this second-century witness.[12] For our purposes, the intriguing thing to note is that Duhm never assumes that the *historical* independence of Second Isaiah necessitates its *editorial* independence as well. This must be proven, in the manner described above. Put in another way, just because Second Isaiah chapters presuppose the Babylonian debacle does not mean they must be independent of Isa 1–39 on compositional grounds. Much material within Isa 1–39 likewise presupposes the events of 587 B.C.E., and yet, according to Duhm's theory this material has circulated within a compositional orbit utterly independent of Isa 40–66, yet wholly at home within the evolving First Isaiah book.

A classic instance of this is to be seen in Duhm's assessment of Isa 13:1—

10. It is a telling observation that very few scholars who follow Duhm on the classic Three Isaiah formulation make reference to this central piece of evidence. Of modern scholars, only Smend (*Entstehung*, 144) mentions the theory, quickly dismissing it: "In passing it was once asserted that 2 Chr 36:22 (= Ezra 1:1 ff.), which calls Cyrus's permission to build the temple the fulfillment of the word of Jeremiah, played on the reference at Isa 44:28 and thus revealed that Isa 40–66 was non-Isaianic and in fact a part of the Book of Jeremiah; but clearly the play is on Jer 25:12; 29:10 (see also 2 Chr 36:21 and Jer 25:11)."

11. Steck makes a passing reference to Duhm's argument on this score (*Heimkehr*, 57) but follows it with a question mark. Smelik interprets the evidence of the Chronicler in exactly the opposite direction, without referring to the theory of Duhm: "It is interesting to note that in Chron. xxxii 32 [*sic*] and Sir. xlviii 17–25 these narratives are considered to be part of the book of Isaiah rather than Kings" ("Distortion," 86, n. 1). In fairness to Smelik's position, 2 Chron 32:32 is open to such an interpretation: "Now the rest of the acts of Hezekiah, and his good deeds, behold, they are written in the vision of Isaiah the prophet the son of Amoz, in the Book of the Kings of Judah and Israel"; Duhm stressed the second clause, Smelik the first. Smelik's argument has a certain force, and the logic of Duhm is certainly too restrictive on this point. See my remarks below, chapter 5, note 21.

12. A view not substantially modified in Steck's recent study (*Heimkehr*, 56–57), or Kaiser's Isaiah commentary (*Isaiah 1–12* [OTL Second Edition Completely Rewritten; Philadelphia: Fortress, 1983]).

14:22˚ and 21:1–15, material he dates "contemporaneous with Deutero-Isaiah" (xiii).[13] One might reasonably assume that within the same book, material dated to the same period probably came from the same compositional hand, or at least reflected a common editorial perspective—something that, in my judgment, could well be established about the relationship between chapters 13/21 and 40–66. But Duhm refused to make this kind of move. Historical distance within First Isaiah proper was to be adjudicated independently of historical distance in Isa 40–66. The overt reasons for this were stated above: (1) a theory about First Isaiah's structural resemblance to Jeremiah (LXX) and Ezekiel, and (2) the (odd) external testimony of a much later Chronicler and Sirach, which established for Duhm that Isa 40–66 had not been joined to "Isaiah" until the late second century. If the precise reasoning behind Duhm's theory of three independent Isaiahs (especially Second and Third from First) has been largely forgotten, the theory itself has survived marvelously and made the separate treatment of Isa 1–39 apart from 40–55 and 56–66 all but required.[14]

The question to be raised at this juncture is whether modern interpreters of Isaiah are prepared to follow Duhm at all points on the matter of Second Isaiah's independence from First Isaiah (we leave Third Isaiah to the side for a moment). It is the thesis of the present study that the vast majority of twentieth-century interpreters have been content to accept the theory of Second Isaiah as brokered by Duhm apart from his broader argument for the editorial independence of Second Isaiah from First Isaiah.[15] While historical distance was itself not sufficient to establish the independence of Second Isaiah for a Duhm at work on the whole Book of Isaiah, *it has been sufficient for virtually all who have followed him.*[16] Because Duhm rightly observed that much within Isa 1–39 was contemporaneous with or postdated Isa 40–55 (as had Eichhorn a century before him), he was forced to provide an explanation for the editorial independence of Second Isaiah from its surrounding literary environment, and from chapters arguably contemporaneous with it. For the separation of Second from Third Isaiah, Duhm's argument for the Palestinian

13. See also his earlier work, *Die Theologie der Propheten als Grundlage für die innere Entwicklungsgeschichte der israelitischen Religion* (Bonn: Adolph Marcus, 1875) 301–5.
14. I will examine those basic elements of Duhm's theory that have survived in modern works (Barth, Steck, Kaiser, Bogaert, Vermeylen) below.
15. This is absolutely true in the case of Duhm's use of the Chronicler; it is partially true with respect to the argument for the tripartite structure of First Isaiah (discussion of Barth, Steck, Vermeylen, and Bogaert on this issue will follow).
16. Especially in Anglo-Saxon circles. No mention of the particulars of Duhm's theory for the editorial independence of Second Isaiah can be found in the works of North, Muilenberg, Knight, Hanson, or Clifford—to name just a few of the more popular studies. In the 1979 OTL commentary on Second Isaiah, Westermann is also silent on the topic and contents himself with the customary set of historical observations about Second Isaiah among Babylonian exiles.

provenance of 56–66 would become memorable.[17] All but forgotten are the reasons he so sharply divided Second and Third Isaiah from First.

Once the Three Isaiah model was in place, and the three sections began to be treated independently—first in monograph and then in commentary format—there was little reflection on the editorial logic that functioned inextricably with Duhm's historical sense. This occurred primarily because of a change in the context of inquiry: those who worked on individual sections of the book were no longer obliged to treat historical problems that cut across critically determined borders, as had Duhm in the HKAT format.[18] The historical complexities within 1–39 could be ignored in a commentary on Second Isaiah, even when they might be complexities cut out of the same cloth as those in Isa 40–55. Anyone observing the collective efforts of commentary on three independent Isaiahs might have reasonably concluded that a neat historical scheme explained the present editorial shape of the book (First + Second + Third),[19] so that the "external evidence" arguments and editorial explanations of Duhm could be and were in fact forgotten.

Convenience and simplicity won out as the cleanly historical dimensions of Duhm's theory evolved into one of the "assured results of historical criticism." The complexities of Duhm's theory were not a subject for discussion once the Book of Isaiah stopped forming the broader explicit context within which the theory of Three Isaiahs was defended.

The Emerging Identity of Second Isaiah, Prophet and Book

Of course there were, strictly speaking, reasons other than historical distance or the external testimony of the Chronicler that functioned to give Second Isaiah identity in Duhm's model. In contrast to the scattered, varied

17. For a good summary regarding the gradual emergence of Third Isaiah as a Palestinian prophet, see C.C. Torrey, *The Second Isaiah* (New York: Charles Scribner's Sons, 1928) 3–19. The force of Torrey's broader argument was unfortunately undercut by his polemical style and odd interpolation theory, as well as his broader views on the "fictional exile."

18. In this regard, recent work on redactional levels bridging individual sections is a return to the context in which Duhm worked, with different results. At present the main interest is in the relationship between chaps. 56–66 and 1–39°. See R. Lack, *La symbolique du livre d'Isaïe: Essai sur l'image littéraire comme élément de structuration* (AnBib 59; Rome: Biblical Institute, 1973); J. Vermeylen, *Du prophète Isaïe à l'apocalyptic* (2 vols.; Paris: Gabalda, 1977–78); R. Rendtorff, "Komposition"; O. Steck, *Heimkehr*; M. Sweeney, *Isaiah 1–4: Isaiah and the Post-Exilic Understanding of the Isaianic Tradition* (BZAW 171; Berlin: Walter de Gruyter, 1988). Ackroyd, Clements, and Childs have examined the relationship between First and Second Isaiah sections (Clements, "The Prophecies of Isaiah and the Fall of Jerusalem in 587 B.C.," *VT* 30 [1980] 421–36; "The Unity of the Book of Isaiah," *Int* 36 [1982] 117–29; B.S. Childs, *Introduction to the Old Testament as Scripture* [Philadelphia: Fortress, 1979] 328–33. Also R. Melugin, *The Formation of Isaiah 40–55* (BZAW 141; Berlin: Walter de Gruyter, 1976) 176–78; D. Meade, "The Isaiah Tradition," in *Pseudonymity and Canon* (WUNT 39; Tübingen: J.C.B. Mohr [Paul Siebeck], 1986); and the early study of D.R. Jones, "The Traditio of the Oracles of Isaiah of Jerusalem," *ZAW* 67 (1955) 226–46.

19. See C. Seitz, "The One Isaiah // The Three Isaiahs," in *Reading Isaiah*, 13–22.

additions to Isa 1–39˚, in 40–55 we are presented with what has from the
dawn of the theory itself been viewed as a uniform, sustained composition—
whether in the hands of a Duhm who excepted the "servant songs" from this
uniformity, or a Mowinckel for whom the uniformity or interconnectedness
between form-critical units was wholly mechanical and artificially imposed.[20]
Even at the height of form-critical atomization, the general picture of Second
Isaiah was that of a sixteen-chapter composition, however the origins and
development of that compositional character were conceived and presented
to critical readerships.[21]

Alongside the factor of sustained literary presentation went other features that insured a sharp profile for Isa 40–55. In Duhm's model, one would
have to name first and foremost the strict separation of chapters 56–66 from
40–55, within what had been thought of as a single exilic composition,
embracing all of 40–66.[22] Moreover, to speak of individual prophetic personalities standing behind these two sections went a long way toward isolating their
activity from what was termed the work of "glossators," "redactors," or even
apocalyptic "authors" within chapters 1–39. Trito- and Deutero-Isaiah were
not glossators, but individual prophetic voices on analogy with Amos, Hosea,
or other self-standing prophetic figures.

But these are editorial, literary, and crude socio-biographical factors.
The heart of the theory separating Deutero- from Trito-Isaiah, as one might
expect, involved historical matters in the strictest sense. Put simply: Deutero-
Isaiah chapters were composed earlier and thought to reflect issues that pre-
dated Trito-Isaiah, about whom Duhm could summarily declare: "Already by
his time the Jewish community was long established, Jerusalem occupied, and
the temple built" (390); by default, none of this could be said of Deutero-
Isaiah chapters. Moreover, Trito-Isaiah was active in Jerusalem. By default,
one would assume Deutero-Isaiah to be active in exile. But here Duhm—
nothing if not brilliantly independent—stated with all vehemence: "By no
means did he live in Babylon."[23]

The significance of this view of Deutero-Isaiah as a non-Babylonian

20. S. Mowinckel, "Die Komposition des deuterojesajanischen Buches," *ZAW* 49 (1931) 87–112,
    242–60. Modern proponents for structural intention as well as authorial uniformity include R.
    Rendtorff (*Introduction*, 193–96), T. Mettinger ("Die Ebed-Jahwe-Lieder: Ein fragwürdiges
    Axiom," ASTI 11 [1977/8] 68–76), E. Hessler ("Gott der Schöpfer: Ein Beitrag zur Komposition
    und Theologie Deuterojesajas" [Diss. Greifswald, 1961]), R. Melugin (*Formation*), and to a
    degree C. Westermann (*Sprache und Struktur der Prophetie Deuterojesajas* [Munich: Kaiser,
    1964]).
21. One thinks here of the *Auseinandersetzung* between Gressmann ("Die literarische Analyse
    Deuterojesajas," *ZAW* 34 [1914] 254–97) and L. Köhler (*Deuterojesaja stilkritisch untersucht*
    [BZAW 37; Berlin, 1923), as well as the stimulating work of Begrich ("Das priesterliche
    Heilsorakel," *ZAW* 52 [1934] 81–92).
22. S.R. Driver, *An Introduction to the Literature of the Old Testament* (New York: Charles
    Scribner's Sons, 1891) 217–31. See also the discussion of C.C. Torrey, *Second Isaiah*, 3–13.
23. "He certainly did not live in Babylonia" (*Jesaia*, xviii).

prophet will be taken up shortly. For our purposes it is clear that the non-Babylonian setting[24] had no effect on the otherwise highly individualized portrait of Second Isaiah, to be sharply distinguished from his successor Trito-Isaiah, on the one hand, and the hodgepodge of material to be found within Proto-Isaiah on the other.

The consequence of Duhm's reading is clear: to the degree that the prophet Isaiah receded behind the complex mass of tradition in 1–39˚, Deutero- and Trito-Isaiah stepped forward into prominence. To them could be attributed reasonably well-organized and sustained blocks of literary tradition; their social and historical location was likewise relatively well-focused, compared with that of First Isaiah. It would be fair to say that here too a great chasm divided chapters 1–39 from 40–66, insofar as what could be claimed for the literature of the second part, in classically tradition-historical terms, could not be claimed for the first. While Duhm does not reflect on this reality as informing his decision to keep First Isaiah chapters independent of 40–66, nevertheless his theory quite clearly evolved in this direction. For later interpreters, the sharp profile of Second Isaiah virtually required the sharp editorial separation of 40–55 from 1–39˚, even though Duhm was obliged to demonstrate this separation on other grounds.

The reasons for Duhm's decision to reject a Babylonian provenance for chapters 40–55 are quite persuasive, even though they are virtually ignored in the present climate of Second Isaiah research.[25] His objections will be examined more closely in the course of our study. It is sufficient to note at this juncture the irony that the most unique feature of Second Isaiah as sketched by later interpreters—his prophetic activity among Babylonian exiles—did not form part of the imaginative reconstruction of Duhm, and indeed was rejected by him.

What is of present interest is the question of the degree to which assumptions about the exile, and the place of Deutero-Isaiah within the exilic community in Babylon, have conspired to force a wedge between chapters 40–55 and First Isaiah different in kind than that proposed by Duhm. That a wedge exists between Second and Third Isaiah on these grounds (e.g., geographical displacement) is obvious from the working theory of Duhm, whereby Third

24. Duhm suggested a location "probably at some place in Lebanon, perhaps Phoenicia" (xiii), "perhaps in northern Phoenicia" (xviii), based in part on his exegesis of 49:12 and the identification of the place name *sinim* as Deutero-Isaiah's own location, in Phoenicia (345–46).
25. An exception is H. Barstad, "Lebte Deuterojesaja in Judäa?" *NorTT* 83 (1982) 77–87. Of the older scholars, Mowinckel was equally forthright in his rejection of a Babylonian provenance, preferring a setting in Palestine: "In spite of the prevailing—even combative—opinion, I regard it as excluded that second Isaiah lived amongst the exiles. . . . he addresses Zion-Jerusalem and speaks of the return of the exiles from the perspective of one in Palestine: his home is in Judah; Cyrus's homeland, which borders on Babylon, is for him 'from the rising of the sun' at the uttermost parts of the earth" ("Komposition," 244). Ewald, Hölscher, Bunsen, and Marti all settled on Egypt.

Isaiah's Jerusalem provenance distinguished him from Second Isaiah in Phoenicia. This was but one factor, however, alongside temporal displacement and
theological discontinuity. Nevertheless, as Duhm's model was picked up in
subsequent research, the wedge looked in firmer place on the front than on the
back end of 40–55. This was true because: (1) both tradition blocks 40–55 and
56–66 were traceable in large part to single prophetic figures (cf. 1–39); (2) the
historical distance separating 40–55 from 56–66 was less than that separating
Second Isaiah from First (and less complicated in character); (3) Third Isaiah
was described in the model of Duhm as an imitator (a poor one in his estimate)
of Second Isaiah, where no such relationship was thought to exist between
First and Second Isaiah. Points 2 and 3 were modified subsequent to Duhm in
such a way as to make the relationship between Second and Third Isaiah all
the more intimate.[26]

In other words, the arguments used by Duhm to derive a fixed profile for
Trito-Isaiah, built more on contrast than continuity, were very quickly modified and toned down, once the theory in general terms found adherents.
Deutero-Isaiah's profile had been capable of clear articulation by Duhm
because of the contrast he saw with Trito-Isaiah; but after that profile was
established, it became of incidental interest that Trito-Isaiah was suddenly
both theologically compatible with and a near contemporary of Deutero-
Isaiah. The contrast evolved essentially into a matter of geography, and that
contrast became sufficient for those who followed Duhm.

As we have seen, it was not Duhm's placement of Deutero-Isaiah at a
later period in time, nor the locating of his activity in Phoenicia that brought
about the sharp isolation of Second from First Isaiah chapters. Duhm relied
upon "external testimony" to drive home the independence of both 40–55 and
56–66 from 1–39. It was argued above that the complexities of this argument
were lost once the absolute independence of Second Isaiah was achieved. It is
important to remember, moreover, that working within the narrower context
of chapters 40–66, Duhm won the independence of Second Isaiah by shaving
off chapters 56–66 and by attributing them to a distinct prophetic figure; these
latter oracles were in his judgment separated by several generations, by physical location, and by theological outlook. Later interpreters modified this,
leaving only the physical location argument in pure form, enhanced by Second Isaiah's further dislocation to Babylon.

In sum, Duhm's Second Isaiah emerged (1) because of the distinction he

---

26. See especially the contributions of K. Elliger: *Die Einheit des Tritojesaia (Jesaia 56–66)*
(BWANT 45; Stuttgart: Kohlhammer, 1928); *Deuterojesaja in seinem Verhältnis zu Tritojesaja*
(BWANT 63, Stuttgart: Kohlhammer, 1933). Trito-Isaiah became a disciple of the exilic
Deutero-Isaiah, working in the very next generation back in Judah. Elliger's modification quickly
won the day and is accepted on this score in most recent treatments (Westermann, Hanson,
Pauritsch, Sekine), even as the literary unity of 56–66 is questioned (full citation below, note 40).
See my essay in the *AB* Dictionary, "Isaiah (Third)" (forthcoming).

made with Third Isaiah chapters, and (2) because of his theory of separate tradition-historical developments for 40–66 and 1–39 in the larger Book of Isaiah. For those who adopted the Three Isaiah model, neither of these central arguments proved essential.[27] What emerged was a distinction based almost exclusively on physical dislocation: Second Isaiah was a prophet among exiles in Babylon, and chapters 40–55 reflected prophetic activity in a foreign land. No other section of the Book of Isaiah could claim this kind of notoriety, nor would such interest have been generated had Deutero-Isaiah remained a prophet active "probably some place in Lebanon or Phoenicia," as Duhm had proposed.

As is now clear in retrospect, Duhm's theory regarding Second Isaiah quickly became fused with much broader historical judgments regarding the life of Israel during the exilic period. While Second Isaiah was already quite distinct from First and Third Isaiah in Duhm's model, his swift transformation into a prophet among Babylonian exiles, on analogy with Ezekiel, all but insured that the wedge Duhm put in place on the back end was now hammered in permanently on the front. To talk of an individual prophet, composer of a fixed block of tradition, at work after the events of 587 B.C.E., was to speak of a prophet other than Isaiah of Jerusalem, to be sure. In addition, to place this prophet among Babylonian exiles, within a broader reconstruction of the history of Israel, and isolate his preaching from section 56–66, was to insure his own absolutely distinctive profile.[28] It would also insure that no lines of editorial linkage could be drawn between chapters 1–39˚ and 40–55, even when sections of 1–39˚ were contemporaneous with or postdated Second Isaiah chapters.[29]

The major unintended consequence of Duhm's theory was that "Second Isaiah" was effectively exiled to Babylon. While other sections of 1–39 had been determined by Duhm to be contemporaneous with Second Isaiah chapters, Isa 40–55 alone would claim a foreign provenance, Babylonian exile. An emphasis on life in Babylonian exile was very quickly gaining prominence in

---

27. The exceptions are those who still defend some form of Duhm's point (2). Their views will be taken up shortly.
28. It is true that scholars prior to Duhm thought of "Second Isaiah" as a prophet in Babylon (for example, S.R. Driver). But by this was meant the anonymous author of 40–66, as distinct from Isaiah of Jerusalem. It was the creation of Duhm's Palestinian Third Isaiah that gave even sharper profile to Second Isaiah and caused one to think of the importance of geographical dislocation in new ways. Driver is working basically with two sections of one book, whose distinction is primarily temporal (eighth century and exilic) and only in a minor way geographical. He never engages the editorial problems of the whole Book of Isaiah (especially First Isaiah) in the manner of Duhm. When the old exilic conception from the nineteenth century was added to Duhm's new theory, a transformation was effected in both, and the result was a mixture not exactly continuous with either.
29. The legacy of this extends to the present period, when scholars are willing to acknowledge linkages between First and Third Isaiah, but are reluctant to include Second Isaiah chapters within the same kind of analysis.

historical and theological reconstructions, apart from Isaiah research more narrowly conceived. Duhm had not argued for such a reading, but with his sharp separation of 40–66 from 1–39° on the basis of external evidence, the die had been cast. The subtle points in his argument were lost in the exhilaration that attended the emergence of the poet Second Isaiah, prophet among Babylonian exiles. The geographical distance of 40–55 from the rest of the Isaiah tradition grew, moving Second Isaiah to Babylon, as if to keep pace with the wideness of the editorial chasm that Duhm had argued separated part two (40–66) from part one (1–39). In the wake of these new developments, it would prove impossible to prefer a treatment of chapters 40–55 within the context of the larger Book of Isaiah over a treatment of Second Isaiah as the unique prophetic personality within larger socio-historical reconstructions of the exilic period. When one adds to this the focus of the emerging form-critical method on matters biographical and sociological, brought about by the interest in *Sitz im Leben*, the fate of Second Isaiah, prophet among exiles, was all but sealed. The significance of form-criticism for Second Isaiah research, a development that takes us beyond the time of Duhm, will be addressed shortly.

Summary

Several conclusions are to be drawn on the basis of observations made thus far. First, Duhm remains an important figure in Isaiah research because his treatment of main sections of the sixty-six chapter book occurred only *after* he had made an accounting of the compositional history of the book as a whole. Given the present interest in the redactional unity of Isaiah, there is no small irony in the fact that Duhm reads like a curiously modern figure.

Second, it has been repeatedly emphasized that the logic operating in Duhm's Three Isaiah model was not a matter for serious scrutiny once the Three Isaiah approach took hold, and this is particularly true of the logic we termed editorial. Admittedly, one should expect modifications and even transformations of an original theory. The question is, however, whether there were serious problems with the original theory that were overlooked for the sake of simplicity, or out of inadvertence, as a consequence of the changed climate in which Isaiah research began to take place—that is, as the three new Isaiahs were treated independently of each other. If this is the case, one of the reasons for the present interest in the redactional unity of the entire Book of Isaiah may have been discovered. Were there serious flaws in the original statement that are now coming into greater prominence, especially with a return to the climate in which Duhm himself worked, in which the three Isaiahs required explanation and argument in defense of their existence?

Third, and derivatively, we have focused on two aspects of Duhm's theory that warrant greater scrutiny. Duhm was unwilling to grant the absolute independence of Second from First Isaiah on historical grounds alone, precisely because he recognized how complex was the editorial history of First Isaiah. If that context for discussion is removed—as it has been for virtually all Second Isaiah research, as well as most First Isaiah commentary—then the complexity of the problem is lost, and we have an answer for why Duhm's theory received so little discussion.[30] But is one entitled to let that context be bracketed out, in the name of independent analysis of the Three Isaiahs? Duhm's central hypothesis, based upon the external witness of the Chronicler, seems uncharacteristically weak, if not out-and-out quirky. But did he not honor an obligation ignored by almost all Second Isaiah interpreters—namely, to explain the curious fact that Second Isaiah has not simply been added on to a finished First Isaiah, in the same manner that Third Isaiah found its place next to chapters 40–55? The only way to establish the absolutely independent tradition-history of these two major sections of the book was to find some outside source that would corroborate his judgment. Duhm turned to the Chronicler whose citation of Jeremiah proved that 40–55 were not yet part of "Isaiah."

Related to this, we noted further a significant omission in Duhm's treatment of Second Isaiah: no setting in Babylonian exile. It is a thesis of the present study that that which established the independence of chapters 40–66 from 1–39 for Duhm (his external evidence) was forgotten because it was very quickly overshadowed by another more dramatic reading. By placing Second Isaiah in Babylon among exiles, the independence of chapters 40–55 was brought about on grounds of physical dislocation, to which was added an imaginative reconstruction of the great anonymous poet among exiles, a figure absolutely unrelated to the prophet Isaiah *or the tradition associated with him as it now exists in the Book of Isaiah*. Duhm did not press for such a sharp divide on the grounds of physical dislocation (his Deutero-Isaiah in Phoenicia) because for him this factor was overshadowed by his reconstruction of the literary development of the Book of Isaiah in its entirety. To put the matter directly: Second Isaiah was not independent of First Isaiah because he was a prophet in Phoenicia (or Babylon); chapters 40–55 and 56–66 were independent of 1–39* because they had an absolutely separate tradition-history, only vaguely related to questions of original setting.

To state the obverse of this within the terms of the modern discussion: moves to correlate Third Isaiah (56–66) with redactional activity in First Isaiah (1–39*) are not made on the grounds of common provenance (Jerusa-

---

30. The complexity of historical and literary problems internal to First Isaiah has increased dramatically from the time of Duhm, so that the question of the relationship between First and Second Isaiah is really more pronounced, even though it is still frequently bracketed out, or treated as an independent issue in the manner of Duhm. This now occurs because so much material within 1–39* is assigned a date *later* than Second Isaiah (see esp. O. Kaiser).

lem). Rather, redaction-historical analysis has cut through (or ignored) Duhm's thesis regarding the independent tradition-history of part one (1–39) and part two (40–66) of the Book of Isaiah, thus freeing the interpreter to see literary connections across sections long thought to be independent of each other. Here matters of geographical location recede in importance, as the focus shifts toward redaction-critical analysis and away from the cleanly historical and biographical dimensions of form-criticism. Once again the whole Book of Isaiah forms the context in which interpretive judgments are rendered, and in that sense something of the original flavor of Duhm's analysis returns.

The question to be pursued in this study is whether the recognition of redactional relationships between Third and First Isaiah applies with similar force to Second Isaiah. Seen against the background of Duhm's analysis, has far too great an emphasis been placed on the Babylonian exile as the setting for chapters 40–55? And has this emphasis not also frustrated inquiry into the redactional unity of the Book of Isaiah, precisely because of the singular status accorded these sixteen chapters?

ISAIAH IN THE MODERN PERIOD: THE UNEVEN DUHM LEGACY

Read in detail, Duhm's Isaiah commentary presents the modern interpreter with a host of intriguing theories, not all of equal quality, regarding the historical location and editorial development of passages in the larger book. But the overarching Three Isaiah conception caught hold almost immediately, and subsequent refinements did not alter this basic imaginative construct. As stressed above, the move to treat Isaiah as *three independent sections* and *three separate research areas* changed the context in which the theory first functioned, producing significant omissions and modifications in emphasis, compared with Duhm's analysis.

As a consequence, one can spot at the present period three only roughly coordinated trends in Isaiah research. Where Duhm was forced to bring his analysis of Three Isaiahs before a single arbitrating theory, much was to be left to the side as unclarified or not of interest in the studies that followed, especially regarding the final redactional stages in the composition of the whole book. As such, it is not surprising that the three trends in Isaiah research to be highlighted here are frequently unrelated, mutually inconsistent, or even at odds with each other. Depending upon which section of the book is being treated, and which element of the classic Three Isaiah theory it engages, the respective emphases and conclusions vary.

The Book of Isaiah as Three Independent Books

The distinguishing feature of this trend is that the relationship among the three Isaiah sections (1–39, 40–55, 56–66) is not a main topic of discussion. This may be stated explicitly, or signaled by lack of interest in the question—

that is, the relationship is not treated because there is none, at least not meriting extensive discussion. The three books have come together for reasons that are unclear or accidental, involving matters of simple expedience or preservation (scroll length).[31] The relationship is generally seen to have been imposed from the outside; it did not grow from any intentional efforts within the sections themselves to relate to, respond to, or modify other sections.

In point of fact, the strictest independence—consistent with one aspect of Duhm's argument—is maintained between First Isaiah and Second Isaiah, since Third Isaiah is treated in most monographs as having some conscious relationship to Second Isaiah. Moreover, the independence of the three sections (again, mostly First from Second) is frequently the consequence of format constraints. Commentaries on First Isaiah may feel free of the obligation to discuss matters beyond chapters 1–39 as such. Similarly, commentaries on Second and Third Isaiah rarely speak to the issue of relatedness (or lack of it) among sections in the larger book.[32] When Melugin concludes his careful analysis of the formation of Isa 40–55, he speaks of the need to relate his findings there to matters regarding the larger Book of Isaiah.[33] But the kind of observations he makes seem for the time curious, and a departure from standard operating procedure.[34]

The independence trend functions in its most pristine form in the case of Second Isaiah. Second Isaiah is viewed in this model as the author of chapters 40–55, an anonymous prophetic individual, active in Babylon among exiles, promising their return in the manner of a second exodus. It is hardly necessary to point out what an exhilarating profile has been secured for Second Isaiah in this century using such a conception. The rise of form-critical investigation heralded an interest not just in forms, as such, but also in the man "Second Isaiah," with an intensity of truly special quality and unparalleled preoccupation. At least in the early period, the number of form-critical essays and monographs on the anonymous poet in Babylon easily outdistanced all such studies on the prophets in general.

Form-critical investigation has been concerned to elucidate the precise

---

31. For a summary of possibilities and discussion, see P. Ackroyd, "Presentation," 16–21; R. Clements, "Unity of Isaiah," 117–29.

32. There have been occasional exceptions, the most notable regarding Second Isaiah and chaps. 34–35 of First Isaiah, which are viewed as having some kind of common origin. See Torrey, *Second Isaiah*, esp. 98–104; M. Pope, "Isaiah 34 in Relation to Isaiah 35, 40–66," *JBL* 71 (1952) 235–43; J. Smart, *History and Theology in Second Isaiah* (Philadelphia: Westminster, 1967) 41, 292–94; J.L. McKenzie, *Second Isaiah. Introduction, Translation and Notes* (AB 20; Garden City N.Y.: Doubleday, 1968) 235–43; Fohrer linked these chapters to Third Isaiah (*Das Buch Jesaja* [Zurich] 138). For a monograph analysis of the problem, see the fascinating work by Steck (*Heimkehr*), whose view is yet more complex.

33. "Although chapters 40–55 manifest a literary integrity of their own within the Book of Isaiah, the fact remains that these chapters are somehow related to the whole of Isaiah. Thus our understanding of the kerygmatic significance of chapters 40–55 will remain incomplete until their theological relationship with the entire book is explored" (*Formation*, 176).

34. Seen from a different angle, they represent one of the more engaging contributions of the monograph.

nature of Second Isaiah's preaching/poetry (oral or written; genre designation; exact literary delimitation), but this investigation has not tampered with the general theory as such. For most, Deutero-Isaiah is an oral prophet, similar to preexilic prophets, only active among exiles in Babylon. For the record, Duhm's Deutero-Isaiah was a writer, at work in Phoenicia.[35]

The precise designation of the content of these sixteen chapters has proven a challenge for form-criticism, with opinions differing about the number and delimitation of speech units, the actual origination of the material (oral; written; compositional imitation of oral forms), and the setting in which the prophet worked.[36] The trend at present is to see larger compositional blocks, and to view the prophecy in chapters 40–55 as somewhat special in nature, compared with preexilic prophetic speech.[37] But none of these trends has seriously questioned the basic view that Second Isaiah was an individual prophet active in Babylonian exile. These chapters are still viewed as the most independent of all sections in the Book of Isaiah.[38]

The same is true in a derivative sense for Third Isaiah, who receives his basic identity—again, thanks to Duhm—as a postexilic, nonexilic (Jerusalemite) counterpart to Second Isaiah. Though it is correct to acknowledge a trend among certain exegetes (Rendtorff, Steck, Lack) to interpret chapters 56–66 with an eye toward the larger book, especially chapters 1–39°, the prevailing instinct has been to treat these chapters in relationship to Second Isaiah

---

35. ". . . we have to differentiate three *writers* in chaps. 40–66" (xiii; emphasis mine), that is, Second Isaiah, Third Isaiah, and the author of the servant songs. The notion of Second Isaiah as writer is firmly rooted in nineteenth-century conceptions of prophecy (see Ewald, Budde).

36. The literature is well known. Form-critics (Gressmann, Köhler) stressed the oral and brief nature of the speech units, as compared with the older literary view (Duhm, Driver), and argued over the precise number and location. Mowinckel added to this an explanation for the arrangement of the units. Begrich tightened the genre analysis and introduced the notion of "literary imitation" to explain the distinctive nature of the material. Von Waldow questioned this and pushed for a concrete setting-in-life for the *priesterliche Heilsorakel* in the exilic cult. Muilenburg wished to speak of longer literary units and strophe analysis as appropriate to the literary/rhetorical composition of the poet Second Isaiah. Melugin sought to find the space between Muilenburg's strophe analysis, on the one hand, and the units isolated in form-critical analysis, leaning toward the latter. Gitay ("Deutero-Isaiah: Oral or Written?" *JBL* 99 [1980]: 185–97) enjoined the debate over oral/written and then bracketed it out as inconsequential, thus ignoring the basic historical questions of such theological importance for critics like Westermann. See, for example, Westermann's passionate rejection of Muilenburg's conception precisely over the question of the *nature of the prophetic office*: "The question about the speech-forms of Deutero-Isaiah is at the same time the question about his place in the history of the activity of God with his people and his address to them. This latter concern must have priority over questions of a literary nature if one is prepared to accept these chapters for what they claim to be: the word of God, vouchsafed to the prophet, for a specific point in time in Israel's history" (*Sprache*, 27).

37. See the work of Melugin, Rendtorff, and Mettinger (*A Farewell to the Servant Songs* [Lund, 1983]), for example. Most recently, with an appeal to context as exegetically significant (cf. form-criticism), see P. Wilcox and D. Paton-Williams, "The Servant Songs in Deutero-Isaiah," *JSOT* 42 (1988) 79–102.

38. The recent assault on the theory by J. Vincent had little real effect (almost none in Anglo-Saxon circles): *Studien zur literarischen Eigenart und zur geistigen Heimat von Jesaja, Kap. 40–55* (BEvT 5; Frankfurt/Bern/Las Vegas: Peter Lang, 1977).

chapters, and yet distinct from them. Like Second Isaiah, Third Isaiah has a basic existence as a prophetic individual, but unlike him, he is active in Jerusalem. Form-critical studies and more recent redactional approaches agree that the material in 56–66 is more heterogeneous than what one finds in 40–55. Nevertheless, a rough analogy to 40–55 is still apposite. There is good warrant for treating these chapters independently of what precedes, based upon similar views regarding Second Isaiah's independence from First Isaiah.[39]

First Isaiah chapters contain the most heterogeneous and historically disparate material in the entire Isaiah collection. Nevertheless, until recently commentaries and monographs have been content to analyze chapters 1–39 independently of 40–66. This is true for studies that maximize the extent of material traceable to the historical Isaiah[40] as well as for those which—in the legacy of Duhm—acknowledge the historical and literary complexity of these chapters.[41] Although the prophet Isaiah has receded behind chapters 1–39 in inverse proportion to the emergence of Second and Third Isaiah, most treatments of First Isaiah continue to pursue traditional problems of history and sociology in these chapters as though such a project required no defense, and could be undertaken on rough analogy with such projects in the second half of the book (40–66). An interest in the redactional history of the wider Isaiah collection brings with it new and diverse challenges to this method of approach, whose consequence is yet to be fully appreciated.

Redactional Approaches: Type A

The move to adopt a redactional analysis of the wider Isaiah collection is not without its own internal conflict, nor has it produced any consensus that

---

39. For a sampling, see P. Hanson, *The Dawn of Apocalyptic* (Philadelphia: Fortress, 1975); W. Kessler, *Gott geht es um das Ganze: Jesaja 56–66 und Jesaja 24–27 übersetzt und ausgelegt* (Die Botschaft des Alten Testaments 19; Stuttgart, 1960); K. Pauritsch, *Die neue Gemeinde: Gott sammelt Ausgestossene und Arme (Jesaia 56–66): Die Botschaft des Tritojesaia-Buches literar-, form-, gattungskritisch und redaktionsgeschichtlich untersucht* (AnBib 47, Rome: Biblical Institute, 1973); G. Polan, *In the Ways of Justice Toward Salvation. A Rhetorical Analysis of Isaiah 56–59* (American University Studies VII.13; New York/Berne/Frankfurt, 1986); S. Sekine, *Die tritojesajanische Sammlung (Jes 56–66) redaktionsgeschichtlich untersucht* (BZAW 175; Berlin: Walter de Gruyter, 1989); E. Sehmsdorf, "Studien zur Redaktionsgeschichte von Jesaja 56–66," ZAW 84 (1972) 517–76; G. Wallis, "Gott und seine Gemeinde, Eine Betrachtung zum Tritojesaja-Buch," TZ 27 (1971) 182–200; W. Zimmerli, "Zur Sprache Tritojesajas," in *Gottes Offenbarung. Gesammelte Aufsätze zum Alten Testament* (Munich: Chr. Kaiser, 1963). For a criticism of the traditional view, see F. Maass, "Tritojesaja?" in *Das Ferne und Nahe Wort, Festschrift Leonhard Rost zur Vollendung seines 70. Lebensjahres am 30. November 1966 gewidmet* (BZAW 105; Berlin, 1967) 153–63.

40. J. Hayes and S. Irvine, *Isaiah, the Eighth-Century Prophet: His Times and His Preaching* (Nashville: Abingdon, 1987).

41. A good example is H. Barth, who adopts a sophisticated version of the accident theory when explaining the relationship between chaps. 1–39* and 40–66, the latter simply added on as an extension (*Erweiterung*) without inherent relationship to First Isaiah chapters (*Jesaja-Worte*, 298).

would break down the traditional Three Isaiah approach illustrated above. For simplicity's sake, two basic positions will be sketched out.

Type A is still concerned to keep separate the origin and development of tradition in 1–39° from that in 40–55, if not 40–66, even as the search for redactional unity proceeds. Elements of Duhm's original theory for the "editorial" independence of First from Second Isaiah have been maintained, and are a topic for discussion and minor adjustment. These elements will be discussed shortly. It is difficult to factor in the extent to which the (1) Babylonian provenance and (2) prophetic individual (Second and Third Isaiah) model exerts pressure on the editorial-independence argument; but doubtless the singular status of 40–55 continues to argue for its separate existence.

Several representatives of this view of Isaiah can be isolated. One of the more complex and intriguing studies is that of O. Steck. On the one hand, Steck demonstrates his independence from the classic Three Isaiah model by rejecting the customary terminology. The terms "Deuterojesaja" and "Tritojesaja" are flawed because they imply far too great a literary unity and redactional simplicity for chapters 40–55 and 56–66, respectively.[42] Moreover, they give the appearance of ruling out possible redactional linkages with "First Isaiah"–a term he retains, equivalent to "Proto-Isaiah"—within the larger Isaiah book as such, termed "Grossjesaja" (9). The consciously vague nomenclature "Zweite Jesaja" serves as a designation for the tradition in 40–66°, thus avoiding premature judgments about redactional linkages between the two Isaiahs, "Erste Jesaja" (1–39°) and "Zweite Jesaja" (40–66°) in the evolving "Grossjesaja."[43]

It should be clear from this terminology, however, that a basic independence is still in force for the "two Isaiahs," and in this sense the legacy of Duhm regarding editorial independence applies in modified form.[44] The linkages he sees involve the bringing together of two thoroughly independent Isaiah collections, accomplished by Isa 35, the "redactional bridge between First and Second Isaiah" (11), thus bringing about a critical merger in the Ptolemaic period. As late as the early postexilic period, one is still entitled to speak of an "unconnected juxtaposition" of the core material in First Isaiah and that in Zweite Jesaja (40–62°). In sum, Second Isaiah originated independently of First Isaiah, on all literary, editorial, and tradition-historical grounds.

---

42. *Heimkehr*, 9. Though not stated explicitly, the biographical aspect of form-criticism, with interest in prophetic personalities, seems also to be rejected when the terms "Deutero-" and "Trito-Isaiah" are set aside.

43. Here again, the biographical and cleanly historical dimensions of form-critical analysis recede in favor of redaction-historical investigation.

44. With clear reference to Duhm's theory, Steck asks at one point about Isa 36–39, "should the notice at 2 Chr 32:32 (cf. LXX) lead to a division of Proto-Isaiah from the Isaiah-narratives (in 2 Kings but not yet in Isaiah)?" (*Heimkehr*, 57).

A similar view of the editorial independence of Second Isaiah is held by numerous scholars, some like Steck interested in the redactional history of the whole book, and others who look beyond their labors in First Isaiah to wonder why the book grew as it did. It is here that elements from Duhm's classic theory reemerge, on two fronts: regarding (1) the tripartite structure of the independent First Isaiah Book; and (2) the borrowing of Isa 36–39 from Kings to provide a conclusion for the First Isaiah Book. Both arguments sought to defend the independence of the evolving First Isaiah Book from Isa 40–66. Many have adjusted Duhm's classic position to allow for a different view of Third Isaiah, but the consequences for Second Isaiah remain the same. What is intriguing to note is the *variety* of ways in which Duhm's theory has been adapted, some quite distinct from each other.

Barth is interested in material in Isa 1–35, and the isolation of a major Assyrian redaction at the time of Josiah. Not surprisingly, this leads him to ponder the question of the continuing growth of Isaiah tradition, beyond these chapters and this period in history. Against the position of Lack, he conceives of two Isaiah "complexes" (1–35[39] and 40–66) in "essentially independent development."[45] How these two complexes came together requires a cautious answer, which is stated by Barth in no more than a provisional way. Isa 36–39, as with Duhm, is termed a "historical appendix." The addition of 40–66 appears to be an attempt to accommodate the final structure of Isaiah to the "three known parts" of Ezekiel and Jeremiah (LXX): "c.1(2)-12 Unheil für das eigene Volk—c.13–35(39) Fremdvölkerthematik—c.40–66 Heil für das eigene Volk" (298). In fairness, Barth's main interest remains with the redactional history internal to First Isaiah chapters. His views regarding the larger Isaiah book present no substantive modification of Duhm's original statement; the same priority is given to LXX over MT Jeremiah, 2 Kgs 18–20 over Isa 36–39, and a putative tripartite structure in Ezekiel and Jeremiah. Barth does not mention the external evidence of the Chronicler in his very brief remarks.

What is most significant is Barth's subtle adjustment of the tripartite structure: now it belongs not to First Isaiah as such, nor to arguments for the independence of 1–39˚ from 40–66˚, but to the larger Isaiah book (1–66). As Ackroyd has pointed out, the tripartite concept is a sophisticated version of the accident theory. It is also different in kind from Duhm's position (viz., the designation of 13–35(39) as *Fremdvölkerthematic*).

Another First Isaiah interpreter, O. Kaiser, does not really treat the problem of the redactional history of the Isaiah book in his commentary,[46] though his views can be found in *Einleitung in das Alte Testament*.[47] While he mentions the schema, and speaks of its home in Ezekiel, he is reluctant to

45. *Jesaja-Worte*, 298.
46. Though see his remarks on Isa 36–39 in *Isaiah 13–39* (Philadelphia: Westminster, 1974) 367–68.
47. 5th thoroughly revised edition, Gütersloh: Gütersloher Verlagshaus Mohn, 1984, 232.

see its influence too heavily involved in the final structure of Isa 1–39 (not more than a "larger orienting scheme"). He acknowledges, then: "1–12 contain primarily words against the nation itself, 13–23 words against foreign peoples, 24–35 prophecies of salvation" (232). At the same time, one can spot intrusions into all sections of more apocalyptic themes, so that one is obliged to speak of the book in its "present form as an eschatological proclamation" (232).

Here the tripartite structure is maintained in the form stated by Duhm, while the more untidy dimensions of Isaiah's growth (into the Maccabean period) are factored in. What is important for our analysis is that, as with Duhm, the growth of Isa 1–39 has taken place independently of Second Isaiah. While Kaiser wants to give more room for the eschatological note the book sounds in its final form and final redactional stages (in a manner not unlike Duhm himself), the tripartite structure can still be detected. It functions as it did for Duhm: as an indication of the independent tradition-history of the First Isaiah Book.

In Vermeylen's massive two-volume treatment of the Book of Isaiah, chapters 40–55 are bracketed out entirely.[48] The seven stages of redaction, which he terms "relecture," reach well into the late postexilic period, embracing Third Isaiah chapters; but the core Second Isaiah material stands apart from this process (though it has received its own later relecture at various points). At the opening of his labors, Vermeylen utilizes the tripartite schema as a helpful device, without prematurely endorsing it: (1) oracles regarding Judah and Jerusalem (1–12); (2) oracles regarding foreign nations (13–27); (3) threats and promises for Israel (28–35). As is clear, the third section has been adjusted somewhat,[49] and chapters 36–39 are not included in the schema.

In a recent essay, Vermeylen is more explicit about the structure and independence of First Isaiah, over against chapters 40–55.[50] He concludes that around 480 B.C.E., independent of Second Isaiah, Proto-Isaiah had a structure that explicated a "theology of history": "after the time of misfortune for Judah and Jerusalem (1–12*) comes that of the judgment on the nations (13–27*), as a prelude to the triumph of the people of Yahweh and Zion (28–35*)."[51] Finally, then, a fourth section is to be found in 36–39, borrowed with modifications from 2 Kgs 18–20. These chapters correspond to (1) the final narrative sections in LXX Jer 43–51 (= MT 36–45), which tell of the suffering of the prophet, and (2) Jer 52 (borrowed from Kings), which concludes on a positive note regarding the ultimate fall of Babylon (Jer 52:31–34), as does Isa 39:8. Though

48. *Du prophète Isaïe à l'apocalyptique* (vol. 1, 1977; vol. 2, 1978).
49. See also G. Fohrer, *Einleitung in das Alte Testament*. Fohrer speaks of a third section that has promises framed by threats to Israel, or something to this effect.
50. "L'unité du livre d'Isaïe," *The Book of Isaiah*, 11–53.
51. "L'unité," 34. This third section is clearly different from what was set out in the provisional schema of his 1977/78 study (viz., threats and promises for Israel).

the analogy between First Isaiah and Jeremiah is not perfect, chapters 36–39 do indeed form a conclusion to a Proto-Isaiah Book, "before this was supplemented by Deutero-Isaiah" (34). At another point, Vermeylen acknowledges that these chapters do ease the transition to Second Isaiah, a position argued persuasively by Ackroyd;[52] nevertheless, they in no way presuppose the existence of a Second Isaiah corpus (cf. Ackroyd). A later redactor is responsible for the merger of the two independent Isaiahs, in the period of Nehemiah, to which is then added "a large redactional unit" (chaps. 56–66) and further relecture throughout 1–66.

For our purposes, it is important to note the strict separation of First from Second Isaiah chapters. When after 480 B.C.E. chapters 1–39 receive their first extensive eschatological rereading, the "Deutero-Isaiaic collection was not alluded to in this relecture" (52). The theological interpretation of history that provides structure for a Proto-Isaiah on analogy with Jeremiah does not involve the "theological-political message meant to rally the Jewish population to Cyrus" as it is found in chapters 40–55°.[53] In that sense, the "theology of history" remains imprinted in a meaningful way only on Isa 1–39, while independent Second Isaiah chapters are fused onto this structure with redactional stitching, before the final scribal "prolongation" represented by chapters 56–66 (p. 53).

Vermeylen is convinced that around the time 480 B.C.E. the same school, or redactor, imposed a structure on both Proto-Isaiah and LXX Jeremiah, the distinguishing feature of which is a central eschatological section regarding the fate of the "pagan world" (32), to be detected as well in Ezekiel and Zephaniah, if not Micah. He provides a helpful chart (p. 32) to illustrate the structure:

Oracles of misfortune on Judah and Jerusalem	Oracles of misfortune on the nations	Promises
Isa 1–12	Isa 13–27	Isa 28–35
Jer LXX 1:1—25:13	Jer LXX 25:13—32:38	Jer LXX 33–42
MT 1:1—25:13a	MT 25:13b–38	MT 26–35
	46–51	
Ez 1–24	Ez 25–32	Ez 33–48

What was a suggestion for Duhm—proposed in the space of one paragraph, seen in clearest form in Ezekiel, requiring the independent testimony of the Chronicler on two counts—has become for Vermeylen a complex theory of redaction, extending to Zephaniah and possibly Micah. The best example of

---

52. P.R. Ackroyd, "Babylonian Exile," 329–52; also "Structure and Function," 3–21.
53. "L'unité," 52.

the tripartite theology of history remains in this schema the LXX Jeremiah text, to whose fundamental priority over the MT one finds a commitment no longer requiring any defense.

A similar view of matters is to be seen in the essay of P.-M. Bogaert devoted to the question of structural organization "of the large prophetic collections."[54] Duhm's tripartite theory is mentioned in the opening sentence, and is quickly extended to Zephaniah as well. Bogaert acknowledges that the third section has not worn well the title "promises"—what is one to make of the Baruchschrift in Jeremiah, the complex "Torah of Ezekiel" in Ez 40–48, and the material in Isa 24–35 that does not speak at all of promises? Nevertheless, what is most fundamental is the existence in all three of a central section regarding oracles against nations "suggesting thereby a tripartite organization" (p. 148).

Not content with firm resolve regarding the priority of LXX Jeremiah,[55] Bogaert also sees a threefold structure in the Book of the Twelve, according to the order of the Septuagint (Hosea, Amos, Micah, Joel, Obadiah, Jonah, Nahum, Habakkuk, Zephaniah, Haggai, Zechariah, Malachi). The interest of Obadiah in Edom, Jonah in Ninevah (+), Nahum in Ninevah (-), and Habakkuk in Chaldea signals for him that here too a "central position" is concerned with the fate of the nations.[56] Like Vermeylen, Bogaert feels the original structure (*le plan type*) is best represented in Jeremiah, and then applied by redactors to Proto-Isaiah, Ezekiel, Zephaniah, and the Twelve.

With respect to Isa 36–39, here too Proto-Isaiah resembles Jeremiah. Both books borrow their conclusions from the Deuteronomistic History (DtrH) in order to (1) set the latter's view of prophecy as the final word, and (2) announce the taking of Jerusalem.[57]

Many questions arise from the proposals of Vermeylen and Bogaert. Consistently one sees a preference for LXX texts and structures, as well as the priority of the DtrH over the prophetic books (Jer 52 and Isa 36–39). It is not the place here to analyze these proposals in detail. What is of interest is the manner in which Duhm's tripartite pattern has found its way into arguments for the independence of a First Isaiah Book by those who now are interested in penetrating the redactional logic of the Book of Isaiah in its entirety. We will return to discuss the salient features of these proposals below.

---

54. In the same volume (*The Book of Isaiah* [1989]: "L'organisation des grands receuils prophé- tiques"), 147–53.
55. Obviously MT Jeremiah knows nothing of any tripartite schema on analogy with Ezekiel or Isaiah.
56. Even granting the priority of the LXX order, what is one to make of sections like Amos 1–2 (nations) or Micah 4–5 (promises)? The same odd admixtures within the three sections of the parts applies as much to the Book of the Twelve (LXX) as it does to Jeremiah (LXX). Moreover, why if there was such a clear pattern did MT disturb it, both in Jeremiah and the Twelve, while leaving it intact in Isaiah and Ezekiel?
57. "Grandes recueils," 150–51.

It is necessary in conclusion to return to the work of Steck and, more specifically, to his own proposal for the independence of the "two Isaiahs" within the larger "Grossjesaja" Book. Here one sees the original tripartite theory in far more vestigial form, moving beyond Barth's modest adjustment discussed above. In fact, the theory in pure form has all but disappeared, even while the independence of the two Isaiahs is strictly maintained.

The essential thesis of Steck is that chapter 35 has been closely developed on the basis of chapters 34 and 40, its "Nachbartexten."[58] He concludes that chapter 35 has borrowed and adapted language and themes from both, in order to form a bridge spanning the two Isaiahs.

Naturally one comes to wonder why chapters 36–39 obscure this bridge function in the present shape of the book. In attempting to explain this oddity, Steck presents his own version(s) of the tripartite schema as a structural device in Proto-Isaiah.[59]

At first glance, one would assume that chapter 34 formed the logical conclusion to the Proto-Isaiah Book in Steck's model. Nevertheless, chapter 33 has clear connections with the Isaiah narratives in 36–39, suggesting that they belong to the same "Abschlußschicht" (57). In this case, the "Gesamtkontur" of the "Protojesajabuch" resembles LXX Jeremiah, "in three major subsections":

1) Words concerning the people of God
   (Isa 1–11˚ and LXX Jer 1:1—25:13)

2) Words concerning the foreign nations
   (Isa 13–34˚ and LXX Jer 25:14—32:13–38)

3) Prophetic Narratives
   (Isa 36–39 and LXX Jer 33–51[52])

If LXX Jeremiah is in fact a modification of an earlier MT, then Proto-Isaiah would have provided the model for such an *Umgestaltung*.[60] Note that this tripartite pattern finds no correspondence in the work of Duhm or any of the scholars reviewed thus far. Nevertheless, the search for a pattern, tripartite or otherwise, confirms the fact that Proto-Isaiah is to be taken as a meaningful structure in and of itself, apart from Second Isaiah.[61]

---

58. The main points can be seen in the first section, "Die Beziehung von Jes 35 zu den Nachbar- texten im Jesajabuch," *Heimkehr*, 13–37.
59. *Heimkehr*, 56–59.
60. Ibid., 58, n. 38. Steck is by no means as dogmatic about the priority of the LXX as Bogaert and Vermeylen. In fact, he leans toward the priority of the MT, as will be shown.
61. Steck remains uncertain about the precise status of 36–39 within the redactional stages of Proto and Great Isaiah. It does appear that 36–39 found their place prior to the welding of the two Isaiahs with the help of chap. 35; otherwise, why would the direct line running from 34 to 35 to 40 (so essential for Steck's thesis) have been broken by the insertion of these chapters? Steck does a good deal of speculating on various possibilities before reaching a decision. At one point (57, n. 37) he refers to the nonmention of Isaiah (instead Kings) in 2 Chr 32:32 as possibly inferring that

Alternatively, chapter 34 formed the first real conclusion to Protojesaja. Shortly after this, 36–39 would have been added, still earlier than chapter 35's pivotal role was put into effect. Steck leans toward this view, while keeping the exact status of chapters 36–39 less fixed. In this case, Proto-Isaiah had for its structural model the Book of Jeremiah, *as preserved in the Masoretic tradition*, viz., with the oracles against nations in the final position:

Part One: Jer 2:4–45 (prophet to Israel, so 1:11—2:3)
Part Two: Jer 46–51 (prophet to the nations, so 1:4–10)

—corresponds to—

Part One: Isa 1–11˚ (words concerning the people of God)
Part Two: Isa 13–34˚ (words concerning the nations)

With the addition of Zweite Jesaja, accomplished by the insertion of chapter 35, the bipartite structure of Proto-Isaiah was converted into a tripartite Grossjesaja, on analogy with Ezekiel, and possibly Zephaniah.[62]

In surveying recent attempts to penetrate the redactional logic of the Book of Isaiah, we have isolated those scholars who, like Duhm, insist that the tradition-history of Second Isaiah be kept absolutely distinct from that of First Isaiah, until late in the postexilic period. Even then, the merger of First with Second Isaiah is externally imposed, and does not grow internally out of either tradition complex.

For our purposes, it is striking that some form of structural argument, involving the larger contour of 1–35 as well as the status of 36–39, is generally mounted to defend the independent tradition history of Proto-Isaiah. Here the legacy of Duhm is strong, though his appeal to the Chronicler for help with the independence of 40–55 and 36–39 has been all but abandoned. What is more striking, however, is that there is absolutely no agreement about what that structure is, nor how it is to be aligned with the other prophetic collections, including now Micah, Zephaniah, and the Twelve. The closest thing to agreement exists between Bogaert and Vermeylen. Steck's thesis is the most complex, though in the end his position begins to lean toward that of Barth, with a tripartite structure involving the entire Isaiah collection. But while Barth includes LXX Jeremiah in the scheme, Steck leaves it to the side as a secondary development. Bogaert moves beyond Vermeylen in arguing for a threefold structure in the Twelve (LXX). And they both restrict the tripartite

chapters 36–39 were not yet in Isaiah, a theory that played a central role in Duhm's larger argument for the independence of First Isaiah.

62. But not on analogy with MT Jeremiah. LXX Jeremiah is an adaptation of the original MT to get it to conform to this pattern. Here Steck follows Smend (*Entstehung*, 157) in preferring an original structure in MT adapted in LXX (see also Seitz, "The Prophet Moses," 13–27). The third section in Ezekiel (40–48) corresponds to Isa 35 + 40ff. (also Zeph 3:9–20).

pattern to Isa 1–39, as such, apart from chapters 40ff., in distinction to Barth and Steck.

In sum, while there is agreement about the independence of First Isaiah from Second Isaiah, there is disagreement about how that independence is to be conceived at the structural level. Nowhere is the uneven legacy of Duhm more pronounced than in arguments for the structural shape and editorial independence of First Isaiah.

One explanation for the wide divergence regarding structural independence in First Isaiah is that *no such structure exists*, or to quote Ackroyd: "The whole tripartite pattern appears to be a modern invention."[63] Another way to state the matter is that structural arguments are required because of the presumption that First Isaiah was once an "independent book." As such, it ought to resemble other independent books (Jeremiah and Ezekiel) or collections (the Twelve).[64] If First Isaiah never had a fully independent existence, beyond the period of Second Isaiah's composition, then one would not expect any such structure, and the whole search for one is predicated on the notion that First and Second Isaiah ought to be kept absolutely distinct. As stated above, the theory of Second Isaiah as a prophet in Babylon doubtless contributes to the argument for editorial/structural independence in First Isaiah. But that issue must be addressed separately. Before such a treatment can proceed, it is necessary to examine those contributions to the redactional study of Isaiah that conceive of the relationship between First and Second Isaiah rather differently.

One final note before moving to that overview. In some measure, all modern scholars who defend the strict independence of First from Second Isaiah also view chapters 36–39 as constituting the conclusion of the former. As did Gesenius in the early nineteenth century, they further hold that these chapters had their original home in the Book of Kings.[65] Though Steck provisionally suggested that these chapters were analogous to the prophetic narratives in Jer 33–51 (= MT 26–45), the others agreed that they were to be taken as a historical conclusion (or appendix), on par with Jer 52, itself borrowed from 2 Kgs 25.

This collection of assumptions must be examined in detail. Ackroyd has repeatedly emphasized that the Isaiah prophetic narratives in no way resemble Jer 52, either in terms of content or function. Jeremiah plays no role in the latter, while Isaiah is the key figure in the former.[66] Here Steck's observation

---

63. "Presentation," 20.
64. Eichhorn promoted the view that Isaiah was an anthology like the Twelve, which is why in rabbinic lists (B.Bat. 15b) it is listed next to the Twelve, after Jeremiah and Ezekiel. But he never toyed with a tripartite organizational theory. Moreover, the entire sixty-six chapter Isaiah resembled the Twelve, not just First Isaiah (so Bogaert).
65. W. Gesenius, *Jesaia*, 2.932–936.
66. Jer 52 "does not show that remarkable intertwining of the activity of the prophet with the

concerning the resemblance of Isa 36–39 to Jer 26–45 is closer to the mark.[67] Moreover, the recent essay of Smelik suggests that the time-honored view of Isa 36–39 as drafted from 2 Kgs 18–20 needs further evaluation, quite apart from theories for the structural integrity of a Proto-Isaiah Book.[68] By stressing the special *function* of the Isaiah narrative within the Book of Isaiah, Ackroyd has raised similar cautions.[69] Ackroyd and Smelik point to the close connections between Isa 36–39 and Isa 6–9, as well as the special transitional role the former narratives play in the Book of Isaiah (but not in Kings!). At a minimum, these sorts of observations call into question any simple view of Isa 36–39 as the conclusion to a Proto-Isaiah Book, on analogy with Jer 52.

Redactional Approaches: Type B

The distinguishing feature of this form of redactional approach is the lack of emphasis on the strict independence of First from Second Isaiah in terms of editorial development or theoretical structural identity (First Isaiah as a closed book with a conclusion and tripartite organization). While for several of the scholars to be discussed the independence of First from Second Isaiah appears to be nearly as fixed as it is in Type A,[70] several distinctive features can be noted: (1) minimal discussion of Proto-Isaiah as a closed book, in the manner of Duhm; (2) the likelihood of an earlier "merger" of the two Isaiahs, or the probability of redactional influence running in both directions (from 1–39° to 40–55, and the reverse) without Proto-Isaiah ever becoming its own "book"; (3) the probability that First Isaiah received redactional enrichment intended to key these chapters to Second Isaiah, earlier and with different effect than the model proposed by Vermeylen and others.[71] In sum, Duhm's argument for two distinctive tradition-historical orbits, only subsequently and artificially brought into conjunction, plays no serious role here. For all that, the singular status of chapters 40–55 within the Book of Isaiah is upheld, as is the model of Second Isaiah as prophet among exiles.

Type B redactional approaches are to be distinguished from type A primarily in the conception of First Isaiah. Ackroyd, Becker, Brueggemann,

course of events which is so important a part of Isa. xxxvi-xxxix" ("Presentation," 20). On the nonmention of Jeremiah, see most recently K.-F. Pohlmann, "Erwägungen zum Schlusskapitel des deuteronomistischen Geschichtswerkes. Oder: Warum wird der Prophet Jeremia in 2.Kön.22-25 nicht erwähnt?" *Textgemäss. Aufsätze und Beiträge zur Hermeneutik des Alten Testaments* (Festschrift E. Würthwein; A.H.J. Gunneweg and O. Kaiser, eds.; Göttingen: Vandenhoeck & Ruprecht, 1979) 94–109; also, Seitz, *Theology in Conflict*, 215–21.

67. So also Ackroyd ("Historians and Prophets," *SEA* 33 [1968] 18–54).

68. K.A.D. Smelik, "Distortion," 70–93.

69. In both "Babylonian Exile" (1974) and "Structure and Function" (1982).

70. This is largely due to the hegemony of the traditional Second Isaiah theory, which has "exiled" chaps. 40–55 to Babylon. As we shall see, the flexibility for type B redactional approaches extends primarily to First Isaiah chapters.

71. That is, not after two independent "books" were merged, but as a still evolving First Isaiah collection took form with an eye to Second Isaiah. Chaps. 40–55 are brought within the orbit of First Isaiah chapters prior to their stabilization.

Childs, Clements, Meade, Melugin, Rendtorff, and Sweeney all fundamentally agree that the tradition in 1–39˚ has remained fluid enough that at the time of Second Isaiah's merger, or earlier, this tradition received enrichment meant to key the reader to the themes and presentation of chapters 40–55, if not subsequently to 56–66 as well.[72] Ackroyd has focused on the transitional function of chapters 36–39, introducing the important datum of Babylonian exile;[73] he has also stressed the purposeful way in which chapters 1–12 have been shaped to function in the final form of the entire book;[74] more specifically, he has recognized important links between chapters 6 and 40 that serve to bridge these two collections.[75] With respect to the question of two independent Isaiahs in the manner of Duhm, Ackroyd lodges his own objection: "there is no adequate basis for the common supposition that these chapters (40–55) were added to an already completed book of Isaiah."[76]

In much of this Ackroyd has been guided by the final brief remarks of R. Melugin, made in a 1976 study on Second Isaiah.[77] Melugin argued that these chapters were "never meant to stand alone" and that "the closest thing to a setting for chapters 40ff. is the prophecy of Isaiah to Hezekiah in chapter 39 concerning the exile to Babylon" (p. 177). We will have occasion to return to these remarks shortly, for they suggest a minor variation on the notion that First Isaiah was "outfitted" to anticipate Second Isaiah. Melugin here argues that Second Isaiah was composed *in conscious relationship* to First Isaiah, a theory that obviously goes beyond Duhm, if not many of those we are presently discussing.

As stated above, most scholars in this group argue more simply that chapters 1–39˚ have been shaped in such a way as to prepare the reader for the themes and setting of Second Isaiah chapters, and that efforts at redactional coherence have taken root within First Isaiah tradition. Such a view of matters is at clear odds with the two positions we have discussed thus far. R.

72. In the least subtle form, some scholars have proposed that Deutero-Isaiah was actually the editor of First Isaiah. Such a view was promoted early on by P. de Lagarde, who held that Isa 1–39 was shaped as a chrestomathy for the purpose of validating the new prophecy of Second Isaiah (*Symmicta*, I, 1887, 142). In a more sophisticated form, this is essentially the position of J. Becker (*Isaias—der Prophet und sein Buch* [SBS; Stuttgart: Kohlhammer, 1973]). Unfortunately, the theory is unlikely, impossible to prove, and suffers from a circularity of logic. For an interesting early study of this problem, see also D.R. Jones, "Traditio," 226–46.
73. "As this section of material stands in the book of Isaiah, it appears as a preface to the whole section, from ch. 40 onwards, which is devoted to the message of the unnamed prophet of the exile, the so-called Second Isaiah" ("Babylonian Exile," 338). "The placing of 36–39 where it stands in the book of Isaiah [is] used to provide a contextual basis for the prophecies of chs. 40ff." ("Structure and Function," 20).
74. "Presentation," 47.
75. "With chapter 40 we are thereby presented with a renewal of the Isaianic commission" ("Structure and Function," 6). See also, Melugin, *Formation*, 176; and now, Rendtorff, "Jesaja 6 im Rahmen der Komposition des Jesajabuches," *The Book of Isaiah*, 73–82; Seitz, "The Divine Council: Temporal Transition and New Prophecy in the Book of Isaiah," *JBL* 109 (1990) 229–46.
76. "Structure and Function," 7.
77. *Formation*, 176–78.

Clements has spoken of a major Babylonian redaction in 1–39, to be distinguished from a level of preexilic editorial reworking within First Isaiah, which had been termed "Assyrian" by H. Barth.[78] The Babylonian redaction is essentially a "process of prophetic re-interpretation and development" ("Fall of Jerusalem," 436) for which the fall of Jerusalem in 587 was the pivotal point. It can be seen at various points throughout First Isaiah chapters, and includes anything from minor glosses to more extended compositions, for which the 587 debacle forms the backdrop.

In principle if not also in specifics, Clements's general view of a Babylonian redaction has met with assent from both Meade[79] and Sweeney,[80] as has Ackroyd's larger set of observations—which had already received endorsement from Rendtorff.[81] As if to emphasize the main thrust of this view of Isaiah's development, Rendtorff has spoken of chapters 40–55 as the actual core ("Kern der jetzigen Komposition") of Isaiah tradition, providing the starting point for redactional enrichment in both First and Third Isaiah. In the initial study of 1984, it was not entirely clear what was meant by "First" Isaiah, so anxious was Rendtorff to stress "that the second part of the book, chapters 40–55, hold a dominant position in the book as a whole."[82] Second Isaiah is the stable point "from which and toward which the other two sections were composed and edited" (318). Clearly tradition existed in First Isaiah upon which this redactional influence was exerted,[83] but Rendtorff wished to place special emphasis on the fluid nature of this material, and the redactional impress from Second Isaiah chapters on it. In so doing, he clearly sought to distance himself from a view of Isaiah's development that stressed the independent character of chapters 1–39° over against 40–55.[84]

Thus far we have been reviewing those scholars who, in distinction to Duhm and the two groups above, view chapters 1–39 as never having moved to "book" form, with independent structure and conclusion, in isolation from Second Isaiah. A very different understanding of chapters 36–39, for example, has been proposed by Ackroyd, Melugin, Clements, and their followers. Ack-

---

78. See especially, "Fall of Jerusalem" (1980); *Isaiah 1–39* (NCB; Grand Rapids/London: Eerdmanns/Marshall, Morgan & Scott, 1980), and "Unity of Isaiah" (1982). The subtitle of Barth's 1977 study is: *Israel und Assur als Thema einer produktiven Neuinterpretation der Jesajaüberlieferung.*
79. *Pseudonymity,* 27–31.
80. *Isaiah 1–4,* 11–25. Sweeney also feels that the "Exodus motif" is a constitutive theme in First Isaiah as well as Second Isaiah (18).
81. "Komposition," 296–97; "Jesaja 6," 75.
82. Ibid., 318.
83. See his essay in *The Book of Isaiah* (1989).
84. So strong is his commitment to the centrality of 40–55, Rendtorff feels that: "At most the second part, with its well-planned and integrated composition, could have existed independently before being inserted into the present composition" (*Introduction,* 200). Here is a view of the Book of Isaiah in which the independence belongs in the first place to Second Isaiah; First Isaiah is dependent upon these chapters for its content and shape.

royd in particular has seriously questioned the logic that classified these chapters as a "conclusion" on analogy with Jer 52, as well as the whole notion of "tripartite" structuring for chapters 1–39. Here we isolate an important disagreement over the nature and function of chapters 36–39 within the Book of Isaiah that will have to be addressed in more detail below. In fact, one might say that the argument for "editorial-independence" as conceived by Duhm and adapted by redaction-critical treatments discussed in the previous section stands or falls with the proper interpretation of chapters 36–39. Either these chapters were composed to serve a transitional purpose; or they were a conclusion to Proto-Isaiah. They cannot form the preface to Second Isaiah, much less "the setting for chs. 40ff." (Melugin), and at the same time close off a Proto-Isaiah book that knows nothing of Second Isaiah chapters.[85] The relationship of these chapters to 2 Kgs 18–20 must be reexamined, as well as the question of the date of the various levels of tradition in 36–39.

An important distinction needs to be introduced at this point, which ultimately touches on the matter of Second Isaiah's original status. A Babylonian redaction could have been undertaken in Isa 1–39 as a consequence of the events in 587, and that redaction might well have been coordinated with Second Isaiah chapters. The scholars we have discussed thus far generally agree on this conception. Childs has summarized his own thinking along similar lines in his treatment of "the theological shaping of First Isaiah";[86] Ackroyd's critical studies have met with approval and have been taken up by Childs.

In his treatment of the "former-latter things" motif in Second Isaiah, Childs raises an important issue alluded to in the work of Melugin. He offers a fresh interpretation of the "former things" as "the prophecies of First Isaiah" (329), a position that has been endorsed by Clements, Brueggemann, Meade, Rendtorff, and Sweeney.[87] Such a move heads in the direction of suggesting that Second Isaiah worked in conscious relationship to First Isaiah's prophecies (using a prophetic individual model, still at the preliterary level). When Childs raises the canonical or literary question, he concludes: "In the light of the present shape of the book of Isaiah the question must be seriously raised if

---

85. One might try to argue that Isa 36–39 was a conclusion that has been edited for the purposes of transition (see Vermeylen's cautious reaction to Clements's position ["L'unité," 34]). Sweeney, for example, has suggested that the "plusses" in Isaiah over against Kings are additions and modifications, meant to enable this text to function better in its new Isaiah context (*Isaiah 1–4*, 13–16). It will be necessary to examine this essentially simple view of the relationship between 2 Kgs 18–20 and Isa 36–39 below, especially in light of Smelik's contention that the direction of influence is from Isaiah to Kings, and not the reverse. Even Sweeney's view of matters does not argue for an original conclusion subsequently edited, except as that conclusion was drafted from 2 Kings 25.

86. *Introduction*, 330–33.

87. A version of this proposal was aired by D.R. Jones ("Traditio") and mentioned by C.R. North ("The Former Things and the New Things in Deutero-Isaiah," *Studies in Old Testament Prophecy* [H.H. Rowley, ed.; Edinburgh: T. & T. Clark, 1950] 124–25).

the material of Second Isaiah in fact ever circulated in Israel apart from its being connected to an earlier form of First Isaiah" (p. 329). Here he appears to come close to the position of Melugin, who felt that chapters 40–55 "were never meant to stand alone" (*Formation*, 177).

Still, the language is rather vague ("never meant to"—but once did?), and it is clear that both Melugin and Childs respect the independence of Second Isaiah (prophet and literature) in a manner consistent with the traditional conception. So it is that Childs at an earlier point in his argument, conscious of the original exilic context of Second Isaiah's message, suggests that elements of historical particularity in chapters 40–55 were eliminated as these chapters were assigned a new role in the canonical Book of Isaiah: "the canonical editors of this tradition employed the material in such a way as to eliminate almost entirely those concrete features and to subordinate the original message to a new role in the canon" (p. 325).

Both Ackroyd and Clements have questioned whether removal of "historical vestiges" is really the issue,[88] and have agreed that the stronger dimension of Childs's argument concerns the former/latter things motif, and what it suggests about the putative independence of Second Isaiah. This is particularly true of Clements. It is necessary to look at his remarks in detail, for they suggest an altogether different approach for understanding the place of Second Isaiah within the Book of Isaiah, to be further differentiated from redactional approaches we have designated type B.

BEYOND DUHM:
SECOND ISAIAH WITHIN THE BOOK OF ISAIAH

Picking up on the intriguing suggestions of Childs and Melugin, Clements has argued for a completely new conception of Second Isaiah. He rejects the accidental merger theory, or even the external linking notion as frequently defended by scholars in the second group above, and proposes "that, from the outset, the material in chs. 40–55 was intended to develop and enlarge upon prophetic sayings from Isaiah of Jerusalem."[89] First Isaiah is not just redactionally "outfitted" in light of 587 events and in view of the literary reality of chapters 40–55;[90] rather "from the time of their origin, the prophetic sayings of Isa. 40–55 were intended as a supplement and sequel to a collection of sayings of the eighth-century Isaiah of Jerusalem" (101). Given the redactional complexity of chapters 1–39, one would naturally like to know exactly

---

88. See also B.S. Childs, "The Canonical Shape of the Prophetic Literature," *Int* 32 (1978) 46–55, where he speaks of Second Isaiah as "drained of its historical particularity" (50). Ackroyd levels the same objection at Melugin ("Structure and Function," 4); Clements, "Deutero-Isaianic Development," 112, n. 14.
89. "Deutero-Isaianic Development," 101.
90. So Clements in "Fall of Jerusalem" (1980) and "Unity of Isaiah" (1982).

what those sayings were and what that collection looked like. At a later point in the study, Clements refers to the Assyrian redaction concept of Barth as providing some clue as to the scope and character of Proto-Isaiah, such as might have been available to Second Isaiah. As he puts it: "that the prophecies of Isa. 40–55 should have arisen in a situation where access to *a written collection* of the prophetic sayings of Isaiah of Jerusalem was possible should in no way surprise us" (emphasis mine, 106). For Clements this "written collection" would resemble Barth's Assyrian redaction, or some other intermediate level of written tradition, brought together between the time of Isaiah of Jerusalem and a later Babylonian redaction.

Clements provides two examples of places where Second Isaiah has "carried forward the message of Isaiah of Jerusalem" (106). The theme of blindness and deafness, prominent in Second Isaiah (42:16; 42:18–19; 43:8; 44:18), is based upon the commission in 6:9–10, and demonstrates that Second Isaiah was "familiar with the actual words recorded of Isaiah's call in a section which is usually ascribed to the 'Isaiah Memoir'" (104). Similar logic is operative for Second Isaiah's language of election, which is seen by Clements to be a direct reversal of First Isaiah's language of rejection with respect to Israel.

Naturally, this view of Second Isaiah calls into question the traditional approach, if not the broader conception of prophecy as such. Here we have an instance of prophecy derived from written texts, as it were, and Clements is fully prepared to accept this as "related to the very nature of prophecy itself, in which particular words and images could be regarded as fraught with special power and significance" (110). Here, too, we stumble onto the sense of Clements's choice of words for the title: "Beyond Tradition-History." For in distinction to von Rad's notion of the prophets being under the influence of traditions—for Second Isaiah these were Zion and David—Clements is suggesting that in Second Isaiah's case that influence is from *written prophetic texts*, from within the evolving First Isaiah book.

At this juncture, one must realize the difficulty such a view presents for the "Second Isaiah among Babylonian exiles" model. For in the tradition-historical model as practiced by Mowinckel,[91] the link between First and Second Isaiah was a crude sociological one: the traditions of First Isaiah were carried by disciples, of which Deutero-Isaiah was presumably one, in Babylonian exile.[92] But Clements rightly rejects this model because it does not really penetrate to the heart of the literary and redactional problems across all of Isa 1–55: "it retains the idea of a connection based upon authorship . . . without requiring *any truly intrinsic connection of content* between the various blocks of material" (emphasis mine, 97). How, then, does First Isaiah tradition

---

91. *Prophecy and Tradition* (Oslo, 1946).
92. See also Jones ("Traditio") and J.H. Eaton, "The Origin of the Book of Isaiah," *VT* 9 (1959) 138–57.

in written form work out its influence on Second Isaiah in exile? Just exactly what kind of model is Clements proposing for Second Isaiah?

It is here that only tentative suggestions are put forward. Clements notes the time-honored observation of Second Isaiah's use of psalmic and lyrical modes of expression; he speaks of the frequent address to Zion, and of the problem such address has caused for a view of Second Isaiah in Babylon; and related to this, he wonders "whether scholarship has been correct for positing for all of chs. 40–55 an origin in Babylon" (109). Put another way: Has the individual prophet in exile model been chiefly responsible for the inability to see "any truly intrinsic connection of content" between First and Second Isaiah? Conversely, if Clements is correct, and one can spot intrinsic relationships from Second back to First Isaiah, is it then necessary to revise many of the time-honored assumptions about the great prophet of the exile, not the least of which is the Babylonian setting and the emphasis on historical context apart from literary context within the Book of Isaiah?[93] On the positive side, would recognition of the reciprocal relationships between Second and First Isaiah help to explain many of the factors that have long puzzled interpreters of chapters 40–55, including matters of literary form and structure, the exegesis of individual passages, and the question of prophetic agency?

These remarks of Clements made in a 1985 essay are intriguing, and point to yet a third possibility for redactional analysis of the Book of Isaiah, for the sake of consistency to be termed type C. Consistent with type B, one finds a rejection of the thesis that Proto-Isaiah developed into an independent book, derivative of an independent tradition-history. As in type B, Proto-Isaiah is seen to have undergone a specific redactional development intended to shape the material toward chapters 40–55, in reflection on the events of 587 B.C.E. (a Babylonian revision). Beyond type B, however, Melugin, Childs, and especially Clements have raised the possibility that Second Isaiah, *from its inception*, was composed in relationship to First Isaiah. With this view of the dependence—not independence—of Second Isaiah, Clements has gone further to question the Babylonian setting of the prophecies in chapters 40–55. Suddenly a completely new perspective on the redactional development of the Book of Isaiah is raised for discussion, with the most profound consequences for that section of the book called Second Isaiah.

SUMMARY AND PROPOSAL

In two respects, we have come full circle. The Book of Isaiah, in its entirety, has again become the context in which discussion of the individual

93. In a recent study on holiness in the Old Testament, J. Gammie has elected to use the designation "Isaiah of Babylon" for the author of 40–55, a notion he picked up from H. Beebe (*The Old Testament: An Introduction to Its Literary, Historical and Religious Traditions* [Belmont, Calif.: Dickenson Publishing Co., 1970] 241, 352, 364) (J. Gammie, *Holiness in Israel* [OBT; Minneapolis: Fortress, 1989] 97).

sections takes place, as was the case with Duhm. Redaction critics (type A and type B) are divided over the question of the nature and degree of Proto-Isaiah's independence within the book, but the larger redactional development of the Book of Isaiah remains the topic of specific interest for both groups, whether they follow Duhm or propose greater interpenetration between 1–39˚ and 40–55. With the emergence of type C, especially as articulated by Clements, the firm conclusion of Duhm regarding the setting of Second Isaiah also comes to mind: "certainly he did not live in Babylon." It must be determined whether the provenance of Second Isaiah has any significant bearing on the question of redactional dependence on First Isaiah.

The question of setting is not just important in its own right; it forces us to reassess the relative status of arguments for the editorial independence of Second Isaiah, as against arguments for the historical, geographical, and form-critical singularity of Second Isaiah within the Book of Isaiah. Is the singular status of chapters 40–55 due to its having originated in Babylonian exile, under the inspired aegis of an anonymous individual prophet (the first two groups above)? Is the singular status to be enhanced further by seeing no tradition-historical relationship between First and Second Isaiah collections, as well as no inherent redactional linkage (Duhm and especially the second group)? What was the nature of Duhm's argument against a Babylonian setting, and would it have any—even ironic—bearing on the possibility put forward by Clements, that Second Isaiah developed in close relationship to First Isaiah? Has the proposal of a Babylonian setting potentially confused the issue regarding editorial dependence or independence for Second Isaiah?

In the 1985 essay, Clements is not dogmatic about the centrality of the provenance question. He states:

> The place of origin would seem to be a question that is not so readily capable of resolution as may at first appear. In any case my own purpose will have been achieved if a strong case can be made to show that the evidence that the prophecies of "Second Isaiah" reveal a conscious dependence on earlier sayings of Isaiah of Jerusalem is firm and reliable. [*Deutero-Isaianic Development*, 109]

Even from this statement it is clear that the issues are related, and that the broader traditional conception of Second Isaiah would have to be adjusted if one wished to claim the kind of "conscious dependence" of Second on First Isaiah proposed by Clements.

This chapter has revealed two basic problems confronting Isaiah research at present. One trend has been isolated, with roots in Duhm's original work. It emphasizes the editorial independence of First from Second Isaiah; this trend stands at one side of a division over the proper approach to Isaiah's redactional unity. We have examined in detail the arguments of type A redaction critics, as these touch on the independent status of 1–39˚. It is clear that the editorial independence argument is based in no small measure on a fixed view of the status of chapters 36–39 in the Book of Isaiah, and the role these chapters presumably play in contributing to a tripartite organizational structure in the Book of Isaiah as a whole, or in the proto-Isaiah chapters. As such, it is clear that the origins, compositional development, and function of chapters 36–39 require further study in order to determine whether these chapters (1) close off a Proto-Isaiah Book, (2) enhance an editorially imposed structural organization, or (3) reveal a basic transitional character, assisting the movement into 40–55 and following.

But the problem is more complicated still. In order to give more room for Clements's conception of the redactional development of the Book of Isaiah, whereby the composition of Second Isaiah chapters has from its inception been keyed to the written prophecy contained in First Isaiah, it is necessary to determine in more precise terms what is meant by "First Isaiah." Here again chapters 36–39 play a critical role, on two counts. First there is the simple problem of whether Isa 36–39 should be considered part of an Isaiah to which Second Isaiah is allegedly related. For even those who reject the tripartite structure as a meaningful redactional index (Ackroyd), preferring to view Isa 36–39 as serving an important editorial function within the development of the Book of Isaiah (Ackroyd, Clements, Melugin, Childs, Sweeney), may choose to view these chapters as (1) only obliquely related to the tradition-historical development of Isa 1–35°, (2) editorially supplied *after* Second Isaiah's position in the book was secure, and (3) comprised of much late and extraneous tradition, postdating both 1–35° and 40–55, and giving evidence at points of theological concerns that are by no means well-integrated into the larger movement of the Book of Isaiah. As such, apart from the fact that these chapters do not "conclude" a First Isaiah book, the position of type B and C redaction critics suddenly is not that different from type A approaches in the legacy of Duhm. At a minimum it is clear that further work must be done on Isa 36–39 in order to fully understand the function these chapters serve in the Book of Isaiah.

The second way in which chapters 36–39 play a critical role is more familiar. Given their interest in the events of 701, the deliverance of Jerusalem, and Zion theology, a vast literature already exists that treats of problems in 36–37. Both in these chapters and in 38–39 the question of the relationship to 2 Kgs 18:13—20:19 is a matter of particular complexity and special importance. That importance extends to the fact that the content of this prose complex both confirms and contradicts, stands both in continuity and discontinuity with the traditions of 1–35°. In many respects, correct interpretation of Isa 36–39 strikes at the very heart of the problem as to what comprises the essential message of the prophet Isaiah. Not surprisingly, then, it is critical that we determine how these chapters are to be understood within the larger framework of Proto-Isaiah. It will hardly be possible to talk about Second

Isaiah's conscious relationship to First Isaiah without clarifying the relationship of these pivotal chapters to that corpus.

The proposal of Clements calls into question the traditional picture of Second Isaiah as an individual prophet among exiles, on analogy with the preexilic prophets. At a minimum, one must recognize in his essay the lineaments of a new form of prophetic activity, one based upon the written oracles of another prophet (cf. tradition-historical approaches).[94] This raises important new interpretive options for the exegesis of material in 40–55, even as it raises the question of the scope and character of Proto-Isaiah.

In this study we are interested in the scope and rationale of First Isaiah, with special emphasis on the correct evaluation of Isa 36–39, as critical to understanding Second Isaiah's relationship to First Isaiah and the rationale of the Book of Isaiah as a whole. Barth's thesis of a coherent preexilic collection of Isaiah's oracles, redacted and supplemented during the reign of Josiah, has not gone unchallenged and is in special contrast to those recent studies of Isaiah that see massive *postexilic* redactional supplementation within chapters 1–39° (Vermeylen, Kaiser). More precision is desired in locating the Proto-Isaiah collection, especially its conclusion, which might have served as constitutive of the "former things," to which Second Isaiah is itself a response (Childs, Clements, Melugin). In the final chapter, it must be determined when this dimension (relatedness to First Isaiah) should exert its influence over exegesis of Second Isaiah, and where should it be left to the side in favor of other contexts.[95]

In the final chapter we will return to issues concerning the relationship between Second and First Isaiah, involving the exegesis of chapters 40–55, the larger structure and thematic development of Second Isaiah, as well as the provenance of the material and the sociological model appropriate for understanding its origins and delivery. More important, however, is a consideration of the quality and extent of Second Isaiah's relatedness to First Isaiah. In my judgment, this dimension can be fully appreciated only when the origin, composition, and function of Isa 36–39 is properly understood, not as part of a separate tradition-historical inquiry, but as a problem involving the rationale of the Book of Isaiah as a whole. Chapter 2 attempts to place the analysis of Isa 36–39 within this new interpretive framework.

---

94. Cf. Seitz, "New Prophecy" (1990) 229–46.
95. Clements confesses at the outset, "I shall certainly not be able to argue that all of the material of Isa. 40–55 can be explained in this fashion, but this is not of itself necessary" (101). How might one explain more precisely the character and extent of the relationship?

C H A P T E R   T W O

"Former Things"—
The Scope and Rationale
of Proto-Isaiah

ISA 36–39: THE NATURE OF THE PROBLEM

A detailed treatment of the many problems attending the interpretation of First Isaiah would take us considerably afield of our purpose: an assessment of the theory that Second Isaiah has taken shape in conscious relationship to a Proto-Isaiah collection, with an evaluation of the exegetical implications such a relationship would have for chapters 40–55. As stated above, it is critical that we gain a clear sense of what is meant by Proto-Isaiah, in order to determine how Second Isaiah is related to it. Among other things, it would be helpful to know the exact scope of the literary corpus, since it is clear that chapters 1–39 contain much material that already presupposes the 587 debacle, as well as oracles that postdate Second Isaiah. Nevertheless, a chapter-by-chapter determination of the original Isaiah tradition, and any preexilic additions, is a separate task, massive in scope and already the subject of considerable debate.[1]

Given the narrower objectives of this study, it is necessary to isolate several specific dimensions of the problem as to what constitutes Proto-Isaiah. As we have seen, the correct interpretation of Isa 36–39 has serious implications for the manner in which the relationship between First and Second Isaiah is to be conceived. These chapters will therefore be the subject of detailed treatment, and will constitute the heart of our inquiry into Isaiah's redactional rationale.

The complex of literary, historical, and theological issues raised by these important chapters is of a piece with issues raised elsewhere in 1–39, involving

---

1. The work by J. Hayes and S. Irvine (*Isaiah the Eighth-Century Prophet*, 1987) marks the *ne plus ultra* of maximalist approaches to First Isaiah from a historical perspective, at least in the modern period. Practically all of the material in 1–39 is traceable to the prophet Isaiah. At the other end of the spectrum one finds the commentary of O. Kaiser, who limits the original Isaiah tradition to scattered verses in chaps. 1 and 28–31 (*Isaiah 1–12*, 1–3).

the role of Assyria, so-called Zion theology, and the depiction of Hezekiah. H. Barth has devoted a monograph to the first of these issues, and has argued that during the period of Josiah the original oracles of Isaiah underwent a "thoroughgoing, well-planned redactional processing," focusing on the imminent defeat of Assyria.[2] However, he refused to include any of chapters 36–39 in his analysis because he concluded, in the manner of Duhm, that these chapters had no integral relationship to Isaiah tradition, but were simply spliced in before chapters 40–66 were added.[3] Clements has recently challenged this view of matters, even as he has endorsed Barth's general conception of a pre-exilic, post-Isaiah redaction within 1–39°.[4] In his view, the report of the 701 crisis in Isa 36–39 cannot be isolated from other Isaiah tradition concerning the role of Assyria on the grounds that this material has its primary location in 2 Kings.[5] This is true for Clements even as he generally accepts the view that chapters 36–39 were first located in Kings; nevertheless, his avoidance of the notion that they were mechanically brought over to function as a conclusion means that he interprets their relationship to other Isaiah tradition differently.[6] Here it is clear that the larger conception of the development of the whole Book of Isaiah influences theories operative within First Isaiah alone.

Because Clements adopts the notion that these chapters have a transitional function within the Book of Isaiah, he views their insertion between First and Second Isaiah as postdating the composition of 40–55.[7] Here Clements works with a more complex view of the tradition-history of Isa 36–39 than exists for Barth. On the one hand, tradition in 36–37 is related to other Isaiah material in 1–35, especially involving the role of Assyria (14:24–27; 17:12–14; 29:5–8; 31:5); on the other hand, these linkages are rather late, as is the insertion of 36–39, and they postdate Second Isaiah entirely.[8]

---

2. *Jesaja-Worte*, 209.
3. Ibid., 298; on the independence of 36–39, Barth remarks at the outset (4, n. 5): "'Proto-Isaiah' in this work stands for chaps. 1–35. The narratives in chaps. 36–39 are their own complex with their own independent tradition-history and redactional-history apart from the development of chaps. 1–35. They will not be treated in our work."
4. In "Isaiah 14,22–27: A Central Passage Reconsidered" (*The Book of Isaiah*, 1989, 243–62); here he extends his work from *Isaiah and the Deliverance of Jerusalem* (1980) with some modifications.
5. Though for Clements the report of Jerusalem's deliverance is a later elaboration of the Josianic redactors' view of Isaiah's theology (10:5–15°)—that is, it is two stages removed. Clements further departs from Barth's position by regarding virtually all positive Zion theology as the work of Josianic editors, subsequent to and based upon the "deliverance" in 701, itself a modest affair (for a summary, see *Deliverance*, 50). In this, Clements's conclusions recall the older liberal position, which "interpreted the Zion tradition as a later reflection on Jerusalem's narrow escape and assigned all such passages to the postexilic period" (Childs, *Crisis*, 51). Childs is more sanguine about detecting links between the Zion theology of Isaiah and that found in 36–37.
6. "Unity," 53; *Isaiah 1–39*, 277–80.
7. "They have been inserted before chapter 40 at a relatively late stage in the compilation of the book and thereby assist the reader in making the transition from the 'Assyrian' part of the book (1–35) to the 'Babylonian' part (40–66)," "Unity," 53.
8. In a recent work ("Central Passage") Clements endorses the position of F. Goncalves regarding the so-called B2 report in 36–37—namely, that it "has attained its final form after the

As if to complicate matters further, Smelik has recently (1) rejected the division of 36–37 into the traditional two sources (B1 and B2), and (2) argued for the original location of this material in Isaiah, not Kings. But like Clements, he opts for the date of composition of this "literary unity" at a period "after the completion of the Second Isaiah in order to create a bridge between the two parts of the book."[9] In sum, while several scholars accept the transitional role of these chapters and reject Duhm's thesis, in essence they agree that all or part of chapters 36–39 were inserted quite late.

The debate is important since it has an impact on the question of the scope and rationale of Proto-Isaiah, and the relationship of Second Isaiah to First Isaiah chapters. Ackroyd and Melugin have stressed the prefacing role of chapters 38–39 vis-à-vis Second Isaiah. These chapters appear to have circulated together with chapters 36–37; at a minimum, this is the impression one gets from their present location in the Book of Isaiah. Is this literary complex 36–39 to be excluded from the Proto-Isaiah collection precisely because its "transitional character" has urged some to argue for its later editorial position, while others have simply stressed its essentially foreign character in the Book of Isaiah? If there are elements of 36–39 that are preexilic, what are they (account A; account B1)? Alternatively, should we view 36–37 as a literary unity (Smelik), whose original home is in Isaiah, not Kings; and are we compelled like him to date the unified narrative after 587 B.C.E.? Finally, can one detect any substantial part of these Isaiah narratives that could be part of a Proto-Isaiah collection? Is the "transitional" or "prefacing" quality these chapters exhibit only a function of later editorial enhancement, or is there any integral way in which the Isaiah narratives in chapters 36–39 both (1) round off a Proto-Isaiah collection[10] and (2) call for an intended continuation into Second Isaiah?

THE PUZZLE OF ISAIAH'S GROWTH

A second dimension of the Proto-Isaiah problem goes beyond the more technical determination of its actual scope and literary content. Here too we touch on the question of Second Isaiah's relatedness to First Isaiah. A consideration of this subject caused Ackroyd to pose the question: "Why is there so substantial a book associated with the prophet Isaiah?"[11]

One might specify the question as involving primarily the filling out of chapters 1–39 with 40–55, as well as 56–66. If Clements is correct, and the

destruction of 587 B.C." (261), or in Goncalve's words, "B2 must be dated to the period described" (*L'expédition de Sennachérib en Palestine dans la littérature hébraïque ancienne* [Paris: Gabalda, 1986] 541).

9. "Distortion," 85.

10. Without conscious structural analogy to LXX Jeremiah, Ezekiel, or LXX Twelve, and prior to the addition of chaps. 40–55.

11. "Presentation," 21.

addition of Second Isaiah also occasioned a Babylonian revision of First Isaiah, we are however still left with a narrower question: Why did chapters 1–39 themselves grow, prior to exilic period additions? Put in another way, it is one thing to raise the question as to how prophecies from the eighth century have given rise to extensive additions from the exilic period, and beyond. Within the Twelve, additions like this tend to be much more modest; the time gap separating primary tradition and editorial supplementation in Jeremiah is also much narrower. Why then did original Isaiah tradition move not only into the exilic period, but more modestly, beyond the lifetime of Isaiah himself?

Barth has answered this question by positing a substantial revision of original Isaiah tradition focused on the correlation of Isaiah's message with the imminent downfall of the Assyrian empire, Isaiah's "rod of fury" (10:5). By placing this revision at the period of Josiah, Barth further stipulates its intention as ennobling the theological and political claims of a new Davidid, to whom fresh hopes attached. The key text for him in this regard is 8:23b—9:6, as well as 32:1–5.[12] One consequence of this reading is that Barth helpfully bridges the gap over which original Isaiah tradition must leap before its further utilization in the exilic period. By claiming a synthetic (*planvolle*) revision in the seventh century, the "Isaiah words" find a staging point in the "Josiah period" before their subsequent utilization in the sixth century.

In this instance, the reason for the extension of Isaiah tradition involved a new set of historical and theological realities regarding the role of Assyria in God's plans vis-à-vis Israel. A limit was set on the quality and nature of Assyria's function as instrument of Yahweh, after the death of Isaiah and with the birth of Josiah, and hopes associated with him. While one might contest the historical conclusions reached by Barth, there has been a general consensus regarding the correctness of his literary and redaction-critical conclusions, so that the general notion of a preexilic, post-Isaianic revision within Proto-Isaiah seems likely.[13] It will be necessary to look more closely at the theory below, especially in respect of his exegesis of 8:23b—9:6 and 32:1–5.

Here we return to the question posed by Ackroyd, regarding extensive additions made to the Book of Isaiah. Why has the Book of Isaiah continued to grow—even beyond a putative seventh-century revision? While Ackroyd is rightly critical of the circular way in which other scholars have answered this question,[14] it is difficult to avoid the impression that he has answered it in the

---

12. *Jesaja-Worte*, 141–78, 213–15.

13. This is true for scholars who, like Clements, make significant modifications in the literary scope of the Assyrian redaction (*Deliverance*, 28–51).

14. "It is begging the question to say, as G. Fohrer does; '...in the later period Isaiah was often considered the prophet par excellence.' That he was so considered is likely to derive in part from the very attribution to him of so large a collection" ("Presentation," 22–23; the Fohrer quote is from *Introduction to the Old Testament* [Nashville: Abingdon, 1968] 375).

same way: "[Isaiah] has been given that status by the presentation in i-xii."[15] It is still not clear: Why were later interpreters interested in enhancing this prophet's status, through the "presentation" of him in Isa 1–12?[16]

Ackroyd likewise rejects notions of a prophetic school as helpful in answering such a question,[17] and in this he is joined by Meade and Clements, whose criticisms are decisive.[18] The notice at 8:16 is forced to do heavy service in defense of a theory of disciples (itself not implausible), with virtually no further literary corroboration. In the end, the same circularity of logic is required: Why did Isaiah have such a singular status that disciples attached themselves to him, especially when we know very little of their relationship to other classic prophets?

As has been shown, interpreters following Duhm have used the editorial structure argument in a variety of ways to explain the growth of Isaiah. Proto-Isaiah grew in order to achieve a certain "canonical" structure, in imitation of Ezekiel (Duhm), or LXX Jeremiah (Vermeylen) and LXX Twelve (Bogaert); or the entire Book of Isaiah grew in conformity with external models, MT Jeremiah (Steck) or LXX Jeremiah and Ezekiel (Barth). The diversity of "external models" is itself an argument against this theory, beyond the obvious problems with a tripartite structure as such.[19] And in its classic form (Duhm, Vermeylen, Bogaert) it only applies to Proto-Isaiah, and therefore does not get at the question of growth into 40–66.[20]

A most convincing argument for the growth of Isaiah has appeared in Clements's work. Clements argues persuasively that "Isaiah's prophecies were thought to shed a great deal of light upon the situation that befell Judah, Jerusalem, and the Davidic dynasty in 587 B.C."[21] He concludes his study of the Babylonian revision of 1–39 with the question: "Can we not conclude then that it was precisely because Isaiah's prophecies were felt to have an important bearing upon the fate of Jerusalem and the Davidic dynasty that chapters xl ff. have become linked with an earlier collection of Isaiah's prophecies?"[22]

Clements's proposal has a decided force, though one might request even further stipulation regarding the "important bearing" Isaiah's prophecies were thought to have than he has provided. His suggestion that the fate of

15. "Presentation," 46.
16. See also the criticism of D. Meade (*Pseudonymity*, 32).
17. "Presentation," 28–29.
18. "Unity," 52; *Pseudonymity*, 32.
19. See Ackroyd, "Presentation," 18–20.
20. A variation of this structural argument comes from an entirely different direction. Both Childs (*Introduction*, 325–38) and Brueggemann have suggested that the present shape of the Book of Isaiah testifies to the full theological reality of God's dealings with Israel, and anything less would truncate that theological reality ("Unity and Dynamic in the Isaiah Tradition," *JSOT* 29 [1984] 89–107).
21. "Fall of Jerusalem," 434.
22. Ibid., 435.

Jerusalem was involved, if not also the Davidic dynasty, moves in a direction of more specificity.[23] Further specification is critical if one wishes to adopt the view of Clements, Childs, and others that the "former things" of Second Isaiah are the prophecies of First Isaiah. In other words, the growth of the Book of Isaiah somehow involves the question of the integrity of the prophetic word as preserved in First Isaiah, or to use more traditional language, the fulfillment of the word of God, only loosely associated with the actual historical figure of Isaiah.[24] In his treatment of Second Isaiah, Childs put the issue directly: the meaning of chapters 40–55 "does not derive from a referential reading based upon events in the sixth century; rather, its message turned on the fulfillment of the divine word in history."[25] The notion that the Book of Isaiah grew in respect of the fulfillment of the divine word suggests more than that the oracles of First Isaiah "were thought to shed a great deal of light" on the events of 587 B.C.E., or even that they had "an important bearing" on these events. Clements is surely correct in seeing the connection between Isaiah's word of judgment in 701 and 587, but this alone does not explain why the words of Isaiah pressed themselves upon later interpreters, occasioning further growth in the book. Why were similar connections not made elsewhere in the prophetic canon? What was it about Isaiah's prophecies that lent themselves to such extensive *Vergegenwärtigung*?

Clements is correct that certain specific thematic concerns of First Isaiah are shared by the author of chapters 40–55, central among them the fate of Zion.[26] If one adopts his view regarding the status of Second Isaiah, and argues that the "former things" referred to there are the oracles of First Isaiah, it appears that the question of the fulfillment of earlier prophecies is a central concern—repeated at several points in the first half of the collection (chaps. 40–48)—and that God's own reliability in this regard stands in the balance (see 40:27—41:4; 41:21–29; 43:15–21; 44:6–8). What was it about the prophet's argument from history, concerning the "former things," that occasioned such passionate defense? What was it in the Proto-Isaiah collection that gave rise to a conviction of final fulfillment, of the latter end of the "former things" (41:22), from the perspective of Second Isaiah?

At points the "former things" seem to involve prophecies regarding the fall of Babylon (41:2; 41:25; 45:1–7), though this hardly exhausts their range

---

23. Also compare below, where Clements regards concern over the Davidic dynasty in 36–39 (as well as 14:24f. and 31:8) a postexilic development, associated with matters of theodicy ("Central Passage," 262). In this case it is difficult to see how integral such concerns were in the Isaiah tradition itself, to which Second Isaiah is related.

24. Meade speaks of the prophetic word as a "geistiges Eigentum" (*Pseudonymity*, 42–43); see also Isa 40:8 and 55:11.

25. *Introduction*, 328.

26. See also Meade, *Pseudonymity*, 32. Thematic arguments also worked well in the older tradition-historical model (see J.J.M. Roberts, "Isaiah in Old Testament Theology," *Int* 36 [1982] 130–43).

(43:18; 48:3). In another context, Clements speaks of his certainty that one element of Isaiah's preaching involved "the eventual overthrow of the Assyrians," so it is possible that a secondary identification of Assyria with Babylon could have led to the notion that the "calling of Cyrus" was a fulfillment of the divine word spoken by Isaiah.[27] But this may be oversubtle, since it requires a necessary transparency in the role exercised by Assyria. Moreover, it limits the range of the "former things" and does not fully explain the urgent tone that attaches to this material in Second Isaiah.

Although C.C. Torrey long ago promoted the view that chapters 36–39 were inserted to join together First and Second Isaiah (40–66), the theory has enjoyed a fresh currency largely at the urging of Melugin and Ackroyd.[28] Ackroyd has focused his attention on the two narratives in 38–39,[29] as well as on the fuller complex extending from 36 to 39.[30] At times Ackroyd hints at a complex tradition-history internal to these four chapters, with the suggestion that in their original form the figure of Isaiah was not so prominent and that Hezekiah was the key person around whom the legends grew and developed. Both he and Clements stress the transitional function these chapters have at present (esp. 38–39), but it is clear that this function has been redactionally introduced. Ackroyd states: "As this section of material stands in the book of Isaiah, it appears as a preface to the whole section, from ch. 40 onwards."[31] Yet he makes it clear that this juxtaposition is the work of a compiler and his references to an "older narrative" imply that the "transitional outfitting" came at the point *after* the composition of chapters 40–55, when they needed a preface or setting.[32] Clements is much less subtle on this point; the narratives were inserted after chapters 40–55 were brought into play.[33] Furthermore, in a recent essay he makes it clear that the composition of the B2 strand in 36–37 (as well as 14:24–25 and 31:8) "owes its origin . . . to the desire to re-establish the rationale for restoring the Davidic kingship and for rebuilding the temple in the wake of what happened to both institutions in 587 B.C."[34] This aetiological judgment extends to chapter 39 as well: "An awareness of what happened to the Davidic royal house in 598 B.C. permeates the story of the coming of the emissaries from Babylon to Jerusalem" (261). In sum, Clements argues that the content and logic of the narratives in 36–39 are based upon post-587

27. "Unity," 56. More specifically, Childs notes that "the description of God's 'stirring up' Cyrus from the north (41:25) picks up the same verb used in 13:17, 'I am stirring up the Medes.'" (*Introduction*, 330). Is this linkage granted exegetical significance from a canonical perspective only, or was a conscious allusion made to Isaiah tradition, in order to demonstrate the fulfillment of the divine word? See also Seitz, "Making Sense," 112.
28. *Second Isaiah*, 100–103.
29. "Babylonian Exile" (1974).
30. "Structure and Function" (1982).
31. "Babylonian Exile," 338.
32. "Structure and Function," 3, 14.
33. See note 7 above.
34. "Central Passage," 262.

circumstances and reflection. The influence is not from Proto-Isaiah to Second Isaiah, but the reverse. Nothing in 36–39 is to be considered a "former thing," to which Second Isaiah is a response.

Ironically, an interest in highlighting the transitional function of Isa 36–39 as contributing to the redactional unity of Isaiah—in contrast to Duhm's view of Proto-Isaiah—has brought with it arguments for the late date of these same chapters, after the composition of 40–55. When Melugin suggested that the "closest thing to a setting for chapters 40 ff is the prophecy of Isaiah to Hezekiah in chapter 39 concerning the exile to Babylon" he had in mind a preexistent literary account. This is made clear by his reference to a redactor's choice of placement for Second Isaiah, next to "the last concrete historical reference in the Book of Isaiah" concerning "the prophecy to Hezekiah of the exile to Babylon."[35] For Melugin, the narratives of 36–39 have a forward influence on 40–55; they were not merely generated for redactional purposes.

The distinction between the views of Melugin, on the one hand, and Ackroyd and Clements, on the other, is an important one for several reasons. Ackroyd has gone to great pains to establish that chapters 36–39 play a functional role in the Book of Isaiah, which is the consequence of their internal structural arrangement. At a minimum one can detect linkages that urge the intepretation of these four chapters as a composite block, and Ackroyd has helpfully explained the odd chronological development within 36–39 as enhancing the functional significance of these chapters in the Book of Isaiah.[36] At the same time, Clements has encouraged a view of Second Isaiah that emphasizes the relationship of chapters 40–55, from their inception, to First Isaiah, in stark contrast to the old independence model. He has also stressed that the view of Assyria and Zion theology found in chapters 36–37 cannot be isolated from related tradition in 1–35, even when these connections are late and depend upon views of Zion introduced by Josianic (and still later) editors.

The question to be posed at this juncture concerns the scope and rationale of Proto-Isaiah. Are chapters 36–39 excluded from a Proto-Isaiah collection that constitutes the "former things" to which Second Isaiah is related? The question is critical because of the content of these chapters, especially the oracle from Isaiah about Babylonian exile (39:5–7), but also the broader conception of the fate and destiny of Zion (37:35) and the remnant within it (37:31–32). If these chapters form part of the Proto-Isaiah collection, if not its essential conclusion, then might we have some clearer answer to the question posed by Ackroyd: Why is there so substantial a book associated with the

35. *Formation*, 177.
36. "Structure and Function," 9–14.

prophet Isaiah? The answer would turn on the fulfillment of the divine word. Why?—because Isaiah spoke of the future assault on Zion by Babylon (39:5–7), and because he also spoke of God's abiding protection over that same Zion (37:35). The first was fulfilled, allowing God to speak again from the divine counsel about a judgment that had been rendered (40:2).[37] Concerning the second there were serious questions, but here too the "former things" were the witnesses to which the prophet turned to defend the cause of Zion (44:26).[38]

In order to establish the general foundation of such a thesis, a detailed examination of the Hezekiah-Isaiah narratives (chaps. 36–39) is required. At issue are the puzzle of Isaiah's growth, the scope and rationale of Proto-Isaiah, and the character of the "former things" to which Second Isaiah makes frequent reference.

PROSPECTIVE

The following chapters pursue a wide variety of critical questions associated with the interpretation of Isa 36–39. Especially with respect to chapters 36–37, considerable attention has already been paid to such questions, entitling one to speak of a history of critical exegesis in mature form, rooted in the work of Gesenius (1821) and Stade (1881), passing through a form-critical phase in the work of Childs (1967), with a tradition-historical adaptation by Clements (1980), and culminating in the recent period in a host of historical, literary, and redaction-critical investigations (Goncalves, Dion, Smelik, Wildberger, Hardmeier), which confirm, modify, and reject traditional conclusions.[39] It will be necessary to examine the fuller history of inquiry and these newer studies in detail.

At the same time, the foregoing discussion should have made clear that the sorts of problems associated with Sennacherib's 701 invasion, Hezekiah's capitulation (2 Kgs 18:14–16), Zion theology, the report of a visit from Merodach-baladan's envoy, or the correct evaluation of Hezekiah's sickness according to Isa 38:1–22 or 2 Kgs 20:1–11—all these problems are to be analyzed toward a different end and with a very different final purpose. The direction of inquiry has already largely been set—even with due allowance for some of the newer, more provocative proposals (especially C. Hardmeier)—and it will be followed here, sometimes in painstaking detail and hopefully in ways that will influence the approach to studying these chapters that is content to proceed without any interest in the redactional rationale of the larger Book of Isaiah. But it is finally this latter perspective and the

37. Seitz, "New Prophesy," 243–45.
38. See the discussion in chapter 4 of the dissonance created by *Heilsprophetie* in the Isaiah traditions (p. 222).
39. For full citation, see chapter 3.

potential it holds for interpreting the Book of Isaiah that commends our
interest. The analysis of Isa 36–39 to follow is undertaken in order to get some
purchase on the problem of how best to understand Second Isaiah's relationship to Proto-Isaiah. It is to that question that we shall finally return, after a
thorough analysis of chapters 36–37, 38, and 39 has been completed.

By the same token, we would insist that a fresh investigation of Isaiah
36–39, with an eye toward the potential redactional integrity of the Book of
Isaiah as a whole, is warranted in and of itself, as a way of pushing beyond the
traditional inquiry, especially in respect of chapters 36–37, and the impasse to
which it not infrequently leads (compare Smelik and Hardmeier with Dion
and Goncalves). We would judge the monograph a success if it is able to offer
a fresh proposal for interpreting these four chapters within the context set
forth thus far, involving the redactional unity of the Book of Isaiah and the
general inadequacy of a strict 1,2,3 Isaiah model of interpretation.[40]

40. See my previous remarks in "Making Sense," 105–26.

CHAPTER THREE

No Escape For a Blasphemer (Isaiah 36–37)

INTRODUCTION

Virtually all studies of the narrative tradition in Isa 36–37 focus on historical questions, either in the first instance or following some form of critical literary analysis. Actually one should speak of the narrative tradition in 2 Kgs 18:13—19:37, rather than Isaiah 36–37. The priority granted the Kings account is consistent with the priority given to the task of historical analysis.[1] The distinction between historical analysis, strictly speaking, and the history-of-traditions (*traditionsgeschichte*) is an important one, but for our purposes the results have been the same at several key points. Revealing in this respect is the choice of title for the many diverse treatments of these narratives, whether from a purely historical or a literary-critical (form- and redaction-critical) perspective.[2] References in these titles are to the basic historical issues at stake: the Assyrian King Sennacherib, his invasion, the Rabshakeh, the date 701, possibly later campaigns, Jerusalem's deliverance, Hezekiah's revolt, and so forth.

---

1. On this, see the following section.
2. Of more recent titles: P. Dion, "Sennacherib's Expedition to Palestine," *Eglise et Théologie* 20 (1989) 5–25; A. Laato, "Hezekiah and the Assyrian Crisis in 701 B.C.," *SJOT* 2 (1987) 49–68; C. van Leeuwen, "Sencherib devant Jerusalem," *OTS* 14 (1965) 245–72; A. van der Kooij, "Das assyrische Heer vor den Mauern Jerusalems im Jahr 701 v. Chr.," *ZDPV* 102 (1986) 93–109; H. Wildberger, "Die Rede des Rabsake vor Jerusalem," *TZ* 35 (1979) 35–47; B.S. Childs, *Isaiah and the Assyrian Crisis* (1967); R. Clements, *Isaiah and the Deliverance of Jerusalem* (1980); O. Kaiser, "Die Verkündigung des Propheten Jesaja im Jahre 701. I. Von der Menschen Vertrauen und Gottes Hilfe. Eine Studie über II Reg 18,17ff, par Jes 36,1ff. 1. Das literar- und textkritische Problem," *ZAW* 81 (1969) 304–15; A.K. Jenkins, "Hezekiah's Fourteenth Year. A New Interpretation of 2 Kings XVIII 13–XIX 37," *VT* 26 (1976) 284–98; R. Liwak, "Die Rettung Jerusalems im Jahr 701 v. Chr.," *ZTK* 83 (1986) 137–66; F. Goncalves, *L'expédition de Sennachérib en Palestine dans la littérature hébraïque ancienne* (1986); H. Tadmor, "Sennacherib's Campaign to Judah: Historical and Historiographical Considerations," *Zion* 50 (1985) 65–80 [Heb]; W. Shea, "Sennacherib's Second Palestinian Campaign," *JBL* 104 (1985) 401–18; C. Cohen, "Neo-Assyrian Elements in the First Speech of the Biblical Rab-shaqe," *IOS* 9 (1979) 32–48. The same is true of older titles, for example: L.L. Honor, *Sennacherib's Invasion of Palestine. A Critical Source Study* (New York, 1926).

The recent exception of Smelik proves the rule. Even though the literary-theological analysis he employs leads ultimately to tradition-historical conclusions, these involve the Book of Isaiah rather than the Books of Kings.[3] One can see in his analysis that a reassessment of the heavy priority given to Kings has led to a shift away from emphasis on strictly historical matters. In Smelik's view the basic point the narratives wish to make, from start to finish, is a theological one: "A blasphemer is nowhere safe from the power of the omnipotent God" (84). Historical references in Isa 36–37 may point to external events that are verifiable from the standpoint of modern science, but their main purpose is to serve a specific function within the present narrative framework.[4] Forms of traditional historical/literary analysis have obscured this purpose and have ignored features contributing to the literary unity of the passage.

Smelik's analysis must be examined in more detail below. At this juncture, I signal agreement with him in two key respects: (1) we are finally interested in the function of these narratives in Isaiah (not Kings), for reasons clarified above, and (2) it is clear that certain forms of historical analysis obscure the main point the narratives wish to make as a literary unity—and that point is a thoroughly theological one. The title of this section owes much to Smelik's literary/theological analysis. Before we can move to his study, however, it is necessary to examine the traditional approach to these narratives.

THE PRIORITY OF KINGS

Gesenius introduced the notion, later adopted by Duhm, that the Book of Isaiah was comprised of internal booklets, the third one of which closed off the "First Isaiah" collection (chaps. 24–35). To this was then added an appendix concerned with events in the prophet's life (36–39) on analogy with the function and placement of Jer 52. As with Jer 52, Isa 36–39 was drawn from the Book of Kings.[5]

For confirmation of this theory of Isaiah's composition, a comparison of Isa 36–39 with its parallel at 2 Kgs 18:13—19:37 was critical, since the opposite view of origin and development would not work with his appendix notion, or the supposed analogy with Jer 52. Gesenius's mode of argument, consistent with critical moves in the eighteenth and early nineteenth century, was *text-critical*, with additional logical observations thrown in.[6]

3. "Distortion of Old Testament Prophecy" (1986).
4. It is too early to determine whether Smelik's literary analysis will be judged a success by the broader field, though the historical instincts of Dion were not seriously affected ("Sennacherib's Expedition," 12, n. 34).
5. *Philologisch-kritischer und historischer Commentar über den Jesaia* (Leipzig: F.C.W. Vogel, 1821) 22, 932.
6. Gesenius's text-critical analysis is summarized and critiqued by Wildberger in light of Qumran and other developments (*Jesaja*, 1371–72).

Essentially, Isaiah is a text that has smoothed out difficulties in Kings, by means of shortening, consistency of rendering (*Gleichformigkeit*), and general tidying up (*Erleichterung*). In a classic argument, "the difficult text" has priority, except where clumsy transpositions (*ungeschickte Versetzungen*) signal that an original sense has been disturbed (Isa 38:21, 22).[7] To this Gesenius added his own logical observations: (1) the narratives conform to the style and larger plan of Kings, not Isaiah; (2) the Book of Isaiah continued to develop after Kings was completed, thus making the direction of dependence from Kings to Isaiah, not the reverse; (3) Isa 36–39 is analogous with Jeremiah 52. Since he began with points 2 and 3, the centrality of his text-critical arguments for establishing the direction of dependence remains.

Gesenius's decision to regard Isa 36–39 as derived from Kings has proven fateful for subsequent research. On the one hand, German scholars up to the modern period (see H. Barth) have often refused to treat these chapters as part of a broader analysis of the Isaiah traditions.[8] On the other hand, shifting the interpretation of 36–39 into the territory of Kings has meant a decided interest in strictly historical matters, in isolation from literary developments within Isaiah, to be sure, but also in isolation from literary developments in Kings outside the narrower unit 18:13—19:17.

Nevertheless, for Gesenius matters of literary and textual development in both Kings and Isaiah merit close attention in and of themselves. Most notable in this regard is his treatment of the unit 18:14–16. He discusses the unit within the broader context of text-critical examination and therefore views it as one fairly prominent example of *Abkürzung* in the Isaiah text.[9] Moreover, its location in Kings potentially disrupts the flow of the narrative. Why did the Assyrians attack *after* tribute had been given? Here Gesenius provides his own crude historical/psychological answer: they thought better of leaving their back unprotected in view of future plans for an Egyptian campaign.[10] Nowhere does Gesenius discuss the special *historical* worth of this missing episode.[11]

Two factors caused this shift. The first was initiated by Gesenius, in his insistence that Kings had priority over Isaiah on text-critical and logical grounds. Simply put, 2 Kgs 18:14–16 took on special prominence because it was a "plus" over against Isaiah, and therefore could figure in no discussion of those chapters as such. The second factor involved the role of the Assyrian records: because there appeared to be a surprising correspondence between 2 Kgs 18:14–16 and an external record, the annals of Sennecherib, and because the latter was considered an "objective" record compared with the "subjec-

7. *Jesaia*, 934.
8. See note 3, above.
9. Its "Streben nach Kürze" (938).
10. *Jesaia*, 937.
11. He does suggest that it was eliminated by the Chronicler for reasons of content (*Jesaia*, 937).

tive" quality of much biblical reporting (and especially the remainder of the account in 2 Kgs 18:17—19:37), 2 Kgs 18:14–16 suddenly took on special importance.[12] What was for Gesenius a potentially troubling retention in Kings, of no special historical value, was to become Account A, distinguished from B1 or B2 on the grounds of historical veracity, or just B on the grounds of multiple campaigns.[13]

By shifting the emphasis to Kings, 2 Kgs 18:14–16 took on special importance and the concept of gradations in historical veracity (from objective annalistic record [A] to edifying story [B1] to near mythological legend [B2]) was introduced. It is difficult to see how such a philosophical scheme might have caught on in the context of Isa 36–39 alone.

Recognizing the limitations of text-critical comparisons, and granting the priority of Kings over Isaiah, Stade shifted the investigation to an internal analysis of the Kings account.[14] His division of the main narrative into two sources has survived remarkably well, adopted by historians (Goncalves), form-critics (Childs), and tradition-historians (Clements) alike.

In contrast to these three modern representatives, however, Stade refused to see one account as more "historical" than the other: "neither one can lay claim to giving a historical presentation of dependable character; both are legendary" (179). The sort of incidental detail that might prove historical is shared in equal measure by both accounts. Stade's chief contribution was literary-critical: he provided an explanation for the existence of three separate prophecies over the fate of Sennacherib (19:7, 19:28b, 19:33) by detecting a seam at 19:9. He concluded that 18:13, 17—19:9 was "an independent narrative of Jerusalem under threat, now robbed of its conclusion" (175). The missing conclusion has been supplied by subsequent scholarship in a variety of ways, and the two-source theory has received its own modifications.[15]

Stade's view on the status of 18:14–16 is similar to that of Gesenius. On the basis of comparisons with the Assyrian records, Stade does render a favorable judgment over the historical quality of this brief notice. In distinction to Gesenius, he also speaks of this unit as an "addition," and quickly defends its historicity as based on "another truly dependable and ancient source" (172). Like Gesenius, he is quick to note that the unit disturbs the flow of the narrative. Because of this choice of placement, between v. 13 and v. 17: "it appears as though Sennacherib dispatched the Rabshakeh with his message

12. As did theories of a significant Hezekiah revolt—a theme dependent more on the annals than the Bible.
13. The two-campaign theory has a long and venerable history. See the studies of Childs and Clements for an overview. Recent attempts to sustain the theory are discussed by Dion.
14. "Miscellen. Anmerkungen zu 2 Kö. 15–21," *ZAW* 6 (1886) esp. 170–89.
15. See Childs for a conclusion to B1 (*Crisis*, 73–78). Disagreement exists over whether B2 utilizes B2 as a literary source, some arguing in favor (Kaiser, *Isaiah 13–39*, 383; Dion, "Sennacherib's Expedition," 22), others against (Childs, *Crisis*, 103).

and demand for Jerusalem's surrender *after* Hezekiah had already given up and had even sent the presents mentioned in v. 14 with a plea for pardon" (181). Stade's decision to move beyond text-critical logic means that he views 18:14–16 as more than a unit "eliminated" in a smoother Isaiah; it is an insertion, whose placement could have been better executed.

The decision of Stade to regard 18:13 and 18:17 as belonging together (172) is significant. It implies a very different status for 18:14–16. This unit and its framing verses must be examined in detail, for the following reasons: (1) this notice is lacking in Isaiah 36; (2) granting it a high degree of historicity, aided by comparisons with the Assyrian annals, encourages a view of the development of 2 Kgs 18:13—19:37 along chiefly historical lines (A to B1 to B2); this also ensures that the discussion will focus on Kings, and only derivatively on Isaiah; (3) it must be determined if 18:14–16 is an insertion, strictly speaking, or if it forms part of a larger Account A, including 18:13. The latter question is crucial for one's understanding of the growth of tradition in 2 Kgs 18:13—19:37. For if 18:14–16 can be shown to be a literary insertion, then the evaluation of it need not follow Stade's optimistic historical tendencies. If the unit is simply a "plus" in the basic sense of the word, whose insertion could be explained on grounds other than historical, or annalistic,[16] this would have serious consequences for the theory of Kings's priority over Isaiah. Its inclusion might be explained as due to editorial considerations internal to Kings, thus freeing one to examine the function of Isa 36–39 in the Book of Isaiah without persistent deference to the parallel Kings passage and its alleged textual and historical priority.

THE STATUS OF 2 KGS 18:14–16— ANNALS NOTICE OR EDITORIAL SUPPLEMENT?

The question of the proper delimitation of the opening unit in 2 Kgs 18:13—19:37 is an important one. It has been answered differently from the time of Gesenius, though the historical reliability of the passage—defined either as 18:13–16 or 18:14–16—has been defended by virtually all scholars.[17]

13 In the fourteenth year of King Hezekiah Sennacherib came up against all the fortified cities of Judah and took them.

14 And Hezekiah king of Judah sent to the king of Assyria at Lachish, saying, "I have done wrong; withdraw from me; whatever you impose on me I will bear." And the king of Assyria required of Hezekiah king of

---

16. Anticipating our discussion, Dion puts it nicely: "it is difficult to imagine what kind of official records may have preserved the memory of military defeats and other humiliations suffered by the Hebrew kingdoms" ("Sennacherib's Expedition," 10).

17. The views of two exceptions (Provan and Hardmeier) will be examined below. Both helpfully separate the question of historicity from that of compositional integrity, preferring to focus on the redactional function of these verses.

Judah three hundred talents of silver and thirty talents of gold. 15 And Hezekiah gave him all the silver that was found in the house of the LORD, and in the treasuries of the king's house. 16 At that time Hezekiah stripped the gold from the doors of the temple of the LORD, and from the doorposts which Hezekiah king of Judah had overlaid and gave it to the king of Assyria.

17 And the king of Assyria sent the Tartan, the Rabsaris, and the Rab-shekah with a great army from Lachish to King Hezekiah at Jerusalem.

It should be apparent that the literary question is of one piece with the question of historical reliability, and with the proper evaluation of the Kings narratives vis-à-vis their counterpart in Isaiah. If the unit is defined as 18:13–16, then it is generally not regarded as an "insertion"—clumsy or otherwise. If, however, the narrower piece 18:14–16 is regarded as the proper form-critical unit, it is difficult to avoid the impression that the narrative flow has been disturbed—whatever one wants to claim for the historical value of the "insertion."

There is also a text-critical problem, in that (1) Isaiah here has a "shorter text," moving directly from v. 13 to v. 17 (Isa 36:1 to 36:2); and (2) the orthography of "Hezekiah" in 18:14–16 is distinct (*ḥizqiyyāh*) over against that found in the framing verse 18:17, in Isa 36:1 and 36:2, and in quite a few Hebrew manuscripts at 18:13 (*ḥizqiyyāhû*).[18] This latter evidence has been evaluated differently. Some argue that the long reading is "the more difficult" and should be given priority.[19] This would give ground to the "insertion" theory, since the short form would be indigenous to 18:14–16, the long form to the framing verses 18:13 and 17. Others tend to view the evidence as less than perspicuous for resolving the literary-critical problem, or simply privilege the shorter reading of BHK3 and BHS.[20]

A separate problem exists with the date of 18:13, the fourteenth year of King Hezekiah, and its correlation with other biblical and extrabiblical notices.[21] However, it impinges on the literary question in a peripheral way, and can be safely left to the side at this point. All are agreed that the date works in conjunction with the notice at 20:6, which speaks of fifteen years being added to the life of a penitent Hezekiah, thus bringing the total 29 into

18. Compare the long form of the "Bomberg Edition" of Jacob ben Hayim (1524–25), followed by BHK (editions 1 and 2), with the short form of Leningrad codex B 19A, adopted by the 3d edition of BHK and by the BHS. The short form is also found in the Aleppo codex, and in 22 Kennicott manuscripts. The long form, however, appears in all Kennicott manuscripts from before 1200 (see S. Norin, "An Important Kennicott Reading in 2 Kings XVIII 13," *VT* 32 [1982] 337). 1QIsaa is of no help on this issue since it systematically eliminates the theophoric *yāhû*.

19. See Norin (note above); A. Laato, "Assyrian Crisis," 50: "the longer reading seems the likelier alternative."

20. See, for example, Goncalves (*Expedition*, 355, n. 2); Wildberger (*Jesaja*, 1485); Childs (*Crisis*, 69–70).

21. For example, see most recently, A.K. Jenkins, "Hezekiah's Fourteenth Year" (1976) 289–98.

conformity with the opening summary at 18:2. Wildberger, who argues for the general text-critical priority of the Isaiah narratives in the present MT, nevertheless feels that the account of Sennacherib's invasion was first composed for Kings. 2 Kgs 18:13 (= Isa 36:1) belongs together with vv. 14–16. The redactor of the Isaiah book, then, only utilized the opening verse as an introduction to 36:2, perhaps in the process disturbing an earlier introductory notice that must have preceded 36:2 ("and he sent . . ."). Whatever problems exist with chronology, therefore, are due in part to the larger redactional principles at work in Kings.[22]

In seeing an original unity in 18:13–17, Wildberger represents a wide spectrum of scholarship, including those who would not agree with his text-critical conclusion regarding the priority of Isaiah. For the majority of these scholars, the unit is also designated Account A, to be contrasted with B1 and B2,[23] or a unified B,[24] but in either case with a better claim to historicity, and in remarkable agreement with the Assyrian records.[25] No disruption is seen in the flow of the narrative: Sennacherib raids Judahite cites (v. 13), Hezekiah is frightened and sends (by messengers?) a message of confession to him at Lachish—presumed by most to indicate he had previously been in revolt—upon which occasion Sennacherib exacts a tribute (v. 14), whose means of acquisition conclude the account (vv. 15–16). If any problem exists with the narrative logic, it follows v. 16, in the manner described above by Gesenius and Stade: Why did the Assyrians press the attack *after* tribute had been sent? To put it more directly: Why does the Rabshakeh harangue Hezekiah about his "confidence," his "strategy," and his rebellion (vv. 19–25) if he has just sent tribute and confessed his wrong? The answer traditionally given trades on the broader source-critical conception, whereby A, B1, and B2 are viewed as only crudely juxtaposed, giving rise to a certain unevenness at the join between A and B1 (18:16 and 17). In other words, the simple proliferation of sources has disturbed the historical and logical sense of Account A, taken by itself. This view of matters is held by virtually all modern interpreters.[26]

Stade, with whom the theory of sources originated, saw matters differently. The major seam in his reading occurred at 19:9, giving rise to his separation of the main portion of the narrative into two sources, later termed B1 and B2, neither of which was particularly "historical." The passage 18:14–

---

22. *Jesaja*, 1385.
23. So Childs, Goncalves, Clements, and Dion.
24. So Smelik.
25. Though see J. Geyer, "2 Kings XVIII 14–16 and the Annals of Sennacherib," *VT* 21 (1971) 604–6.
26. Typical is A. Laato, who accounts for the problem by positing a missing conclusion: "Since tradition A is incomplete, some kind of continuation must be assumed. But the redactor of 2 Kgs did not include it in the conjoined story; instead he replaced the end of A with a combination of tradition B1, B2 (without 38:1–8) and C. How A ended cannot be said" ("Assyrian Crisis," 56–57).

16 was an insertion, likely to be historically valuable because of its resemblance to the Assyrian annals. But for both Stade and Gesenius, the literary-
critical and text-critical evidence confirmed that (1) 18:14–16 was a unit; and
(2) the original movement was from 18:13 to 18:17, the beginning of the B
account.

A similar view of the literary and text-critical problems in 2 Kgs 18:13–
17 was set forth by Kuenen, to whom Wellhausen makes reference when he
states: "The verses of 18:14–16 are lacking in the parallel text of Isaiah 36
where 18:13 is immediately followed by 18:17."[27] It was Kuenen who pointed
out the text-critical oddity "that Hezekiah not less than five times is spelled
חזקיה while v. 13 and v. 17 have חזקיהו" (290). Typical in his high evaluation of
18:14–16 as a historical source is Burney, who because of the shorter orthography regards these verses as an insertion.[28]

As Childs and Goncalves have pointed out, the text-critical evidence is
difficult to evaluate in this particular instance, since the Hebrew manuscripts
are internally divided over the status of *ḥizqiyyāh* and *ḥizqiyyāhû* at 18:13.
Nevertheless, it should be observed that long forms are the rule in the remainder of the account (18:17, 19, 22, 29, 30, 31, 37; 19:1, 3, 5, 9, 10, 14a, 14b, 15,
20). There is no debate over the status of the long form in Isa 36:1 and 36:2.
What is peculiar is the short form, occurring five times in the space of three
verses, in 18:14–16. Norin may have a point, therefore, when he regards the
long form at 18:13 as correct, and 18:14–16 as an insertion, in agreement with
older scholars, among them Stade, Wellhausen, Burney, and Jepsen.[29]

The text-critical argument requires support on form-critical grounds if
it is to win consent. In the older literary-critical climate, Stade and Gesenius
had agreed that vv. 14–16 interrupted the flow of the narrative; even if the
verses had a claim to historical reliability (Stade), their placement was odd
and produced confusion. This argument was countered on source-critical
grounds by positing a unity for 18:13–16 and isolating the roughness in
narrative flow to v. 17. Yet the older literary-critical observation has some
force. Why introduce the notion of tribute and then follow it with a report of
rebellion and siege; why abut an original "historical" narrative with an
account that presupposes revolt? What does one make of the logic inherent in
the Isaiah narrative in the movement from 36:1 to 36:2ff.? Even Wildberger
recognizes the need to posit an original introduction before 36:2, lost when
36:1 was brought over from Kings (= 2 Kgs 18:13).

The logic of the Isaiah narrative, or the Kings account lacking 18:14–16,

---

27. *Die Composition des Hexateuchs und der historischen Bücher des Alten Testaments* (4th ed.;
   Berlin: Walter de Gruyter, 1963) 290. For Keunen's view, see *Historisch-kritische Einleitung in
   die Bücher des alten Testaments hinsichtlich ihrer Entstehung und Sammlung. Zweiter Teil*
   (Leipzig, 1892) 74–78.
28. *Notes on the Hebrew Text of the Books of Kings* (Oxford: Clarenden, 1903) 339.
29. *Die Quellen des Königsbuches* (Halle, 1953) 77.

is clear. Sennacherib raids Judahite cities (36:1) and then turns his attention to Jerusalem (36:2). The Rabshekah is dispatched by Sennacherib from Lachish; the Assyrian envoy confronts the envoy of Hezekiah, at the scene of an earlier moment of decision, for Hezekiah's predecessor Ahaz: at "the upper pool on the highway to the Fuller's field" (Isa 36:2b//Isa 7:3b). No capitulation is recorded, thus permitting the Rabshakeh's language about rebellion to refer to Jerusalem's option to hold out against a planned attack from the Assyrians (36:18–20). As the story goes on to record it, in either one account (Smelik) or two (Stade), Hezekiah prays for deliverance and for a sign that YHWH is God alone (37:14–20), in clear contrast to Ahaz.[30] The prophet Isaiah announces the decision of the God of Israel, in response to Hezekiah's faithful prayer (37:21), and the remainder of the account tells of deliverance, loyalty to Hezekiah, vindication on Sennacherib, and the blasphemous claims he makes in the name of his gods (37:36–38).

Is there further form-critical evidence that the unit 18:14–16 is intrusive, and stands outside an essentially coherent narrative, still intact in Isaiah? If so, what was the motivation for its inclusion in Kings—can one detect any redactional logic for its placement at the head of this narrative?

In terms of content, the negative—most assume frank—thrust of the notice, that Hezekiah confessed wrongdoing and stripped the temple, has been construed as evidence of the historicity of the account, on the theory that that which is pernicious in one's own records must be true. Laato puts it succinctly:

> Tradition A (2 Kgs 18:14–16) is generally acknowledged as the most reliable OT source about Sennacherib's campaign in Judah. This is incontestable, since account A tells the dark side from Judah's point of view concerning the year 701. ["Assyrian Crisis," 56]

The rule of "more difficult reading" is here transferred to the realm of historiography. Dion has questioned the wider assumption that such an account was found in annalistic records (further enhancing its claim to reliability), because "it is difficult to imagine what kind of official records may have preserved the memory of military defeats and other humiliations suffered by the Hebrew kingdoms."[31] Childs offers a slight variation on this notion: "the biblical account rests upon an archival source which preserved the material chiefly because of its concern with the temple and the treasury."[32] Childs's assessment is more likely, though the tradition-historical conclusions to be drawn from this could run in the opposite direction, as we shall see (with a date for Account A subsequent to that for B). The bulk of the account (vv. 14b–16) is

---

30. P. Ackroyd, "Structure and Function," 17–18; K.A.D. Smelik, "Distortion," 73.
31. "Sennacherib's Expedition," 10, n. 26 (contrary to Goncalves).
32. *Crisis*, 73.

concerned with recording precisely what Hezekiah paid Sennecherib, and from what sources. In that sense, Childs's hunch may be correct.

In addition to the distinctive orthography (*ḥizqiyyāh*), the account also repeats three times the expression, *melek-yĕhûdāh*, which stands in contrast inside the account to *melek-'aššûr*, and outside the account, in the frame verses, to *hammelek ḥizqiyyāhû*. Similar phraseology (King Hezekiah) is found at 19:1 and 5, while the remainder of the verses that contain *ḥizqiyyāhû* do not include any further predication.

The single exception to this is found in the second speech of the Rabshakeh (19:8–13). The Assyrian envoy makes reference to the king of Ethiopia, the king of Hamath, the king of Arpad, the king of the city of Sepharvaim, the king of Hena, and the king of Ivvah, whose collective impotence stands in contrast to the powerful "kings of Assyria" (19:11). Not surprisingly, in this abusive context, the Rabshakeh refers to Hezekiah as a *melek-yĕhûdāh* (19:10). Only here and in the notice termed Account A does the phrase appear, within the larger tradition complex 18:13—19:37.

On the other hand, the phrase is well-known from the rubrics that introduce the kings of northern and southern kingdoms, where not surprisingly the phrase *melek-yĕhûdāh* is employed in contrast to *melek-yiśrā'ēl*. This would seem to confirm the suspicion that whoever composed 18:14–16 worked in the same manner—call it archival—as the redactor responsible for 18:1–2.[33] At a minimum, (1) the triple mention of *melek-yĕhûdāh* in 18:14–16 is striking, (2) it stands in contrast to 18:13 and 18:17, and (3) it seems to be a way to contrast Hezekiah, "the king of Judah," with Sennacherib, "the king of Assyria" (18:14a, 14b, 16), even when the final effect is somewhat overloaded: "At that time Hezekiah stripped the gold from the doors of the temple of the LORD, from the doorposts which Hezekiah king of Judah had overlaid and gave it to the king of Assyria" (18:16).

Still more striking is the similarity of Account A to an earlier notice of capitulation, in the reign of Ahaz during the Syro-Ephraimitic invasion (16:5–9):

> 5 Then Rezin king of Syria and Pekah the son of Remaliah, king of Israel, came up to wage war on Jerusalem, and they besieged Ahaz but could not conquer him. [6 At that time the king of Edom recovered Elath for Edom, and drove the men of Judah from Elath; and the Edomites came to Elath, where they dwell to this day.] 7 So Ahaz sent messengers to Tiglath-Pileser king of Assyria, saying, "I am your servant and your son. Come up and rescue me from the hand of the king of Syria and from the hand of the king of Israel, who are attacking me." 8 Ahaz also took the silver and gold that was found in the house of the LORD and in the

33. Goncalves, *Expedition*, 367.

treasures of the king's house, and sent a present to the king of Assyria. 9 And the king of Assyria hearkened to him; the king of Assyria marched up against Damascus and took it, carrying its people captive to Kir, and he killed Rezin.

Following the lead of Ackroyd and Smelik, we have had occasion to note the conscious way in which Hezekiah has been contrasted with his predecessor Ahaz in the main account of the 701 invasion (Isa 36–37; 2 Kgs 18:13, 17— 19:37).[34] In this prose account, we return to the scene (36:2b) where hearts once shook "as the trees of the forest shake before the wind" (7:2), and where signs were refused (7:12), to see a new Davidid respond in prayer and faithfulness, and receive a new, positively received sign of God's attention (37:30). So it is curious that in 18:14–16, it is not contrast with Ahaz but continuity that is highlighted.

The form-critical similarity of 2 Kgs 16:5, 7–9 to 18:13–16 is unmistakable:

1. Notice of invasion (16:5; 18:13)
2. Royal contact is made with the "king of Assyria" (16:7; 18:14)
3. First-person capitulation speech (16:7; 18:14)
4. The collection and sending of tribute (16:8; 18:15–16)

The language parallels are also striking:

A *wayyišlaḥ 'āḥāz mal'ākîm*
  'el-tiglat pĕleser melek-'aššûr (16:7)
B *wayyišlaḥ ḥizqiyyāh melek-yĕhûdāh*
  'el melek-'aššûr (18:14)
A *wayyiqqaḥ 'āḥāz 'et-hakkesep wĕ'et-hazzāhāb hannimṣā' bêt-YHWH*
  ûbĕ'ōṣĕrôt bêt hammelek (16:8)
B *wayyittēn ḥizqiyyāh 'et-kol-hakkesep hannimṣā' bêt-YHWH*
  ûbĕ'ōṣĕrôt bêt hammelek (18:15)

Even where 16:8 mentions both silver and gold "found in the house of the LORD," while 18:15 mentions only silver, there is in 18:14b a reference to both silver and gold (*šĕlōš mē'ôt kikkar-kesep ûšĕlōšîm kikkar zāhāb*) exacted by the king of Assyria, thus maintaining the close correspondence between the two accounts.

It should also be noted that the inclusion of 18:14–16 not only disrupts the narrative flow in the report of the 701 invasion; from a redactional perspective it also functions in a similar manner as the final Hezekiah anecdote (20:12–19; Isa 39:1–8). Provan theorizes that the addition of 18:14–16 is

34. Ackroyd, "Structure and Function," 17–18; Smelik, "Distortion," 73.

"part of an attempt, which may also be noted in 20:12–19, to tone down the rather exaggerated picture of Hezekiah which is given in the same account."[35] I will have occasion to return to his remarks and the question of Hezekiah's depiction below.

It appears that Account A was constructed in part to demonstrate the continuity between Ahaz and Hezekiah, even though in so doing it interrupted the narrative of 2 Kgs 18:13—19:37*, introducing a tribute payment before the "siege."[36] Furthermore, one would have to explain why an account that stresses Hezekiah's exemplary behavior—everywhere in contrast to his predecessor Ahaz—grew out of Account A, which depicts him in precisely the opposite terms.[37] Focus on Zion theology and the supposed growth of Zion's legendary status in order to account for the existence of B1 and B2 has confused the issue.[38] That which unites the several narratives in Kings (18–20) and Isaiah (36–39) is the figure of Hezekiah.[39] Singular in its negative assessment of him is the so-called Account A. The evidence begins to point in the direction of interpreting that singularity as a sign of intrusion, not of historical reliability. But in order to establish this, it is necessary to push beyond the exegesis of 18:14–16 as such.

A summary of my findings in respect of the Kings "plus" at 18:14–16 is in order at this point. With Gesenius and Stade I view these verses as intrusive in their present location. Against Stade and all who have followed him, I reject the view that "Account A" is more historical, and precedes tradition-historically the composition of B1 and B2.[40] To the text-critical evidence for the distinctiveness of 18:14–16 have been added two literary and form-critical observations. The use of the term *melek-yĕhûdāh* (compare *hammelek ḥizqiyyāhû*), three times in three verses, is striking; together with the short *ḥizqiyyāh*, it sets these verses off from the broader account (18:13, 17—19:37), and highlights the coherent way in which the Isaiah narratives, lacking this brief notice, function at present (so Jepsen). Close language parallels can also be seen in a previous notice concerning Ahaz's capitulation (16:5, 7–9). The

---

35. I. Provan, *Hezekiah and the Books of Kings: A Contribution to the Debate about the Composition of the Deuteronomistic History* (BZAW 172; Berlin: Walter de Gruyter, 1988) 122, n. 82.

36. Hardmeier identifies the redactional tendency in 18:(13)14–16 as concerned with making a connection between Hezekiah and Zedekiah. I will discuss his provocative study, and especially his explanation for the redactionally motivated "misplacement" of 2 Kgs 18:13–16, in detail below. C. Hardmeier, *Prophetie im Streit vor dem Untergang Judas. Erzählkommunikative Studien zur Entstehungssituation der Jesaja- und Jeremiaerzählungen in II Reg 18–20 und Jer 37–40* (BZAW 187; Berlin: Walter de Gruyter, 1990).

37. See our full discussion below, chapter 5, 2d section.

38. In the spirit of Clements, *Deliverance* (1980).

39. In fundamental agreement with Ackroyd, "Structure and Function," 16; and with aspects of his argument in "Death of Hezekiah," 219–22.

40. Smelik's view that B1 and B2 form an essential unity is compelling and will be taken up below.

formal similarity of the two accounts suggests that they were composed by the same hand, or the second was modeled on the first.

One hypothesis is that a later editor (post-B) noted a similarity of theme (foreign hostility) in both accounts (16:5–20 and 18:13, 17—19:39), and especially in the introductory verses (16:5 and 18:13). Yet the accounts are quite different. In the first, it is reported that the Syro-Ephraimite coalition *failed* to conquer Ahaz (16:5), and that he asked for Assyrian aid anyway (16:7–8), and went further and had a copy of a foreign altar made (16:10–16) and ended up stripping much of the temple "because of the King of Assyria" (16:18). This same Assyria shortly eliminates the northern kingdom (2 Kgs 17). In stark contrast, Hezekiah receives the strongest possible endorsement (18:5) and it is recorded that "he rebelled against the king of Assyria and would not serve him" (18:7; cf. 16:7: "I am your servant and your son"). The truth of this is illustrated in narrative form in 18:13, 17—19:37. The only possible explanation for the intrusive note at 18:14–16 is that these verses were spliced in to bring 18:13–16 into formal correlation with 16:5–9 and to suggest that— contrary to the exultant tone of 18:1–8 and 18:13, 17—19:37—Hezekiah had a moment of capitulation analogous to Ahaz. Somewhat like Ahaz, he paid tribute as a hedge. But the splice never worked in Hezekiah's case, since Hezekiah is not depicted in the rest of the narrative as kindly disposed toward Assyria (cf. Ahaz). It just looks as though he paid tribute and the act was ignored (which may be the effect the final editor wanted to achieve, even when it does not work that well—see 18:19–20).[41]

I would further speculate that the attempt to depict Hezekiah in the same terms as Ahaz on the matter of Assyrian capitulation has a larger purpose in the Book of Kings (but not in Isaiah). First, it attempts to account for the fact that, despite Hezekiah's stalwart opposition and faith in YHWH, the Assyrian threat is not brought to a final end with the death of a blasphemer: Esarhaddon his son reigned in his stead (19:37). The final editor of Kings is aware of the reign of Manasseh, of ongoing foreign influence, and of behavior reminiscent of Ahaz and others before him (21:1–9). The verdict over Manasseh keeps the threat of ultimate foreign devastation alive (21:12–15).

Second, and related to this, is the subsequent reign of Josiah. We have noted the "insurpassability" evaluation of Hezekiah: "there was none like him among all the kings of Judah *after him*, nor among those who were before him" (18:5). Yet about Josiah it is ultimately concluded: "*Before him* there was no king like him, who turned to the LORD with all his heart and with all his soul and with all his might, according to the law of Moses." Is it the subsequent verdict over Josiah that has occasioned the notice of capitulation now found in

41. See our remarks below regarding Hardmeier's treatment of Account A, and especially chapter 4, 5th section.

18:14–16? There is no similar blemish on Josiah's record, and we know that the verdict of judgment is one for which Manasseh, not Josiah, is accountable (23:26–27).[42]

This hypothesis is set forth as an attempt to account for the intrusive quality of 18:14–16. In so doing, we touch on problems that more properly belong to a discussion of the Deuteronomistic history. But such a hypothesis has clear implications for the interpretation of the Book of Isaiah, and for the narratives that conclude so-called First Isaiah chapters (36–39). No longer does the text-critical evidence favor a privileging of the parallel Kings narratives (Wildberger, Smelik). Rather than viewing 18:14–16 as a more historical, annals citation, tradition-historically prior to accounts B1 and B2, I see it as a later addition motivated by concerns indigenous to the Book of Kings.

Such a thesis has wide-ranging implications for the regnant view of tradition-historical developments in 2 Kgs 18:13—19:37. Most have assumed that Account A gave an unbiased, historical picture of Hezekiah, and that such an account was consistent with his depiction in the Book of Isaiah (esp. chaps. 20–32), though he is never explicitly mentioned in these chapters.[43] Hezekiah was involved in intrigue with Assyria, and also Egypt.[44] Accounts B1 and B2 were legendary enhancements keyed to a growing interest in Zion theology, but they also embellished the profile of Hezekiah, which was far more equivocal in fact.[45]

---

42. In this context, it seems quite possible that the first main edition of the Deuteronomistic history climaxed with the reign of Hezekiah (lacking 18:14–16), and not with Josiah as is commonly held. As such the narratives of Isaiah 36–39 were composed with a dual intention: as a conclusion to "First Isaiah" and counterpoise to the Ahaz narratives (Isa 6–8) and as a prophetic evaluation of Hezekiah for the Book of Kings. See my detailed remarks below, in chapter 5, 6th section. For the notion of a "Hezekiah recension," see H. Weippert, "Die 'deuteronomistischen' Beurteilungen der Könige von Israel und Juda und das Problem der Redaktion der Königsbücher," *Bib* 53 (1972) 301–9; B. Barrick, "On the 'Removal of the High-Places' in 1–2 Kings," *Bib* 55 (1974) 257–59; Dion, "Sennacherib's Expedition," 25; I. Provan, *Hezekiah and the Books of Kings* (1988).

43. Ackroyd is appropriately cautious: "Material which might originally have involved a negative appraisal of Hezekiah's policy—so chapter 20 and 22, 8b–13 and perhaps also the very problematic 22,15–25—contains no direct reference to him" ("Death of Hezekiah," 221); Childs, too, avoids undue emphasis on Hezekiah in his treatment of the oracles of Isaiah (*Crisis*, 20–68). More on this below.

44. Clements, *Deliverance*, 28–32. Hezekiah's rebellion against Assyria, reported at 2 Kgs 18:7 in an altogether positive context, is presumed by Clements to have been negatively appraised by Isaiah, and to have involved Egyptian alliances—two bits of speculation that find no corroboration in Kings. This is curious since Kings (esp. Account A) is supposed to contain the frank realities of history, before they were theologized. Clements fails to note that in the Isaiah passages he treats (30:1–5; 31:1–3; 29:1–4; 31:4; 22:1–4; 1:4–8), Hezekiah is never mentioned, nor does the term *melek* ever appear.

45. Clements, *Deliverance*, 28–32; Ackroyd ("Death of Hezekiah," 220) is typical in treating 18:14–16 as intentionally "eliminated" for use in Isaiah: "The effect is immediately to modify the picture of Hezekiah from a rebel and a political contriver—implicit in the 2 Kings text—to that of a king of absolute faith and trust when confronted by the Assyrian onslaught." Surely Ackroyd has overstated the degree to which 2 Kings could be summarized as depicting Hezekiah as a rebel. The only verses that suggest such a thing are 14–16. The bulk of the account describes Isaiah in the same manner as Isa 36–37. And the rest of 2 Kings (18:1–8) is more positive still.

In contrast, I am suggesting that the positive picture of Hezekiah was there from the beginning, firmly anchored in Israel's tradition. The contrasting picture of Ahaz and Hezekiah has been sketched out in our discussion of 2 Kgs 16:5–9 and 2 Kgs 18:14–16. But it also forms an essential part of the Book of Isaiah, as has been recently emphasized, in the twin prose sections (chaps. 6–8 and 36–39). Clements has argued that a similar contrast can be seen between the House of David during the reign of Ahaz (chaps. 6–8) and the immediately following oracle at 8:23—9:6, with whom he associates the figure Hezekiah.[46] I agree with his interpretation at this point, and would further speculate that the positive depiction of Hezekiah in 36–37 stands in the same tradition-historical orbit—that is, it is not a secondary embellishment from the postexilic period, but is of a piece with 8:23—9:6, 11:1–10, and 32:1–8.[47] In sum, a strong possibility exists that the initial editorial work on Isaiah traditions came not during the period of Josiah (who is never mentioned in the book), but during the reign of Hezekiah, at the end of Isaiah's own lifetime (contrary to Barth).

Several issues must be treated in order to test this thesis. (1) What is Isaiah's view of Hezekiah? (2) Is Account B two separate narratives, or one unified report (Smelik)? (3) When should Account B be dated? (4) What is the relationship between chapters 36–37 and 38 and 39? (5) What about the seeming correspondence between "Account A" and the annals of Sennacherib? As this last issue is the most compact, it will be treated first.

I conclude my treatment of 2 Kgs 18:14–16 at this juncture. More will be said below, especially in light of Hardmeier's recent analysis. I will also return below to evaluate the theory that Hezekiah was increasingly idealized in later redactional levels of the text.

ACCOUNT A AND THE ANNALS OF SENNACHERIB

One could claim that the notice at 18:14–16 was historically reliable apart from the evidence of the annals of Sennacherib (AS). Goncalves's analysis of "Account A" (18:13–16) posits a high degree of reliablity for the notice primarily on internal evidence, because it appears to be "an official contemporary document."[48] Before the evidence of AS was brought to bear on the issue, Gesenius merely speculated that in its "urge to shorten" the Isaiah text had eliminated material that he characterized as "minor, largely inconsequential,

---

46. So too Ackroyd ("Death of Hezekiah," 221) who mentions 11:1–10 and 32:1ff. as well.

47. Ackroyd correctly notes the linkages between Isaiah oracles concerning Hezekiah (8:23—9:6; 11:1–10; 32:1–5) and the narratives in 36–39, but he views the latter as secondary developments, made near the time of Second Isaiah. In no small measure, it is the priority of 18:14–16 that has influenced his reconstruction of the Hezekiah tradition-history—viz., from candid historical portrayal to idealization. Nevertheless it is clear that some early "idealization," to stick with this language, can be identified in Isaianic material he regards as genuine. So the movement is more complex than he suggests.

48. *Expedition*, 371.

but authentically historical or authentically traditional details"[49]—2 Kgs 18:14–16 presumably belonged in the category "authentic-historical."

Quite apart from hunches and internal arguments for the official, archival, or annalistic character of 18:(13)14–16, most have argued that the Kings's plus was historically reliable because it found confirmation in an external source (AS). Already Stade is of this mind, though he uses AS to defend the placement of 18:14–16 following 18:13.[50] For two-campaign theorists, AS and 18:14–16 agree about an invasion in 701, while the remainder of Kings reports a second campaign in the 680s, thus enabling the seeming anachronisms regarding Tirhakah (19:9a) and Sennacherib's death (19:37) to stand.[51] In respect of the use of AS to corroborate "Account A," even single and two-campaign proponents are in basic agreement, and the same can be said of those who agree with or debate Stade's classic division of Account B into two narratives.[52]

The basic conformity of the two accounts is, then, defended by a variety of modern scholars. Clements states: "In all essentials the report [AS] . . . can be reconciled with that given in 2 Kings 18:13–16."[53] Though he acknowledges that a "full-scale siege" is not reported in AS, the point is not significant; the same is true about Account A: "Similarly the lack of any explicit mention of a siege in 2 Kings 18:13–16 may be taken to give an adequate perspective" (13). Finally, regarding the historical reliability of Assyrian records—about which there has been surprisingly little doubt, compared with biblical reporting— Clements is equally confident: "The arrogant tone of the Assyrian account should not mislead us into supposing that it is in serious factual error" (13). In the most recent treatment of the problem from a historical perspective, the author similarly concludes: "All in all, 2 Kgs 18:13–16, a terse report which makes no bones about the Assyrian conquest of all the fortified cities of Judah and the heavy payment exacted by the conqueror, agrees well with Sennacherib's account of the invasion."[54] Childs, whose method of literary analysis of Account A has been picked up in Goncalves's study, reaches the cautious conclusion: "the essential accuracy of the facts reported seems assured by the essential agreement of the two accounts."[55] Nevertheless, Childs also notes important divergences:

49. *Jesaia*, 933.
50. "Miscellen," 180.
51. J. Bright, *A History of Israel* (3d ed.; Philadelphia: Westminster, 1981) 298–309; recently, W. Shea, "Sennacherib's Second Palestinian Campaign," *JBL* 104 (1985) 401–18. For an assessment of recent attempts to defend the two-campaign theory, see Dion ("Sennacherib's Expedition").
52. Bright, who otherwise disagrees with Stade, says of Account A: "What is important is that II Kings 18:14–16 (not in Isaiah), and it alone, is remarkably corroborated and supplemented by Sennacherib's own account of the campaign of 701" (299).
53. *Deliverance*, 13.
54. Dion, "Sennacherib's Expedition," 10.
55. *Crisis*, 73.

Other problems are raised, however, by the failure of the annal to mention Lachish, the apparent chronological schematization of the annal which mentions the restoration of Padi before Hezekiah's capitulation, and by the inordinately high number of captives reported. [*Crisis*, 72]

In 1971 J. Geyer devoted a short note to dislodging Bright's summary statement that Account A "parallels perfectly" the AS, and that "no mentionable conflict exists between the two."[56] Geyer merely pointed out the obvious—namely, that while AS speaks of a siege, Account A speaks of tribute; conversely, Account A speaks of Hezekiah "sueing for terms at Lachish" (606), while AS mentions nothing about this. Account B, on the other hand, does speak of a siege—one that failed dramatically. As many have pointed out, AS does not speak of a siege that ended successfully, even as it arrogantly boasts of assaults on Judah and *later* tribute from Hezekiah. In fact, many have noted the rather lenient treatment Hezekiah received in comparison to other defeated monarchs.[57] But even a subtle agreement between Account B and AS over the noncapture of Jerusalem has not been the point at issue.

What Account A and AS agree about is that Hezekiah paid tribute, though they are in considerable disagreement about the timing, circumstances, and actual amount of that tribute. For the purpose of comparison, the relevant lines of AS are reproduced here from *ANET* (3d edition). Discussion of more technical aspects of the record will be left to the side except where pertinent.[58] Those sections of the text that treat of Jerusalem only are indented:

> As to Hezekiah, the Jew, he did not submit to my yoke, I laid siege to 46 of his strong cities, walled forts and to countless small villages in their vicinity, and conquered [them] by means of well-stamped [earth-] ramps, and battering-rams brought [thus] near [to the walls] combined with the attack by foot soldiers, using mines, breeches as well as sapper work. I drove out [of them] 200,150 people, young and old, male and female, horses, mules, donkeys, camels, big and small cattle beyond counting, and considered [them] booty.
>
> > Himself I made a prisoner in Jerusalem, his royal residence, like a bird in a cage. I surrounded him with earthwork in order to molest those who were leaving the city's gate.[59]

56. Bright, *History*, 299; J. Geyer, "2 Kings xviii 14–16 and the Annals of Sennacherib," 604–6.
57. Especially Sidqa, king of Ashkelon, who was deposed, taken captive, and replaced by Sharuludari; Luli, king of Tyre, fled for his life to Cyprus and was replaced by a puppet Ethbaal. See Seitz, *Theology in Conflict*, 31–33.
58. For example, the high count of deportation from Judahite cities and villages (200,150) has been the subject of much discussion. For an illuminating proposal, see S. Stohlmann, "The Judaean Exile after 701 B.C.E.," in *Scripture in Context II: More Essays on the Comparative Method* (W.W. Hallo, J.C. Moyer, and L.G. Perdue, eds.; Winona Lake, Indiana: Eisenbrauns, 1983) 147–75. Also, Seitz, *Theology in Conflict*, 31–33.
59. Geyer notes that taken by itself, the language "like a bird in a cage" (*kima iṣṣur kuppi esiršu*) need not imply a full-scale siege (so Gray, *I & II Kings* [OTL; Philadelphia: Westminster, 1964]

His towns which I had plundered, I took away from his country and
gave them [over] to Mitinti, king of Ashdod, Padi, king of Ekron, and
Sillibel, king of Gaza. Thus I reduced his country, but I still increased the
tribute and the *katru*-presents [due] to me as his overlord which I imposed
[later] upon him beyond the former tribute, to be delivered annually.

Hezekiah himself, who the terror-inspiring splendour of my lordship
had overwhelmed, and whose irregular and elite troops which he had
brought into Jerusalem, his royal residence, in order to strengthen [it],
had deserted him, did send me, later, to Ninevah, my lordly city,
together with 30 talents of gold, 800 talents of silver, precious stones,
antimony, large cuts of red stone, couches [inlaid] with ivory, *nimedu*-
chairs [inlaid] with ivory, elephant-hides, ebony wood, boxwood [and]
all kinds of valuable treasures, his [own] daughters, concubines, male
and female musicians. In order to deliver the tribute and do obeisance
as a slave, he sent his [personal] messenger.

Account A speaks of a presiege capitulation and offer of tribute (18:14),
presumably as a means of suing for peace (that, when read with Account B,
fails!). Conversely, AS states explicitly that "Hezekiah, the Jew, did not submit
to my yoke." In its present narrative form, the clear implication is that this
obdurance on Hezekiah's part—not capitulation as Account A has it—was the
reason for Sennacherib's siege of "46 of his strong cities," the "driving out and
counting as booty" of 200,150 citizenry and much property from the same,
and the eventual (unsuccessful) siege of Jerusalem. In fact, the only success
that AS mentions, personally related to Hezekiah and the capital, is a subsequent sending of tribute to Sennacherib *at Ninevah*.

The general thrust of AS is that Hezekiah, who did not submit, nevertheless lost a massive portion of Judahite territory and some special troops
through desertion, and was suitably awed by Sennacherib's show of force.
Tribute payments were increased, according to Sennacherib, and this tribute—again in considerable disagreement with the silver and gold payments of
Account A—was sent by personal messenger to Ninevah. One gets the sense
that Sennacherib wants to memorialize the fact that the cities of Hezekiah, the
Jew, received rough treatment, in contrast to his own "lordly city" Ninevah,
final recipient of transferred goods and personnel from Hezekiah. But
nowhere does the report indicate that the siege of Jerusalem, "his royal residence," was successful in the obvious military sense. For this, the near contrast
with the siege of forty-six walled cities and the plundering of the Judahite
countryside is striking.

Whatever else one makes of his reported victories over Judah, it cannot

611); he argues, however, that taken together with the following expression "surrounded him
with earthwork" (*URU ḫalṣu MEŠ elîšu urakkisma*), the 701 siege of Jerusalem is meant (2
Kings XVIII 14–16 and the Annals of Sennacherib, 606). In this he is probably correct, but it says
nothing about the success of the siege—AS itself suggests that the point of the earthworks,
intended or not, was "to molest those who were leaving the city."

be forgotten that this was at best a grand consolation prize for the Assyrian king. This may explain in part the exaggerated tone of success in AS (though not unusual for this type of annal record), as against the (pregnant) silence regarding Hezekiah's retention of the throne, and Jerusalem's exemption from final assault and plundering. One must wonder if the concluding claim to have taken Hezekiah's daughters as tribute is not in "serious factual error" after all (contrary to Clements). The point is that AS is shot through with an arrogant and exaggerated character that might be explained in this instance as due to Sennacherib's offended pride at not having captured Jerusalem and meted out to Hezekiah, king of Judah, the same treatment he reserved for Sidqa, king of Ashkelon, and Luli, king of Tyre. Such an interpretation at least merits equal consideration along with other speculations.

The granting of objective, historical status to AS runs against the obvious subjective nature of this and other reports in the Assyrian records and stems from a curious reflex among biblical interpreters. In this case, that reflex was assisted by the all too eager desire to designate the Kings plus at 18:14–16, different in tone from its surrounding narrative and lacking in Isaiah, as a frank and therefore historically accurate notice of Sennacherib's 701 successes. But the lack of agreement between the two accounts would be immediately noted were they both found in the biblical record, and were a formal analysis to be as rigorously applied to AS as to Account A.[60]

A more fruitful approach would try and account for the subjective character of both AS and the biblical record, in order to determine if there are actual points of agreement, as well as disagreement. Determining "what really happened" has traditionally meant privileging one account over another, rather than examining the subjective and functional nature of all reports. It has also frequently meant that the broader literary structure in which such reports function has frequently been ignored.[61]

Both AS and Account A agree that Hezekiah paid tribute to Sennacherib. They also both agree in their assessment of Sennacherib's devastation of Judahite cites, and in the nonmention of Jerusalem's defeat (esp. Account B). The bulk of the Kings report has not surprisingly highlighted this latter reality (Account B), while it appears to be a frustrating silence in the report of AS. Account B also fills in the silence with remarkable detail concerning a massive Assyrian defeat, approaching legendary quality.

The question is: Why did the apparent reality of Hezekiah's tribute payment, made at some point during his twenty-nine-year reign (Account A),

---

60. See esp. A.R. Millard, "Sennacherib's Attack," 61–77.
61. At least Goncalves compares Account A with other notices of capitulation in Kings (*Expedition*, 368–670), following T. Vuk, "Wiedererkaufte Freiheit. Der Feldzug Sanheribs gegen Juda nach dem Invasionsbericht 2 Kö 18,13–16" (thesis, Pontificium Athenaeum Antonianum. Facultas Hierosolymitana Theologiae Biblicae, 1979—not available to me).

or annually (AS), finally make its way into the biblical record, now as a notice of capitulation *prior* to any assault (//16:5, 7–9)? It is easy to account for why it was left out—Hezekiah is viewed as a king without peer in the record provided by the Dtr historian. Why would the historian mention such an episode, especially given the altogether positive record that had grown up about his faithful demeanor during the 701 invasion, when YHWH proved more powerful than the gods of other nations and their blasphemous representatives? In other words, one central consideration for the modern historian who works with the Bible involves the principles of selection and omission with which the ancient biblical reporter worked. It is possible to regard Account A as "an official contemporary document" as does Goncalves, for example, and still argue that it has been *secondarily* inserted into a fuller narrative (Stade), either B1 or a unified B (Smelik). I have tried to account for its inclusion above, as governed by principles at work in the final editorial structuring of the Book of Kings.

In sum, it is the peculiar placement of 18:14–16 that produces tension both with Account B and AS, because it introduces the notice of tribute payment in a manner at odds with AS and the narrative logic of B. The formal similarity with 16:5, 7–9 on this score suggests the hand of a later redactor, who may well have been working with information that had a basis in fact (i.e., Hezekiah paid tribute to the king of Assyria). But this information was introduced at a period after the composition of Kings regarding Hezekiah's reign (18:1—20:17°), in order to coordinate Hezekiah's reign with that of Josiah. Such a theory would confirm the essential integrity of the Isaiah narratives as they now stand, lacking Account A in their depiction of 701 events. It is to those narratives, called Account B in the context of Kings, that I now turn.

ISA 36–37 ("ACCOUNT B"):
A UNIFIED NARRATIVE?

The unity of Isa 36–37 ("Account B") has been defended by Smelik in a recent study.[62] Stade's basic division of 2 Kgs 18:13—19:37° into two narratives (2 Kgs 18:17–19, 9a, 36 and 2 Kgs 19:9b–35) has met with general assent in the last century,[63] so much so that Smelik's study comes as something of a surprise. The massive treatment of Sennacherib's invasion by Goncalves, for example, proposes essentially no new variation on the literary division of Stade (B1 = 2 Kgs 18:17—19:9bα, 36–37; B2 = 2 Kgs 19:9b–20, 32aβ–b,34–35).[64] As the complexity of his versification demonstrates, the isolation of a conclusion for both accounts has been an ongoing problem. Childs does a good

---

62. "Distortion of Old Testament Prophecy" (1986) 70–93.
63. With the exception of many two-campaign theorists, for whom it stands at the periphery of the perceived historical task (Bright).
64. *Expedition*, 373–76 and 445–48

job summarizing the older (minor) adjustments on Stade, and he himself adopts a standard division: B1 = 18:17—19:9a, 36f. and B2 = 19:9b–35.[65] Given the frequency with which the theory has been rehearsed, it is not necessary to provide a fresh summary here.

The question of literary unity is an important one in its own right, and it will be treated as such; but it also has an important bearing on historical matters that ultimately affect one's view of the redactional history of Isaiah. Many of those who accept Stade's division and date portions of the narrative (Account B2) after the composition of Second Isaiah[66] are nevertheless willing to date the primary material (generally B1) to the preexilic period.[67] Smelik has argued for a unified narrative, but he dates the whole thing *after* the composition of Second Isaiah, for several of the same reasons B2 was placed at this period:

> In the first place: the date of the narrative has to be established again. Up till now there was no agreement on this point; distinction was made between earlier and later strands. But if the text is a literary unity, we have to opt for the Persian period because some passages are rather similar to the Second Isaiah. Also Isaiah xxxix cannot have been written

---

65. *Crisis*, 73–76.
66. Goncalves, *Expedition*, 480ff.; R. Clements ("Central Passage") accepts his conclusion: "What I find to be significant in the study of Goncalves is the contention that the B2 narrative of Jerusalem's deliverance in 701 B.C. is a composition that has attained its final form after the destruction of the city in 587 B.C." (261). This appears to be a modification of the view he presented in *Deliverance*: "Detailed investigation of the Account B, however, shows that it is a composite narrative, written in its present form more than half a century after 701" (91)—viz., still relatively close to the events themselves. In *Deliverance*, Clements focuses on the Josiah period as a time when major theological composition occurred (so also Barth). Dion, "Sennacherib's Expedition": "the language of Hezekiah's prayer [in B2] . . . is reminiscent of the monotheistic rhetoric found in II-Isaiah" (21).
67. R. Clements, *Deliverance*: "(B1) has obviously been written up at some time later than 701 as is shown by the mention of Sennacherib's death, which took place after 681" (55)—but still in the preexilic period: "If we had only this B1 account there would be very little serious difficulty in interpreting its contents as conformable to the picture that we have elsewhere of Jerusalem's escape from any serious destruction in 701" (56). Dion, "Sennacherib's Expedition": "B1 could have been written as early as the middle of the VIIth century" (19); "Its preservation of a few likely details about participants and its felicitous characterization of Assyrian psychological warfare require a date close enough to the Neo-Assyrian domination of Judah. However, the irreproachable faith attributed to Hezekiah and his people in contrast to the disapproval voiced in many authentic oracles of Isaiah ben Amoz, and the anachronistic inclusion of Sennacherib's murder (681 B.C.), preclude the ascription of B1 to an eyewitness" (19). I will treat the topic of Isaiah's disapproval of Hezekiah below. On the preexilic date of B1, just after the Josiah period, see also Wellhausen (*Composition*, 289–90); Goncalves (*Expedition*, 442–44). Childs does not assign fixed dates, though "a large layer of the material [in B1] . . . reflects ancient tradition with a genuine historical setting" together with "newer elements" under the influence of a "Dtr. author" (*Crisis*, 93). B2 is from the "postdeuteronomic period" and one can see in it language that parallels Deutero-Isaiah (100). A. Laato ("Hezekiah and the Assyrian Crisis") argues for a preexilic date for both B1 and B2; about the former he states: "Sennacherib's murder took place in 681. Thus tradition B1 took its final form only after 681. It presents the historical events and spiritual atmosphere of the year 701 so well that I think it probable that it solified [*sic*] into its final form soon after 681" (60). B2 "received its final form some time in the second half of the 7th century" (64).

earlier than the Persian period because in its present form it predicts that the Davidic dynasty will not be restored to the Judaean throne. These chapters were probably written after the completion of the Second Isaiah in order to create a bridge between the two parts of the book. ["Distortion," 85]

What if Smelik is correct in his literary observations, but wrong in his historical and tradition-historical conclusions? Is it possible to defend the literary unity of Account B, and date it in the same period as others have been willing to date B1 (Laato, Dion, Wellhausen, Clements)? Much of the dating of B2 turned on the ability to draw tradition-historical distinctions with B1;[68] if those distinctions are removed (so Smelik), does it simply follow that a unified B is to be dated after Second Isaiah "added to an almost complete book of Kings"?[69]

It is clear from Smelik and others (Childs, Dion, Clements) that language from B2 is frequently compared to Second Isaiah, and thought to be tradition-historically dependent on that work. Recent interest in the function of Isa 36–39 (Melugin, Ackroyd) suggests that proper interpretation of "Account B" is of a piece with broader redactional considerations in the Book of Isaiah, and with the proper conception of the conjunction of 36–37 with 38 and 39 (see the citation from Smelik above). Analysis of the literary unity of Isa 36–37 has a central bearing on the question of the relationship of Second Isaiah to the "former things" of First Isaiah. Did chapters 36–39 conclude "First Isaiah," or were these chapters inserted after Second Isaiah had been brought into the same tradition-historical orbit as the Isaiah traditions? Do chapters 36–39 form an essential part of the "former things" to which Second Isaiah makes reference, or were they redactionally generated after the formation of 40–55? What is the direction of literary and traditional influence?[70] The answer to these questions ultimately turns on one's assessment of the literary shape of Isaiah 36–37 ("Account B").

The classic two-source theory has not been without its problems. Childs provides a succinct statement of these in his treatment.[71] They include: (1) determining the proper ending of B1; (2) assignment of the final verses of chapter 19; (3) the seeming incompleteness of the separated sources; (4) the fragmentary nature of B2 (esp. 19:21–28 and 29–31). The question of the motivation for Sennacherib's return to Ninevah, upon which the conclusion of the separated Account B1 is predicated (in the movement from 19:9a to 36–37), continues to call forth discussion. Naturally, a legendary account depends

68. Especially Childs, *Crisis*, 99–103.
69. "Distortion," 85.
70. In this regard, the language and content of Isa 37:26 is striking ("Have you not heard that I determined it long ago? I planned from days of old what now I bring to pass?") in its similarity to Second Isaiah.
71. *Crisis*, 73–75.

on surprising details and twists of fate for its genius, though the roughness of B1 is not capable of explanation on this logic alone, nor can one claim that in this roughness is to be found its essential difference from B2. As Smelik puts it: "Would the Assyrian king who had defeated the Egyptians at Eltekah . . . have been seized with panic by the appearance of an 18 years [*sic*] old boy? It is hard to believe" (76). The problem is serious enough, even allowing for literary and formal considerations, that Laato has searched for the motivation (his "factor X") elsewhere in Account B, finding it at 19:35 (= Isa 37:36):

> In terms of both content and ideas, 37,36 would fit into B1 as factor X.
> It would explain why Rabshakeh left Jerusalem (without an army!). [55]

Laato shifts all of 37:9 (= 2 Kgs 19:9) to B2, where it forms the beginning of the account; B1 then comprises:

$$\text{Isa } 36{:}1 \text{---} 37{:}7 \text{ [insert } 37{:}36] \text{ } 37{:}8, 37\text{--}38 =$$
$$2 \text{ Kgs } 18{:}14 \text{---} 19{:}7 \text{ [insert } 19{:}35] \text{ } 19{:}8, 36\text{--}37$$

But such a solution is rather mechanical,[72] and Laato's redactional explanation for the transposition of "factor X" to its present location in the narrative (Isa 37:36; 2 Kgs 19:35) is unsatisfactory. Another possibility is that "factor X" is missing because Account B should not have been divided; namely, "factor X" is to be found if one reads continuously from 19:9a on into "Account B2." This is the direction Smelik wishes to push the discussion.

Whatever else might be said against it, the study of Laato (and Smelik) has helpfully reminded us that Stade's initial argument for two sources was primarily focused on the seam that was alleged to divide the two accounts. Much water has passed under the bridge since he published his remarkably brief (approx. 10 pp.) assessment over a century ago, especially when one considers the size and sheer number of treatments that have used his division as a point of departure—whether for historical, form, tradition-historical, or redaction-critical purposes. In this regard, it also bears consideration that Stade judged both accounts (B1 and B2) to be legendary, of little or no historical value.

In trying to account for the existence of three oracles prophesying the return of Sennacherib to Assyria (19:7, 19:28b, 19:33), Stade reasoned that 19:7 seemed to bring one account to a conclusion, in the same way that 19:33 did. The report (*šĕm'ûāh*) that Sennacherib was to hear (19:7) he does hear (*wayyišma'*) in 19:9a—"and with this narrative is brought completely to its conclusion" (175). The complete fulfillment of the first prophesy, "and I will cause him to fall by the sword in his own land" is not, however, mentioned, because the account (B1) "has been disturbed at its conclusion by a later hand

---

72. Although no more mechanical, one might argue, than supplying a conclusion for B1 from the end of B2—something even Stade resisted (see below).

in order to fuse on the second narrative, at whose conclusion is an extensive report of how Sennacherib died in his own land" (175). Not fully satisfied with an incomplete B1 as hypothesized by Stade, later interpreters snatched part of the "extensive" conclusion of B2 (usually vv. 36–37 of 19:32–37) and utilized it for Stade's "story robbed of its ending" (175), so-called Account B1.

Smelik does a convincing job demonstrating that repetitions in the account—indications for Stade of discrete sources—are in fact literary devices that provide structure for the whole narrative. Stade argued that the first prophesy (19:7) was fulfilled immediately in Sennacherib's "hearing" at 19:9, together with his sudden withdrawal and violent death (the critical ending that is unfortunately missing). Smelik correctly shows that another interpretation is possible, one that works with the text in its present form and is not forced to posit missing conclusions, transpositions from 19:36–37, or a "factor X" from 19:35. By means of the first oracle and its possible fulfillment already at 19:9 ("and he *heard* concerning Tirhakah"), the author intentionally retards the action in order to emphasize for the reader the possibility that the alliance with Egypt, referred to and roundly disparaged by the Assyrian official at 18:21, might in fact prove the means of Jerusalem's deliverance after all.[73] Such a possibility is deliberately ambiguous, for while it would mean deliverance, it would also call into question the manner by which Israel is to be saved and the proper foundation of Israel's trust—matters that are correctly and obediently illustrated later in the narrative, by the righteous King Hezekiah, in his direct appeal to YHWH (19:14–19). As the narrative stands in its present form, the report of a second embassy to Jerusalem in "Account B2" (19:9b–13) is not a repetition signaling a second source, but a literary continuation consistent with the logic of the story, so that the proper staging for Hezekiah's act of obedience (19:14–19), in stunning contrast to Ahaz, might be set.[74]

The fulfillment of the first oracle promising retreat and defeat for Sennacherib (19:7) does not come about at 19:9a, but only after the logic of the narrative, with its focus on the question of YHWH's power and the obedience of the house of David, has been able to properly unfold. Stade's last two oracles do not come until the end of B2 (19:28b, 19:33). They are in sufficient literary proximity as to form two sides of one coin. They remind the reader of the promise of defeat uttered back at 19:7, in the second half of the verse, after the retarding action of 19:7a has been allowed its full effect. Sennacherib does

---

73. "Distortion," 77. As he cleverly puts it: "By supposing that in the first account the news of Tirhakah's arrival ended Sennacherib's attack, Stade actually walked into the trap the author has set for the reader" (77).

74. Childs has correctly noted that there is not that great a tradition-historical distance between the second speech of the Rabshakeh in chap. 18, and B2's blasphemous depiction of YHWH as one god of the nations (*Crisis*, 90). The earlier distinctions he claims to identify (*Crisis*, 89), insofar as they are substantive, are again capable of explanation using the model Smelik employs—viz., as determined by the logic of the narrative as a literary whole.

hear a rumor; he does finally return to his own land; and he is finally done in there. The return is more forcible than 19:7 had allowed (so 19:28), perhaps as a consequence of events that unfolded in the meantime, but the defeat of Sennacherib is as promised (19:36–37). Moving this final notice back to 19:9a destroys the effect the author wished to achieve. The notice of the widespread devastation of the Assyrian army at 19:35, whatever one makes of it as a historical datum, simply provides the motivation for Sennacherib's return to Ninevah. It also functions as a confirmation of the promise to Hezekiah at 19:32–34, in fairly dramatic terms.

The appeal of Stade's literary argument was its easy adaptation to an evolutionary scheme that explained the interplay between historical and legendary elements in the narrative. Stade never pursued this line in any sustained fashion. But in the hands of others, the argument was mounted of decreasing historicity from A to B1 to B2. Account A resembled the AS and presented a "dark account" whose reliability was not to be questioned; the assessment of B1 has been divergent, though most date it in the preexilic period, as a fairly reliable historical report (Goncalves, Clements, Dion, Laato); increasingly, B2 is thought to postdate Second Isaiah, and its tradition-historical distinctiveness over against B1 has been frequently asserted.

Smelik's essay calls into question the basic literary argument of Stade, thus requiring a reassessment of historical and tradition-historical conclusions as well. The propriety of granting absolute historical reliability to Account A on the basis of the traditional arguments has been challenged above. Smelik dates a unified Account B in the postexilic period, in agreement with the arguments used by others for assigning B2 to this period. Many of those same arguments drew for support theories whose evaluation of the history of Hezekiah traditions is equally evolutionary, moving from negative portrayal (Account A and Isaiah's oracles), to more neutral depiction (B1), to legendary status (B2, Chronicles, Sirach).[75] Because I have called into question the starting point for this evolutionary process (Account A) and now question phase two (with Smelik's convincing proposal for B), it is necessary to consider the evaluation of Hezekiah in Isaiah's oracles, which are thought to agree with Account A as a dark portrayal, or one certainly more negative than what is found in Isa 36–37. Since the Book of Isaiah does not contain "Account A," and since I have argued this notice was supplied after the fact in Kings to coordinate Hezekiah's reign with that of Josiah, it will be interesting to see if the picture of Isaiah is elsewhere in agreement with Account A. Alternatively, if the evidence does not favor such an interpretation, then our theory regarding

---

75. See Childs, Clements, Laato, Ackroyd. Laato's new study pursues a similar tack, *Who is Immanuel? The Rise and Foundering of Isaiah's Messianic Expectations* (Åbo: Åbo Akademis Förlag—Abo Academy Press, 1988). Laato argues that Hezekiah was made to conform to Isaiah's portrayal of Immanuel, after hopes associated with the latter never materialized.

Account A's purpose in Kings will be bolstered, since only Kings will offer negative testimony in respect of Hezekiah.

KING HEZEKIAH'S FOREIGN ALLIANCES (ISA 36-37, 38)

Setting to the side the altogether positive depiction of Hezekiah to be found in Account B (esp. 2 Kgs 19:14-19; Isa 37:14-21),[76] I have had occasion to note other evaluations in Kings that stress Hezekiah's singular obedience and altogether righteous deportment. The unsurpassability notice at 18:5, as well as the broader context in which it is found (18:3-8), is particularly noteworthy in this regard.

While interpreters frequently confuse rebellion against Assyria with the making of foreign alliances,[77] the latter uniformly denounced in Kings and the Book of Isaiah, it is clear that the notice at 18:7 ("he rebelled against the king of Assyria and would not serve him") is to be interpreted narrowly and positively. The opening of the verse leaves no doubt about this ("and the Lord was with him, wherever he went forth, he prospered"), as does the broader context in which it is found. As noted above, the expression wĕlōʾ ʿăbādô is in obvious contrast to Ahaz's terse confession in 16:7: ʿabdĕkā ûbinĕkā ʾānî. Whereas the negatively evaluated Ahaz (16:2-4) formed an alliance with Assyria (16:7), the positively evaluated Hezekiah (18:1-7) did not (18:7). Rebellion is here a virtue, and does not involve alliances with Egypt, or other foreign countries for that matter (as the concluding verse [18:8] indicates). In sum, it bears repeating that Account A alone introduces the notion of foreign alliances in Kings—though not with Egypt, but with Assyria itself.

Before examining the argument for Isaiah's alleged denunciation of Hezekiah on this score, it is necessary to examine one section of Account B that departs from the positive depiction of Hezekiah, in an oblique but nonetheless striking manner. In the initial speech of the Rabshakeh to the assembly that went out to meet him (18:19-25), the Assyrian official makes reference to reliance on Egypt and the pharaoh, "that broken reed of a staff" (18:21). The opening charge "Say to Hezekiah" makes it clear that the accusation is leveled at the king, not at the envoy,[78] and that it comes directly from Sennacherib ("thus says the great king, the king of Assyria").

But the official begins to extemporize at 18:22ff. (in a manner consistent

---

76. The negative remarks of the Rabshakeh concerning alliances with Egypt (2 Kgs 18:20-21) will be taken up shortly.

77. Clements, *Deliverance*: "So far as the first of our questions is concerned, that concerning Isaiah's attitude to Hezekiah's joining the coalition that rebelled against Assyria in 705, the answer is clear and definite. Isaiah condemned it firmly and decisively" (29). Clements everywhere assumes that rebellion against Assyria presupposes alliances with Egypt, as though the matter was to be evaluated in something of the same spirit as the Assyrian annals.

78. So too the 2d m.s. forms: ʾāmartā, bāṭaḥtā, māradtā.

with the brilliant craftsmanship of the narrative) in that he begins to address the members of the envoy quite apart—and necessarily so—from Hezekiah: "But if you [2d m.pl.] say to me, 'We rely on the Lord our God,' is it not he whose high places and altars Hezekiah has removed" (18:22).[79] In other words, the formality of speech to Hezekiah is quickly dispensed with in order to expose what is, from the author's perspective, the crafty nature of the Rabshakeh's "appeal." The Rabshakeh is not just a mechanical mouthpiece for Sennacherib, as might have been implied by his opening words. By shifting the indirect address to Hezekiah to direct address to the envoy, he seeks to drive a wedge between Hezekiah and his people—hence the charge about his destruction of high places, and the concern of the envoy regarding the "hearing of the people who are on the wall" (18:26).

Given this context, how is one to evaluate the Rabshakeh's charge about Hezekiah's reliance on Egypt? Is this absolute fact, or an accusation that functions to anticipate the rumor regarding Tirhakah (19:9)? Moreover, what is one to make of the factual nature of Rabshakeh's address when he concludes his remarks on a note that is surely to be construed as bombast and manipulation: "Is it without YHWH that I have come up against this place to destroy it? YHWH said to me, Go up against this land and destroy it" (18:25). Whether or not this item can be classified as historical, it clearly functions in the narrative to indict the Rabshakeh as a blasphemer. Given this, it is difficult to accept the Rabshakeh's charge of reliance on Egypt as objective proof of Hezekiah's foreign policy. Moreover, as we shall see, the notion of reliance on Egypt is fairly prevalent in Isaiah's oracles. The question is whether *Hezekiah* is ever denounced by Isaiah for entering into alliances with Egypt, or any other foreign power. In other words, the notion of Egyptian reliance is in and of itself not fantastic, not even in the mouth of a crafty Assyrian official. But whether the same official is to be trusted when he charges Hezekiah with such a policy, given both the circumstances of siege and the logic of the narrative that reports it, is far less likely.

Our interpretation of the Rabshakeh's charge finds striking confirmation in the second speech he makes (18:28–35). Here he thoroughly dispenses with the notion that his words are meant only for Hezekiah, or even for the envoy:

> Has my master sent me to speak these words to your master and to you,
> and not to the men sitting on the wall, who are doomed with you to eat
> their own dung and drink their own urine? [18:27]

That a certain logic and development mark the Rabshakeh's persuasive art is clear from the content of his second try. No longer is Hezekiah indicted for foreign alliances. Rabshakeh gets to the heart of the matter: Hezekiah has urged the people to rely on YHWH (18:30), and it is *that* reliance the Rab-

---

79. The forms are therefore appropriately plural: *kî-tōʾmĕrûn, ʾĕlōhênû, bāṭāḥnû*.

shakeh means to ridicule in the presence of Jerusalem's citizenry. "Do not listen to Hezekiah when he misleads you saying, The Lord will deliver us" (18:32).

In sum, it is not possible to use the Rabshakeh's charge of foreign alliances with Egypt as objective proof of Hezekiah's policy (one that would be at odds with the prophet Isaiah) without similarly accepting his characterization of Hezekiah as the one man (not Isaiah) whose counsel to trust in YHWH threatens to mislead the people. The Rabshakeh may be correctly depicted as wily, and he may even inadvertently tell the truth. But his second charge against Hezekiah has as much claim to objectivity as his first, read within the constraints of the narrative that contains them both. In fact, given the manner in which Hezekiah responds, first in penitence (19:1–4) and then in prayerful appeal (19:14–19)—when finally the Rabshakeh gets back to the task at hand and addresses him directly—it is difficult to avoid the impression that the second charge was the correct one. Tirhakah even threatens to put in a personal appearance (19:9), allowing for the possibility of Hezekiah acting in conformity with the Rabshakeh's first charge. But nothing is mentioned about Hezekiah's interest in foreign aid. Instead he receives the letter of abuse and goes to the house of the Lord (19:15), proving by his act of prayer that reliance on "mere words" (*'ak-dĕbar-śĕpatayim*), to adapt a phrase of the Rabshakeh himself (18:20), is in fact good "strategy and power for war" (*'ēṣāh ûgĕbûrāh lammilḥāmāh*). As such, the Rabshakeh's second characterization of Hezekiah as one who trusts in YHWH, and counsels others to do so, is clearly the one the narrator wishes to hold up as accurate. The charge of foreign alliances, at least in this narrative, proves groundless in the end.

It should not be lost on the reader that while Hezekiah requests intercession from the prophet Isaiah,[80] and while Isaiah responds with a favorable oracle (19:7), it is the king's own intercessory prayer that is acknowledged by Isaiah as leading to God's final sentence of judgment against Assyria (19:20–21), delivered as a prophetic word in 19:21b–28. King and prophet together accomplish the necessary intercession and proclamation of deliverance. There is no hint of antagonism or rebuke, from either side, or for reasons of past history or prior failure. In the ensuing narrative (20:1–7), to be treated shortly, Hezekiah's prayer has the effect of altering the prophet's word, changing a death sentence to a sentence of new life, which, strikingly, is then related to the earlier deliverance of Jerusalem (20:6). The prayer of Hezekiah is clearly depicted as a force to be reckoned with, and no "mere word of the lips" (18:19). At a minimum, in these narratives the relationship between prophet and king is complementary, not antagonistic, with the central role occupied by the righteous Hezekiah.

80. Compare use of the motif in Jeremiah (C. Seitz, "The Prophet Moses," 3–27), where prophetic intercession is disallowed for Judah's last kings.

The larger thrust of Isa 36–37 (and 38) makes the alleged denunciation of Hezekiah by Isaiah, in the matter of foreign alliances, seem curious. Interpreters who have advocated such a view have necessarily dated Account B at some distance from the events it depicts, though much of the success of this reconstruction depends upon a division of Account B into two sources. The Hezekiah of Isa 36–37 is a legendary figure, to be contrasted with the Hezekiah of authentic Isaiah oracles.[81] The positive depiction of him there, as we have underscored it in our assessment of the Rabshakeh's charges, is a later development at odds with historical facts.

KING HEZEKIAH'S FOREIGN ALLIANCES (ISA 1–35*)

It would be presumptuous to attempt a full historical analysis of Judahite foreign policy in the period of Isaiah's activity, and it would move us far afield of our narrower concern to determine the place of Isa 36–39 in the redactional history of Isaiah. Such studies already exist, including some recent, full-scale ones.[82]

Moreover, the two larger aspects of such an analysis have little or no bearing on the question at hand. Of specific interest to this study is whether the picture of Hezekiah found in Isa 36–37 stands in such tension with that found in Isaiah's oracles that the former must be judged secondary—even secondary to material in 40–55. The two aspects that are only partially related to this question are: (1) Isaiah's attitude toward the nations in general, and Judah/Israel's relationship to them in particular; and (2) Judah's actual relationship to foreign powers as can be reconstructed in general ANE history. It is clear, for example, that Isaiah takes a consistently negative view of foreign alliances (10:20; 18:1–7; 22:3; 28:11–13; 30:1–7; 30:16; 31:1), especially as these are considered signs of lack of faith in YHWH (1:4; 7:9; 22:11; 30:8–14; 31:1–3). But of interest to the question raised here is whether Isaiah condemns *Hezekiah* for such alliances. This matter alone impinges on the interpretation of Isa 36–37, and the contrast that is thought to exist between various portrayals of Hezekiah.

As to the second aspect: it may well be that ANE records report Hezekiah's alliances with Assyria or Egypt.[83] But the biblical notices are not chiefly interested in reporting "history," at least not to any greater degree than ANE

---

81. So, for example, Clements (*Deliverance*), Goncalves (*Expedition*).

82. Among others: F. Huber, *Jahwe, Juda und die anderen Völker beim Propheten Jesaja* (BZAW 137; Berlin: Walter de Gruyter, 1976); W. Dietrich, *Jesaja und die Politik* (BEvT 74; Munich, 1976); Goncalves, *Expedition*, 3–269; M. Hutter, *Hiskija König von Juda: Ein Beitrag zur judäischen Geschichte in assyrischer Zeit* (Graz, 1982). The standard histories of Israel also treat this issue in detail (Noth, Bright, Hayes/Miller, Donner).

83. Hezekiah is viewed in most standard histories as a participant in a widespread revolt following Sargon's death. See, for example, J. Bright, *History*, 283. These historians are dependent upon Sennacherib's records for the actual details of the "revolt."

sources; at a minimum, both are selective and work toward ends that are obviously not objective in any modern sense.[84] It is necessary to determine what the *Book of Isaiah* says about Hezekiah, and how it interprets his relationship to foreign powers and Israel's God. Isa 36–37 (and 2 Kgs 18:1–7, 13, 17—19:37) depict Hezekiah in favorable terms, making explicit the connection between these two possible objects of reliance: Hezekiah trusts in YHWH, not in foreign alliances. Is such a view at odds with the oracles of Isaiah that appear earlier in the book?

For those working principally on questions of the growth of Isaiah tradition, Isaiah's denunciation of Hezekiah is clear and can be confirmed at several points in chapters 1–35. Bright's position is typical:

> In spite of the earnest warnings of Isaiah, who branded the whole thing folly and rebellion against Yahweh, Hezekiah joined in and sent envoys to Egypt to negotiate a treaty (cf. Isa. 30:1–7; 31:1–3). In fact he became a ringleader in the revolt. [283]

Laato states the standard view this way:

> It is often stressed that the picture of Hezekiah in this legendary narrative [Account B] is completely different to the image of the historic Hezekiah, who has been regarded as the wicked king by Isaiah, because of his planned rebellion which was not according to Yahweh's will (see Is 30,1–5.15–17; 31,1–3). ["Assyrian Crisis," 49]

After adjusting the date of B1 and B2 closer to events of 701, Laato concurs with the standard view:

> These traditions have been created among Isaiah's disciples, who certainly knew Isaiah's critical attitude against Hezekiah's rebellion in 701 B.C. The only possible explanation is that the historical events in 701 have caused the idealization of Hezekiah's role in these traditions. [66]

Dion speaks of Hezekiah's role as "ringleader of a Palestinian coalition," "in league with Sidqa of Askelon" and with a "revolutionary junta that seized power in Ekron." The oracles of Isaiah (18:1–2, 4; 30:1–5, 6b–8; 31:1–3) indicate "the prophet's disapproval of the Egyptian alliance."[85] Clements and Goncalves are in essential agreement with the views here cited.[86] It is the theory of Hezekiah's alliances, denounced by Isaiah, that enables one to draw

---

84. See A.R. Millard, "Sennacherib's Attack on Hezekiah," *TynBul* 36 (1985) 61–77.

85. "Sennacherib's Expedition," 6.

86. *Deliverance*: "concerning Isaiah's attitude to Hezekiah's joining the coalition which rebelled against Assyria in 705, the answer is clear and definitive. Isaiah condemned it firmly and decisively, and foretold that it would lead to ruination" (29). *Expedition*: "From Isaiah's point of view, Hezekiah's attitude and his court's attitude differ in no way from that of Ahaz at the time of the Syro-Ephraimite invasion. Only the actors are different. In the same way that Ahaz relied on Assyria to remove the Syro-Ephraimite danger, Hezekiah relied on Egypt" (264). Here Goncalves promotes exactly the opposite view of Ahaz/Hezekiah as was defended above, where the Ahaz/Hezekiah *contrast* was at issue.

such a compelling contrast with Isa 36–37 and thereby classify B (Smelik) or B1 and B2 (Laato, Goncalves, Clements, Kaiser) as an edifying legend, whose approving picture of Hezekiah stems from the fact of subsequent deliverance in 701.

One might argue that the conclusion reached by these various scholars is the consequence of a certain fixed order of investigation. One begins with the general picture of Assyrian domination in the Levant, as refracted through the annals, moves to a discussion of Judah's vassalage under the same, treats Hezekiah's reign and revolt (based on the annals), and then discusses Isaiah's attitude to the revolt, the testimony for which is to be found in sections of 1–35 that speak of foreign alliances— chiefly in chapters 30–31, but also (with the proper exegesis) in chapters 18, 22, 29, and 1. This is precisely the order of investigation in Goncalves's recent work, though he is hardly to be credited with its genesis.[87] Gaps in one set of documentation (Isaiah or the ANE sources) are filled in with information from the other.

As has been noted, apart from Account A there is no mention in Kings or Isa 36–37 of Hezekiah's paying tribute to Assyria.[88] Apart from the references in the Rabshakeh's speech, there is no mention in Kings of an alliance with Egypt. So too, there is no explicit mention of Hezekiah's role in foreign alliances, as these are condemned in the Book of Isaiah. On the other hand, it is not surprising that the Assyrian records might be read as confirming this suspicion. Obviously any resurgence would be regarded in such records as evidence of royal assertion in the name of Judah. And it must be stressed again that we are not interested in "objective facts," but in Isaiah's perspective on this issue and the possibility that it stands in tension with what is found in Isa 36–37.

It will not be necessary to examine all the material in 1–35 for signs of Hezekiah's foreign alliances, nor is an examination of Isaiah's "Zion theology" relevant to the question at hand, strictly speaking.[89] There is a general consensus about the passages that reflect Isaiah's denunciation of Hezekiah. We will begin with the three to which Clements and others make frequent appeal (30:1–5, 31:1–3, 29:1–4), mindful of the central role they play in adjudicating matters of tradition-history and reliability in Isa 36–37:

> If, as a result of this study, we find that the picture given of Isaiah and
> his preaching in the narrative account B (2 Kings 18:17–19:37) is in line

---

87. Chaps. 1–5 proceed exactly in this order.
88. In its present location, Account A actually speaks of a "bribe," in the strict sense, not a regular payment.
89. The two issues are frequently linked (so Clements, *Deliverance*, 28–51), though the difficulty with extrapolating a consistent Zion theology for Isaiah means that its linkage with views on Hezekiah and Davidic kingship will always remain tentative. Are the prophet's harsh—or for that matter promissory—words to Zion evidence of his attitude toward Hezekiah and his putative foreign alliances?

with what we otherwise know of him, then we should have a strong basis for accepting the evidence of the narrative as historically reliable. [*Deliverance*, 29]

The logic of Clements's remarks here is clear: Did Isaiah preach a sufficiently distinct message to Hezekiah prior to 701 that we must judge Account B to be an "idealization"—to use Laato's phrase?

Clements describes 30:1–5 as "the prophet's bitter condemnation of the negotiations with Egypt which formed Hezekiah's main hope of support."[90] Childs, who links this passage with the following 31:1–3 and classifies them both as invective-threat, is more circumspect. A decision is to be made between Yahweh and Egypt (31:1), between Israel's plan and God's plan (30:1). Isaiah's invective-threat (*hôy*) is meant to drive home the serious way in which Israel's misplaced trust is judged by God and doomed to failure: "they will all perish together" (31:3).[91]

Using Clements's criterion of discontinuity, it is difficult to see any significant disagreement between Isaiah's words here and in Account B (19:6–7). In the latter, Hezekiah actively chooses the plan of God (compare '*ēṣāh* at 30:1 and on the Rabshakeh's lips at 18:20), ignoring possible Egyptian aid (19:9), seeking instead the counsel of prophet (19:2) and God (19:14–20). It is difficult to avoid the impression that Hezekiah has been consciously portrayed in "Account B" as one whose faith and demeanor are exemplary, in utter contrast to those condemned by the prophet in 30:1–5 and 31:1–3.

Strikingly absent from both oracles of invective-threat is any reference to Hezekiah. The prophet speaks of "rebellious children" (*bānîm sôrĕrîm*, 30:1) and "those who go down to Egypt" (*hahōlĕkîm lāredet miṣrayim*, 30:2). In 29:1–4, another key passage illustrative of "Hezekiah's rebellion" for Clements, it is "Ariel" that is addressed by the prophet's *hôy* (29:1). However one understands the distinctiveness of this term,[92] and regardless of where the oracle is placed diachronically, it is clear that the prophet's invective-threat is directed at a military encampment, and all that it symbolizes. Siege works will be raised against it. How such an oracle could be construed as a denunciation of Hezekiah's foreign alliances is unclear, without a considerable extrapolation from the biblical text, with further assistance from ANE documentation. The same is true of 22:1–4 and 1:4–8. At most they speak of misplaced trust and its consequences. Whether such material can be so closely tied to a denunciation of Hezekiah's foreign alliances is not obvious from the text itself.

By the same token, it must be admitted that the prophet here condemns real and not just hypothetical alliances and apostasy. He addresses "scoffers" ('*anšê lāṣôn*) and "rulers of this people" (*mōšĕlê hā'ām hazzeh*) at 28:14; those

---

90. *Deliverance*, 29.
91. *Crisis*, 32–35.
92. In contrast to Zion, where God has his abode? See Childs's discussion (*Crisis*, 53–57).

"who hide deep from the LORD their counsel" at 29:15; "rebellious people, lying sons" at 30:9; those who say "No! We will speed upon horses" (30:16). A contrast is established with "he who believes" (28:16); "the deaf who hear and the blind who see" (29:18); those who are saved "in returning and rest" (30:15).

Within this larger section (chaps. 28–31), all chapters are introduced by the recurring *hôy* (28:1; 29:1; 30:1; 31:1); so also 33:1. It cannot be coincidental that chapter 32 is introduced with *hēn*, nearly maintaining the pattern but also offering a variation. Only in chapter 32 is the term *melek* found, and not in any of the passages thought to offer evidence of King Hezekiah's alliances. The king is to be found among those the prophet had contrasted with the unfaithful: he reigns in righteousness (32:1), seeing eyes are not closed and hearing ears are not shut up (32:3), that which is noble remains as such (32:5). There will be a period of distress, coming shortly (32:10), but it will be followed by a period of righteousness and peace (32:15–20). The account in Isa 36–37 of widespread destruction in Judah (36:1) and the deliverance of Jerusalem and the remnant—based sheerly on the grace of God and the righteouness of God's servant Hezekiah—fits strikingly as the consummation of Isaiah's oracles in 28–33. Far from offering a contrasting picture of Hezekiah, or of Isaiah's preaching, these chapters bring to a stunning conclusion both the promises and the denunciations that precede.

Enormous debate persists over proper interpretation of chapter 32 and other passages in this section (28–33). It would be unfruitful at this point to enter fully into that debate. I only wish to make some provisional observations about the denunciations and promises found in these chapters, as a means of calling into question the procedure of assigning most denunciations to a backdrop of Hezekiah intrigue and foreign alliances. The evidence is far from clear that Hezekiah is being condemned. He is never mentioned by name. The royal house is never singled out by the prophet for attack, and in fact the opposite is true. That Isaiah was fully capable of making explicit his charges against the royal house is well illustrated in the case of Ahaz (Isa 6–8).

Who is Isaiah condemning? Who are the rulers and various officials who espouse and carry out plans of foreign alliance? The answer is purely a matter of conjecture. Doubtless there were those who counseled Hezekiah and the military to engage in political intrigue as a means of overthrowing Assyrian domination. That there was dissent over proper strategy at such a time is clear from analogous circumstances reported in the biblical record.[93] The AS themselves report that, as a consequence of Sennacherib's assault on Jerusalem, Hezekiah lost through desertion his own "irregular and elite troops which he

---

93. See Seitz (*Theology in Conflict*, 14–120) for a treatment of internal political conflict in the preexilic period, and especially within the monarchy. That forces beyond the king had an impact on political alignment is clear from the biblical record (including the "Queen Mother," the *'am hā-'āreṣ*, and a variety of other official and semiofficial figures).

had brought into Jerusalem, his royal residence, to strengthen it" (ANET, 288).

The AS and the biblical record agree that Hezekiah resisted Assyrian invasion. The former also tells of those who deserted Hezekiah's cause. If one were seeking objective verification of dissension among the ranks, before and during events of 701, this notice is as good as any. Those who counseled a plan other than the plan of YHWH, revealed to God's servant Isaiah, and who went down to Egypt for aid—these the prophet condemned. As Isaiah made clear in an earlier oracle, those who gloated over the escape of their rulers (22:1-4) had misunderstood their ultimate fate. Moreover, there should be no rejoicing, inasmuch as "the covering of Judah" had been taken away (22:8). Political intrigue may not have meant final disaster for Jerusalem, but it did for Judah. Jerusalem was not spared because of the wisdom of its people and the faithfulness of its leaders, but because of the grace of God, in response to King Hezekiah, and "for my own sake and for the sake of my servant David" (37:35).

In sum, I see no evidence for the kind of contrast Clements and others seek to establish regarding Isaiah's attitude toward Hezekiah. In its place, I offer the proposal that "Account B" was composed precisely to illustrate the faithful conformity of King Hezekiah to the will of God as proclaimed by Isaiah. He is a king who rules in righteousness (32:1), who believes and is not in haste (28:16), who is saved in returning and rest (30:15). "Account B" exists in the present shape of the Book of Isaiah as chapters 36–37, viz., lacking the notice of Kings (18:14–16) termed "Account A." As such, the terms are now inappropriate. Only "Account A," taken by itself, reports Hezekiah's capitulation to Assyria. There is no evidence in the biblical sources of Hezekiah's alliances with Egypt or Isaiah's condemnation of them.

Various arguments have been advanced for a late date for B2 (Clements, Goncalves), for a unified B (Smelik), or even for B1 (Kaiser). In some measure, all of these derive from a starting point in which Account B is contrasted with the "historical" Account A.[94] Both my analysis of Account A and my conclusions about Isaiah's view of foreign alliances in 1–35° call this contrast into question. Moreover, Smelik's argument for a unified Account B means that the contrast between B1 and B2, on tradition-historical grounds, falls to the side. Yet how is one to date "Account B"? What of the notion that language in B is dependent upon Second Isaiah? Is the view of the monarchy found in B evidence of its late date? Does Hezekiah's prayer speak of God in terms more appropriate to a later period and later conceptions? What of the long poetic

---

94. On this score, Dion's summary remarks are characteristic: "Confronted with the duality of a deliverance story and the grim report of Hezekiah's failure [Account A], one might be wiser to imitate the restraint of the deuteronomists; they simply appended B1 as a kind of supplement to 2 Kgs 18:13–16, and renounced the task of harmonizing such heterogeneous sources" ("Sennacherib's Expedition," 23).

unit at 37:22b–29—is this a late intrusion? What of the alleged anachronism at 37:38? These questions must be addressed before a date can be assigned with any confidence.

THE LITERARY INTEGRITY OF "ACCOUNT B"

The Prayer of Hezekiah (Isa 37:14–20; 2 Kgs 19:14–19)

The analysis of Account B, above, confirmed the view of Smelik that Isa 36–37 is essentially a unified narrative. Stade's theory of two separate sources, based on an alleged seam at 2 Kgs 19:7 (= Isa 37:7), was challenged. Using a fresh literary approach, it has been shown that elements in B2 are indispensable for the logic and movement of B1; by the same token, B2 cannot exist in isolation from B1 except as an artificial construct. That Account B admits of division into two narratives (the first requiring a transposed ending, the second a fuller beginning) is not evidence that behind it lie two independent sources, crudely joined, but rather that a certain staging has been crafted into an original unified narrative, giving it an intentionally episodic character. It belongs to the logic of the present narrative that Tirhakah emerge as a potential threat to Assyria, and as an ambiguous "ally" in Hezekiah's cause.[95] The sending of a second envoy to Jerusalem (37:9) is no more a sign of a second source than the Rabshakeh's second speech (36:13–20) is grounds for yet further subdivision in B1. It belongs to the logic of the narrative, in its original form, to slowly move to the heart of the matter from the Assyrian perspective: Hezekiah's false trust in YHWH (37:10). Division of the narrative at 37:7 (= 2 Kgs 19:7) is artificial and destroys the episodic movement of the story, by which the author introduces complexities before moving to the central issue (37:10–13) and its final resolution (37:36–38).

The notion that significant theological contrast exists between the two sources was initially predicated on the theory that B2 was strictly independent of B1.[96] But how does one explain cross-references such as the one at 37:12–13 back to 36:18–20? Even those who suggest that B2 presupposes B1 in literary form still press for theological discontinuity between the two.[97] Dion speaks in

---

95. Historical realities are definitely at work behind the narrative. Tirhakah's appearance at this point in time is, however, a bit premature, according to the standard reckonings (for bibliography, see Goncalves, *Expedition*, 129–30; for summary, Dion, "Sennacherib's Expedition," 12–13). This fact must be taken into consideration in any attempt to date "Account B." The same is true of the final note (37:38), in fulfillment of the prophecy at 37:7, regarding Sennacherib's murder in Ninevah, dated 681. See S. Parpola, "The Murderer of Sennacherib" in *Death in Mesopotamia* (B. Alster, ed.; *Mesopotamia*, Copenhagen Studies in Assyriology 8; Copenhagen: Akademisk Forlag, 1980) 171–82. More on the impact of these matters on the tradition-historical question below.

96. For example, Childs, *Crisis*, 103: "The many non-tendentious variations would rule out a literary relationship." Childs goes on to acknowledge the possibility of "mutual influencing of the two sources" (103) at a literary (or editorial) level.

97. Dion, "Sennacherib's Expedition": "B2 has to be regarded as an exilic creation based on B1" (22). Goncalves (*Expedition*, 478–79) stresses the relationship between B1 and B2 at 2 Kgs 18:29aβ, 30aab, and 19:10aβb.

classic terms of the contrast between "historical reliability" and "theological presuppositions"—B2 heavily influenced by the latter and in contrast to B1 in respect of the former. A quote from his work will serve as representative of this line of analysis:

> B2 is not rich in narrative content; the political debate between concrete protagonists, which was still at the forefront in B1, is now replaced by a theological debate with a solution provided by God himself. Whereas in B1 the *rab-shaqeh* took YHWH's power for granted and denied his willingness to help an impious Hezekiah, in B2 it is YHWH's very ability to protect that is at stake. [21]

Elsewhere he speaks of the "monotheistic focus" and "monotheistic rhetoric" of B2.[98]

Yet the question must be asked: How meaningful is the distinction between politics and theology as stressed in Dion's analysis? Is it fair to say that B1 is (even marginally) more concerned with political matters than B2, or that B2 is somehow more theological or monotheistic in its thrust than B1? Apart from a potential heuristic value, this is an imposition of categories foreign to the biblical world in general, and to this narrative in particular. It is to be conceded that the Rabshakeh introduces his appeal with reference to Israel's reputed political affiliation with Egypt (36:6).[99] But he quickly, and craftily, moves to the subject of Hezekiah's religious reforms (36:7a) and the wisdom of relying on a God who prefers just one altar and whose royal representative does not build high places but removes them (36:7b).

Moreover, it is impossible to restrict the question of YHWH's "very ability to protect" to the "second source" ("B2"). If the matter seems muted in the Rabshakeh's first speech—and this is questionable—it could not figure in greater prominence in his second (esp. 36:15, 18–20). The obvious correlation between 36:18–20 ("B1") and 37:11–13 ("B2") has already been noted. Does the mention of kings, in contrast to gods, at 37:13 mean that B2 is here uncharacteristically "political," matching B1's slip into a more "theological" mode at 36:19?[100] In sum, the distinction is not relevant to the genre of the material, and does not issue into a clean separation of sources in any case, as is illustrated by the comparison of 36:19 with 37:13. It belongs to the logic of the unified narrative that a dramatic point is reached with Hezekiah's prayer, where the question of YHWH's ability to save is brought before the one counsel that can render a final verdict, that of God alone (37:16–20). To call

98. "Sennacherib's Expedition," 21.
99. Though *after* he raises the single question that runs across any putative source division: "On what do you rest this confidence of yours?"
100. Isa 36:19: "Where are the gods of Hamath and Arpad? Where are the gods of Sepharvaim? Have they delivered Samaria out of my hand?"; 37:13: "Where is the king of Hamath, the king of Arpad, the king of the city of Sepharvaim, the king of Hena, or the king of Ivvah?"

this more "theological" is gratuitous, and it has no significant bearing on the question of source division at the strict literary level.

More serious is the objection of Dion and others that the language of Hezekiah's prayer reflects the influence of Second Isaiah.[101] A quote from Dion will again serve as a point of departure:

> The language of Hezekiah's prayer, with expressions like "You are God, you alone" (vv. 15a, 19b), "you have made heaven and earth" (v. 15b), "they are the work of a human hand, wood and stone" (v. 18b), is reminiscent of the monotheistic rhetoric found in II-Isaiah, the late deuteronomistic writings, and psalmic literature. [21]

It is not to be denied that the language of the prayer is similar to language found in texts generally dated to a later period.[102] It would not be fruitful to enter into a discussion about the dating of the deuteronomic and deuteronomistic literature, or seek to address the objections raised by modifying the larger religio-historical framework in which they function.[103] For our purposes, it is necessary only to demonstrate that the language of Hezekiah's prayer cannot be restricted to a later period, as derivative of Second Isaiah and other later influences. Moreover, if it can be shown that the language of the prayer is determined in large measure by the literary context in which it now functions, especially in response to issues raised in B1 (with which it is held to be in clear contrast), then the appeal to a larger religio-historical framework will prove less decisive for adjudicating the matter at hand. Put in another way: the argument for literary unity in Account B, as advanced by Smelik and adapted here, is a sword that cuts in two directions. The same literary features that assist in effecting unity and logic within the narrative can be appealed to against arguments for distinctive language in Hezekiah's prayer, and a late date for it.

It should be added that this question, involving the correct understanding of the direction of influence from "First" to "Second" Isaiah in the narrower scope of Hezekiah's prayer (37:14–20), lies at the heart of the wider problem we are addressing in this study. Has Hezekiah's prayer felt the "back-influence" of themes and language from Second Isaiah, consistent with the model sketched out more broadly by Clements in his 1980 essay?[104] Or, conversely, has language from Hezekiah's prayer had a forward influence on Second Isaiah, in the manner described by Clements in a later study[105] but

101. "Sennacherib's Expedition," 21; Childs, *Crisis*, 99–103; Smelik, "Distortion," 85; Clements, "Central Passage," 261 (with reference to his earlier views); Goncalves, *Expedition*, 478–80.
102. Childs mentions Isa 43:8ff. and 45:5ff. (*Crisis*, 100).
103. Childs's argument, for example, functions within a set reconstruction of the deuteronomic movement and "Dtr. theology" (*Crisis*, 99–103). So too Clements, *Deliverance*, 72–108.
104. "The Prophecies of Isaiah and the Fall of Jerusalem in 587 B.C.," *VT* 30 (1980) 421–36.
105. "Beyond Tradition-History: Deutero-Isaianic Development of First Isaiah's Themes," *JSOT* 31 (1985) 95–113.

rejected in this specific case?[106] It will be necessary to examine the language of Isaiah's oracle (37:22–29) as well, especially the question at 37:26, which bears unmistakable resemblance to Second Isaiah: "Have you not heard that I determined it long ago? I planned from days of old what now I bring to pass" (cf. 40:21, 28; 41:22–23; 44:7; 45:21). Does the language of Second Isaiah find its point of reference in Isaiah's oracle, or has the theme simply been grafted into Account B after the events of 587 and the composition of 40–55?

Pursuing this last question, it is intriguing to note the language of Second Isaiah in more specific terms. If one wished to find the kind of precise parallels that would give evidence of editorial influence from 40–55 on 37:16–20, such parallels are lacking. It is true that passages in Second Isaiah speak of YHWH as the only God:

I, I am the LORD and besides me there is no savior (43:11)
'ānōkî 'ānōkî YHWH wě'ên mibbal'āday môšia'

Beside me there is no god (44:6)
mibbal'āday 'ên 'ĕlōhîm

Is there a god beside me (44:8)
hăyēš 'ĕlôah mibbal'āday

I am the LORD, and there is no other
'ănî YHWH wě'ên 'ôd
besides me there is no god (45:5; cf. 45:6)
zûlātî 'ên 'ĕlōhîm

There is no other god besides me
wě'ên-'ôd 'ĕlōhîm mibbal'āday
there is none besides me (45:21)
'ayin zûlātî

For I am God, and there is no other (45:22)
kî 'ănî-'ēl wě'ên 'ôd.

But assuming direct editorial influence, it is striking that a fairly uniform vocabulary in Second Isaiah (*wě'ên 'ôd; zûlātî; mibbal'āday*) is not directly put to use in Hezekiah's prayer: "Thou art the God, thou alone" (*'attāh-hû' hā'ĕlōhîm lěbadděkā*).[107] The additional predication, "of all the kingdoms of

---

106. "There is much to be said in support of the claim of Goncalves that the B2 account of how Jerusalem was divinely protected in 701 B.C. has been composed in its extant form after the catastrophe of 587 B.C." ("Central Passage," 261).

107. Isa 37:16 (= 2 Kgs 19:15). A similar expression is found after the final *kî*-clause (2 Kgs 19:19): "all the kingdoms of the earth shall know that you YHWH are God alone" (*wěyēdě'û kol-mamlěkôt hā'āreṣ kî 'attāh YHWH 'ĕlōhîm lěbaddekā*). Isa 37:20 seems abbreviated, lacking *'ĕlōhîm*, though it may simply mean: "that you are YHWH, you alone," corresponding to the use

the earth," is nowhere to be found in Second Isaiah. The same is true of the opening address: "O LORD of hosts, God of Israel, who art enthroned above the cherubim" (37:16). If one were searching for common language and background, Isa 6 would serve the purpose better than Second Isaiah (6:1–2, 6).

In this same light, it is striking that much of the polemic of Second Isaiah against idols and idol manufacture assumes a fairly specific background (40:18–20; 41:5–7; 41:24, 29; 42:17; 44:9–20; 45:20; 46:5–7). The vocation of idol making, and all that it represents, is ridiculed by the prophet. Idolatry is not taken seriously—it is a crass and superstitious affair, meriting abuse and denunciation. Hezekiah's prayer never pursues this logic. Idolatry is mentioned with reference to the "laying waste of all the nations and their lands" (37:18), in which undertaking Assyria cast idols into the fire and burned them (37:19). The prayer is quick to add that "they were no gods, but the work of men's hands, wood and stone; therefore they were destroyed."[108] As shall be shown, this footnote serves a particular purpose within Account B. But it is different in terminology and in form than what we find in Second Isaiah.

Finally, while Second Isaiah speaks of YHWH as creator, as the one "who made all things; who stretched out the heavens alone, who spread out the earth" (44:24; cf. 40:22), it never uses the precise phrase of 37:16: "who made the heavens and the earth" (*'attāh 'āśîtā 'et-haššāmayim wě'et hā'āreṣ*). Again, if one were to adopt the view of direct editorial influence from Second Isaiah back to Hezekiah's prayer, it is striking how flexibly the language has been adapted. Moreover, would one wish to argue that such language— YHWH of hosts, God of Israel, who dwells upon the cherubim, the only God for all the kingdoms of the earth, who made the heavens and the earth— belongs only to late monotheistic rhetoric?

This question can be pursued from an altogether different angle than language comparisons and religio-historical reconstructions permit. If one grants that a prayer from Hezekiah, whatever its content, is consistent with the logic of the narrative—the feature of spreading out the letter (37:14) is frequently regarded as "authentic," based upon ANE parallels[109]—what kind

of final *lěbaddekā* at 37:16 and 2 Kgs 19:15. If this is the case, it is difficult to view either of these expressions (37:16 and 37:20) as proposing a "pure monotheism," as the classic argument has it. At 37:16 the thrust is, you are the god, you alone, for all the kingdoms of the earth; 37:20 puts it, all the kingdoms of the earth shall know that you are YHWH, you alone. Does Hezekiah's prayer really involve a "pure monotheism"—or is the concern with revelation and identity? Even the note at 37:19, "though they were not gods," sounds like a cautionary addendum, the subject of "their gods" having been broached by the pious Hezekiah. Might one even translate: "and he threw their gods into the fire—for they were not God, but the work of mortal hands, wood and stone"? Whatever the proper translation, it is difficult to see this as an intrusion of later monotheistic thinking, on a par with the logic of Second Isaiah.

108. And see the preceding note.

109. In a learned note, Dion remarks: "Some motifs of the B2 narrative itself are not devoid of historical plausibility. Thus, the scene of Hezekiah spreading the letter in front of YHWH

of prayer might one have expected to hear from Hezekiah? At two separate points the challenge has been put quite clearly as involving the past record of Sennacherib and other Assyrian kings (36:18–20; 37:10–13). One falls in "B1," the other in "B2." Assyrian kings have been successful in defeating other nations; the gods of these nations have not delivered; peoples and kings have been defeated; YHWH will not deliver or save. Hezekiah makes explicit reference to the "words of Sennacherib" in his prayer (37:16), and asks God to hear them and defend his honor. In vv. 18–19 the language is not determined by reference to later editorial theologizing, as some would have it, but by reference to charges leveled in Account B. Assyria has laid waste nations (37:18; cf. 36:18; 37:11) and their gods have not delivered (37:19; cf. 36:19; 37:12). If YHWH delivers Israel, all the kingdoms will know YHWH as the only God. The prayer is remarkably free of gratuitous theologizing. The blasphemous challenge of Sennacherib, repeated twice in Account B for emphasis, is referred to succinctly in the prayer, occasioning only the note at 19b regarding the disposal of gods of wood and stone, which is fully consistent with the logic of the narrative. At a minimum, this note seems a great distance from Second Isaiah's diatribe against idol manufacture, and it lacks the expansiveness of his "monotheistic rhetoric," if one should call it that.

The lack of precise parallels with Second Isaiah, and the prayer's terse consistency with the logic of the narrative, argue against the view that the prayer has been shaped with reference to chapters 40–55.[110] Childs has noted the distinctive role exercised by Hezekiah here, vis-à-vis Isaiah, and has argued as a consequence that it "fits completely into the framework of Dtr.'s theology" (100). This is further evidence of the cogency of Stade's source division:

> In B1 Hezekiah's concern is to acquire the intercessory prayer of the prophet. However, in B2 Hezekiah does not even inform Isaiah, but enters the temple, and approaches the very presence of God, and offers as a royal priest the prayer of his people. Here the parallel with David (II Sam. 8.18), and Solomon (I Kings 8.14ff.) is striking. [*Crisis*, 100]

Childs has rightly isolated the distinctive role Hezekiah is depicted as exercising at this juncture in the narrative. But is this evidence of a second source, or must the focus eventually fall on Hezekiah given the constraints of the narra-

---

(19:14) has a precedent in the Tukulti-Ninurta epic, where the king of Assyria is portrayed laying down before Shamash the tablet sent by his Kassite enemy, and asking for a divine decision between the two of them" ("Sennacherib's Expedition," 15). Though many note the abrupt way in which the letter is introduced, following an oral message (37:10–13), there is little will for breaking up B2 into even smaller sources. The problem is generally isolated at the oral stage. It should be noted, however, that the messengers do not deliver the oral message; the readers know its content by dint of "hearing" Sennacherib's address to them (37:9).

110. In agreement with Smelik's literary analysis and in disagreement with his tradition-historical conclusions.

tive, the groundwork for which is laid out in "B1" and extended into "B2"? From the very beginning of the narrative, in the opening speech of the Rabshakeh, it is made clear that the matter at hand involves two chief figures: Sennacherib, king of Assyria, and Hezekiah, king of Judah. Isaiah's role is not preempted in B2 in accordance with Dtr. theology, any more than his role overshadows Hezekiah in B1. It belongs to the logic of the narrative that the matter is finally between Hezekiah and YHWH, and on the basis of the king's stance the outcome of the contest with Sennacherib is to be determined.

Isaiah's role in "B1" is to respond with a word to the crisis facing the king, due to the threat of military defeat, but also to the threat from blasphemy unleashed (37:4). Hezekiah requests a prayer (37:4b), and the prophet responds with an oracle (37:6–7). But the oracle appears to fail, since the king hears a report as promised (37:9), but he does not "return to his own land" (37:7). Instead he issues a fresh challenge (37:10–12), repeating much of what his own envoy had earlier said (36:18–20). The prayer Hezekiah originally requested from Isaiah (37:3) he himself makes on behalf of "the remnant that is left" (37:3; 37:14–20). It is not clear that Isaiah is being "replaced" here, as it were. Rather, his role seems complementary, as in "B1." Hezekiah prays; Isaiah responds with an oracle from YHWH, the God of Israel "because you have prayed to me concerning Sennacherib" (37:21).

A similar illustration of the interchange between royal prayer and prophetic word can be seen in chapter 38. There too we see the same pattern: prophetic oracle (38:1), royal petition (38:3), fresh oracle (38:4) in response to the prayer ("I have heard your prayer," 38:5), as at 37:21. As if we were not to miss the pattern, reference is made to the deliverance and defense of the city (38:6) beyond the promise of new life out of death for the king (38:5). This in turn is followed by a sign (38:7–8), rather obscure in nature, which confirms the divine word.[111] In sum, the role exercised by Hezekiah in 37:14–20 is not evidence of a second source, or of a different view of royal prerogative such as is found in B1. The logic of a unified Account B is confirmed elsewhere (Isa 38:1–8), as exhibiting a pattern of royal and prophetic exchange.

As to the similarity of depiction of Hezekiah and David and Solomon, the continuity is conceded.[112] But this need not imply a late, postexilic date, consistent with theories that contrast "B2" with "B1." The role of Isaiah is not preempted, but rather he functions in the same manner as in "B1" and 38:1–8. Lacking so-called Account A, it is clear that the report of Kings, consistent with the logic of Isa 36–37, understands Hezekiah as a king who acted in accordance with "all that David his father did" (18:3), whose trust in YHWH the God of Israel merited the fulsome endorsement at 18:5. That Isa 36–37

---

111. Handled differently in 2 Kgs 20; more on this below.
112. Childs, *Crisis*, 100.

depicts Hezekiah as the righteous king whose trust can save a city or whose prayer (38:5) can avert a sentence of death is clear, and in this it is in full agreement with 2 Kgs 18:5, which proudly reports Hezekiah's unparalleled trust. But his depiction in 37:14–20 is not such as would warrant a source division based upon contrast, or the assignment of a late date based upon distinctive Dtr. theology. The point of the unified narrative is to hold up King Hezekiah as one who does not "rely on Egypt for chariots and horses," to use the words of the Rabshakeh (36:9) or the prophet Isaiah (31:1), but who relies on YHWH, as Isaiah had demanded (31:1). Hezekiah does consult YHWH (37:14–20) as Isaiah had counseled (31:1), and as a result the city is saved, as Isaiah puts it in YHWH's name: "for my own sake and for the sake of my servant David."

This final note (37:35) is not evidence of a "doctrine of Zion's inviolability," by which the city is spared but which also seems in contrast with Isaiah's earlier words of judgment.[113] Rather, it is a reference to the covenant with David, and in this context it has broader application to the royal figure Hezekiah. The language "for my own sake" (*lĕma'ănî*) preceding "and for the sake of my servant David" (*ûlĕma'an dāwid 'abdî*), functions within this narrative context to fully counter the blasphemy of Sennacherib, in response to the appeal of Hezekiah. It should not be extrapolated and used in service of a theory of Zion's inviolability. Nothing prevented YHWH from allowing the Assyrians to overrun Zion, as Isaiah had always proclaimed and as the later events of 587 would demonstrate. But in this case, YHWH protected Zion "for his own sake," viz., because his own honor was at stake, and "for the sake of his servant David," who at this critical juncture was ably represented by King Hezekiah.

Further Additions in Isa 37:21–38 (2 Kgs 19:20–37)

The previous observation about a pattern at work in both Isa 36–37 and Isa 38, involving a prophetic oracle (38:1), a royal prayer (38:2–3), a fresh oracle (38:4–6), and a sign of its trustworthiness (38:7–8), assists with the analysis of Isaiah's oracle in 37:22b–29 (frequently termed a "mocking song"). Not surprisingly, both the oracle itself and the sign that follows it (37:30–32) have been considered secondary additions that interrupt the movement from v. 22a to v. 34 (= 2 Kgs 19:21a to 33).[114] Dion, for example, considers the latter a "chain of post-exilic additions," which is "headed by the announcement of a

---

113. The literature that works this line of approach is vast. See as an example, G. von Rad's treatment of Isaiah, in *Old Testament Theology* (vol. 2; New York: Harper & Row, 1965) 155–69.

114. Childs: "It has long been noted that the message of Yahweh to Hezekiah through Isaiah which begins in v. 21 has been broken off and continued again in v. 33" (*Crisis*, 96). In such an analysis, Isa 37:33 (2 Kgs 19:32) is left hanging, and must be taken together with the preceding sign oracle (37:29–31) as part of an expansion.

long-term 'sign,' out of context in such an emergency as Sennacherib's threat."[115] Using similar historical logic, he considers the possibility that the mocking song of Isaiah is older than B2 and might be "authentic" to Isaiah's preaching, but he finally rejects this view on the grounds that the reference in v. 24 to drying up the streams of Egypt can only refer to Esarhaddon.

What is curious, however, is that the first-person speech of vv. 24b–25 is not an excerpt from the Assyrian records, but precisely the opposite: words on the lips of an Israelite prophet in a self-consciously styled mocking song directed at the hubris of Assyrian kings. Is it appropriate to search for clear historical allusions in this manner in a song whose chief purpose is to put on display the arrogance of Assyrian kings? Can the claim to drying up the streams of Egypt belong only to one fixed historical referent? Other elements in the song fit the narrative framework quite well, including the reference to servants who mock YHWH (v. 24; so 36:4–10, 13–20), the destruction of fortified cities (v. 26; so 36:1), and the turning back of Sennacherib on the way he came (v. 29; so 37:7).

As for the sign at 37:30–32, mention of the "remnant of the house of Judah" (v. 31) and the remnant and survivors of Jerusalem (v. 32) conforms well with Hezekiah's plea to Isaiah to pray "for the remnant that is left" (37:4). The timetable introduced is no more unusual than what is found in 7:14–17. Indeed, with others I agree that the sign serves a particular purpose beyond its role in the 701 crisis: it points up the contrast between Hezekiah and Ahaz, previous representative of the house of David (7:13) who refused a sign (7:12).[116] Together with other features ("by the conduit of the upper field," 36:2; 7:3; the groundless fear of Ahaz and the legitimate piety of Hezekiah),[117] the sign assists in clarifying the distinctive obedience of Hezekiah—"the effect is thus to stress the propriety of the conduct of Hezekiah."[118] In this regard, it is striking to note the final colophon in the sign pericope: "the zeal of the LORD of hosts will accomplish this" (*qin'at YHWH ṣĕbā'ôt ta'ăśeh-zō't*). Only here and at the conclusion of the royal oracle at 9:1–6 does the phrase appear.[119] The royal figure in this oracle, whose placement next to the Ahaz material we judge to be significant for similar reasons of contrast, has been the subject of much speculation, although I agree with Clements, Ackroyd, and others that a strong case can be made for Hezekiah.[120] The promise of a righteous king who

---

115. "Sennacherib's Expedition," 20.
116. Melugin, *Formation*, 178; Ackroyd, "Structure and Function," 18; Smelik, "Distortion," 73.
117. Ackroyd, "Structure and Function," 19.
118. Ibid.
119. Ibid. Because this verse so clearly closes off the unit, the following verse (37:33) should not be included with it (against Childs, Dion, and others). Rather, 37:33 belongs with the following verse. Traditionally, 37:22a has been treated as the introduction to 37:34, on the grounds that the mocking song has been interpolated without its own introduction.
120. Laato's recent contribution to this question seems unnecessarily clever (*Who is Immanuel?* 1988). The oracle concerns an Immanuel who never makes an appearance in history; as a

will establish and uphold the throne of David (9:7) is made on the basis of the *qin'at YHWH ṣĕbā'ôt* (9:6), as is the promise of a remnant that will go forth from Jerusalem (37:32). It can hardly be accidental that apart from 9:7 only here, in an oracle addressed to Hezekiah, the same precise expression is used by Isaiah. Would it be too much to suggest that Isaiah's promise of a remnant, scattered throughout 1–35 and now interwoven with post-587 material, finds its culmination here, in the sign given to Hezekiah?[121]

The purpose of my remarks is not to defend Isa 36–37 as a seamless whole, composed by an eyewitness in a single sitting.[122] Clearly a process of tradition building has gone on, centered on the wondrous events of 701 but more specifically on the figure of Hezekiah, depicted in steady contrast to an Ahaz who faced similar decisions at an earlier time of crisis. The very existence of chapters 38 and 39, the former a composite work in itself, attests to such a tradition process. By the same token, a strong case has been made by Smelik for the literary unity and coherence of "Account B" (Isa 36–37). The mocking song and the sign retard the movement from 37:21 to the oracle at 37:33–35, and may represent "an extension of the narrative material."[123] The question is what the character of that extension is, and how to locate it diachronically.

To take the example of the sign (37:30–32). The location and function of the sign has already been discussed, and on these grounds there is no reason to regard its existence as peculiar at this juncture, as is often maintained. Does the content of the sign give indication of its date? It is difficult to see what purpose the three-year timetable (v. 30) would serve from a later, post-587 perspective. There is strong formal evidence in favor of regarding vv. 30–32 as a single unit.[124] The expression "surviving remnant of the house of Judah" (*pĕlêṭat bêt-yĕhûdāh hanniš'ārāh*) forms no part of the vocabulary thought to be standard in post-587 redaction of Isa 1–35°, for example, the pairing "Judah and Jerusalem" (in that order) at 1:1 and 2:1.[125] Moreover, "house of

response to this "cognitive dissonance," later editors adjust the material in Isaiah, esp. 36–39, so that Hezekiah now appears to be Immanuel (a standard rabbinic view), thus saving these "failed" prophecies. I prefer to view the prophecies as having to do in the first instance with Hezekiah.
121. The "Remnant will return" (7:3) is to be one of the "signs and portents in Israel from the LORD of Hosts who dwells on Mount Zion" (8:16).
122. Anymore than this is true of the material in Isa 6–9:6. It does not belong to the nature of biblical narrative to talk about "eyewitnesses" in the modern sense. Moreover, mention of the death of Sennacherib in a notice (37:38) that is integral to the narrative (it is the fulfillment of 37:7), an event dated 681, means that the narrative took final form not many years after Hezekiah's death (687 B.C.E.). More on this notice and its putative status as an anachronism below.
123. Ackroyd, "Structure and Function," 12.
124. Contrary to Dion, "Sennacherib's Expedition," 20 (following Goncalves). The passage 37:33 is frequently left hanging as a consequence of the interpolation theory (37:21a linked directly to v. 34).
125. D.R. Jones, "Traditio," 239; so also Kaiser, *Isaiah 1–12*, 3 (among others). The language of 4:2–6, judged by many to be a post-587 editorial addition, is distinctive over against 1:1, 2:1, and the passage under discussion (so too 10:20–27).

Judah" exists separately outside the paralleled items Jerusalem/Mount Zion of
v. 32, itself striking in its unique use of language: "For (*kî*) out of Jerusalem
shall go forth a remnant, and out of Mount Zion a band of survivors." The
separate mention of "house of Judah" in v. 31 is consistent with the note at 36:1
and the historical reality that although Sennacherib failed to capture Jerusalem, he overran Judah. The prophet promises that the "surviving remnant"
will recover, will enjoy harvest by the third year, and will be joined by the
remnant from Jerusalem and Mount Zion. Admittedly, the sign may well have
resonated for readers in a post-587 situation—and there is every reason to
believe it did—but it is difficult to see based on the content of the oracle how
these verses can be excluded from referring to 701 events.[126] So far as the sign
is concerned, it is difficult to view it as an interruption in terms of content or
on historical grounds.

I have already discussed the mocking song (37:22–29) and its relationship to the surrounding narrative at several points (vv. 24, 26, 29). Ackroyd
argues that the song is "clearly also at certain points closely related to Deutero-
Isaiah."[127] The problem is somewhat similar to what we encountered in Hezekiah's prayer, regarding the manner in which direction of influence is determined. It should simply be noted again that the song is a unified composition,
and that within that unity the alleged language from Second Isaiah is not
uniformly distributed ("daughter of Zion," v. 22; "I planned from days of old
. . .," v. 26). The notion of Assyria's hubris is the most uniformly articulated
theme (vv. 22–25, 28–29) and this is by no means foreign to oracles considered
authentic to Isaiah, most notably 10:5–11. The reference to the "plan from
days of old" (*mîmê qedem wîṣartîhā*) and the bringing to pass of what was
determined long ago is certainly similar to expressions found in 40–55.[128] On
the other hand, neither of the elements of the familiar pair "former" and
"latter/new things" (41:22; 42:9; 43:18; 46:9; 48:6) of Second Isaiah appears
here, and the notion of a plan of God is firmly rooted in Isaiah tradition
(14:24), involving to no small degree the role of Assyria as instrument of
judgment (5:26; 10:5) as well as the limiting of that role due to Assyria's
arrogance (10:16–19; 10:33–34). Both elements are referred to in the song
(37:26–27 and 37:29).

It may well be that the reference to the plan's venerable quality is
determined by the internal diachronic context of the Book of Isaiah in which
it functions—viz., that from the perspective of 701 events, it is a plan "from
beforehand" (*lĕmērāḥôq*) and from "former days" (*mîmê qedem*) spoken of

---

126. It may well be the case that 4:2–6 belongs to a later redactional level, itself based on 37:30–32.
127. "Structure and Function," 12.
128. Although the precise phrase never appears there. The expressions "things of old"
(*qadmōniyyôt*) and "of old" (*miqqedem*) appear at 43:18 and 45:21, and beyond that a wide
variety: *mērō'š* (41:26); *mē'āz hišma'tîkā* (44:8); *mē'ôlām* (46:9); *lipnê-yôm* (48:7).

earlier in the book (chaps. 5, 10–14*) during the reign of previous kings (Uzziah, Ahaz). In this respect, the language functions rather differently here than in Second Isaiah, where the ability to see the linkage between former things and their outcome is part of the challenge put to rival deities, and part of the way Second Isaiah has been linked with First Isaiah traditions.[129] Here the language is used as a way of taunting Assyria, inasmuch as Israel's God, YHWH, commissioned it for a goal about which it feels privately boastful. YHWH, however, is the one who knows Sennacherib's "going out and coming in" (v. 28) and the Assyrian king is about to "go out" in disgrace and humiliation (v. 29). In sum, it may well be the case that the motif of 37:26 has been picked up and extended to new purpose in 40–55, but it has its own specific function within Isa 1–39* and cannot simply be attributed to the "back-influence" of Second Isaiah.

The tradition has accumulated in such a way that the mocking song (37:22b–29) and sign oracle (37:30–32) now precede the oracle to Hezekiah at 37:33–35, but not in such a way that warrants the description "interruption." Moves to regard Hezekiah's prayer as secondary (B2 vs. B1) are of the same order as objections to the song and the sign as interruptions. The response of Isaiah at 37:21 is clearly aimed at smoothly incorporating the taunt song into its present context, since it refers specifically to Hezekiah's prayer "concerning Sennacherib king of Assyria." That prayer raised specifically the issue of YHWH's having been mocked by Sennacherib's words (v. 17) and of Assyria's indisputable track record as destroyer of nations ("of a truth, O LORD"). Both of these issues are directly addressed by the mocking song, which is introduced as YHWH's word to Sennacherib.[130] As such, the song is a response to the prayer and to issues it has raised for YHWH's attention. YHWH attends to the concerns of his servant Hezekiah before he deals with the fate of the city itself, in the sign and in the oracle at 37:33–35. Far from interrupting the flow, issues are treated in appropriate order. Only by eliminating the prayer would the elimination of the song and the sign follow.[131] To do so because of historical logic (does it make sense to give a long-term sign at a time of siege?) is to misunderstand the literary form in which the report of the events of 701 comes to us.

From that perspective, moreover, the siege *never in fact takes place.*

---

129. On this, see the following chapter.

130. 37:22a should be retained as the introduction to the mocking song, and not spliced off to introduce the oracle at v. 34, leaving v. 33 hanging.

131. Movement directly from 37:22a to 37:34 would prove abrupt in its own way, skirting entirely issues raised in Hezekiah's prayer. Eliminating Hezekiah's prayer would solve the problem, of course, but with a loss of a great deal of the narrative's dramatic quality, upon which the story depends for its theological force. Cleaning up the narrative in such a way as to reconstruct "historical events" violates the genre of the literature, and results in a truncating of the narrative and its theological point. Moreover, the secondary nature of Hezekiah's prayer has been proposed within the climate of distinctions between B1 and B2, and not within B2 itself (cf. 37:22b–29 and 37:30–33).

The oracle at 37:33–35—which cannot now be eliminated without losing the story altogether—makes this clear: "He shall not come into this city, or shoot an arrow there, or come before it with a siege, or cast up a siege mound against it" (v. 33). In contrast to Judah's fate, Sennacherib neither "comes up against" nor "takes" Jerusalem (cf. 36:1). The problem of the siege's nonmention is only partially solved by considering this one verse (37:33) a yet further addition to the original ending of B2, itself "secondary" to B1. Account B2 allegedly concludes with the assault on the Assyrian camp (37:34–36) and is to be kept separate from the notice of Sennacherib's return and death at 37:37–38, which forms the conclusion to B1. Yet the problem with the distribution of verses from the end of the narrative (37:33–38) into two sources is as old as the two-source theory itself. A look at Goncalves's recent literary division, adopted by Dion, gives good illustration of how complex the problem is.[132] Stade had the good sense to regard the conclusion to the first source as lost, thus avoiding many of these problems.

There is, moreover, no reason to question the formal integrity of the unit 37:33–35, apart from the need to (1) find two separate endings in one Account B, and (2) posit a direct continuation from 37:22a to 37:34.[133] I have argued above that 37:22a forms the proper continuation to 37:21 and issues raised in Hezekiah's prayer (37:16–20). It introduces the mocking song (37:22b–29), which specifically addresses the content of Hezekiah's prayer. Only then does Isaiah deliver an oracle regarding the fate of the city in military terms (33–35). It is also the case that 37:33 is regarded as secondary (to B2 and B1), because it so clearly states that the siege never took place—a fact at odds with a "historical" evaluation. Reference to Sennacherib's not casting up a siege mound is particularly striking, given the report of AS.

Yet is it at odds with the rest of Account B—either B1 or B2? Sennacherib has left Lachish and removed to Libnah (37:8). He is still not in the near vicinity of the capital. He has laid siege to Judahite cities (36:1), but no such activity has yet occurred to Jerusalem. The assault has been verbal, and verbose—first from the Rabshakeh, and then indirectly from Sennacherib. As such, from the standpoint of Account B (or even Account A), siege preparations have not yet taken place. According to 37:33, and the entire unit 33–35, they never do.

It is also difficult to separate the final unit from this logical depiction (37:36–38), or further subdivide it along the lines of 37:33–35.[134] Isa 37:33–35 reports that the Assyrians will not enter or even approach Jerusalem. Clearly

132. See p. XX, above. Also Wildberger, *Jesaja*, 1416.
133. Wildberger, *Jesaja*, 1417: "die ursprüngliche Einleitung zu dem kurzen Orakel steht bereits in 22a."
134. Most separate the "mythological" notice of 37:36 from what follows, placing it with 37:34–35 as the conclusion to a more legendary B2. Vv. 37–38 are sober history, though anachronistic in their reference to the "immediate" death of Sennacherib, thus preventing the author of B1 from being an "eyewitness" (Dion, "Sennacherib's Expedition," 19).

one concern is to depict the assault from YHWH's angel as occurring beyond the environs of Jerusalem and Zion (the angel went forth, *wayyēṣē'*). The assault occurs not from Sennacherib, on the "camp" of Israel—as the Assyrian king had boasted—but on the "camp of the Assyrians" (37:36), who were last mentioned as at Libnah, twenty-five miles away. What Jerusalem, its king, and its citizenry were to have experienced, as arrogantly proclaimed through the agency of Rabshakeh and anonymous Assyrian messengers (*mal'ākîm*, 37:9), the camp of the Assyrians experiences at the hand of YHWH, through the agency of his messenger (*mal'ak YHWH*, 37:36). Sennacherib finally does return home (37:37), as Isaiah had once prophesied to Hezekiah (37:37). Isa 37:38 reports the final fulfillment of the prophet's word: Sennacherib is slain by the sword in his own land (37:7b), while worshiping the god "that is no god, but the work of men's hands" (37:19). He is slain not by YHWH's angel, but by his own sons. There is finally no escape for a blasphemer.

Conclusions

Division of the final verses of chapter 37 into two sources, giving rise to a theory of yet further glossing (37:22b–29; 37:33), is consistent with the historical and source-critical logic that has dominated the interpretation of Isa 36–37 for the last century. The fundamental issue raised by the analysis of Smelik is whether elements that occur in formally distinct units are nevertheless essential to the logic of the narrative in its entirety. There is no question that Isa 36–37, as it presently stands, is a composite work derived from a tradition process whose precise character is a matter for reasoned speculation. It is not a work authored in a single sitting, or by an eyewitness concerned with reporting "what really happened" in some objective sense.

An outline of the formal structure of Isa 36–37 reveals a series of Assyrian challenges, two from the Rabshakeh (36:4–10 and 36:13–20), and then one from Sennacherib himself via messengers (37:10–13). Interspersed within these challenges are responses from representatives of Hezekiah (36:11–12, 21–22), Hezekiah (37:1–4), and Isaiah the prophet (37:5–7). Finally Jerusalem's king must respond directly to the challenge of Assyria's king, in a prayer to Israel's LORD and king (37:14–20). Other sections of the narrative (36:1–3; 37:8–9) provide the necessary circumstantial information to allow the narrative to unfold in a logical fashion.

At the conclusion of Hezekiah's prayer, the narrative moves toward a resolution of the contest. The prophet addresses an oracle to Hezekiah, in response to his prayer (37:21–29). The oracle is confirmed by a sign (37:30–32), whose effects will begin almost immediately and will continue for a three-year period.[135] Then an oracle concerning the military threat is delivered

---

135. Compare the sign of Exod 3:12, which is to *follow* the deliverance from Egypt.

(37:33–35), introduced by the customary formula (*lākēn kōh-'āmar YHWH*). The oracle promises that the Assyrian king will advance no further and will return "by the way he came" (37:34), in confirmation of Isaiah's earlier promises (37:7, 29). The promise is grounded in God's own honor and "for the sake of my servant David."

The final verses of the narrative (37:36–38) tersely report the fulfillment of the oracle. YHWH's angel assaults the Assyrians in their camp. Since this event, strictly speaking, goes beyond the oracles at 37:7 and 37:29, which focus on the return of Sennacherib as well as his death "in his own land" (37:7), it probably speaks to a matter whose source lies in historical events—however one accounts for the large number reported slain (185,000).[136] Such an event may well have been regarded as a fulfillment of what Isaiah had proclaimed at 10:16 ("The LORD, the LORD of hosts will send a wasting sickness among his stout warriors"), thus accounting for its placement here, its unusual form (slain first, dead bodies the next morning), and the large number recorded as slain.[137] In the strict sense, then, only the final verses (37–38) report the concrete fulfillment of the oracle spoken by the prophet Isaiah. They tell of the return of Sennacherib to Ninevah and his death by sword there.

It is most likely that behind this narrative lies an extended oral legend, going back to the miraculous events of 701 themselves.[138] Sennacherib failed to take the city and was forced to return by the way he came, as Isaiah had maintained (37:7; 37:29; 37:37). An "angel of YHWH" went forth and struck the camp of the Assyrians, again in fulfillment of Isaiah's earlier word (10:15). In contrast to Ahaz during the Syro-Ephraimitic debacle, King Hezekiah was a model of obedience and piety during the crisis. These three factors comprised the foundation of the oral legend.

However, the artistry and craftsmanship of the narrative in its present form owe much to literary influences. The narrative may once have been briefer in scope (as a literary work), but this is impossible to determine. Clearly an interest in final editorial coherence and unity marks the present text, so that sections that appear to have developed independently (37:22b–29)

---

136. Close to the number Assyria reckoned to have "counted as booty" in the AS (200,150).

137. Isa 37:36 reads "And the angel of YHWH went forth (*wayyēsē'*) and smote in the camp of Assyria 185,000 men; and they arose in the morning, and behold they were all dead bodies." The *hinnēh* clause should be read as reporting an event that occurred just subsequent to the waking up. The subject of *wayyaškîmû* is not clear, though it must either be (1) men in the Assyrian camp who were not slain, but who observed the dead bodies of their fellow Assyrians; or (2) those who awoke, and then very quickly died (cf. RSV, which makes it sound as though unknown men went and observed these bodies). Making a logical interpretation, 2 Kgs 19:35 adds at the front "now it was during that night" (*wayhî ballaylāh hahû'*), further stressing the delay between the slaying and the death itself. Is the "gradual death" what is implied by a wasting sickness (*rāzôn*) at 10:16? The Niphal of *rzh*, "to make lean," appears at Isa 17:4 in a description of Jacob's fat flesh growing lean (*mišman běśārô yērāzeh*). In other words, 37:36 may have been made to conform more closely to 10:16, whatever its origin in historical events.

138. On questions of dating the narrative, see the following section.

nevertheless are carefully integrated into the present narrative. Central to the narrative in its final form, in all its sections, is the challenge put to YHWH and Hezekiah by the arrogant Assyrian king, and the final punishment of Sennacherib and the Assyrian militia.[139] This has meant that a considerable focus now falls on Hezekiah, who is depicted in steady contrast to the Ahaz of Isa 6–8. That focus is maintained into chapters 38 and 39, which are the subject of sections to follow.

MATTERS OF FUNCTION, DATE, AND PROVENANCE

We have rejected the division of the narrative into two sources (B1 and B2) and the tradition-historical assumptions that follow from it, whereby B2 is assigned to the exilic or postexilic period. The question of Second Isaiah's influence on both the prayer of Hezekiah and the taunt song has been addressed, and the argument has been put forward that the direction of influence runs exactly counter to what is traditionally claimed. At a minimum, the language in the prayer and the taunt song is distinctive over against Second Isaiah, and is appropriate to the context in which it now appears.

The terminus a quo for the growth of the account is obviously the year 701 B.C.E. The oral account doubtless goes back to this date. The present unified narrative is marked by the kind of literary features and composite quality that precludes its being dated too closely to 701. Yet as has always been recognized (at least for B1), the degree of specificity at several points in the narrative is such as to argue against its simply being a cult legend or a later mythologized "drama of deliverance."[140]

The feature of Hezekiah's centrality is a factor that must be reckoned with and, despite the arguments of source-critics, that centrality is as much a feature of a unified B as a putative B2. It has become a commonplace to describe the heightened interest in Hezekiah an "idealization" from a later day;[141] this in turn assists in assigning a terminus ad quem for the finished narrative. The degree to which source-critical analysis is purely responsible for such a reconstruction is difficult to test, though Smelik's final reading offers an interesting control, since he defends the unity of Account B. He dates Account B to the later period because of the Second Isaiah similarity. As

---

139. In this, it resembles the Goliath legend and foreshadows the contests between Daniel and the blasphemous detractors of YHWH in Daniel 2–6, especially the Belshazzar legend in Dan 5 (which does not end with a confession of YHWH as one LORD over all the kingdoms of the earth, but with the death of Belshazzar "that very night").

140. On the "authentic" details of B1 (including matters of language/dialect, "Assyrian contacts," and "other specific bits of information"), see Dion, "Sennacherib's Expedition," 13–19.

141. Ackroyd has pursued this logic in all of his works, beginning with "Historians and Prophets," 18–54 (and see note 143 below). Also Laato, *Who is Immanuel?* (1988); Childs, *Crisis*, 103; Clements, *Deliverance*, 65; Dion, "Sennacherib's Expedition," 22; Goncalves, *Expedition*, 480; Wildberger, *Jesaja*: "Previous exposition has made it clear that over against the first report the second increases the piety of Hezekiah and allows Isaiah to proclaim the deliverance of Jerusalem" (1438).

additional evidence he cites the conclusion of chapter 39, which he takes to predict the end of the Davidic dynasty, which signals for him a date in the Persian period.[142]

The reference to chapter 39 is important, since it implies rather clearly that matters of dating in 36–37 cannot be handled apart from the interpretation of 38–39. While there is a certain correctness in this view, as shall be shortly demonstrated, the reference to 39:7 can, however, be interpreted differently than as an aetiological note from a period when kingship had come to an end.

What is curious about Smelik's analysis is that two different *tendenzen* seem to be at work in the same body of tradition (Isa 36–39). On the one hand, there is a concern to trace the end of kingship to Hezekiah's obscure action in chapter 39, at the same time he is presumably being idealized in 36–37. One might well argue that the tradition-history of chapter 39 is distinct from 36–37 (and 38), but then it would be impossible to use a reference in the former (39:7) to help date the latter. Anticipating, I agree with Smelik that the dating of 36–37 is affected by proper interpretation of chapters 38–39, but it is difficult to see how Hezekiah has been idealized in Account B and made curiously responsible for the 587 assault, if not the end of the Davidic dynasty, in chapter 39. The issue is further complicated by the fact that Smelik argues for the priority of Isa 36–39 over 2 Kgs 18:13—20:19, a position with which I concur. But the presentation of Isa 38 continues the altogether positive portrayal of Hezekiah, in some contrast to 2 Kgs 20:1–11. In that sense it is consistent with Isa 36–37, even as it stands in tension with chapter 39.

To his credit, Smelik tends to avoid the language of "idealization" in speaking of Hezekiah in Account B, or chapter 38. But for the many scholars who adopt such a view of the tradition-history of Isa 36–37, the question remains: Why is Hezekiah idealized at a later point in history, when at the same later period he is curiously denounced in chapter 39? Ackroyd's solution—to view chapter 39 in terms other than denunciation—is helpful at this point.[143] But the question can be put even more narrowly: Why bother to

---

142. "Distortion," 85.

143. "Babylonian Exile," 336–38. By the same token, in "Death of Hezekiah" (1981), Ackroyd summarizes his older position and demonstrates how pivotal the A/B1/B2 theory is for his own reconstruction: "The effect (in Isaiah) is immediately to modify the picture of Hezekiah from a rebel and a political contriver—implicit in the 2 Kings text—to that of a king of absolute faith and trust when confronted by the Assyrian onslaught. This provides a marked contrast with the portrayal of Ahaz in Is 7 which, in fact, presents Ahaz as a king who lacks faith, a picture markedly darker than that provided in the corresponding 2 Ki 16. Ahaz has already moved down the scale, approaching the low point reached in the vivid picture of 2 Chr 28; Hezekiah has moved up the scale towards the idealisation to be found in 2 Chr 29–32, in Sir 48 and beyond" (220). It is difficult to agree with the neatness of this "scale" reconstruction, esp. in respect of Ahaz, who seems to be equally negatively portrayed in both Isaiah and 2 Kgs 16. What is important for our purposes is the degree to which the whole theory of a "scale" derives from the isolation of "Account A" as the foundational (negative) report, away from which the "idealization" moves.

idealize Hezekiah at all?[144] The question is especially pressing if the view promoted above is adopted, whereby the movement in Kings is not toward idealization but precisely the opposite, as witnessed in the so-called Account A, toward adjustment in the light of Josiah's subsequent career and the wider history and final demise of kingship in 587 B.C.E. It is far easier to assume that Hezekiah's positive portrayal was an essential part of the original narrative and the legend that underlies it than that this portrayal grew up in the postexilic period, when other evidence might have been read to the contrary (e.g., 2 Kgs 18:14–16; 20:1–19). The positive portrayal is of one piece with the positive outcome in 701. The city was delivered, as both accounts ("B1" and "B2") have it. That deliverance was predicated in no small measure on the righteous deportment of King Hezekiah, in conformity with Isaiah's word both within and outside the narrative proper.

Other theories for the lateness of B2 are equally suspect. Dion, for example, argues that B2 is "an exilic creation based on B1."[145] Such a view is based on the literary theory of Stade, and on the following aetiological conception:

> In addition to the punishment of Sennacherib's blasphemy, the exemplary protection extended to the monotheistic Hezekiah may have been of great significance to the author and his audience, who could feel its contrast with the ruin visited upon a kingdom fallen into idolatry. [22]

Using similar "palimpsest" logic, Clements argues with respect to Isa 39: "An awareness of what happened to the Davidic royal house in 598 B.C. permeates the story of the coming of the emissaries from Babylon to Jerusalem in 2 Kgs 20, 12–19 (= Isa 39)."[146] Also following Goncalves, Clements feels that B2 was composed after the catastrophe of 587 B.C.E.:

> The narrative is designed to show that, under the obedient response of a faithful king, God does act to protect and uphold his people. [261]

Is it possible, however, to distinguish between a theoretical later interpretation of an earlier narrative, on the one hand, and a narrative whose original purpose was to have the oblique effect proposed by Clements? We agree that the narrative is designed to illustrate the obedient response of a faithful king, as Clements puts it. But this theme belongs to a unified B (so Smelik), not a B2 nearly on the end of a scale of idealization (cf. 2 Chron 32 and Sir 48) at whose other end is Account A.

---

144. Laato's theory that Hezekiah was artificially pressed into service as "Immanuel"—assisted by his portrayal in B2—in order to offset "cognitive dissonance" suffers from lack of concrete evidence for such dissonance (*Who Is Immanuel?* 313–26).

145. "Sennacherib's Expedition," 22. Dion acknowledges his dependence on Goncalves's conclusions (*Expedition*, 480).

146. "Central Passage," 261. Actually, it would be a reverse palimpsest, in that what appears below the surface of the text is a later, not earlier, message.

The date of the unified narrative at Isa 36–37 must be sufficiently far from the events of 701 to allow two "anachronisms" to make their way into the literary presentation. The first is the mention of Tirhakah at 37:9. This detail itself is striking and argues for an essential rootage in actual events, even for a literary elaboration that allows itself considerable temporal flexibility. Rejecting two-campaign theories or complex reconstructions of co-regencies, Tirhakah was simply too young to have been more than a prince during the 701 expedition.[147] The author of the narrative, however, saw obvious value in using an actual figure from history, who later made life difficult for Assyria, at this point in the story, thereby eliciting a direct message from Sennacherib to Hezekiah, focusing the challenge as between these two kings, and between trust in YHWH or trust in Egypt. The author was not refusing to be "historical" or "objective"—historical events were simply used flexibly in service of the narrative and its larger theological presentation.[148]

The second anachronism causes more historical tension, though its origin can be explained along similar lines. The final notice at 37:38 reports that Sennacherib was murdered by his sons, an event that is to be dated at 681 B.C.E.—that is, some six years after the death of Hezekiah. Attempts to collapse the period separating his return and his death might lessen the tension with 37:7, but they do not solve the basic historical problem. Alternatively, since the time period separating Sennacherib's return (37:37) and his murder (37:38) is not stipulated, his return could be dated to 701 and his death at 681. But this still places the date of the unified narrative after 681, and raises questions about the oracle to Hezekiah at 37:7, which links the return and the death and places them both long before Hezekiah's death. The reference to Sennacherib's death in 37:38 is problematic from a historical standpoint. Can it be explained from a literary standpoint?

One possible explanation is that the author of Isa 36–37 worked after the death of Sennacherib, and with knowledge of his assassination—a fact for which we have confirmation in extrabiblical sources.[149] Yet for the purposes of the narrative, he portrays the murder as roughly coterminous with Sennacherib's departure and the deliverance of 701 (37:37 + 37:38). The murder was viewed as unusual and auspicious. Its prediction was therefore attributed to

147. The ruler was Shabaka (for bibliography and discussion, see Dion, "Sennacherib's Expedition," 12–13).
148. C. Hardmeier does an excellent job analyzing this type of historical flexibility in narrative presentation, and he offers a brilliant, provocative alternative to the source-critical approach in the recent *Prophetie im Streit vor dem Untergang Judas: Erzählkommunikative Studien zur Entstehungssituation der Jesaja- und Jeremiaerzählungen in II Reg 18–20 und Jer 37–40* (BZAW 187; Berlin: Walter de Gruyter, 1990). While I share many of his criticisms of historical analysis, his own proposal—seeing 701 events in narrative form as derivative of a later *Erzählsituation* just prior to the fall of Judah (reported in Jer 37–40)—lacks an important form and tradition-critical dimension. An extended analysis of this important monograph follows in the next section.
149. See S. Parpola, "The Murderer of Sennacherib," 174.

Isaiah, together with his (sufficiently) wondrous prediction of Sennacherib's return and Jersualem's deliverance, which formed part of the original oral account (now found at 37:7a and 37:29) and which finds (sufficiently) wondrous fulfillment at 37:37. Like the mention of Tirhakah, precise chronology has been sacrificed in service of the narrative and its theological burden.[150] The later fact of Sennacherib's murder was seen to be perfectly consistent with the proclamation of Isaiah regarding his humiliation and forcible removal (37:29). In fact, it provided striking testimony of the ultimate fate of a blasphemer, a theme around which the narrative is organized and toward which it now moves inexorably.

Taking into consideration these two "anachronisms," it is possible to date the present narrative in the first decades of Manasseh's long reign (687–642 B.C.E.).[151] The notice of Sennacherib's murder in Ninevah, with which the narrative concludes (37:38), marks the terminus a quo of the composition of Isa 36–37 in its present form (681 B.C.E.). Did the choice of Manasseh's birthname signify hopes for the reunification of Israel, as may have found expression in Isaiah's oracles (11:13)? Manasseh was born just after the 701 crisis (699 B.C.E.) and he took the throne at only twelve years of age (2 Kgs 21:1). Hopes associated with the deliverance of 701 may have been transferred to Hezekiah's son Manasseh and may have affected the decision to place this young boy on the throne (there were probably other sons—Hezekiah was forty-two when Manasseh was born).[152] This means that for the opening years of his reign, and at least until Sennacherib's death in 681, Manasseh ruled as an adolescent and was doubtless assisted by various parties and advisors in Jerusalem.[153]

150. Similar temporal flexibility can be seen in both Isa 38 and 39 (see below).
151. One of the weaknesses of Hardmeier's monograph is that while he correctly spots tensions in the narrative of a historical nature—tensions I have highlighted in the present study—these are capable of explanation for him only by placing the narrative's origin in close proximity to the Jeremiah prose tradition and the similar events of 597–587, when (1) Egyptian aid caused a temporary Babylonian withdrawal (Jer 37:5; cf. Isa 37:9 and the reference to Tirhakah), and (2) tribute was given by Zedekiah prior to his rebellion (Ez 17:15; 2 Kgs 24:20b; cf. 2 Kgs 18:13–17, which tells of Hezekiah's tribute *before* the siege). In this manner he is able to account for the odd placement of "Account A" (2 Kgs 18:13–16)—a problem I addressed above. Hardmeier is right to argue that 587 events have had an influence on the presentation of Hezekiah now found in Kings (esp. at 18:14–16 and 20:12–19). But it is more likely that the account I regard as central and original (Isa 36–37) had a *forward* influence on the prose traditions of Jeremiah, even as those later traditions, and esp. their depiction of Zedekiah and the fall of Judah, back-influenced the record of 2 Kings 18–20. In other words, the historical "anachronisms" concerning Tirhakah and the death of Sennacherib are different in kind than the problem of Account A. They belong to an original historical/theological narrative composed during the early Manasseh period (contrary to Hardmeier, *Prophetie im Streit*, 162–64). The existence and location of "Account A" next to the basic Hezekiah-Isaiah narrative (2 Kgs 18:14–16 + Isa 36–37) belongs to a larger set of problems within the development of the DtrH. Hardmeier's thesis will be examined in more detail shortly.
152. See Seitz, *Theology in Conflict*, 14–71.
153. Similar circumstances obtained at the accession of Josiah, who was only eight when he took the throne (Seitz, *Theology in Conflict*, 72). The "people of the land" are credited with placing him in power and avenging the assassination of Amon his father (2 Kgs 21:23–24).

Since the principle of primogeniture could be set aside in Judah, and frequently was, it is an open question as to what motivated the selection of a younger son, especially one quite young (as in the case of Josiah and Manasseh). One obvious possibility was the desire to have the right impact on the young king, on the part of those who insured his selection, for good reasons or for matters of expedience (2 Kgs 21:23–24; 1 Kgs 1:11–40).

Barth has argued for a major level of redaction in Isaiah to be dated roughly coterminous with the accession of Josiah, and with hopes associated with the collapse of the Assyrian empire. The royal oracles in Isaiah are to be dated to this period as summarizing the hopes placed in King Josiah. Barth left the Isaiah narratives (36–39) out of discussion, based on his conviction that these chapters belonged in Kings and were only brought over to Isaiah, at the latest period of its development, to serve as a "conclusion" for Proto-Isaiah on analogy with Jer 52. The fact that Josiah is never mentioned in the Book of Isaiah did not dissuade Barth from associating the first full-scale redaction of the book with him.

As has been demonstrated in my treatment of Isa 36–37, it is difficult to analyze the sorts of questions raised by the interpretation of these chapters without at the same time discussing material in 1–35˚, especially as it is related to Hezekiah. In this, I stand in agreement with a wide range of scholars.

Although it remains in the realm of reasonable speculation, I would substitute for Barth's conception of a Josianic redaction an edition culminating in Isa 36–37 (38–39) and the figure of Hezekiah.[154] As to the narrower question of the provenance and function of 36–37, I return to the central role played by Hezekiah in the narrative. Clements has seen in him a model of obedience and faith, whose depiction was meant to demonstrate to the post-587 community that "God does act to protect and uphold his people"; similarly, Dion sees the postexilic portrayal of the "monotheistic Hezekiah" keyed to concerns with "a kingdom fallen into idolatry."[155] Arguing for a date after the death of Hezekiah, in the early years of Manasseh's reign, another option is possible for this essentially correct view of the narrative's interest in Hezekiah as exemplary king. Apart from celebrating Jerusalem's deliverance in 701 in and of itself, the narrative seeks to hold up Hezekiah as the model of faith, whose obedience in YHWH helped avert a crisis. The pedagogical target of such a message is not just the average citizen, as is implied in post-587 readings, but the royal house itself. For whom was that message particularly apposite, if not for the young Manasseh, son of Hezekiah? That Manasseh ultimately does not heed such a message, and is judged to be the worst king in Israel before his fifty-five-year reign is over (2 Kgs 21:1–18), is not to the point. In fact, the argument could be made that who but Manasseh needed to be

---

154. At this juncture we do not want to exclude chaps. 38–39 from such an edition; see the following sections.
155. See above, p. 98.

reminded of the faith and obedience of his father Hezekiah, whose reform work the historian tells us he undid before his long reign was over (2 Kgs 21:3).[156]

Barth has made much of the fact that the Josianic redaction was stimulated by hopes associated with the downfall of the Assyrian empire—hence the term "Assyrian redaction." There is no reason to assume that such hopes were not also generated at other periods in time, including the one under discussion. The momentum produced by the 701 deliverance doubtless gave rise to hopes for a lessening of Assyrian dominance, or even a complete turning back of Assyria, consistent with what Jerusalem had experienced in Hezekiah's fourteenth year. It would be pointless to suggest that such hopes required concrete verification of the kind that analysis of ANE history might produce.[157] Hopes need not be realistic, especially when judgments based on hindsight and broader historiographic perspective are not weighted more than they deserve. More to the point, the factor that was fully within Judah's ken was the awareness that Jerusalem had been spared by divine grace, royal obedience, and prophetic word. What was critical was the possibility that such a set of circumstances might obtain again, to the same good effect. It is this possibility that the Isaiah narratives seek to inculcate, in Hezekiah's successor, Manasseh; or in any successor who would seek to do the will of YHWH and thereby assure his protection over Zion.[158]

To pursue this hypothesis regarding date, function, and provenance for Isa 36–37 further, it is interesting to return to Gesenius's original argument for the priority of 2 Kgs 18:13—19:37 over the Isaiah narratives. Apart from his text-critical judgments (which are rejected by many today), Gesenius made the general observation that the Isaiah narratives seemed curious in the context of the Book of Isaiah ("an extensive appendix to the Isaiah oracle collection," 932), while they were quite appropriate in the historical Books of Kings. As Smelik has recently pointed out, such an observation does not work as well as might appear at first glance.[159] The relevant factor for Gesenius was doubtless the sharp contrast between prose and poetry (Isa 35 marked the end of the

---

156. Apart from its historical accuracy, one might trace the literary origin of the Martrydom of Isaiah to this kind of interpretation, which may be latent in the biblical material in its synchronic form. The silence of the biblical record on Isaiah's ultimate fate (cf. Jer 37–45) is filled in by this martyr legend, in which King Manasseh hunts down the prophet Isaiah (cf. Jer 26:20–23) and has him sawn in two.

157. Compare Barth, *Jesaja-Worte*, 239–65.

158. A similar judgment has been rendered about a first edition of Kings that would have ended with the reign of Hezekiah: "The aim of this production was to inculcate the right mode of behaviour for Judaean kings to follow, in the light of and in order to avoid the fate that had overtaken Israel" (A.D.H. Mayes, *The Story of Israel between Settlement and Exile: A Redactional Study of the Deuteronomistic History* [London: SCM, 1983] 122). Also Iain Provan, *Hezekiah and the Books of Kings* (1989). I assume that the narratives of Isa 36–37 (38–39) were composed for the Book of Isaiah, but were also meant to be used for the reign of Hezekiah in the Books of Kings, with material relevant to that context and its broader royal evaluation added subsequent to the fall of Jerusalem. More on this shortly.

159. "Distortion," 72.

"oracle collection"), obvious as one moved from Isa 35 to Isa 36, but less than conspicuous in the movement from 2 Kgs 17 to 2 Kgs 18. But beyond this, how accurate is the judgment of Gesenius?

Smelik has raised several interesting objections.[160] He notes, for example, that this is the only place in Kings where a prophet whose sayings are collected in the latter prophets makes an appearance—a fact that is particularly striking when one thinks of the close relationship between the Dtr. history and the Book of Jeremiah.[161] Second, the poetic sections of the Isaiah narratives are hardly unusual in the Book of Isaiah—indeed, we have tried to argue there is much similarity between themes in the taunt song and those that appear in Isaiah's oracles—while the poetry of 2 Kgs 19:21b–28 is exceptional in the Books of Kings. Third, and somewhat less obvious, Smelik argues that the account of Hezekiah's illness is better composed in Isaiah than in Kings; we have yet to take up this important question. The more relevant issue concerns the relationship between Isa 36–37 and chapters 38 and 39. Smelik treats the tradition complex as a whole, and is therefore able to register one final strong objection to the theory of Gesenius. Picking up from Ackroyd and Melugin the notion that the tradition-complex Isa 36–39 serves a bridge function in the Book of Isaiah, one is able to see linkages between these chapters and material preceding and following in the Book of Isaiah, where no such linkages exist in similar fashion in Kings.[162] Moreover, according to Smelik, one could mount an argument for the proper order of these chapters being: (1) Hezekiah's illness (38); (2) the visit of a Babylonian envoy upon his recovery (39); (3) the 701 invasion (36–37). The only explanation for the present order is that the account of the Babylonian envoy had to come last in order to introduce the theme of Babylonian captivity. But such a placement serves no purpose in Kings and is therefore evidence of the priority of Isaiah in respect of 36–39.

There is much to be said for the corrective value of Smelik's objections in a climate where the priority of Kings is frequently taken for granted. I have argued above that the root cause of this is the theory of gradations in historical reliability, from Account A to B1, to B2. Because Isaiah does not contain Account A, the tendency has been to regard Kings as the proper arena in which to discuss the 701 invasion. Smelik does not mention this, because he adheres in residual measure to a similar conception, at least as regards Account A and a now unified Account B.[163] The benefit of Smelik's observations is that a broader perspective is opened up onto the question of the

160. Ibid., 72–74.
161. The distinctive thing about narratives in Kings that are close parallels to narratives in Jeremiah is that the prophet *does not appear* in the former (2 Kgs 24–25).
162. I disagree with Smelik and Ackroyd that the "bridge function" indicates that these chapters postdate Second Isaiah, but I agree that linkages can be identified in Isaiah that are less conspicuous in Kings.
163. "[A historical] reconstruction must be based on 2 Kings xviii 13–16 and the Assyrian sources" (85).

function of Isa 36–39 in Isaiah vis-à-vis 2 Kgs 18:13—20:19 in Kings. Ackroyd had already made important inroads on this matter.

The question of the order of accounts in 36–39 is an important one, and it will be taken up shortly. Anticipating a bit, I see the matter as more complex than Smelik sets it out, at least for adjudicating the priority of Isaiah over Kings. Nevertheless I am in general agreement that the Isaiah narratives are related both to what precedes and what follows, and in that sense they have not been artificially spliced in, based on a putative analogy with Jer 52. What must finally be addressed is the question of *how* Isa 36–39 is related to 40–55, and whether the former was composed to serve a bridge function it did not originally possess prior to Second Isaiah. As stated above, I am inclined to view the bridge function of 36–39, if one should call it that, rather differently than Smelik and Ackroyd.

The way Smelik has posed the question, moreover, has meant the creation of an artificial choice. If one brackets out 2 Kgs 18:14–16, it is striking how essentially similar are the two accounts of the 701 invasion, not to mention the remaining material in 38/39.[164] Is it then possible to raise a third option for understanding the relationship between the Isaiah narratives and their counterpart in Kings? Noting the absolute uniqueness of the situation, whereby an extended narrative from a prophetic book is also to be found in the Book of Kings, is it possible to assume that this uniqueness is no accident? Was the Hezekiah tradition composed for two sources from its inception, for Isaiah and for Kings, and not just for one or the other? What sort of implications would this have for the authorship and provenance of Isa 36–37//2 Kgs 18:13, 17—19:37?

In a recent study,[165] C. Hardmeier refers to the material in 2 Kgs 18–20 as the "Hiskija-Jesaja-Erzählungen" (HKJ-Erzählungen), a term he borrows from Wildberger,[166] on the following grounds:

> The customary designation of this tradition-complex as "Isaiah legends" obscures the fact that not Isaiah but rather Hezekiah (with his ministers and their particular religious-theological politics) occupies center stage. [1, note 1]

He further designates what he considers to be the core of the material (2 Kgs 18:9f.,* 13—19:37*) the "Erzählung von der assyrischen Bedrohung und der Befreiung Jerusalems" (ABBJ-Erzählung, "the narrative of Assyrian threat and the liberation of Jerusalem"). The Isaiah version of the former he simply terms the "J-Version."

Quite apart from the complexities of Hardmeier's thesis, to be taken up

---

164. The differences between Isa 38 and 2 Kgs 20:1–11 are the subject of the following section.
165. *Prophetie im Streit* (1990).
166. *Jesaja*, 1369.

shortly, the recognition that Hezekiah plays a central role in the narrative, along with his ministers, is an important one and justifies the designation "Hezekiah-Isaiah Narratives"—not for 2 Kgs 18–20 in contrast to a separate ABBJ narrative, but for the narratives under discussion here—viz., Isa 36–39 and their parallel in Kings (lacking 18:14–16). This is the sense in which Wildberger employs the term. What the designation emphasizes is the special focus on Hezekiah in the narratives, without excluding the prophet Isaiah. In fact, the portrayal of the complementary functions of king and prophet is what sets these narratives off from other accounts in the latter prophets or the Book of Kings. In either context, the most familiar way in which prophet and king are depicted is in tension or outright conflict (Amos 7; 1 Kgs 11:26–40; 17–19; 21). The conflict is particularly intense in the Book of Jeremiah (19:1–15; 21–24; 26; 36; 37–39) and also in the Book of Isaiah (chaps. 7–8). This makes the exemplary depiction of Hezekiah, obedient to the divine word proclaimed by Isaiah, all the more striking.[167]

Moreover, the memory of Hezekiah's righteous deportment is not restricted to the Book of Isaiah. Like Isaiah, the Book of Micah never specifically condemns King Hezekiah for the sins that must lead to Zion's destruction (3:12); rather, it is the "heads of Jacob, and the rulers of the house of Israel" that are addressed (3:1; 3:9), along with (false) prophets and seers (3:5; 3:7). A critical text in this regard is Jer 26. When it is urged upon the "princes of Judah" (26:10) to render the death sentence in the case of Jeremiah, who had pronounced judgment on Jerusalem and the temple, external testimony is given in his defense by the "elders of the land" (26:17). The prophecies of Micah are recalled (Mi 3:12) from "the days of Hezekiah king of Judah" (26:18) as a precedent for Jeremiah's own prophetic message. Equally important is the recollection of Hezekiah's righteous response to the message of judgment:

> Did Hezekiah king of Judah and all Judah put him to death? Did he not fear the LORD and entreat the favor of the LORD, and did not the LORD repent of the evil which he had pronounced against him? [26:19]

The memory of Hezekiah's entreaty that diverted a sentence of judgment corresponds perfectly to the thrust of the Hezekiah-Isaiah narratives. Hezekiah forms an exact counterpoise to Jehoiakim, whom the narrative tells us had the prophet Uriah hunted down and brought back to Jerusalem for royal execution (26:20–24).

The reason Micah's prophecy is recalled and not Isaiah's is difficult to determine, since it requires an argument from silence.[168] As the story has it, the elders who rose to Jeremiah's defense were from Moresheth, home of

---

167. His curious reaction to Isaiah's word in 39:8 will be taken up in chapter 4.
168. See Ackroyd, "Presentation," 23–24.

Micah—perhaps there is some basis in history for the notice at Jer 26:16–19. More significant for the tradition-process behind Jer 26 may have been the realization that in the Hezekiah-Isaiah narratives, the prophet Isaiah did not take an adversarial role toward Hezekiah. Micah's message is cited because of its sharp judgment against Zion, as such. The text avoids saying that the message was directed at Hezekiah in particular, only that it was uttered while he was king (26:18). Hezekiah responded in prayer and fear, thus bringing about YHWH's repentance.[169]

The interest in King Hezekiah in Jeremiah traditions is significant for another reason. Gesenius felt that the largely narrative quality of Isa 36–39 was not appropriate to the context of Isaiah's oracles, but fit better in Kings. Admittedly, the central role that Hezekiah plays would be consistent with the narratives of Kings, though then Isaiah's role would prove singular, for the reasons mentioned above. Moreover, the intentional contrast that is now argued to exist between Isa 36–39 and the similarly prosaic Isa 6–8 on thematic, formal, and linguistic grounds would present a significant problem for Gesenius's theory. Seen from a different perspective, the Hezekiah-Isaiah narratives in 36–37 are by no means conspicuous in the broader prophetic corpus when one considers the prose sections of Jeremiah, including the long narrative just cited (chap. 26). Particularly when one appreciates the unity of the Hezekiah-Isaiah narratives, as is the case in this study, the features held in common by the prose tradition in Jeremiah and Isa 36–37 are numerous and striking.

First, the interest in details, sometimes incidental, often marks the Jeremiah narratives, especially in chapters 37–43, and this feature can be seen in Isa 36–37 as well.[170] In an effort to further clarify the standard classifications

---

169. Hardmeier's insistence that the ABBJ narrative was composed on the basis of Jer 37–40 (a narrative he terms the "Erzählung von der Gefangenschaft und Befreiung Jeremias," the "GBJ-Erzählung") and other Jeremiah prose tradition runs into a problem at Jer 26. The reference to Hezekiah's piety in 26:19 presupposes the traditions of Isa 36–37. While it is possible that Jer 26:19 refers to traditions in oral form only, it is unclear why the record of Hezekiah's exemplary deportment during the 701 crisis never took literary, or at least a mature oral form, similar in shape to what now exists at Isa 36–37. The form-critical dimension is lacking in Hardmeier's otherwise provocative treatment.

170. Seitz, *Theology in Conflict*, 231–35. Hardmeier acknowledges this dimension in both the ABBJ and GBJ narratives, but in the case of the former, "such concreteness in the depiction of the situation and in the provision of personal names is no guarantee of the authenticity of historical memory" (225). In contrast to Jeremiah prose tradition, the ABBJ is a "Tendenzerzählung" (1), a "fictive account which makes a 'historical' claim" (287), "a clear propaganda piece" (461), "a narrative which at its inception was literarily conceived in order to make a claim of historicality" (462). In other words, where the *Konkretheit* and *Detaillierung* of Jeremiah are signs of historicity, similar features in the Hezekiah-Isaiah narratives are only fictively constructed, betraying their real *Erzählsituation* as the events of 597–587. The discrepancy Hardmeier sees is forced on him by faulty literary and tradition-historical assumptions. See the following section.

"biographical" (B) and "deuteronomistic" (C), it has been argued in an earlier study that the former belong to a specific genre of composition, termed the "scribal chronicle," and a specific circle of tradents close to Jeremiah whose position on the fate of the exiles or the need for life in Judah to come to an end through further Babylonian onslaught after 597 B.C.E. is rather neutral.[171] The term "scribal chronicle" was chosen for two reasons: because of the interest the narratives show in the scribal family of Shaphan (including most centrally Shaphan, Ahikam, and Gedaliah), and because of the literary form of composition employed, which is less theologically reflective than other prose compositions influenced by an exilic perspective (the Golah redaction) and more interested in the fate of Jeremiah and the post-597 community in Judah, as such, quite apart from broader theological considerations regarding the fate of the wider Israel, including the community in exile.

What is important in assessing the Hezekiah-Isaiah narratives is not the theological or formal distinction between the scribal chronicle and Golah redaction—these distinctions are apposite because of certain historical, sociological, and theological realities that pertain to the Book of Jeremiah and the twin crises of 597 and 587. It is the fact of *exile* and *the division of the community* following 597 that hovers over the Jeremiah tradition complex, in a way for which there is no fit analogy for the Hezekiah-Isaiah narratives.[172] What is relevant, however, is a certain broad resemblance between the way a theological message is communicated in narrative form in Isa 36–37 and in the prose traditions of Jeremiah, whether from the Golah redaction or the scribal chronicle. The possibility I wish to entertain is that the composition of Isa 36–37 initiated a form of scribal narrative theology that was imitated in the tradition process of the Book of Jeremiah, in two diverse ways, and then extended beyond to the Book of Ezekiel and other postexilic compositions. The common prose format does not issue into common theological positions,

---

171. *Theology in Conflict*, 201–96.
172. Hardmeier's thesis that the Hezekiah-Isaiah narratives were composed as propaganda by the opponents of Jeremiah (and Ezekiel), in order to counter the message of capitulation to Babylon, fails to distinguish between the very different historical contexts of 701 and 587, and two very different prophetic messages (Isaiah and Jeremiah). Jeremiah's proclamation of judgment by the foe from the north lies at the heart of his message, and it finds a consistent corollary in his admonition to "serve the king of Babylon" and accept Babylonian authority (Jer 27:1–11). There is no fit analogy for this type of proclamation, with its various nuances, in the earlier period of Isaiah. Assyria may be the "rod of my anger" (10:5), but Assyria's dominion is always circumscribed by the distinctive element of Isaiah's message that is later transformed in the preaching of Jeremiah: so-called Zion theology. The whole weight of the Jeremiah tradition suggests that an earlier theology of Zion must now be set to the side, because of developments that took place in the life of Israel after Isaiah's prophetic career. The very real tension between the deliverance of 701 and the nondeliverance in 587—involving Zion's final destiny—collapses if the Hezekiah-Isaiah narratives are seen only as *Tendenzerzählungen* from the period before the fall of Judah. This tension may in fact be the central reason for the development of the Isaiah traditions beyond 1–39*, concerned with the question of Zion's final destiny.

or standardized productions, as a comparison between Ezekiel and Isa 36–37 demonstrates. The creativity of the author and the age remain as agents to be reckoned with.

The interest of the Jeremiah and Hezekiah-Isaiah narratives in specific details has already been mentioned. This feature can be seen in the enumeration of defeated gods and nations (36:19; 37:12–13), in the specific locale for the encounter ("by the conduit of the upper field on the highway to the fuller's field," cf. 7:3), in the crafty logic of the Rabshakeh (36:12), in the notice of Sennacherib's removal to Libnah (37:8), in the concern with date (36:1), and in the precise listing of Hezekiah's envoy ("Eliakim the son of Hilkiah, who was over the household, and Shebna the secretary, and Joah the son of Asaph, the recorder," 36:3; 36:22). The same features appear in the prose traditions of Jeremiah, which frequently relate specific information regarding location (esp. in 37–41), precise dates (26:1; 27:1; 28:1; 32:1; 36:1), persons, and functions.[173] In the latter case, one thinks especially of the interest in various minor officials in chapter 36, including "Gemariah the son of Shaphan the secretary" (v. 10), "Micaiah the son of Gemariah, son of Shaphan" (v. 11), "Elishama the secretary, Delaiah the son of Shemaiah, Elnathan the son of Achbor, Gemariah the son of Shaphan, Zedekiah the son of Hananiah, and all the princes" (v. 12), "Elishama the secretary" (vv. 20, 21), and others ("Baruch the secretary" and "Jerahmeel the king's son"). In 36:16 it is reported that upon hearing the scroll read, these officials "turned one to another in fear" (36:16) and insisted that the king hear as well; but when the scroll is read "neither the king, nor any of his servants who heard these words, was afraid, nor did they rend their garments" (36:24).

By contrast, upon hearing the message of the Rabshakeh, the envoy from Hezekiah is faithful to the king's command and answers not a word in response (36:21). Then it is reported of Eliakim (*'ašer-'al-habbayit*), Shebna (*hassōpēr*), and Joah (*hammazkîr*) that they "came to Hezekiah with their clothes rent" (cf. Jer 36:24) and reported what Rabshakeh had said (36:22). King Hezekiah's response is entirely appropriate and in clear contrast to that of Jehoiakim at hearing Jeremiah's word received from the hand of Elishama the secretary—neither he nor his servants was afraid nor did they rend their garments (Jer 36:24) Even when urged by Elnathan, Delaiah, and Gemariah not to burn the scroll, Jehoiakim arrogantly refuses and demands that Jeremiah and Baruch be brought before him (36:26). By contrast, Hezekiah rends his clothes, covers himself with sackcloth, goes to the temple, and asks Isaiah to be brought—not for execution—but that he might "pray for the remnant that is left" (37:1–4). The command not to intercede, which is fully developed in the Book of Jeremiah, stands in clear contrast as well to this request from

---

173. See charts 1 and 2 in *Theology in Conflict*, 9–11.

Hezekiah for a prayer—a request that is not refused by the prophet, nor denied as a mode of prophetic activity by God (cf. Jer 7:16; 11:14; 15:1).[174]

The kind of features that Isa 36–37 and the prose traditions of Jeremiah hold in common cut across chapters in Jeremiah that are frequently assigned different tradition-historical backgrounds (usually "B" and "C"). This means that there is no one obvious way to link the Hezekiah-Isaiah narratives to coherent theological developments that take place in the Book of Jeremiah.[175] All that can be safely said is that certain distinctive prose features in Isa 36–37 can be spotted as well in the Book of Jeremiah. The most obvious conclusion to be reached is that Jehoiakim and Zedekiah have been portrayed in strict contrast to King Hezekiah, whose actions and deportment are exemplary. We judge similar moves with respect to King Josiah (2 Kgs 22:11–13) to be a correlative development, based upon Hezekiah's portrayal in Isa 36–37.

As to the role of the various officials in Jer 36 (and beyond), Isa 36–37, and 2 Kgs 22, it is striking that (1) they are explicitly named and (2) their offices are given, even when they play very little (verbal) role in the narrative.[176] In the Hezekiah-Isaiah narratives, they speak only once (36:11), to request that the Assyrian flaunting be carried on in Aramaic; beyond that, they have basically a silent role.[177] Yet the narratives are concerned with depicting their actions as proper to the occasion (36:22; Jer 36:16, 25; 2 Kgs 22:9–10).

It also bears notice that in all three of these cases the office of the scribe (*hassōpēr*) is consistently mentioned, whether filled by Shaphan (2 Kgs 22:3, 8–10; cf. Jer 36:10), Elishama (Jer 36:12, 20, 21), Baruch (36:26), or Shebna (Isa 36:3), the latter joined by a record keeper (*hammazkîr*) named Joah, the son of Asaph, and Eliakim, who was over the household (*'ăšer-'al-habbāyit*). Eliakim, son of Hilkiah, is the recipient of a promissory oracle at 22:20–25, which in its present form may involve a redactional gloss at v. 25, involving his ultimate rejection.[178] Also mentioned in the oracle is Shebna (22:15), who is

---

174. C. Seitz, "The Prophet Moses," esp. 5–18.

175. Hardmeier, who sees the direction of influence running from 587 to a fictively portrayed 701, argues that the ABBJ narrative was composed as a *Tendenzerzählung* whose purpose was to counter the theological stance of Jeremiah on capitulation to Babylon (= Assyria), as recorded in the GBJ narrative. The ABBJ narrative teaches that capitulation *leads* to siege (so the odd placement of "Account A"); God will protect Zion without the need for capitulation or alignment with foreign powers. The narrative was produced by "nationalreligiös-heilsprophetischen" circles opposed to Jeremiah and Ezekiel (461). The theological and historical problems with this scenario will be discussed shortly. We are only interested in establishing that a *formal* similarity exists between the Hezekiah-Isaiah narratives and the later prose traditions of Jeremiah. Where theological issues are raised, they have to do with the contrast between Hezekiah and Judah's last kings, in that *forward* direction of influence (so Jer 26:19).

176. Their verbal role is most developed in Jer 36 (vv. 14–19), and even there it is quite succinct.

177. When they speak at 37:3–4, they are only a mouthpiece for the king ("Thus says Hezekiah")— more on this below.

178. Or, vv. 24–25, which is the view of most commentators. See Kaiser, *Isaiah 13–36*, 158–59; Clements, *Isaiah 1–39*, 190–91; Wildberger, *Jesaja*, 849–51.

called steward (*hassōkēn*) and the one over the household ('*ǎšer-'al-habbāyit*), the term applied to Eliakim at 36:3, which is transferred to him from Shebna at 22:20.[179]

The literary and redactional complexities of Isa 22:15–25 are the subject of detailed treatment in the commentaries. Matters such as the date of the passage, the possibility that Eliakim was secondarily introduced into an anonymous eschatological oracle (22:20–23), and the interpretation of the final verse, or vv. 24–25, as a later gloss are treated in some detail, as are the various historical theories regarding the status and function of the '*ǎšer-'al-habbāyit*.[180] For our purposes, only two specific issues are important: (1) Is the same Shebna spoken of in 22:15–19 and in 36:3, 22? (2) How does the description of Eliakim in 22:20–23 relate to the proper interpretation of his role in the Hezekiah-Isaiah narratives?

The two questions are related. All that pertains in a positive sense to Eliakim in 22:20–23 is set in contrast to Shebna. Shebna is condemned; he is to be hurled away, thrust from office, and cast down from the position given to Eliakim son of Hilkiah. His crime is the preparation of a tomb on the height (22:16), presumably equivalent to the placing of false trust in "the weapons of the House of the Forest" mentioned earlier in the chapter (22:8b); reference is also made to his splendid chariots at 22:18 (*markĕbôt kĕbôdĕkā*), with which he will die in a broad land ('*el-'ereṣ raḥǎbat yādāyim*).

No mention is made of any of this in the Hezekiah-Isaiah narratives. Shebna appears along with Eliakim. He is called a secretary (*hassōpēr*), not a steward or "one over the house" as in 22:15. That position is filled by Eliakim. Two possibilities, therefore, exist: (1) the transfer has already taken place, and Shebna has become a secretary, following Eliakim's assumption of his former position as promised at 22:20;[181] or (2) Shebna the steward and Shebna the secretary are in reality two different people.[182] Because the tone of 22:15–19 is so unequivocal about the final judgment over Shebna—which did not include his becoming secretary, much less "second in command" according to some theories!—the first possibility seems to be ruled out. Of course, if one dates the oracle at 22:15–25 *after* the events of 36–37,[183] then neither of these options is

179. For a discussion of the literary problem at 22:15b ('*al-šebnā*' following the command *lek-bō*'), see Wildberger, *Jesaja*, 832–34. He also gives a summary of the discussion regarding the term "steward" from the hap. leg. *sōkēn* (835–36).

180. For a typical theoretical treatment, see H.J. Katzenstein, "The Royal Steward (Asher 'al ha-bayith)," *IEJ* 10 (1960) 149–54.

181. By weaving together a variety of texts in which the terms *sôpēr* and '*ǎšer-'al-habbāyit* appear, it is often assumed that this represents a movement from something like "head of state" to "second in command" (see the discussion of Katzenstein, "The Royal Steward," 152–54).

182. Most prefer some version of the former option. Wildberger summarizes the discussion well: "It is naturally not excluded at the outset that he deals with two distinct bearers of the name Shebna. One is able, however, to summarize that Shebna degraded the writer, or for a different reason a change in occupancy of the highest office in the land occurred, so that 22:15–18 must be temporally situated around an individual for whom the conversation with Rabshakah, described in chap. 36, occurred" (*Jesaja*, 836).

183. Or assumes that what Isaiah prophesied need not have occurred in any strict sense.

necessary. But the problem would still remain: Why speak of Shebna as steward (*sōkēn*) and *'ăšer-'al-habbāyit* when that position is so clearly held by Eliakim in 36–37? Moreover, the oracle speaks of a transfer of power to Eliakim ben Hilkiah (22:19), a transfer that is presupposed in the references at 36:3 and 36:22. Why would a later oracle introduce a tension such as this?

Based upon the limited evidence we possess, it is impossible to determine whether Shebna the scribe and Shebna the steward are one and the same person. Theories regarding demotions and modifications of Isaiah's uncompromising oracle at 22:19 are attempts to deal with the tension that exists if one regards 22:15 and 36:3, 22 as speaking about the same Shebna. But we have seen no reason at other points to regard the Hezekiah-Isaiah narratives and Isaiah's oracles as in tension, and there seems to be no effort made whatsoever in Isa 36–37 to clarify Shebna's sudden change in status over against 22:15–19. As I have noted above, he and Eliakim and Joah are exemplary in their behavior, just as their counterparts are in Jer 36 and 2 Kgs 22. The evidence favors regarding Shebna the scribe as a different figure than Shebna the steward, Eliakim's denounced predecessor. Eliakim, on the other hand, is depicted in terms that are perfectly consistent with 22:20–23, thus maintaining the same kind of continuity we have spotted elsewhere between Isaiah's oracles and the Hezekiah-Isaiah narratives in 36–37.

The continuity between the positive depiction of Eliakim ben Hilkiah in 22:20–23 and 36–37 is precisely what makes the alleged discontinuity with respect to Shebna difficult to accept, in view of the fact that he and Eliakim are depicted side-by-side in the Hezekiah-Isaiah narratives. None of the three figures—Eliakim, Shebna, Joah—has any separate or special activity. All three appear before Hezekiah with clothes rent (36:22). Their reaction is one with the reaction of Hezekiah, who in addition covers himself with sackcloth and goes into the house of the LORD (37:1). Then the king sends the two men Eliakim and Shebna—now clothed like Hezekiah with sackcloth—together with the senior priests to the prophet Isaiah (37:2). These "servants of King Hezekiah," as they are called in 37:5, faithfully convey the message from king to prophet, and from prophet to king.

Two features in this brief unit (37:1–7) call for special comment. First, Eliakim and Shebna are depicted as one with Hezekiah in their reaction to the crisis (clothes rent—sackcloth). Second and related to this is the precise role they play in conveying the royal message to Isaiah. As the narrative sets it out, we are privy to Hezekiah's appeal to Isaiah only through the direct speech of the envoy to the prophet, introduced by "thus says Hezekiah" (37:3). On the other hand, Isaiah responds directly to the speech of the envoy with the words, "say to your master, 'Thus says the LORD'" (37:5). In other words, the envoy speaks directly on behalf of the king in a manner that is subtly altered when Isaiah speaks, on behalf of YHWH. They do not report the word of God, mediated by Isaiah, to Hezekiah; rather, Isaiah speaks directly the message that is to be conveyed—a message that *is* conveyed in the narrative world to the reader, with no further notice of the return of the envoy to Hezekiah. As the narrative is structured, the clear implication is that as the prophet speaks for YHWH, mediating the divine word directly ("thus says YHWH") without third party, so too the envoy of Hezekiah speaks directly for the king: "they said to him, 'Thus says Hezekiah'" (37:3). In this manner royal speech and divine speech come to the fore, mediated on the one hand by the "servants of Hezekiah" and on the other by "the servant of YHWH."

If this interpretation of the narrative technique in 37:1–7 is correct, the oracle to Eliakim at 22:20–23 can be seen in a fresh light:

> In that day I will call my servant Eliakim the son of Hilkiah, and I will clothe him with your robe, and will bind your girdle on him, and will commit your authority to his hand; and he shall be a father to the inhabitants of Jerusalem and to the house of Judah. And I will place on his shoulder the key of the house of David; he shall open, and none shall shut; and he shall shut, and none shall open. And I will fasten him like a peg in a sure place, and he will become a throne of honor to his father's house.

The oracle continues in a manner that urges most interpreters to consider these final verses (22:24–25) a historicizing gloss.[184] Whether they depict as severe a judgment as is often implied is another question. For our purposes, the interesting feature—about which there is no debate—is the overwhelmingly positive depiction of vv. 20–23.

Verses 20–21a depict the transfer of power to Eliakim ben Hilkiah "my servant" (cf. 37:5). Verse 21b speaks of Eliakim's position vis-à-vis the "inhabitants of Jerusalem and the House of Judah" (cf. 37:31–32), in which capacity he is to be as a "father" (*lĕ'āb*). Verse 22 speaks of Eliakim's more specific relationship to the house of David. The expression of conferral of authority, "on his shoulder" (*'al-šikmô*), is familiar from the royal oracle at 9:5. The imagery of the key (*maptēaḥ*) and the language of opening and shutting in 22b together emphasize Eliakim's role in granting access or denying it. In this role, he will become a "throne of honor" (*kissē' kābôd*) for his father's house (22:23), as such fully justifying the transfer of authority to him (22:20).

The language of 22:20–23 is not just impressive in what it conveys about the power granted to Eliakim in his office, it also is striking in its use of imagery from royal contexts elsewhere in Isaiah. He will be a father—similar to the portrayal of the Davidid in 9:5. The key will be on his shoulder, as is the government on the royal shoulder in 9:5. As the Davidid of 11:5 wears a girdle of righteousness, so too Eliakim is clothed in a girdle and robe (22:20). He will even be a "throne of honor," just as the king of 9:6 occupies the throne of David "to establish it and uphold it." Verse 24, which is often taken together

184. See note 178, above.

with the following v. 25 as a later gloss, may simply speak of the weight that the "peg in a sure place" (20:23) is capable of bearing, for the successors who come after him from his father's house. This would correspond in a positive sense to the note of perpetuity that concludes the royal oracle of 9:1–6. The final verse speaks of an ultimate giving way of the peg "in that day" (*bayyôm hahû'*), and of its being cut down and felled. But on the other hand, the net effect of all this is that the burden that was once on it (*hammaśśā' 'ăšer-'ālêhā*) is cut off. So while the authority of Eliakim and his house extends only to a fixed point in history, and is then taken away, the final note is not as severe as is often implied. The burden that was placed on it is finally lifted. The implication may simply be that the responsibility of Eliakim and his progeny was finally limited to one period in history, after which it had no further purpose.

The manner in which Eliakim ben Hilkiah is portrayed, together with Shebna the secretary, is in perfect conformity with the oracle of 20:20–23(24). What the king does, Eliakim, *'ăšer-'al-habbayit*, does. Eliakim and the envoy speak directly on the king's behalf in a way the narrative judges to be perfectly appropriate. In something of the same sense of 22:22, Eliakim grants access to the royal house, as he goes forth with Hezekiah's word to the prophet, and is sent back to Hezekiah with a fresh word from Isaiah. In this role, Eliakim anticipates the activity of the various scribes and officials in Jer 36, whose access to King Jehoiakim meets with altogether different effect. More specifically, Baruch the scribe has the function of mediating the prophetic word on Jeremiah's behalf (36:5–8), in part because of the threat on the prophet's life.

The role Baruch fills in the narratives of Jeremiah, as well as the function he executes in the redactional extension of Jeremiah's message, appears to be somewhat similar to the role that is set forth for Eliakim in the Book of Isaiah.[185] But whereas Baruch's role as scribe is tied closely to the prophetic office, Eliakim's role as *'ăšer-'al-habbayit* is tied closely to the royal office. Moreover, the circumstances under which Baruch functions, with the relationship between king and prophet at its nadir, stand in utter contrast with those that obtain during the 701 crisis. At every point where Hezekiah acted in obedience and trust, Jehoiakim acted in complete rebellion. Consequently, the Hezekiah-Isaiah narratives convey not just a different picture of the relationship between king and prophet, but also a different picture of the mediatorial Eliakim. Baruch is modeled on Jeremiah, in a similar way as Joshua is modeled on Moses, and the upshot is that Baruch must follow Jeremiah in suffering and sacrifice (Jer 45:1–5). Eliakim is spared such a

---

185. On the role of Baruch as a redactional "aide" in the composition of the Book of Jeremiah, see Seitz, "The Prophet Moses," 17–24.

depiction in the Book of Isaiah. He is the obedient mouthpiece of his obedient master, and the one who is granted special access to the royal house (22:22).

I am in a position to summarize my findings regarding the function, date, and provenance of Isa 36–37. The function of the narrative is to hold up Hezekiah as the model for obedient kingship, as the king who through penitence and prayer averts a merited sentence of judgment. This is the Hezekiah recalled in Jeremiah prose tradition (26:19).

The two anachronisms at 37:9 and 37:38 suggest that the narrative achieved its present form after the death of Sennacherib in 681. I conjectured that the early years of Manasseh's reign would have been a good time to memorialize Hezekiah and hold up to the young king the example of his righteous father, whose prayer and deportment were recalled as pivotal in turning back the Assyrians and saving Jerusalem. The message would have remained all the more relevant, even urgent, as Manasseh's reign grew longer and his disobedience more pronounced.

The largely silent but nevertheless central role played by Eliakim and his fellow officials in the narrative would also prove significant during such a period. Eliakim, Shebna, and Joah faithfully carry out both the will of the king and the will of the prophet. Through their actions they assist the king and together with him they share in the deliverance of the city. The oracle to Eliakim at 22:20–23 memorializes his role in the Hezekiah-Isaiah narrative as *'ăšer-'al-habbayit* and royal steward. It remains a prophetic endorsement of a royal office, and as such is consistent with the larger thrust of the Hezekiah-Isaiah narratives. Unlike the later prose narratives of Jeremiah, which draw on many of the features of Isa 36–37, the Hezekiah-Isaiah narratives are able to portray the royal office in a favorable light and hold up Hezekiah as a model for a later day. It is in just that spirit that Jer 26:19 looks back on the King Hezekiah of Isa 36–37 when it states: "Did he not fear the LORD and entreat the favor of the LORD, and did not the LORD repent of the evil which he had pronounced against them." Here the Jeremiah prose tradition captures the essence of the Hezekiah-Isaiah narratives, as it has been handed down to us in Isa 36–37.

It is difficult to be more specific about matters of authorship and provenance in Isa 36—37 without an unnecessarily high level of speculation. I have observed the largely peripheral yet essential role played in the narrative by the figures of Eliakim, Shebna, and Joah. Isa 22:15–25 assists in providing further perspective on the office of *'ăšer-'al-habbayit*, especially as related to the house of David. I have further conjectured that just as the figure of Hezekiah has been set forth as a model for future kings, so too these royal officials are portrayed sympathetically, as discharging the responsibilities given to them in a manner appropriate to their station.

In an intriguing rabbinic citation dealing with the authorship of biblical books, the Book of Isaiah is said to have been composed by "Hezekiah and his retinue" (b. batra. 14b, 15a).[186] Obviously the citation functions in a context of inquiry at great distance from the one in which we are working, with an altogether different set of constraints and final concerns. Yet ironically, it is the position of this study that if one wished to speculate further about the "author" of Isa 36–37, in its present form, circles represented by the steward, the scribe, and the record keeper would be a logical choice. They stand to the side of the prophet and the king in this narrative, responsible at one key point for communicating the word of Hezekiah to Isaiah (37:1–5). They are obediently silent before the Assyrian official (36:21), but fulfill their responsibility in conveying the content of the blasphemous speeches of Rabshakeh (36:4–10; 36:13–21) to the king (36:22). Even their plea to the Rabshakeh to speak in a foreign tongue (36:11) could not be construed by posterity as anything more than an expedient attempt to constrict the range of the blasphemy to their own learned circle.

In short, no one would have been in a better position to recall and preserve the original 701 traditions, ultimately shaping them into their present, carefully structured form, than the circles associated with the triad of Eliakim, Shebna, and Joah—steward, scribe, and record keeper.[187] It is a further question whether circles associated with this same "contingent of Hezekiah" also had the responsibility for redactional activity beyond the narrower context of the Hezekiah-Isaiah narratives, in an emerging Proto-Isaiah collection.

In conclusion, what the rabbinic citation may suggest is that from one early interpretive perspective a close connection was seen to exist between "Hezekiah and his retinue." Whether "Eliakim, Shebna, and Joah" were representatives of such a following is difficult to determine, but it certainly cannot be ruled out as one possible interpretation. Secondly, the rabbinic citation suggests a close connection between "Hezekiah and his retinue" and the traditions of Isaiah. Why Isaiah is not cited as having compiled his own

---

186. Rashi's conjecture that Isaiah failed to author his own book because he was killed by Manasseh is apparently based on the Martyrdom of Isaiah. What is curious is how "Hezekiah and his retinue" were chosen as substitutes, also responsible for "authoring" (e.g., put into writing) Ecclesiastes, Song of Songs, and Proverbs. Proverbs contains a reference to the "men of Hezekiah" (Prov. 25:1) who copied the proverbs of Solomon, again suggesting that the phrase "Hezekiah and his retinue wrote" be understood as "compile" or "put into writing" rather than "author" in the modern sense. Rashi's explanation is curious since according to the legend Isaiah was martyred *after* Manasseh had become king, thus creating similar "authorship" problems for "Hezekiah and his retinue."

187. Hardmeier's decision to interpret these figures as pure fictional constructs requires greater evidence (437–50). He claims that the names Eliakim and Shebna—"fictive, historicizing provision of names"—were created on the basis of the names given in chap. 22 (440). On the other hand, he is correct to state: "The names most probably give evidence of the specific location of that circle responsible for the narrative and its theological-political traditions" (440). Yet in my view the names give evidence of actual—not fictional or representational—figures in such an "Erzählerkreis"; they are not just a "fictive representation of the narrative" (449).

book (cf. Jeremiah) is unclear, though similar questions may be considered to exist with regard to the Book of Ezekiel.[188] What is clear is that Hezekiah was capable of choice as "author" along with his "followers." The same could be said of very few kings; only Josiah comes to mind from the later preexilic period.

In sum, the rabbinic citation reflects one obvious interpretation of all the relevant biblical material (2 Kgs; Isa; 2 Chron; Prov) read at the synchronic level—viz., that Hezekiah and Isaiah were aligned as closely as any king and prophet in the history of Israel, so much so that he and his retinue could be credited with having put into writing the Book of Isaiah, as well as the Song of Songs, Proverbs, and Ecclesiastes—traditions associated with another significant Judahite king who never reached the heights of Hezekiah (2 Kgs 18:5).

The formal structure and literary organization of the Hezekiah-Isaiah narratives is sufficiently complex to argue that its composition was the result of careful scribal activity. This is not prophecy in a classic mode: brief oral speech delivered spontaneously, generally in the form of invective-threat and judgment. Rather, this is "prophecy" as we see it later in the Book of Jeremiah—viz., narrative chronicle (*Kurzgeschichte*) and rhetorical prose, traditionally categorized in that context as "B" and "C."[189] Like the material in Jeremiah termed "scribal chronicle," the Hezekiah-Isaiah narratives take an interest in the prophet as a figure depicted within the narration itself, and only one among others. In Jer 37–43 the prophet is joined by enough other figures that it is difficult to argue that he occupies center stage; these include the king (Zedekiah), scribal figures (Baruch), and other minor officials (Ebed-Melech; Gedaliah). Similarly, in Isa 36–37 the prophet Isaiah is joined by King Hezekiah as well as the triad Eliakim, Shebna, and Joah. As in Jer 37–43, we find it most likely that the "authors" of Isa 36–37 are to be sought among the scribal families of Judah, whose representatives are depicted in the narrative. Their purpose in composing this "scribal prophecy" was to hold up Hezekiah as a model of kingship for Manasseh and his successors, with the hope that obedience to the divine word would lead to continued deliverance from Assyrian miltary threat and blasphemy.

THE HEZEKIAH-ISAIAH NARRATIVES: CONCLUSIONS

We have looked at a classic problem of interpretation in Isa 36–37 from a variety of traditional angles, but to a different final purpose—namely, to determine the role such narratives might play as part of the conclusion to a

188. Jeremiah wrote his own book and Kings. The Book of Ezekiel was authored by the Men of the Great Assembly.
189. N. Lohfink, "Die Gattung der 'Historischen Kurzgeschichte' in den letzten Jahren von Juda und in der Zeit des Babylonischen Exils," *ZAW* 90 (1978) 319–47. Hardmeier, *Prophetie im Streit*, 466.

Proto-Isaiah collection now influencing Second Isaiah chapters. In discussions of the classic problem, this final question has been touched on only obliquely, as part of a larger set of interpretive questions involving the direction of influence from Second Isaiah chapters, in Hezekiah's prayer (37:14–20) and in the taunt song of Isaiah (37:22–29).

At the same time we have approached these older interpretive questions in a new and different context, in which the narratives of Isa 36–37, together with 38–39, are the focus of special attention due to their possibly functional role in the redactional history of the larger Book of Isaiah. As a fresh treatment of the classic problem has demonstrated, it is no longer possible to regard these two areas of inquiry as separate and to discuss the interpretation of Isa 36–37 apart from larger questions of the redactional purpose of Isa 36–39 in the Book of Isaiah as a whole, and specifically with reference to chapters 40–55.

In reexamining the classic problem of interpretation in Isa 36–37 from this new perspective, the various traditional questions—historical, text-critical, source-critical, form-critical—have been addressed, as well as those raised by newer redaction-critical and literary approaches. In particular, arguments for the unity of Account B, as it has been traditionally called, have been viewed appreciatively, especially as these have led to greater understanding of the place and function of Isa 36–37 within the larger Book of Isaiah—a view that had been thoroughly obscured by the heavy priority granted to the narratives in 2 Kgs 18:13—19:37.

Here too some of the older issues have resurfaced. The priority given to Kings on classic historical grounds, especially as derived from the source-critical argument for three decreasingly objective accounts (A, B1, and B2), has had an important corollary in Isaiah studies: chapters 36–39 have been regarded as an addendum to a finished Proto-Isaiah book on reputed analogy with Jer 52. Alternatively, even as the special function of these narratives in Isaiah is being reconsidered, the older source-critical conclusions have been retained in sufficient measure to insure that the redactional purpose isolated for Isa 36–39 nevertheless still postdates Second Isaiah chapters.

I have argued for a different conception. Adopting the literary analysis of Smelik, I have argued for a unified narrative now essentially represented by Isa 36–37. The composite quality of the narrative, long-recognized by form-critics, is not to be denied, especially at certain junctures in Isa 37:21–38. Nevertheless, these several formally distinct units (37:21–29, 30–32, 33–35, 36–38) function in such an integral way in the final form of the material that it is difficult to conceive of a narrative capable of making its point effectively lacking even one of them. Undoubtedly the tradition process behind Isa 36–37 was a gradual one. Yet I have seen no reason to date the narrative in its present form much later than the death of Sennacherib (681), with which it comes to a stunning close.

The hegemony of the source-critical approach and the historical conclusions that follow from it continue to exert a formidable influence over all analysis of Isa 36–37. The recent treatment of Goncalves offers what is in essence only a massive tightening up of the theory as it had been brokered by previous scholars. Given such a climate, portions of the argument advanced here, if not the whole theory itself, will doubtless be judged faulty and quite outside the accepted form of approach. There has been virtually no scholar in this century who has questioned the historical veracity of 2 Kgs 18:(13)14–16 or doubted that it formed the proper starting point for all historical reconstruction (cf. Provan, Hardmeier). Along with such an appraisal has gone the assumption that Account A and the annals of Sennacherib are in essential agreement. On these two matters the most conservative scholar and the more skeptical interpreter have found rare common ground. I have challenged both these tenets of historical analysis, and am sure that such a challenge will meet firm resistance, if not outright rejection, from one or both camps.

Yet it is hoped that the larger conception of Isa 36–37 as representing a coherent literary and theological unity will not be rejected *tout court*. For then the possibility will exist that the broader ramifications of such a position, with all that it portends for the interpretation of Hezekiah, the date of the narrative, the correct assignment of provenance and proper understanding of function in the context of the larger Book of Isaiah, will not be lost in a skirmish over details that were essential in the climate of traditional historical analysis. Only then will the wider possibility be kept open that the function of Isa 36–37 might be understood in new and fruitful ways, vis-à-vis Second Isaiah chapters and the Book of Isaiah as a whole.

Before it is possible to look at this specific question, issues similar to those that have arisen in 36–37 must be treated in chapters 38 and 39 as well. Yet there is one final question that must be faced from the narrower perspective of chapters 36–37 alone. The puzzle of Isaiah's growth was a topic addressed at the opening of this chapter. One approach to understanding the growth of the Book of Isaiah as a whole involved the possibility that a correlation was seen to exist between 701 and 587 events. In Hardmeier's recent monograph, this correlation has been the point of focus from a new and provocative angle. As such, it is appropriate at this juncture to return to the puzzle of Isaiah's growth, with the possibility that a correlation between 701 and 587 events gave rise to the extension of Isaiah tradition beyond the lifetime of the prophet to the events of the exile and beyond.

CHAPTER FOUR

The Destiny of Zion
(701 and 587 B.C.E.)

THE PUZZLE OF ISAIAH'S GROWTH RECONSIDERED

In chapter 2 the question was raised, with reference to Ackroyd's 1978 study, why so substantial a book came to be associated with the prophet Isaiah.[1] The notion that Proto-Isaiah (or Isa 1–66) developed in order to conform to a "canonical" tripartite structure was judged to raise more problems than it solved. On the other hand, the arguments of Ackroyd, Clements, and Meade were viewed more positively. These scholars pressed for an understanding of prophecy that explained the growth of Isaiah as due to "the vitality of the word of God."[2] More specifically, Isaiah grew because "a connection was seen to exist between certain of Isaiah's prophecies and the fall of Jerusalem in 587."[3] Ackroyd notes that such a view of Isaiah was quite familiar in precritical conceptions (Sir 48:23). What is of interest to the modern interpreter is how Isaiah might properly be understood as the "prophet of the exile" and why such a conception of him developed in the first place.[4]

There are two specific dimensions of such an inquiry that now press themselves forward, given the analysis of Isa 36–37 just undertaken. The first has already been referred to in a general way; it involves the way the direction of influence is conceived within sections of the developing Book of Isaiah, and the nature of that influence. Clements has put forward a strong case for seeing in Isa 1–39˚ "a fairly homogeneous redaction in the wake of 587 events."[5] Yet

---

1. See Ackroyd, "Presentation," 21.
2. From Ackroyd's work by the same title, "The Vitality of the Word of God in the Old Testament," *ASTI* 1 (1962).
3. Clements, "Fall of Jerusalem," 421.
4. Ackroyd introduces his remarks in a 1982 study with the observation: "It would, I believe, be not inappropriate to give this study the alternative title. of 'Isaiah: Prophet of the Exile'" ("Structure and Function," 3).
5. "Fall of Jerusalem," 423.

the reasons Proto-Isaiah, and not some other prophetic book, underwent such a redaction are never entirely clear. Clements speaks of "some sort of connection between certain prophecies given by Isaiah and the destruction that came upon Jerusalem in 587 B.C." (423) and indicates that these prophecies included "sharp and decisive threats against the city and inhabitants of Jerusalem" (422). He qualifies the last remark by continuing, "although not specifically including a threat against the destruction of the temple."

At this point the prophet both Ackroyd and Clements mention as a logical target for secondary development comes to mind: Micah. Since 587 events did include the destruction of the temple, and since "sharp and decisive threats" were uttered by Micah to this effect (Mi 3:12; cf. Jer 26:16–19), the question remains: Why were the prophecies of Isaiah seen to have "some sort of connection" with "the destruction that came upon Judah in 587 B.C." and not the prophecies of Micah? If one wanted to speak of the vitality of the prophetic word as the cause of secondary interpretation (*relecture; nachinterpretation*), it remains unclear why Isaiah was chosen. Anticipating our second point, here too the status of Isa 36–37 comes into play. Is Clements right when he qualifies his characterization of Isaiah's prophecies by excluding threats against the temple? And if so, should one go even further and on the basis of Isa 36–37(38) see Isaiah as a *Heilsprophet* in respect of Zion?[6]

The question is particularly acute in the case of Isa 36–37. But bracketing out the controversy surrounding proper interpretation of these chapters, problems still remain with Clements's explanation for the growth of Isaiah. In fairness, it is an explanation that works basically in the context of 1–39˚, clarifying the existence of glosses and other redactional insertions now found at scattered points in these chapters, and assigning them to a more homogeneous level of editorial work. But it leaves open the question of Isaiah's further expansion into chapters 40–55 and beyond. And even within 1–39, the glosses do not involve the *fulfillment* of Isaiah's prophecies so much as explanation and pedagogical assistance given 587 events, as Clements himself puts it: "A sixth-century writer, working with inherited material about Isaiah, had clearly wanted to show that the tragic events of his own day could be understood more fully with the help of the prophecies of Isaiah" (423). This sort of *relecture* in 1–39 is to be distinguished from the puzzle of Isaiah's growth beyond Proto-Isaiah chapters, into Second Isaiah and beyond.

In point of fact, the sort of glossing and redactional supplementation identified by Clements in 1–39˚ exhibits sufficient variety to call into question

6. On the origin of *Heilsprophetie* in the Book of Isaiah, see the helpful summarizing discussion of Hardmeier (*Prophetie im Streit*, 1–8). Does *Heilsprophetie* originate with the historical Isaiah, with the *Assur-Redaktion* (Barth, Clements, Hardmeier), or with prophecies in a *postexilic* 36–37 (O. Kaiser, *Isaiah 13–19*; W. Werner, *Eschatologische Texte in Jesaja 1–39. Messias, Heiliger Rest, Völker* (*Forschung zur Bibel* 46; Wurzburg, 1982])?

any one single reason for the extension of Isaiah's message. Some passages speak of near extinction (1:9), others of idolatry and the terror of YHWH (2:18, 20; 8:21–22), still others of a delayed punishment about to take place very soon (6:12–13; 23:13; 22:25). Words of hope find their way into Isaiah's message together with words of coming judgment. Even if both kinds of supplementation belong to a "homogenous redaction in the wake of the events of 587" (423), it still remains unclear (1) why Isaiah's proclamation received such enrichment, and not another prophet's, and (2) why such enrichment was called for in the first place.

Somewhat closer to the context of chapters 36–37, the passage relating the visit of a Babylonian envoy from Merodach-Baladan (Isa 39) has frequently been considered a key piece in the puzzle regarding Isaiah's subsequent development. Ackroyd in particular has stressed the function of this passage in the larger Book of Isaiah, as it demonstrates that "the consequences of Hezekiah's actions in 39 . . . as it were, guarantee the exile, and thereby provide an appropriate occasion for 40ff."[7] His views have met with endorsement by Clements and others.[8]

Ackroyd has moved in a similar direction with his interpretation of Isa 38:

> The illness of Hezekiah and the death sentence upon him thus become a type of judgment and exile, and in that measure they run parallel to the theme of judgment which is found in the ambassador story which follows; but the theme of restored life and continuing rule which follows upon Hezekiah's strong appeal to the deity, is a pointer to the possibility of such a restoration for the community. ["Babylonian Exile," 346]

Yet because Ackroyd is concerned to tie chapter 38's function closely to that of chapter 39, *both* are treated as redactional supplements to Proto-Isaiah. Once again a certain circularity emerges in the analysis of Isaiah's growth: passages that raise the kinds of issues that are picked up and developed in the extension of Isaiah's message in chapter 40 and following are determined to have been added on to a Proto-Isaiah collection so that "the experience of exile when it comes may be understood to have been foretold in prophetic judgment."[9] Ackroyd may well be right about the function of chapter 39 (and 38) in the Book of Isaiah. But this does not answer the question as to why Isaiah was chosen for redactional enrichment that would ease the transition to Second Isaiah, and why anyone would bother with such enrichment in the first place. The question still remains: Why juxtapose chapters 40–55 with a Proto-Isaiah

---

7. "Structure and Function," 5; "Babylonian Exile," 332–43.
8. "Fall of Jerusalem," 423; Smelik, "Distortion," . 72; Meade, *Pseudonymity*, 28; Melugin, *Formation*, 177; Sweeney, *Isa 1–4*, 12.
9. "Babylonian Exile," 341. Also: "Once Isaiah prophesied the Babylonian exile to Hezekiah, it becomes less amazing that he is also supposed to have announced the return of the exiles in the days of the Persian king Cyrus" (Smelik, "Distortion," 72).

collection apparently ill-suited for such a purpose, necessitating comprehensive redactional supplementation? Put conversely: Was there any element inherent in the proclamation of Isaiah that occasioned its further development?[10]

To point up a contrast in approach to this sort of question, the later essay of Clements is helpful.[11] Here Clements is concerned with the way Second Isaiah chapters pick up and extend "themes" and language from First Isaiah. Strictly speaking, this sort of inquiry is better suited to get at the puzzle of Isaiah's growth, since it moves from a generally agreed upon Isaiah core forward to material in chapters 40–55. Yet as was pointed out in the previous chapter, Clements's conception of the developmental process is essentially one of "enlargement" and "supplementation" whose final consequence is "sequel" collections being placed side by side.[12] This is a more casual process than one that turns on the fulfillment or nonfulfillment of the prophetic word. It seems there was no real necessity for Isaiah to develop beyond an eighth-century setting, beyond its general suitability for such enlargement. Yet at issue is how that suitability is to be defined. More specifically, how the correlation Clements spoke of between 701 and 587 events forms a part of this developmental process is never made clear. It seems to be a factor at work within the redactional supplementation of 1–39°, but has no impact on the extension of Isaiah's message into Second Isaiah and beyond.

At this juncture the critical role that Isa 36–37 may play in the development of the Book of Isaiah should be obvious, especially if that growth involves some sort of correlation between 701 and 587 events, the former of which is the special concern of these chapters. It is quite likely that the correlation—or even noncorrelation—of 701 and 587 events was a key factor in the development of the Book of Isaiah; this possibility will be examined shortly. As concerns chapters 38 and 39, an examination must be undertaken of the Hezekiah-Isaiah narratives in order to determine the exact nature of their relationship to these two concluding chapters of Proto-Isaiah. Obviously if chapter 39 were shown to be part of the Proto-Isaiah collection—even its conclusion—it would be easy to see how the prediction of Babylonian exile found there (39:7) might have given rise to an extension such as we find in 40–55.[13]

While it may prove unlikely that chapter 39 formed an integral part of an original Proto-Isaiah collection, the distinction between chapter 38 and

10. See p. 43 above on the possibility that Isaiah's promise of an end to Assyrian domination was seen as having been fulfilled in the calling of Cyrus.
11. "Deutero-Isaianic Development" (1985).
12. Ibid., 101.
13. See Melugin, *Formation*, 172. This possibility is ruled out by most on the theory that chap. 39 was redactionally supplied *after* Second Isaiah chapters were brought into play, making 39:7 a classic *vaticinium ex eventu*.

chapter 39 should be kept clear with respect to *function* in the larger Book of Isaiah. Strictly speaking, the function of chapter 38 as highlighted by Ackroyd vis-à-vis Second Isaiah chapters is typological: the illness of Hezekiah and the death sentence upon him are a "type of judgment and exile." As such, chapter 38 might properly be said to "anticipate" the situation of 40–55. This is a very different sort of functional role than what is exhibited in chapter 39, where a direct prophecy is issued concerning future Babylonian assault, if not also the end of the Davidic line. The very different way in which chapters 38 and 39 "anticipate" Second Isaiah (typology and prophecy-fulfillment) suggests that they may have formed different stages in the redactional development of the Book of Isaiah. In this regard it is important to remember that while chapters 38 and 39 share certain common features, even greater commonality may exist between the Hezekiah-Isaiah narratives (36–37) and the story of Hezekiah's illness (38). That possibility will be examined in the following chapter.

To summarize: it may be the case that a correlation was seen to exist between the events of 701 and 587, and this correlation may explain the extension of Isaiah tradition beyond an eighth-century setting to include chapters 40–55. If this is the case, it becomes all the more necessary to determine the status of Isa 36–37, where the traditions concerning 701 events find their clearest statement. Put negatively: if there is very little authentic tradition associated with the 701 deliverance of Jerusalem in Proto-Isaiah, then it can hardly be the case that a correlation was seen to exist between the fall of Jerusalem in 587 and that earlier event. Precisely in order to avoid circular argumentation, we exclude from consideration the possibility that Proto-Isaiah was redactionally supplied with an interest in 701 events—events which then in turn were correlated with the fall of Jerusalem in 587 B.C.E. While such a possibility cannot be ruled out in theory, if it is admitted we will not have made any advance on the puzzle of Isaiah's growth. The question will simply be begged: Why supply an interest in 701 events that was not there to begin with? As shall be shown, precisely this question is begged in several recent studies.

THE CORRELATION OF 701 AND 587 EVENTS

On the face of it, the correlation between 701 and 587 events would appear to be antithetical: Zion was delivered in 701—it was destroyed in 587. A synchronic reading of Isa 36–37 would defend such an interpretation, and a flat reading of Isa 38 would do the same. The insightful observations of Ackroyd notwithstanding, the focus of chapter 38 remains on Hezekiah's recovery—not illness (= exile). This does not exclude the possibility that his sickness was viewed as a metaphor for 587 destruction, but both in 38:1–8 and 38:9–22 Hezekiah receives a positive remedy for his "exiled" state. That conclusion is the final word of both accounts.

Unfortunately, even a synchronic or postredactional reading of Isa 1–39 does not produce one perspicuous interpretation of how 701 and 587 events are related. Meade, for example, speaks of a "formal parallel between the Babylonian destruction of Jerusalem and Isaiah's threatened judgment by means of Assyria."[14] Here the connection is between threatened judgment (eighth century) and judgment executed (sixth century). While it is a plausible reading, Meade is forced to hang the interpretation on one key text and one significant diachronic decision. Isa 22:1–4, 12–14 is taken as Isaiah's reaction to Hezekiah's having "cut a deal" with Sennacherib, the evidence for which Meade must provide outside Isaiah in the controversial 2 Kgs 18:13–18. The citizens are rejoicing over their "deliverance" when they should be mourning; consequently, "this iniquity will not be forgiven till you die." Meade concludes with the main thrust of his argument for correlation: *"In other words, in light of the circumvention of his original prophecies against Jerusalem, Isaiah threatens with a future judgment"* (emphasis Meade)—a judgment that takes place in 587 B.C.E.[15]

To his credit, Meade has produced a possible interpretation of how Isaiah's preaching was seen to be relevant to the later crisis of 587. Unfortunately, the interpretation requires no small degree of assent to his diachronic reconstruction, which trades on a much broader—and more controversial— view of the historical circumstances surrounding 701 events. Several problems emerge: (1) the use of 2 Kgs 18:13–18 as evidence of Hezekiah's historical capitulation to Assyria; (2) the theory that that capitulation led to Assyrian withdrawal (contrary to 2 Kgs 18:18); (3) the odd (synchronic) placement of Isa 22 in the present structure of 1–39; and (4) perhaps most controversial, the notion that Assyrian withdrawal amounted to a circumvention of prophecies against Jerusalem, in the eyes of the historical prophet who uttered them, Isaiah. There is a long history of interpreting Isa 22:1–4, 12–14 against the backdrop of Jerusalem's deliverance, though not exactly as Meade proposes. The rejoicing condemned by Isaiah is usually linked not to 2 Kgs 18:13–18 (*sic*), but to the 701 deliverance as such (minimally, "Account B1").[16]

Without entering into the massive discussion regarding Isaiah's Zion theology, it is not to be conceded in the manner of Meade that Isaiah's oracles against Jerusalem were circumvented by 701 events or a putative Hezekiah "deal."[17] On the other hand, it may well be the case that Isaiah's preaching was sufficiently complex—if not ambiguous—on the topic of Zion's destiny and on

14. Ibid., 28.
15. Ibid.
16. Most recently, Clements, "Fall of Jerusalem," 429–30; *Deliverance*, 33–34.
17. For a good survey of the problems associated with reconstructing Isaiah's Zion theology, see Childs, *Crisis*, 20–68.

several other topics, that precisely this complexity has given rise to later extension of his proclamation, beyond the events of 701.[18]

The complexity of Isaiah's message can be illustrated rather simply, without detailed diachronic analysis. The historical Isaiah may well have seen in Assyria "the rod of YHWH's anger"; the oracles associated with him certainly enshrine that view (10:5). By the same token, other oracles speak clearly of a careful circumscribing of Assyria's role in judgment (10:15–19), in a manner that stands in some contrast to the preaching of Jeremiah on "the foe from the north" (Jer 4:5–8). So too, Isaiah speaks of a coming judgment against Jerusalem, but at the same time a special distinction, however one understands it, seems to exist with respect to Zion as such.[19] There is a "reaching to the neck" (8:8), a "booth in a vineyard" (1:8), a "shaking of the fist" (10:32)—to choose less controversial texts (compare 29:8, 31:5, which stretch the ambiguity to the limit). The "covering of Judah" is taken away (22:8), Ariel, the city where David encamped, is distressed (29:2), there is no sure trust in the "weapons of the House of the Forest" (22:8b) or the "reservoir between two walls" (22:11)—even as "a stone, a tested stone is laid in Zion" (28:16), and as YHWH promises to "protect Jerusalem, he will protect it and deliver it, he will spare and rescue it" (31:5). It has always been difficult to construct a diachronic grid that will sort out this complexity and set Isaiah's preaching in some coherent staging according to historical or evolutionary principles— quite apart from designating certain texts *vaticinium ex eventu*, drawn up as a consequence of the 701 deliverance.[20] But precisely because this is the case, Meade's notion that Isaiah's prophecies against Jerusalem were "circumvented" by events of 701 must remain tentative and open to challenge on both the synchronic and diachronic front.

Several features of Meade's analysis commend themselves for further study. One cannot give pivotal status to the interpretation of Isa 22 without at the same time wrestling with the content and function of Isa 36–37, as an integral part of Proto-Isaiah and as possibly the single most important piece in the puzzle of Isaiah's growth, as has been maintained in this study right along. Melugin had concluded his work on Second Isaiah with a recognition of the

---

18. From another direction, Childs summarizes this complexity well: "It remains perplexing how to relate the message of unmitigated disaster to sinful Israel with the assertions of Zion's inviolability and Assyria's defeat" (68). Certain uses of the term "inviolability" with respect to Zion may in fact introduce a false distinction, as Childs notes in another context.

19. Childs, concerned to avoid false distinctions between the "spiritual" Zion and the "political" city, nevertheless does recognize that in 29:1–8, one of the more controversial texts: "the besieged city in v. 1 with its busy cult is designated only as the place where once David encamped. It is not the holy city in which Yahweh has his eternal abode" (*Crisis*, 57).

20. See Childs's appropriate final caution on the difficulty of assigning a historical setting for these passages, from which is then reconstructed a proper diachronic scheme to handle all the tensions inherent in the tradition (*Crisis*, 68).

centrality of these chapters in any reconstruction of the redactional history of the Book of Isaiah as a whole:

> I suggest that the redactor understood the sparing of sinful Judah in Hezekiah's time as a delay of the full punishment announced by Isaiah until the time of the Babylonian exile. [*Formation*, 177]

Like many statements in the concluding section of Melugin's 1976 study, this one is particularly pregnant. By "full punishment" we would take Melugin to mean that one dimension of the complex Isaiah tradition that stressed the need for purging judgment, at the hands of Assyria. By "delay" is recognized that a deliverance was really accomplished in 701, and that the narrative recording such a deliverance had made its way into Isaiah tradition, if not forming one central dimension of it, well before the time of Second Isaiah and the "decision" to juxtapose chapters 40–55 with the material preceding, of which chapters 36–37 formed an important part.

At this point the puzzle of Isaiah's growth gains one essential (theoretical) piece of information that may explain why it was chosen for development and not another preexilic prophetic corpus. The irony has been noted above and in other studies that at the trial of Jeremiah the preaching of Micah against Zion was cited, and not that of Isaiah—around whom is subsequently developed a prophetic collection that dwarfs by a considerable degree that of Micah. In considering the puzzle of Isaiah's growth as a book, it was also pointed out that if one were looking for a neat correlation between judgment oracles delivered in the eighth century and their subsequent fulfillment in the sixth, several other candidates could as readily stand redactional extension as Isaiah. In other words, what may prove to be the oddity in Isaiah tradition is not its singular potential for conforming to a "judgment threatened" (eighth-century) and "judgment executed" (sixth-century) pattern—a pattern that could be developed, and has been developed in small measure, in a variety of preexilic prophetic witnesses (Ho 14; Am 9:11–15), including Micah (4:1—5:15). What is unique about Isaiah tradition is *precisely the material it contains that frustrates such a pattern*—namely, *Heilsprophetie* regarding Zion and the containment of Assyria. These two related themes find their stunning and appropriate conclusion in the narrative of Zion's deliverance in the 701 debacle, now found in chapters 36–37.

By raising the relatively recent question concerning the "reciprocal relationships" among sections of the larger Book of Isaiah, a new perspective is opened up on the development of Proto-Isaiah tradition and the Hezekiah-Isaiah narratives as such. If Isaiah's growth is largely accidental or unconscious, there is no "puzzle" concerning its development that has a meaningful solution. On the other hand, if one grants a certain redactional coherence and intentionality to the developmental process of the book at large, then a new angle is provided on the interpretation of individual passages across sections traditionally kept separate.[21]

It is the thesis of this study that the Proto-Isaiah collection, far from being amenable to direct redactional extension inclusive of 587 events, actually stood in some tension with such an extension. The tension was created by the existence of *Heilsprophetie* concerning Zion's destiny and the limiting of Assyria's role in judgment. Most specific in this regard was the narrative of Zion's deliverance in 701, found now in Isa 36–37. This collection of tradition, firmly imbedded in the Proto-Isaiah material, created sufficient dissonance given the overruning of Zion in 587, that an extension was necessitated—an extension that not only involved enlargement and supplementation, but also a serious, sustained wrestling with the nature of prophecy in general, the reliability of YHWH's word in history, and Isaiah's prophecies concerning Zion's destiny in particular.

Such a thesis will finally require support from the direction of Second Isaiah chapters—not just those sections concerned with "former things" and the reliability of prophecy, but also more especially the second half of the Second Isaiah collection, where the destiny of Zion is discussed from the other side of 587 (chaps. 49–55). The final chapter will look more closely at this subject. Such a thesis obviously trades on a view of the growth of the Book of Isaiah, and especially Second Isaiah's relationship to First Isaiah, which until recently would have found very little support. In the narrower context of Isa 36–37, what it suggests is that if dissonance concerning Zion's final destiny is the root cause for the growth of Isaiah tradition, then there must be sufficient tradition dealing with the subject of Zion's near destiny in positive terms to raise questions about its final status, given 587 events. This argument will avoid the charge of circularity if it can be shown (1) that the puzzle of Isaiah's growth is capable of meaningful solution, (2) that such a solution involves the question of Zion's near and final destiny as addressed in Isa 36–39° and 49–55, respectively, and (3) that the Hezekiah-Isaiah narratives form an essential part of the preexilic Isaiah collection, as argued above.

Before the place and function of chapters 38 and 39 can be examined, an alternative view of the growth of the Book of Isaiah and the place of chapters 36–37 in that growth must be critically surveyed.

ALTERNATIVE CORRELATION (701 AND 587)

In his 1980 study, Clements reaches the conclusion that Zion theology is preexilic, but derivative of the 701 deliverance. That deliverance is recorded in the preexilic document Account B1, which is supplemented in the Josiah

---

21. See my remarks at the conclusion of "The Divine Council: Temporal Transition and New Prophecy in the Book of Isaiah," *JBL* 109 (1990) 243–47.

era by Account B2, in the same climate when Zion theology flourishes.[22] In his more recent essays, the emphasis has shifted to the exilic period as the time during which (1) creative work on the Isaiah traditions in 1–32 took place, and (2) the Isaiah narratives in 36–39 received their essential form.[23]

With this shift in emphasis an alternative model begins to emerge for understanding the growth of Isaiah tradition, and the place of Zion theology in it. The contrast between 701 and 587 is one that begins to have its real effect in a reverse direction, as a consequence of the fall of Jerusalem and the end of kingship:

> There is much to be said in support of the claim of Goncalves that the B2 account of how Jerusalem was divinely protected in 701 B.C. has been composed in its extant form after the catastrophe of 587 B.C. The narrative is designed to show that, under the obedient response of a faithful king, God does act to protect and uphold his people. ["Central Passage," 261]

Still more significant are his remarks about 14:24ff.—which are directly linked to the diachronic perspective on B2 and a Babylonian redaction in 1–32—and what they portend about Zion theology. I will quote at some length in order to set forth clearly the contrast with conclusions he reached in *Deliverance* (1980):

> [Isa 14:24ff.] too has been composed after 587 B.C. and its purpose is thereby revealed as a concern to provide a qualified re-affirmation of the importance of the Davidic dynasty and the city of Jerusalem in the divine plan. By contrasting the fate of the city and its king in 587 B.C. with what took place in 701 B.C. it was thought to be possible to retain a positive role for both the Davidic kingship and the temple of Mount Zion in the divine plan for Israel. By such means the desirability of restoring both institutions was affirmed. . . . We may venture to draw the conclusion therefore that the "anti-Assyrian" saying of Isa 14,24f. owes its origin, along with the comparable saying of Isa 31,8 and the B2 narrative now combined in 2 Kgs 18,17—19,37 to the desire to re-establish a rationale for restoring the Davidic kingship and for rebuilding the Jerusalem temple in the wake of what happened to both institutions in 587 B.C. There is also an inseparable element of theodicy implicit in such an undertaking which cannot be ignored. Both Davidic kingship and Jerusalem temple were valuable instruments of divine protection, but only when accepted and used in a context of faith and obedience. ["Central Passage," 261–62]

Unfortunately, Clements does not clarify how this post-587 Zion-royal theology, if it might be called that, is to be related to the preexilic Zion theology sketched out in his earlier study. The effect of his emphasis on Zion-royal traditions as part of a post-587 restoration program is that preexilic statements along the same line are suddenly overshadowed, and the force of

---

22. *Deliverance*, esp. chapters 4 and 5.
23. "Fall of Jerusalem" (1980) and "Central Passage" (1989).

the Hezekiah-Isaiah narratives is quickly shifted to an exilic setting. Whether this was Clements's intention is not fully clarified. What is clear from his remarks is that a special interest in Davidic kingship and Zion, which did not form an original part of the preexilic tradition, was created as a consequence of the 587 debacle. This model for correlating 701 and 587 events is at clear odds with the one sketched out in the preceding section, whereby a preexilic Zion theology, culminating in Isa 36–37, created a tension over Zion's final destiny that was resolved in chapters 40–55.[24]

A somewhat similar view of historical matters is set forth by Smelik when he dates the unified Hezekiah-Isaiah narratives in the exilic period. Yet his theological/political conclusions are precisely the opposite of those reached by Clements. Because chapter 39 speaks of the *end* of Davidic kingship, neither it nor the narratives in 36–38 with which it is closely associated could "have been written earlier than the Persian period, because in its present form it predicts that the Davidic dynasty will not be restored to the Judaean throne."[25] It seems that even late aetiological explanations for the royal-Zion traditions in Isa 1–39 do not produce consistent interpretations.[26]

The move to date a significant portion of the Isaiah tradition to the exilic and postexilic period, modestly anticipated in the narrower work on 36–37 and Account B2, and in the remarks of Smelik and Clements just reviewed, has found its *ne plus ultra* in the recent commentary work of Kaiser. Not sure whether even minimally the material in chapters 28–31 is Isaianic, Kaiser speaks of the possibility that an "anonymous prophecy from the last years of the kingdom of Judah" that warned against trusting in Egypt (i.e., chaps. 28–31) was subsequently attributed (viz., for reasons other than historical accuracy) to the prophet Isaiah "in order to make him see beyond his own time to the downfall of the kingdom, because the situations of 703–701 and 589–587 were essentially similar."[27] In a curious kind of way, Kaiser too argues that the correlation of 701 and 587 events led to the development and extension of Isaiah tradition.

Kaiser is able to retain for Isaiah some rootage in the 701 debacle

24. I do not want to exclude at this point chap. 38, or for that matter chap. 39, from consideration as part of the Proto-Isaiah collection. The inclusion of chap. 38 in Clements's view is meant only to provide an example of obedience in the royal house, so that kingship might be resuscitated after the events of 587 ("Central Passage," 261).

25. "Distortion," 85.

26. Ironically, interest in the late dating or exilic theological force of Isa 36–39 tends to collapse the two groups of redaction critics isolated in chapter 1, since in both models these four chapters begin to stand to the side of the tradition process at work in both Proto- and Deutero-Isaiah. Clements's earlier work stressed the relationship between Isa 36–37 and 1–35* in the area of Zion theology. For Clements (1989), Ackroyd, Smelik and others, the real purpose of Isa 36–39* is to bridge two sections of the book otherwise separated, or to wrestle with problems in the exilic or postexilic community. Although no reference is made to tripartite theories for the structuration of Isaiah, 36–39 begin to take on a quite separate identity.

27. *Isaiah 1–12*, 2.

because the narratives relating his participation are found in the Deuteronomistic history, which in at least residual form (B1) are to be judged historically
valuable for the reconstruction of Isaiah tradition. Partly because in those
narratives Isaiah and Hezekiah are on the same side, "it was easy to assume
that at that point he had warned against the policy which proved so disastrous
for the kingdom and forecast its consequences as the punishment of Yahweh"
(2). On the basis of this slim tradition, the entire Isaiah corpus unrolls in the
postexilic period:

> In the last resort the whole process of tradition, which caused the
> collection continually to expand, can only be understood against the
> background of the loss of living authorities in post-exilic Judaism and the
> consequent enhancing of the reputation of antiquity, as being well-tried
> and fundamental. [2]

So while a correlation between 701 and 587 events got the tradition process
moving, it required only a minimal shove from scanty authentic traditions at
the point of origin, after which it rolled along with very little assistance from
traditions inherited from the preexilic period or the historical Isaiah. The need
for "the reputation of antiquity" was apparently sufficient to account for the
development of such a massive block of tradition in the name of the prophet
Isaiah.

As a consequence of this reconstruction, the Hezekiah-Isaiah narratives
play an important role, since they alone contain the seed tradition regarding
the prophet Isaiah, which "proved responsible for the formation of the whole
of the tradition handed down in the prophet's name" (2). A correlation between the events of 701 and 587 emerged primarily on the basis of the
judgment tradition contained in narratives relating the former, since in
Kaiser's view this judgment tradition was confirmed by the 587 destruction:
"it was easy to assume that at that point [viz., 701 B.C.E.] he had warned against
the policy which proved so disastrous for the kingdom"—that is, disastrous as
the kingdom fell before the final Babylonian assault in 587 B.C.E.

Quite apart from the more radical aspects of Kaiser's tradition-process
model for Isaiah, questions arise even with respect to the core tradition in Isa
36–37. In the narrower context of our discussion of the correlation of 701/587,
it is curious how even a quite reduced narrative concerning 701 (B1) could
have been construed primarily as judgment tradition by later interpreters
seeking to extend the reputation of Isaiah. But for our purposes, the more
relevant piece of data is Kaiser's recognition that "the situations of 703–701
and 589–587 were essentially similar," and that the record of the former
situation exists in Isa 36–37, even in reduced form.

Kaiser's views are rehearsed at this juncture in part because they form
the backdrop for Hardmeier's recent monograph.[28] While disagreeing with

---

28. *Prophetie im Streit* (1990).

Kaiser over the extent of preexilic Isaiah tradition (including *Heilsprophetie*), Hardmeier is nevertheless in agreement with one key aspect of Kaiser's reconstruction: the notion that the correlation of 701 and 587 is a central feature in the Isaiah tradition-process, especially affecting the composition of the Hezekiah-Isaiah narratives. Against Kaiser, Hardmeier adopts the basic reconstruction of H. Barth in respect of a widescale preexilic Isaiah collection, which included *Heilsprophetie* in the form of Zion theology as well as judgment oracles against Assyria.[29] But also unlike Kaiser, he refuses to see Isa 36–37 as containing any preexilic traditions to this same effect. In many respects, like Barth and Vermeylen, Hardmeier refuses to discuss Isa 36–37 in the same orbit as developing Isaiah tradition in the preexilic period. But unlike them, he offers an extremely provocative thesis regarding the origins of the narrative in Isa 36–37—or as he prefers to refer to it, the ABBJ narrative (Erzählung von der assyrischen Bedrohung und der Befreiung Jerusalems) whose principal location is in 2 Kgs 18:9f., 13—19:37*.

Obviously, then, Hardmeier rejects the priority of Isa 36–37 and focuses his attention on the narrative tradition in Kings, and its surrounding context (viz., 2 Kgs 18:9–12* and 20:1–19).[30] Other elements of the classic theory are retained, but with a wholly different flavor due to Hardmeier's impressive use of narrative theory in evaluating both diachronic and final-literary-form dimensions of the Hezekiah-Isaiah narratives.[31] The basic division into two main strands is maintained, but lacking the old nomenclature (B1 and B2), the source-critical grounding, and most particularly the historical/theological reconstruction.[32] At one point Hardmeier asks:

> It remains without satisfactory explanation why all theological reflections are to be regarded as "late"; moreover, for what tradition-critical necessity must an untheological-historical *Grunderzählung*, such as O. Kaiser reconstructs, be rooted in oral tradition? The differentiation of theological from untheological Kaiser has picked up from B.S. Childs. [*Prophetie im Streit*, 10, n. 30]

Actually, in defense of the older theory, Hardmeier's division into two strands on literary grounds alone, with no appreciable historical or theological distance separating them, seems idiosyncratic. At this point, it seems an unnecessary holdover from a source-critical approach against which Hardmeier's broader thesis is directed.[33]

---

29. Ibid., 3–4; 466.
30. For the text-critical argument in favor of the priority of Kings, see, for example, *Prophetie im Streit*, 116–17.
31. Chapter 2 (23–86) is devoted to *Erzähltextanalytische Grundlagen*.
32. Hardmeier has an interesting assessment of the old Account A (18:13–16), which I will return to below.
33. ". . .19:9*3–36*2 did not originally belong to the ABBJ narrative and were only secondarily supplied as a later interpretation" (*Prophetie im Streit*, 134). [Hardmeier uses a star, instead of Greek letters, to indicate verse subsections].

That broader thesis rends particularly asunder the traditional historical conclusions regarding a preexilic B1 (his "Haupterzählung"). Remaining consistent with the priority granted to Kings over Isa 36–37, Hardmeier moves beyond the traditional boundaries assigned to the 701 narrative to examine the framing units ("Rahmennotizen") in 2 Kings 18:1–12. He makes the observation that 18:9f. resembles rather strikingly the notice that introduces the ABBJ narrative, traditionally termed Account A (18:13–16). Both speak of a siege, one in the fourth year of Hezekiah which proves successful, and one ten years later that fails—the first against the northern kingdom, the second against Judah and Jerusalem. At the same time, Hardmeier correctly notes that 18:13–16 has been misplaced, since it speaks of tribute paid *before* the siege ever takes place—and in this it contradicts the annals of Sennacherib.[34]

In attempting to account for these several features—the contrast between northern and southern kingdoms, the ten-year separation between Assyrian assaults (18:9 and 13), the capitulation that leads to siege—Hardmeier identifies another historical/compositional situation ("Erzählsituation") that conforms better than 711–701 to the narrated events ("erzählte Situation") in this series of episodes.[35] That situation is reflected in the Jeremiah prose tradition, especially chapters 37–40 (the GBJ narrative), and it involves the historical events from 597 to the fall of Jerusalem, another critical ten-year period in Judah's history. Jer 37:5 reports that the Babylonians had withdrawn because of an Egyptian approach. This historical notice has given rise to the literary feature in 2 Kgs 19:9, where the possibility that Egyptian aid might lead to an alleviation of Assyrian threat is raised.

To put it bluntly, as does Hardmeier, the ABBJ narrative is a propaganda work ("Propagandaerzählung")[36] whose main purpose is to show that submission (18:13b–16) only leads to siege (18:17—19:9). It was drawn up by national-religious ("nationalreligiös-heilsprophetische") circles before the fall of Jerusalem to oppose the prophetic word of Jeremiah and Ezekiel, the former now contained in the GBJ narrative, who counseled submission to Babylon (see, for example, Jer 38:2b, 17–23).[37] The fate of the northern king-

---

34. See my remarks above, chapter 3, sections 3 and 4. Hardmeier calls 18:13b–16 a "quotation from an old annals source" which was incorporated into the ABBJ narrative at an early point (*Prophetie im Streit*, 116). On the other hand, its incorporation was accomplished in light of "the perspective of the problems and experiences of a narrative situation that can be precisely identified as before the Fall of Jerusalem in 587" and "to this fiction also belongs the artificially constructed date at 18:13a" (114). The date in 18:13a "the 14th year of Hezekiah" ("eine historische Fiktion")—about which the historical problems are already well-known—was created to work in conjunction with the "4th year of Hezekiah" (18:9). See also *Prophetie im Streit*, 291–303.

35. On the distinction between narrative world and the situation of the narrator, see *Prophetie im Streit*, 26–27.

36. Ibid., 461; also: "historische Tendenzerzählung" (460) and "an example of theological-political *Auseinandersetzungsliteratur* in narrative form" (463).

37. For a summary, see *Prophetie im Streit*, 460–67. A favorite text for Hardmeier in this regard is

dom is set out as a warning to Hezekiah (= Zedekiah), just as the previous assault on Judah in 597, leading to the exile of Jehoiachin and Judahite citizenry, should have been a warning to Zedekiah. Zedekiah should follow the counsel of Isaiah as found in the ABBJ narrative, not the counsel of Jeremiah and Ezekiel, which appears in the same narrative "more or less as Assyrian-Babylonian propaganda, here in the dress of the Rabshakeh speech" (461). Support from Egypt should not be viewed negatively (contrary to Jeremiah in 37:8). Such support actually (= fictively) led to Assyrian (= Babylonian) withdrawal in 701, as the ABBJ narrative teaches. Here is where the correlation between 701 and 587 events finds its "narrative-oriented" rationale.[38]

Such a brief summary cannot hope to do justice to the high level of argumentation and the complex exegetical analysis that distinguish Hardmeier's provocative monograph. Doubtless there are portions of our précis that do not accurately reflect the thrust and the sense of proportion that mark the work itself—not to mention the massive critical undergirding and engagement with secondary sources that must be left to the side for our purposes.[39] But in the context of our discussion of the role of Isa 36–37 in the growth of the Book of Isaiah, it should serve to illustrate a radical alternative correlation of 701 and 587 events. Where in the work of Clements and others, 587 circumstances have begun to overshadow the interpretation of Isa 36–37, with Hardmeier these circumstances are solely responsible for the origination and detailed composition of the narrative fictively portraying 701 events.[40] Out of

Ez 17:15, which tells of Zedekiah's wrongful rebellion against Nebuchadnezzar, "whose covenant with him he broke"; therefore "in Babylon he shall die" (17:16). It should be noted that the original title for Hardmeier's *Habilitationsschrift* ("leicht überarbeitet" [v] for the present monograph) was "Die Polemik gegen Ezechiel und Jeremia in den Hiskija-Jesaja-Erzählung" (Bielefeld, 1987).

38. What Hardmeier calls "the thoroughgoing parallelism between the complex of problems and experiences during the 588 break in the seige and the narrative profile of the ABBJ-Erzählung" (288).

39. My earlier work *Theology in Conflict* (1989) deals with much of the same material in Jeremiah (and Ezekiel) covered by Hardmeier. In my view, the "Scribal Chronicle" does assert that submission to Babylon is God's will for the Judahite remnant (and the exilic community), so for example Jer 38:17 or 29:7. From a later historical perspective, the Golah redaction simply makes clear within that Chronicle that the Judahite community refused to submit and therefore merited divine judgment (for example, Jer 37:2). Neither level of tradition argued *against* submission in the manner Hardmeier asserts for the ABBJ narrative—such a view is seen as a rejection of the prophet Jeremiah, as in the case of Irijah, who arrests the prophet on the grounds that he is "deserting to the Chaldeans" (37:13). It is difficult to see how such a document, even veiled in the "past" events of 701, could have gotten a hearing during this tense period "vor dem Untergang Judas," when the challenge to Jeremiah over this issue is consistently depicted as its own kind of "treason" against YHWH and his servant the prophet. One thinks as well of the dastardly murder of Gedaliah, who ruled by Babylonian appointment (41:1–3). Are we to look for the authors of the ABBJ narrative among this *nationalreligiös* circle, headed by the murderer Ishmael (of the royal family)?

40. Hardmeier does reject a post-587 date for the ABBJ (contrary to Clements, Smelik)! Against Kaiser, he accepts Barth's notion of a preexilic Isaiah collection, lacking of course 36–37 (466).

the historical circumstances of the "Belagerungspause von 588" and "derived from the quite specific political-theological conflict during this fateful period" the narrative of Isa 36–37 "was composed down to the most minor details" (460).

In the context of our discussion of the puzzle of Isaiah's growth, the net effect of Hardmeier's reconstruction is to reduce the contribution the 701 deliverance might have made to the solution to nil. The deliverance is a fictive event in a propaganda narrative meant to demonstrate to a Zedekiah in 588–87 options other than submission. In this climate of radical reconstruction, ironically Hardmeier rejects Kaiser's view concerning the nonexistence of Isaiah tradition from the preexilic period containing *Heilsprophetie* (Barth).[41] The "heilsprophetisch" aspects of the ABBJ narrative do presuppose the existence of such an "Assur-Redaktion." Yet one wonders how close a connection actually exists, and what the nature of the connection really is. Since the Hezekiah-Isaiah narratives owe their origin and specific literary shape ("in allen ihren Einzelzügen") wholly to circumstances just before the fall of Jerusalem, it is difficult to see how serious a link exists at the literary or sociological level to such a "retrospectively interpreted, salvation-prophetic Isaiah tradition" (466). In other words, chapters 36–37 remain essentially a stranger to the Isaiah tradition process. Their incorporation was brought about in an essentially derivative manner.

This fact is borne out by the priority given to the DtrH as the proper arena in which to discuss the Hezekiah-Isaiah narratives, and by the decision to work with one basic narrative (ABBJ) whose original location stands outside the Book of Isaiah. It is here that Hardmeier finally paints himself into a corner. He notes that alone among the narratives of Kings, the ABBJ reports the activities of a prophet (Isaiah) from the collection of latter prophets, while it remains silent concerning all the others.[42] He takes this to indicate a concern for *Heilsprophetie* ("Ablehnung der kritischen Unheilsprophetie") in the DtrH and must therefore conclude that the "Deuteronomismus" represented in Kings is of a different flavor than that found in Jeremiah, classically "unheilsprophetisch." "The Deuteronomism that has stamped the Jeremiah redaction is of another sort than that which has stamped the Deuteronomistic History" (467).

Without stepping into the quagmire of Deuteronomism and its reconstruction, it is Hardmeier's decision to treat the Hezekiah-Isaiah narratives (viz., the ABBJ narrative) independently of the preexilic Isaiah tradition (following Barth) that leads to the estrangement of these narratives from both

41. *Prophetie im Streit*, 466.
42. Ibid., 467.

Isaiah and ironically from the DtrH as well—necessitating an explanation for their singular inclusion in both contexts. Too much weight is finally placed upon the correlation with 587 events as the originating agent in the composition of the ABBJ, and derivatively, of Isa 36–37. As has been argued above, the direction of influence is better explained as moving from the Hezekiah-Isaiah narratives to the Jeremiah prose tradition, rather than the reverse.[43] The kind of theological tension Hardmeier claims exists between the two—and indeed gives rise to the former—is better explained within the context (literary, historical, sociological) in which the narratives respectively appear. In that respect, even moving from Isa 36–37 forward to the Jeremiah prose tradition, the influence is more from the side of the development of a new literary medium (prophetic narrative theology), than from theological propaganda and a debate over proper *Ausserpolitik* vis-à-vis Assyria/Babylon. The events of 701 remain tradition-historically and theologically singular, as reported in Isa 36–37, and precisely in that singularity a dilemma is created over the destiny of Zion. That dilemma is what has given rise to the growth of Isaiah tradition beyond 701 to the fall of Jerusalem in 587 B.C.E.

METHOD: HARDMEIER'S NARRATIVE ANALYSIS

One particular strength of Hardmeier's analysis of the Hezekiah-Isaiah narratives is his employment of insights from narrative theory. Hardmeier clearly demonstrates that source-critical analysis (Stade) and newer form- and tradition-critical refinements (Childs, Kaiser) have remained primarily occupied with historical questions, insofar as they plot a literary development that has its origin in more objective tradition, moving toward theological elaboration.[44] Childs and Clements have in his view done a good job shifting the discussion away from the less subtle aspects of historical investigation ("what actually happened in 701 B.C.E.?") toward an appreciation of the traditional and formal aspects of the literature that reports these events. But their work finally remains too rooted in this classic form of inquiry.[45]

On this score there are points of contact between the literary analysis of

---

43. So also K.-F. Pohlmann (*Studien zum Jeremiabuch. Ein Beitrag zur Frage nach der Entstehung des Jeremiabuches* [FRLANT 118; Göttingen: Vandenhoeck & Ruprecht, 1978] 55), with whose position and my own ("The Crisis of Interpretation over the Meaning and Purpose of the Exile: A Redactional Study of Jeremiah xxi–xliii," *VT* 35 [1985] 78–97) Hardmeier takes issue (*Prophetie im Streit*, 178–82). Because Pohlmann dates the "golaorientierte Redaktion" so late (fourth century, 191), Hardmeier rightly sees that such an *Auseinandersetzung* between Jeremiah and Isaiah prose tradition could then only be conceived as "Ausdruck eines akademischen Theologenstreits in spätnachexilscher Zeit" (289)—a characterization that would not hold given my view that the *exilic* period was the time when both the Golah redaction and the Scribal Chronicle took shape ("Crisis of Interpretation," 95–97; *Theology in Conflict*, 282–91).
44. See esp. Hardmeier's insightful remarks in the opening chapter (*Prophetie im Streit*, 8–19).
45. Ibid., 12.

Hardmeier and that of K.A.D. Smelik. Smelik's critique of Stade was focused on his refusal to move from "historical" to "literary" logic when assessing "seams" and "duplications" in the narrative.[46] Stade evaluated the phenomenon of repetition in the narrative against the backdrop of perceived sequentiality in the time-space world, to which the narrative was related and from which the narrative gained its essential logic. So at Isa 37:8–9, where the verb *šmʿ* is repeated, Stade detected a seam that led him to posit the existence of two sources.[47] The theory took its point of focus at 37:7, where the verb *šmʿ* also appears, in conjunction with a promise that the Assyrian king would, upon hearing, return to his own land. Stade therefore found Sennacherib's reaction in 38:9 suspicious: instead of returning to his own land as a consequence of hearing, he sends messengers back to Hezekiah.[48] In other words, the logic of the historical backdrop was disturbed in Stade's opinion. By splitting 39:9 and concluding that the report of an actual return to Assyria had been lost, the positing of sources served both (1) to clarify the disturbed sequentiality and (2) to explain what happened to the original ending, viz., "it has been disturbed at its conclusion by a later hand in order to fuse on the second narrative, at whose conclusion is an extensive report of how Sennacherib died in his own land"[49]

Smelik interprets the repetition not against a putative world of historical reference, but within the narrative world proper, asking the question: "Is it [repetition] possible from a literary point of view?" Here Smelik questions the methodological assumptions of Stade, whereby the logic of the narrative is measured against the logic of historical events to which the narrative theoretically refers. The "friction" at 37:9 is caused by the conjunction of sources in the development of the narrative, each reporting a different series of events according to Stade. By contrast, Smelik considers the repetition of *šmʿ* an intentional narrative device meant to key the reader to an important feature that has been intentionally imbedded in the narrative world. At Isa 36:6, 9 the Rabshakeh had raised the possibility that reliance on Egypt might save Hezekiah and Jerusalem—an option considered pure self-deception. When Sen-

---

46. "Distortion," 74–78.

47. Stade of course worked in the context of Kings, not Isaiah. The text-critical divergence at 37:9 ("and he heard") and 2 Kgs 19:9 ("and he returned") is not critical for the challenge mounted by Smelik. The former would strengthen his emphasis on *smʿ* as a motif word ("Distortion," 75), but it is not required as a preferred reading for Smelik's larger point; the latter reading, preferred by Stade, simply provides a more felicitous transition to the following *wayyišlah*. Both readings indicate that as a result of "hearing," messengers were sent back to Jerusalem by Sennacherib. The Isaiah reading is certainly *lectio difficilior* in this context ("Distortion," 75). Qumran and LXX combine *wayyišmaʿ* and *wayyāšob* (see Talmon, "Aspects of the Textual Transmission of the Bible in the Light of Qumran Manuscripts," *Textus* 4 [1964] 107).

48. "One might think: what a clever field marshall that king of Assyria is! As a precaution against the *Meroiten* catching him from behind he dispatched yet a second emissary to the refractory Jerusalem" ("Miscellen," 174). After pointing out its logic, Stade rejects such a reading; Smelik, from another angle, ends up accepting it.

49. "Miscellen," 175.

nacherib "hears the rumour" (37:7) that Tirhakah has come forth "to wage war," the question is raised for the reader: "Will Rabshakeh's words yet be proven false and will Egypt appear a reliable ally after all?"[50] By *not* having Sennacherib return to his own land, the question remains an open one: Who will Hezekiah trust—YHWH or Egypt? This narrative logic is disturbed by Stade's source-critical dissection, foreshortening the narrative and making the contest between YHWH and Sennacherib the subject of a separate narrative, rather than the logical conclusion to a single, carefully composed presentation. "By supposing that in the first account the news of Tirhakah's arrival ended Sennacherib's attack, Stade actually walked into the trap the author has set for the reader" (77).

Stade and Smelik have put forth two rival theories as to the growth of biblical narrative. With attention to features like "author," "narrative," and especially "reader," Smelik shifts the analysis to another plane.[51] The narrative is more than a window on historical events or even a set of clues from which to discuss what really happened in 701. At the literary level, alleged seams are not evidence of the merger of sources if other explanations can be found to defend the present logic of the material. But the sociological model presupposed by Smelik's analysis is in many ways its most distinctive feature over against that of Stade, even while this is largely unstated. Suddenly the biblical narrative must be accounted for in its present shape, on the assumption that the sociological forces responsible for presenting the material in its final form had in mind a readership which would confront the narrative in its present form, and in just this form. Stade at one point ridicules the narrative for failing to move smoothly from its predictions at 2 Kgs 19:7, 19:28b, and 19:33 to their respective fulfillments, an expectation one would be entitled to "expect even with a writer who was only relatively sophisticated."[52] Stade's source-critical repair work allows him to put himself forward, as it were, as the one who possesses the requisite skill to wrest the logic from the narrative in its garbled form.

It is Smelik's attention to the role of the reader that finally distinguishes his method from that of Stade. For Stade, the "reader" was an accidental or fully external construct, so far as the origins and development of biblical narrative were concerned. The development of the narrative—or better, the sources—went on in such a way as to be fully unconcerned with a reader who would come to the material expecting something like "narrative logic." On the contrary, the origin of the material had to do with events in history, and its development beyond those events was often accidental—even if capable of explanation (Childs, Clements)—and generally resulted in a departure from

50. "Distortion," 77.
51. Use of the term "source" naturally implies a very different sociological model.
52. "Miscellen," 174.

the original historical logic, so that the final form of the material was frequently "verstümmelt" (disturbed) and its "logic" had to be recovered behind the final narrative presentation. For this the narrative required a special kind of reader: one who knew how to restore the "logic" of the narrative by recasting it into historical sources—at least ones in which lost endings and missing pieces were capable of explanation, by reference to the original source-critical theory itself.

Like Smelik, Hardmeier is concerned to shift the attention away from the historical events to which the narrative makes reference (the 701 deliverance), in order that the narrative world with its own internal frame of reference (*Erzählgegenwart*) might be properly evaluated. While Hardmeier is interested in the role of an external readership confronting the narrative in its present form, he never loses sight of the historical implications of such a perspective or the text's abiding diachronic character. Noting that the "narrative world" of the ABBJ Erzählung is full of complexities, including the "misplaced" Account A, the anachronisms concerning Tirhakah and the death of Sennacherib, and other oddities (two sieges ten years apart), Hardmeier does not eschew the quest for historical referentiality. Instead, he seeks to find an appropriate compositional/historical frame of reference ("Erzählsituation") that is capable of accommodating the complexities of the narrative portrayal ("erzählte Situation") represented in Isa 36–37 (viz, the ABBJ narrative).[53] He seizes on the "perspective of the problems and experiences of the 588 break in the siege" as this has been brokered in other biblical narratives (GBJ Erzählung and Ezekiel)—narratives in which there is a far greater claim to congruence between narrative world and historical reference (fall of Jerusalem), in Hardmeier's view.[54]

It is here that Hardmeier's redaction-critical and tendenz-critical interests encroach in obvious ways on his narrative insights. In a more modest way, Smelik too is forced to read the narrative from a very oblique historical angle before all is said and done:

> Where Zedekiah failed to listen to Jeremiah and relied on Egypt, Hezekiah puts his trust in the Lord alone and takes heed to Isaiah's words. This results in a miraculous delivery of Jerusalem in contrast to the terrible fate Jerusalem met in Zedekiah's days. In this way it is clarified to the readers as to why they had to experience exile whereas their ancestors have been spared after Hezekiah's rebellion. Seen from this perspective

---

53. On the distinction in theoretical terms between "Erzählsituation" and "erzählte Situation," see *Prophetie im Streit*, 26–27.

54. See section 4.3.6.1: "Zum Verhältnis von Erzählgestalt und authentischer Erinnerung" (*Prophetie im Streit*, 225–28). Speaking of the ABBJ narrative, Hardmeier states, "in distinction to the GBJ narrative, the larger structure of the ABBJ narrative has not been oriented around actual events that took place" (*Prophetie im Streit*, 287).

the Hezekiah narratives do have a historical background, but a rather different one than it appears at first sight. ["Distortion," 86]

The last sentence illustrates the way in which redaction-critical analysis—even of a particularly literary, narrative, or reader-oriented stripe—is not done with historical referentiality. That referentiality—what Hardmeier terms the Erzählsituation—is simply located in another context than the one reported in the narrative itself ("erzählte Situation").

We also see how remarkably close are the conclusions of Smelik and Hardmeier, in the final analysis: (1) Isa 36–37 is drawn up on the basis of virtually no historically valuable tradition; (2) the narratives are purposely created for another (oblique) context, before the fall of Jerusalem (Hardmeier) or later (Smelik); (3) the contrast between Zedekiah and Hezekiah forms a central concern of the narrative. That contrast could only be fully appreciated in light of the events of 587 B.C.E.

The major methodological question raised by the studies of Smelik and Hardmeier does not involve their criticism of historical and source-critical approaches. There is much to be said for shifting the emphasis from behind the text to in front of the text, as it were: from the text's origins in the *bruta facta* of ANE history to the text's composition/reception in its present, logical form. The interest in a unified narrative, or even one whose unity has been redactionally imposed, enables the interpreter to move beyond the narrow confines of certain forms of diachronic inquiry, and to raise a different set of questions sensitive to (1) the literary context in which the narrative appears and (2) the function of the narrative in its present form and location.

The main issue to be addressed is the discontinuity that is argued to exist between the narrative world (the 701 "erzählte Situation") and the world ("Erzählsituation") of the perceived author/reader.[55] For Smelik and Hardmeier, the Hezekiah-Isaiah narratives depict 701 events and the deliverance of Jerusalem during the reign of Hezekiah, but they address an audience at a considerable distance from that narrative world, in historical terms. It is this audience for whom the narratives were first composed. In historical terms, the narrative's depiction is fictive.[56] The narrative's function is to instruct an audience at a later period, for which the fictive portrayal of 701 has a distinct pedagogical (analogical) value, given the real events of 587 B.C.E. The genre of Isa 36–37 would have to be classified "historicized parable."[57]

---

55. "A fundamental non-correspondence between the narrative flow of events and actual circumstances capable of historical reconstruction" (*Prophetie im Streit*, 168).
56. As Smelik puts it: "the narrative has almost no bearing on the historical reconstruction of the events in 701 B.C.E. This reconstruction must be based on 2 Kgs xviii 13–16 and the Assyrian sources" ("Distortion," 85).
57. Hardmeier: "a narrative which at its inception was composed in order to make a claim of historicality" (462); "a fictive narrative which makes a 'historical' claim" (165).

It is here that legitimate criticism of source-critical approaches and their historical conclusions has produced a more sophisticated literary evaluation, at the price of substituting an oversubtle, tendenz-oriented historical agenda. That later readers might have seen a compelling contrast between the events of 701 and 587 or between the deportment of Hezekiah and Zedekiah is quite likely. But unfortunately the form-critical and tradition-critical underpinning that bore the traditions of Jerusalem's deliverance and Hezekiah's obedience is cut away once the generative forces behind the composition of Isa 36–37 are located on the other side of 587 B.C.E. In the name of acknowledging the correlation between 701 and 587, is it necessary to focus primarily on the reverse influence the fall of Jerusalem and the end of kingship had on the portrayal of 701 events, rendering the core traditions concerning 701 a torso, or a mystery?

If diachronic approaches—and Hardmeier and Smelik clearly belong within this circle of interpretation—are to retain their force, over against newer synchronic and reader-oriented challenges, they must be able to make a virtually airtight case when arguing for great distance between the narrative world and the actual world of historical reference. The recent effort in Isaiah research to date the composition of the tradition in the postexilic period (Kaiser) threatens, if nothing else, to cut away the historical moorings of the tradition in a way not unlike certain synchronic approaches. If one posits a readership at a sufficiently late period, then all problems of a distinctly diachronic nature begin to merge indiscriminately.[58] Moreover, while a degree of speculation always marked the traditional historical approach, at least it had in its favor the commendation of the narrative world, which situated the material in relatively perspicuous historical settings—at least when measured against putative settings in the postexilic period.

A convincing case must also be made in favor of collapsing the distance between narrative world and readership in history. I have attempted to account above for (1) the anachronisms concerning the death of Sennacherib and the reference to Tirhakah, (2) the focus on Hezekiah as obedient royal figure, (3) the diachronic complexity of the tradition in Isa 36–37, and (4) the function of the narrative in its present form, by dating the composition of Isa 36–37 to the early decades of Manasseh's reign. By retaining sufficient—even extensive—traditions concerning Jerusalem's deliverance in 701, we also retain a key piece in the puzzle of Isaiah's growth, which I have argued concerns Zion's final destiny—an issue raised by Zion's deliverance in 701 and called into question by its destruction in 587 B.C.E. As such, I acknowledge that the correlation between 701 and 587 exists as an important datum in the redactional history of the Book of Isaiah. Unlike Smelik, Clements, and Hardmeier, I interpret the evidence as favoring a *forward* direction of influence,

58. See J.D.W. Watts, *Isaiah 1–33* (WBC; Waco, Texas: Word Books, 1985).

from Isa 36–37 to the prose narratives of Jeremiah, the DtrH, and the traditions of Second Isaiah. One major caveat, however, exists with regard to the DtrH. It is to that issue, and Hardmeier's contribution to it, that we now turn.

A QUESTION OF CONTEXT: ACCOUNT A RECONSIDERED

Hardmeier's decision to investigate the Hezekiah-Isaiah narratives through the lens of the Dtr. history proved fateful for his reconstruction of the relationship between ABBJ and GBJ narratives. This can be illustrated in the case of so-called Account A (2 Kgs 18:13–16). Hardmeier rejects this source-critical nomenclature even as he regards the passage (vv. 13b–16) as having been likely drawn from an "Annalwerk" available to the Dtr. historian.[59] What is of singular importance in Hardmeier's study is his investigation of the 701 narratives within the literary context of the DtrH, with special interest in the passages that frame the ABBJ narrative (esp. 18:10–12˙). The connection he sees between the siege notice at 18:10 and 18:13, for example, enables him to gain some purchase on the correlation with 597/587 events. So too, 18:13b–16 is a critical passage because a report of tribute *prior* to siege is peculiar, thus providing for Hardmeier a possible clue to a more appropriate "Erfahrungs-perspektive," viz., one in which submission did not lead to siege but to destruction (587 B.C.E.).

This literary context (18:10–12 and 18:13b–16) and all that it represents for Hardmeier's theory plays, of course, no role in the Hezekiah-Isaiah narrative tradition in Isaiah (36–37). Only the opening verse (36:1) is paralleled in the Kings tradition. In my analysis of the question of priority (Kings or Isaiah), I preferred a third alternative: that an original narrative (now preserved in Isa 36–37) was composed for *both* contexts, the DtrH and a Proto-Isaiah collection. In the former, Hezekiah was seen as a second David, whose prayer and obedience led to the deliverance of Zion. He is set up as a model for his successors, both in the Hezekiah-Isaiah narrative portrayal, as well as in the introductory section (18:1–8). Both of these sections now contained in the DtrH agree on Hezekiah's incomparable stature, as is recorded at 18:5. As noted above, what seems extraneous is the notice at 2 Kgs 18:14–16, which tells of Hezekiah's capitulation (used in historical reconstructions) but more importantly of his turning over treasures and stripping of the temple. Add to this the unusual placement of the notice in the logic of the depiction (tribute preceding siege), and one senses immediately how different are the contexts of the DtrH and the Book of Isaiah.

I argued above, in essential agreement with Hardmeier, that the place-

---

59. "An annal source that was already on hand at the time of the composition of the ABBJ narrative" (*Prophetie im Streit*, 156). Yet he immediately qualifies: "However, this piece is only to be understood as a type of citation which was taken up in order to conform to the structure of the ABBJ narrative and made to fit by the inclusion of the dates at 18:9–10a 1 and 13 1" (156).

ment of "Account A" was both unusual and in disagreement with the Assyrian records.[60] In disagreement with him, I argued that the conclusion to be drawn on the basis of this fact was that the narratives in Isa 36–37 better preserved the "original" Hezekiah-Isaiah tradition regarding 701 events. These Hezekiah-Isaiah narratives (Isa 36–37) contain the important Zion traditions that have given rise to the growth of the Proto-Isaiah collection beyond an eighth- into a sixth-century setting.

In many respects, Hardmeier's entire thesis stands or falls with his argument for the "integrale Zugehörigkeit" of 2 Kgs 18:14–16 within the ABBJ narrative. This argument leads him to view Isaiah 36–37 (the J version) as a shortened version of the Hezekiah-Isaiah narratives, and one that disturbs the internal "Spannung und Dramatik" of the ABBJ narrative original.[61] The passage 2 Kgs 18:14–16 is not an independent "source" (A) but an essential episode in the dramatic movement of the Hezekiah-Isaiah narratives within the DtrH. And precisely in its "integrale Zugehörigkeit" it gives the lie to the "fundamental non-correspondence between historically reconstructed and narratively related events" (168), since tribute *before* siege belongs to the "sequence of events" from before the fall of Jerusalem, not during its deliverance in 701.

The first part of the argument trades on Hardmeier's narrative theory, as it works within the "erzählte Situation." The passage 2 Kgs 18:14–16 is essential to the narrative since it creates a dramatic tension with what follows. By "eliminating" this material, the Isaiah version betrays its secondary ("abgeleitete") quality:

> If, like the Isaiah narrative, one leaves out this passage concerning the tribute and offer of surrender (18:14–16), the entire narrative in no small measure loses its inner drama and sense of tension. This tension has been built up in the narrative through the contrast between what one might ordinarily expect at vv. 14–16 and the resultant threat—even more serious—at v. 17. By eliminating vv. 14–16 the Isaiah version has levelled the dramatic effect originally constructed in the Kings version in 18:17ff. [*Prophetie im Streit*, 154–55]

With expressions like "narratively essential" it is clear that verses thought to comprise an old "Source A" (vv. 14–16) have been retained under very new conditions. So too, the priority of Kings over Isaiah finds an altogether unprecedented line of defense. Conversely, the narrative at whose conclusion (19:37) is to be found the resolution of the tension allegedly introduced in 18:14–16

---

60. Chapter 3, 3d and 4th section. "According to all the relevant sources—excluding the ABBJ narrative—the tribute payment and submission of Hezekiah came only at the conclusion of the crisis . . . only the ABBJ narrative has reversed the chain of historical events in such a pronounced way" (*Prophetie im Streit*, 291).

61. Ibid., 154.

(with the *Leitwort šûb mēʿālî*) is essentially the old Source B1, as this had been traditionally distinguished from B2.[62]

The major problem with this line of argument is the difficulty of determining whether a "narrative tension" alleged to exist in 2 Kgs 18:14–16 (and not in Isaiah) belongs to the level of "authorial" or redactional intervention.[63] More important is the question of whether the kind of dramatic quality seen by Hardmeier in the movement from 18:14–16 to 18:17f. (1) really exists, or (2) belongs so essentially to an "original" narrative that Isaiah must be seen as lacking an episode without which the entire dramatic quality is lost. Surely (2) is overstated; there is no evidence that Isa 36–37 lacks sufficient dramatic quality vis-à-vis the Kings account. As to (1), a major question remains: Why if 18:17ff. was to introduce something unexpected, giving the narrative a dramatic character without which it is judged a torso, was this feature not marked more explicitly in the narration itself? By all accounts, the movement from 18:16 to 17 lacks a measure of expansiveness: without explanation we hear of the king of Assyria, having just received tribute, dispatching an envoy to antagonize, blaspheme, and generally bully the givers of that same tribute. In its favor, the old source-critical approach could argue for a seam here, whose roughness was the consequence of the merger of sources.[64] But Hardmeier cannot move in this direction, having argued for a dramatic quality whose very existence is predicated on the "integrale Zugehörigkeit" of 2 Kgs 18:14–16.

It is dubious whether Isa 36–37, without 2 Kgs 18:14–16, has lost its dramatic quality. At a minimum, no analogous roughness in the opening verses of Isa 36 has ever led to source-critical solutions. Either the abruptness of 18:14–16 is "explained" by reference to a source-critical theory, or the inclusion of these verses is seen as not touching on the question of the dramatic effectiveness of Isa 36–37. Here I agree with the source-critical model in interpreting 18:(13)14–16 as abruptly placed and hardly an essential signal of dramatic effect, without which Isa 36–37 must be judged a torso. I have questioned above the historical logic by which "Source A" has been designated the starting point for literary evaluations of the Hezekiah-Isaiah narratives, weighting the inquiry in favor of Kings instead of Isaiah. But I agree that verses 14–16—far from providing critical dramatic effect—stand in literary

---

62. The old B2 source is termed "sekundäre narrative Nachinterpretation" (*Prophetie im Streit*, 157).

63. See below, p. 160ff.

64. Childs's remarks are representative: "There is widespread agreement that the Account A (II Kings 18.13–16) is followed by material from another source. The change in style from the condensed, descriptive report of the annal to the extended, dramatic representation of events and persons is striking. Moreover, the latter account in II Kings 18.17—19.37//Isa 36.1—37.38 (= Account B) makes no reference to the events in A, and, in fact, takes no cognizance whatever of the reported capitulation" (*Crisis*, 73).

and logical tension with the following report of Assyrian verbal assault. It is worth recalling Gesenius's view that Isaiah was shortened to smooth out problems—not to let essential episodes drop out.[65]

The second objection to Hardmeier's theory involves his assignment of these verses to the *Erzählsituation* before the fall of Jerusalem, on the grounds that they form an integral part of the *Haupterzählung* and betray its inner logic as related to 587, not 701, events—a logic that again reveals Isaiah's derivative character. My objection is leveled specifically at Hardmeier's literary evaluation of 18:14–16 *in the context of the larger narrative*, viz., that it forms an essential part of a wider narrative composed in the light of events before the exile, and as such reveals the true situation of composition *of the whole narrative* as those same exilic circumstances. It might well be the case that Hardmeier's *Erzählsituation* proves helpful for clarifying the existence of 18:14–16—quite apart from the broader narrative and in distinction to it— as isolated in source-critical theories. Then we would penetrate the redactional—not compositional—logic behind the inclusion of these verses in their present, odd location. At the same time, the question of the "priority" of Kings or Isaiah would remain unanswered, since the main narrative (Isa 36–37; 2 Kgs 18:13, 17—19:17) would be unaffected by a narrow decision related to the redactional inclusion of 18:14–16.

The essentially disruptive quality of 2 Kgs 18:14–16 in the larger narrative of Kings was noted above and used as an argument for the derivative nature of the Kings version of the Hezekiah-Isaiah narratives. The roughness of the narrative in Kings was also noted by virtually all early interpreters and explained by recourse to a source-critical theory, based upon certain historical principles. I rejected these principles even as I agreed with the observation of disruption (contrary to Hardmeier). On the other hand, I am willing to entertain the possibility that the odd placement of 2 Kgs 18:14–16 belongs to the logic of the DtrH (following Hardmeier). The question was raised above whether 2 Kgs 18:14–16 was (1) styled on analogy with other notices of capitulation in Kings, and (2) included to offset the incomparability formula of 18:5 in view of the subsequent reign of Josiah. With his attention to the *Erzählsituation* of 587 B.C.E., Hardmeier has identified another set of factors that might have influenced the decision to place 18:14–16 at the opening of the Hezekiah-Isaiah narratives, as a splice at the introduction of Isa 36–37.

Hardmeier's chief contribution to the problem is his provision of an explanation for the odd sequence: first tribute (18:13–16) then siege (18:17ff.). The notion that tribute does not bring deliverance may well have been an important theme for the Dtr. historian working over existing tradition with

---

65. *Jesaia*, 932–94; Gesenius speaks of the "früheren allerdings schleppenden Text" of Kings, shortened by the "Ueberarbeiter" responsible for the "Abweichungen" of Isa 36–37 (940).

knowledge of 587 events and with the example of Zedekiah behind him. But if the unit 18:13b–16 is taken as an integral part of one single narrative, as Hardmeier claims (ABBJ), and not as a redactional splice (18:14–16) into a preexilic Hezekiah-Isaiah narrative tradition, as is maintained in this study, then it might look like tribute does in fact lead to deliverance, as was the case in 701 and as the narrative goes on the record. By seeing 18:14–16 as in tension with its literary environment (so source critics), and as redactionally spliced into a core Hezekiah-Isaiah narrative (Isa 36–37), another explanation is forthcoming. Redactors working from the perspective of the fall of Jerusalem, mindful of Zedekiah's capitulation, wanted simply to demonstrate how ineffectual any form of tribute payment was: it only led to the depletion of the royal treasury and the temple itself (Hezekiah strips what he himself overlaid), and it does not work in any case: Assyria continues to press the siege. In this reading of the redactional motivation behind 18:14–16, it is not necessary to tie the *entire* narrative tradition (Isa 36–37) to the *Erzählsituation* of 587 B.C.E. That portion of the narrative under the direct influence of 587 events (1) is quite minimal, (2) is confined to Kings, and (3) is more broadly related to events depicted in the GBJ than Hardmeier argues.

The only point the redactors of the DtrH wished to make by the inclusion of 2 Kgs 18:14–16 (a point irrelevant in the Isaiah context) was that tribute cannot effectively set aside foreign threat. As Hezekiah demonstrates by his obedient response, only prayer and intercession can lead to graceful divine protection. It may well have been the case that redactors responsible for the inclusion of the Kings-plus (18:14–16) worked with knowledge of events leading up to the fall of Jerusalem and the end of the monarchy (597–587), though they were not as directly controlled by the GBJ narrative in strict literary terms as Hardmeier claims. Jerusalem's defeat is not caused by tribute payment to Babylon, as Hardmeier reconstructs the oppositional propaganda at work behind the composition of the ABBJ Erzählung, but by the accumulated sin and disobedience of king and people, leading to the fateful decision revealed to Jeremiah regarding a new "foe from the north" (Jer 1–6). This is where the analogy between 701 and 587 breaks down, or makes sense only in a forward, not a reverse, direction. Events leading up to the fall of Jerusalem are depicted with an awareness of the 701 deliverance and the pious example of Hezekiah (so Jer 26). But where once Jerusalem was delivered by God's grace and royal obedience, now no intercession can stay the divine verdict (Jer 7:16–20).

Seen in this light, the notice of 2 Kgs 18:14–16 may well have been included to signal for readers aware of 587 events that even in 701 Jerusalem was not delivered because Hezekiah was a savvy statesman. His tribute payment depleted the temple and accomplished nothing, only increasing the military threat and bringing Assyrian blasphemy close enough for all to hear.

As stated above, it is not possible to render judgment on the historicity of the notice; similar problems will accrue in respect of the evaluation of Isa 39, which tells of a visit from another (Babylonian) envoy. What is clear is that the sequence tribute/siege is unusual, and probably signals an important redactional intervention at this point in the DtrH. In the narrower scope of 2 Kgs 18:14–16, I agree in part with Hardmeier's reconstruction of the compositional situation at work behind the text. But I reject his view of the compositional situation for the main Hezekiah-Isaiah narratives, as these have been preserved in Isa 36–37, preferring instead the early period of Manasseh's reign.

CONCLUSIONS: THE DESTINY OF ZION (701 AND 587)

In this chapter I have raised for further discussion the puzzle of Isaiah's growth, as one way to gain a certain kind of perspective on the traditions found in the Hezekiah-Isaiah narratives. I concluded that the one singular feature of Proto-Isaiah traditions, Zion theology, may also have been responsible for the extension of Isaiah's oracles beyond their original eighth-century setting. The growth of Isaiah tradition was not the consequence of some internal suitability that distinguished Isaiah from other preexilic prophetic collections or made secondary supplementation intrinsically more appropriate. Rather, it was the existence of *Heilsprophetie* in the form of oracles (1) limiting the role of Assyria as agent of divine wrath and (2) expressing final divine concern for Zion, that set Isaiah traditions off as unique among preexilic prophetic collections.

These related forms of prophetic expression, scattered throughout chapters 1–35* in their present form, were not of themselves sufficient to create significant problems when Jerusalem finally fell to the Babylonians over a century later. Isaiah's Zion theology was supple and ambiguous enough to allow even for the overrunning of Zion in 587 B.C.E., especially when this theology was seen from the perspective of the extensive Isaiah judgment tradition with which it formed an integral part. It is the existence of a particular form of narrative Zion theology that urges us finally to view the Zion oracles in a less profoundly and unrelentingly ambiguous light. That narrative Zion theology grew up around the events of 701 B.C.E., centered on the military deliverance of Jerusalem and the theological defense of Zion and David. This narrative Zion theology is unrelentingly positive in its depiction, making it difficult from a synchronic perspective not to view Isa 36–37 as the final resolving chapter of a book where the fate of Zion seemed always in the balance.

At the same time, precisely this positive denouement posed a problem. The model of royal obedience that now forms the central focus of the narratives is ignored by Hezekiah's successors, so that even Josiah's righteous deportment can be viewed in the best light as but a delaying action. The problem that is posed is a theological one involving the destiny of Zion. When taken together with the poetic tradition concerning Zion found in 1–35˚, the record of Zion's deliverance in 701 forms a narrative verification that God had not spoken in vain of the final concern for Zion's welfare. The poetic and narrative traditions, when taken together, enrich one another and produce a picture of Zion theology which finally stands in tension with Zion's nondeliverance in 587 B.C.E. At no point is it appropriate to talk about Zion's "inviolability"—neither in the poetic nor the prose traditions, and not in the combination of the two. The Hezekiah-Isaiah narratives maintain a focus on the figure of the king, and it is clear that Zion's deliverance is the consequence of royal obedience as well as divine grace. But "inviolability" says more than the traditions can bear and tends to translate a poetic metaphor (best seen in the Psalms of Zion) into a concrete doctrine presumed relevant, for example, to the question of proper military strategy and general attitude.

It is not Zion's inviolability that is at issue in the Hezekiah-Isaiah narrative traditions, but rather the singular example of divine grace and royal obedience that confirms Isaiah's earlier Zion proclamation and leads to Zion's wondrous deliverance. The key piece in the puzzle of Isaiah's growth is the complex of traditions concerning Zion, as these find expression in the poetic oracles but also especially in the Hezekiah-Isaiah narratives (chaps. 36–37). The fall of Jerusalem and assault on Zion in 587 B.C.E. were not seen as a fundamental rejection of earlier Zion theology. But the events of 587 B.C.E. surely led to a probing of earlier prophetic traditions as these spoke to the fate of Zion. From the perspective of 587 B.C.E., Second Isaiah provides ample testimony of the concern to understand "former things," both in and of themselves and as related to "things to come"—that is, as related to the events of 587 and their aftermath. One sees a specific interest in the question of Zion's final destiny within these same chapters (40:9; 49:14–26; 50:1–3; 51:1—52:10; 54; 55). Especially in chapters 49–55 one sees how burning an issue was the question of Zion's defeat and restoration.

The rhetorical intensity evidenced in Second Isaiah on the question of Zion's destiny is best explained against the backdrop of earlier Zion theology, as contained in the Hezekiah-Isaiah narratives. The growth of the Book of Isaiah was not the consequence of general suitability, or of intriguing *relecture* possibilities, but of the pressing need to hear the divine word regarding Zion in 701 within the context of Zion's defeat in 587 B.C.E. There is strong likelihood that Second Isaiah was from its inception intended to form an extension to the Proto-Isaiah traditions.[66] As a contribution to the puzzle of Isaiah's growth, it is also likely that these chapters were composed within the

66. Clements, "Deutero-Isaianic Development" (1985) 101. Seitz, "New Prophecy," 233–34, 246–47.

circle of influence drawn by Isaiah's Zion theology, especially as contained in the narrative traditions of Isa 36–37 where the "near destiny" of Zion finds positive expression.

I have used the term "Hezekiah-Isaiah narratives" to refer to the long 701 deliverance narrative found in Isa 36–37. These narratives do not, however, conclude the section of the Book of Isaiah classically termed First Isaiah (1–39). There are two further narrative complexes (chaps. 38 and 39) in which Hezekiah retains a central role. These complexes form the subject of the analysis to follow. I wish to determine (1) their place in the Proto-Isaiah collection, (2) their role in the puzzle of Isaiah's growth, and (3) their relationship to Second Isaiah chapters. With this analysis, it is hoped that the rationale for the merger of two Isaiahs will come into better focus.

CHAPTER FIVE

Zion-King:
Death Sentence Diverted
(Isaiah 38)

PRELIMINARY MATTERS: ISA 38 IN ITS LITERARY CONTEXT

The exegesis and interpretation of Isa 38:1–22 cannot take place in isolation from the passages that now frame it: the narrative of Zion's deliverance (Isa 36–37) and the report of the visit of an envoy from Merodach-baladan (Isa 39). The opening words of chapter 38 (*bayyāmîm hāhēm*) temporally link Hezekiah's sickness with the preceding events, and the divine oracle in vv. 5–6 sets the entire episode at the same point in time as Zion's deliverance in Hezekiah's fourteenth year (36:1), with its reference to fifteen years added to Hezekiah's life (37:5) and by the explicit identification of royal recovery with the deliverance of the city (37:6).[1] In its present form, then, clear linkages are established between chapter 38 and chapters 36–37. In fact, the manner in which Hezekiah's recovery has been tied to the deliverance of the city has urged some interpreters to view chapter 38 as chronologically precedent to the narratives of 36–37, even while the significance of the present arrangement is acknowledged.[2] The point to be made is that the composition, or at least the editing, of chapter 38 has taken place with an eye toward the Hezekiah-Isaiah narratives of 36–37.

Similar chronological problems must be confronted in chapter 39, by virtue of similar internal linkages, though this time the connections are between chapters 38 and 39, and run from the direction of the latter to the former. The introductory *bā'ēt hahî'* at 39:1 works to link the Merodach-baladan episode to the preceding chapter, as does the reference to Hezekiah's sickness and recovery, which ties 39:1 to 38:1 and 38:9 in the same way that language in 38:5 is linked to 37:35. Consequently, chapter 39 has something of the same relationship to chapter 38 as the latter does to 36–37. So it would

---

1. The identical expression *wĕgannôtî 'al hā'îr hazzō't* is found at 37:35 and 38:6.
2. Ackroyd, "Babylonian Exile," 332; "Structure and Function," 10; Smelik, "Distortion," 73–74.

seem that interpreters who regard these three narratives as reflecting a common editorial and functional background are justified in treating them as a group for purposes of studying the editorial history of the Book of Isaiah.[3] In his 1974 work, Ackroyd goes beyond redactional commonality to posit a common tradition-historical rootage.

> Behind the present series, there are discernable, on the basis of comparable material, narratives dealing with the major movements of Hezekiah's reign—a Hezekiah-Sennacherib tradition, a Hezekiah illness tradition, and a Hezekiah-Merodach-baladan tradition. ["Babylonian Exile," 350]

A negative observation should, however, be registered at this juncture: there is no direct compositional or redactional relationship between chapter 39 and chapters 36–37, but only one that is established by virtue of chapter 38 and the motif of sickness. This means that the quest for a common tradition-historical background for all three narratives, in the manner suggested by Ackroyd, possibly misunderstands the way the traditions have developed. This is made somewhat clearer when a proper chronological order for the three narratives, as a group, is sought. As most historians have it, a visit to Jerusalem by the Chaldean tribal chieftain Marduk-apla-iddina (unrelated to a Hezekiah illness) is quite plausible, but only prior to 701 events.[4] Aware of these and other complexities, Ackroyd theorizes with regard to the sequence of the Hezekiah "series":

> We recognize that the fourteenth year of 36:1 and the fifteen years of 38:5 tie the narratives with the tradition of a rule of 29 years by Hezekiah. This could mean that the illness preceded the attack by Sennacherib in 36–37. Similarly, if we suppose that Merodach-baladan's ambassadors were in Judah, not really to inquire after the king's health or to offer congratulation, but to gain support for alliance against Assyria, then this would appear likely to belong to the early years of Sennacherib's reign. ["Structure and Function," 10]

Smelik adopts a similar view, and uses it as a means of defending the priority of Isaiah, where the "disorder" of the three accounts at least has some redactional rationale. The relevant passage is rather long:

> In Isaiah xxxviii 6 it is said that YHWH will deliver Hezekiah and Jerusalem out of the hand of the king of Assyria, but such a deliverance has already taken place at the end of the previous chapter. A more logical sequence would, therefore, have been: first the narrative of Hezekiah's illness, and only then the story of Jerusalem's deliverance. In such an arrangement, however, also the account of the Babylonian embassy had to

---

3. Especially Ackroyd, "Isa 36–39: Structure and Function" (1982).
4. See, for example, J.A. Brinkman, "Elamite Military Aid to Merodach-Baladan," *JNES* 24 (1965) 161–66; "Sennacherib's Babylonian Problem: An Interpretation," *JCS* 25 (1973) 89–95.

precede the story of Jerusalem's deliverance, as it is the sequel of the narrative concerning Hezekiah's illness. Such a more logical arrangement would fit in the book of Kings, but not in the book of Isaiah, because it would destroy the connection between the account of the Babylonian embassy and Isaiah xl. We have to conclude that the present arrangement of the Hezekiah-narratives is only understandable from the perspective of the book of Isaiah, not from that of Kings. ["Distortion," 74]

What is pointed up by these two sets of observations is the difficulty of establishing any clear chronological sequence or "more logical arrangement" for the three separate episodes, if they might be called that, when they are considered as a group. If the Merodach-baladan episode is to come first, on historical grounds, then the reference to illness (39:1) must be eliminated. That is easily enough done by viewing the present narrative as redactionally modified to work with reference to chapter 38. But as the setting provided for the visit (39:1) is by no means essential for the narrative to unfold properly, it is difficult to understand why it would be of redactional importance. It merely links the story to chapter 38. Other features in the story are responsible for giving it the character of a finale (esp. vv. 5–8). As such, it is somewhat misleading to talk about a better order in which the Merodach-baladan story came first, on historical or any other grounds.

For various internal reasons, it is difficult to avoid the impression that the Merodach-baladan story never appeared in any other position. The final remark of Hezekiah at 39:8, whatever its more precise import, could only with difficulty appear anywhere but last in the series. The same is true of Isaiah's oracle (39:5–7), which peers into the future in a way that would be heartily inappropriate, and certainly preemptive, before the narratives of 36–37.[5] Only by severely reducing the scope of the account, or reconfiguring it as Ackroyd suggests (eliminating the prophet Isaiah), could one imagine a Hezekiah-Merodach-baladan tradition that appeared prior to chapters 36–37(38).[6]

Similarly, it would not solve the chronological problem of 38:6 to place the entire story of Hezekiah's illness prior to the narratives of 36–37, as Smelik implies.[7] The mention of Assyrian deliverance in 38:6, chronologically curious as it is, requires the preceding story of Assyrian assault for its logic. Only by reducing the story to a brief oral tradition, or by eliminating the odd conflation of Hezekiah's recovery and Jerusalem's deliverance (38:6) would such a

---

5. Whether this means that the Isaiah "trilogy" makes better sense given the placement of 39 next to Second Isaiah (so Smelik), and therefore argues for its priority over Kings, is not entirely clear.
6. "Babylonian Exile," 350; "Structure and Function," 13.
7. Smelik's argument is quite subtle because he only entertains the notion of a "more logical arrangement" as a means of getting a purchase on the "logic" of the present arrangement and what it reveals about the priority of Isaiah over Kings. As such, his "more logical arrangement" is something of a fiction (cf. Ackroyd), since he recognizes the logic of the narratives of 36–39 in precisely their present form—a logic that also betrays the late date of the narratives *as a group* ("Distortion," 85).

transposition really make sense. The notice of an additional fifteen years given to Hezekiah (38:5) would also have to be reconfigured, since the connection with Hezekiah's fourteenth year (36:1) does appear motivated by awareness of the tradition of a twenty-nine-year total reign (2 Kgs 18:2). The implication is clearly that recovery from illness occurred at the same time the city was delivered (viz., 14th year of Hezekiah + 15 = 29).

As such, it is difficult to conceive of an "original series" of early traditions in a particular order—one that has been recast through redactional intervention in both Isaiah and Kings. The chronological "problems" form such an integral part of the compositional force of chapters 38 and 39 that it is misleading to talk of "solving" them through imaginative rearrangement at the preliterary level or by reconstructing earlier traditions. Moreover, the net effect of such a move is to treat the various problems as though they existed at one level only, across all three accounts, implying that a single rearrangement could solve them. The mistake is in trying to posit an earlier, more logical arrangement for all three narratives *as a group.*

It seems far more likely that a distinctive set of compositional and redactional questions attend the interpretation of chapter 38, vis-à-vis chapters 36–37, as over against chapter 39. The references in chapter 38, to (1) deliverance from Assyrian military threat and (2) the provision of fifteen extra years, form an integral part of the account and point to an intended connection with 36–37. In literary terms, chapter 38 is a "sequel" in one special sense only: the same temporal setting that appears in 36–37 is reused in chapter 38, so that the recovery from illness is portrayed as though it would occur at the same time as the city's deliverance. At a minimum, the provision of precise temporal sequence, in the strict sense (which came first, the illness or Assyrian assault?), has taken a back seat to a different concern. That concern is seen precisely in the conflation (not sequencing) of recovery from illness with deliverance from military threat. Far from needing to be excised, the reference to delivery of king *and* city belongs to the very rationale of the story from its inception.[8] The opening temporal indicator "in those days" (38:1) seeks to assign in the most general terms the passage to the same period as that of chapters 36–37, when Zion "recovered" from Assyrian threat.

What this also means is that chapter 38 and the relationship it has to 36–37 must form the subject of an investigation quite separate from chapter 39, on both internal and external grounds. Not only is the content of chapter 39 distinct compared with that of chapter 38, so is its alleged function in the Book of Isaiah. The whole point of the narrative in chapter 39 is the final oracle and response (39:5–8). There is no real interest in the military possibilities repre-

8. Gray implies through his text-critical annotation that reference to the city should be eliminated (*I & II Kings*, 697).

sented by a visit of ambassadors from Merodach-baladan, except as these help illuminate the force of Isaiah's oracle—a force that is specifically directed to the future, and not to the events of Hezekiah's own day. The functional role this episode may play in the larger Book of Isaiah is thereby revealed. But chapter 38 is far less perspicuous in this regard, even when a redactional function is argued to exist in the composition of the story of Hezekiah's illness.[9]

But more to the point is the simple observation that chapter 39 has only a very loose connection to chapter 38, and none at all to 36–37, while chapter 38 has been consciously linked through the motif of illness/recovery to the long narrative of Zion's 701 deliverance. As such, there is a limit to the wisdom of treating all three stories as if they were part of an originally intended series, a kind of tradition-critical triptych. In Ackroyd's work, this has had the corollary of treating chapters 38–39 as though they belonged together, on analogy with 36–37.[10] By then moving in the direction of late dating for 36–37, suddenly all three narratives, with only a vague tradition-historical base, share the same redactional function.[11] That function in turn becomes the guarantor of a mode of interpretation that places all three narratives on one basic level (Isa 36–39).

I wish to move in an entirely different direction, based upon the foregoing interpretation of Isa 36–37. It remains to be seen, on the basis of an internal analysis, how chapter 38 is in fact related to the Hezekiah-Isaiah narratives that precede it. My plea at this juncture is to keep quite distinct the interpretation of chapter 39 from that of chapter 38, so that the episode of Hezekiah's illness might not be peremptorily assigned a redactional function on the same level as chapter 39.

HEZEKIAH'S IDEALIZATION

As we have seen, the status of Hezekiah in various literary presentations has served to determine the relative date of the material, on the theory that Hezekiah was increasingly idealized as one moved from earlier to later tradition. This was true in the context of 36–37 in respect of the differentiation of B1 from B2, and specifically in the assessment of Hezekiah's prayer (37:16–20). But a similar set of considerations has also come into play in the interpretation of chapter 38, and in connection with the sorting out of chapter 38's relationship to its framing narratives (36–37 and 39). What is intriguing is the clear way in which the various proponents of such a method disagree over the finer points of this type of inquiry.

Clements, for example, regards the "proper spiritual" deportment of

---

9. Clements, "Central Passage," 261; Ackroyd, "Babylonian Exile," 343–45.
10. "Babylonian Exile" (A Study of 2 Kings 20, Isaiah 38–39).
11. Ackroyd, "Structure and Function," 14–21. Smelik, "Distortion," 72–74, 85–86.

Hezekiah in B2 as a sign of the narrative's exilic composition and its intention "to show that, under the obedient response of a faithful king, God does act to protect and uphold his people."[12] The same is true by extension of Isa 38 and its counterpart in Kings (20:1–11). Clements concludes:

> The city of Jerusalem could, it was believed, be supernaturally protected by the very angel of Yahweh (cf. Isa 14,32) when the proper spiritual conditions were fulfilled. The fulfilling of these conditions through the agency of a devout and obedient king of the Davidic royal house is the primary purpose of the inclusion of the story concerning Hezekiah's sickness (2 Kgs 20,1–11 = Isa 38˙). ["Central Passage," 261]

In its favor, at least the interpretation of chapter 38 is linked by Clements with the preceding chapters 36–37, if only in residual (B2) form. Whether the link is as late and is occasioned by the sort of circumstances Clements reconstructs in the exilic period is another question.

Working with similar redactional assumptions for all of 36–39, Smelik adopts a very different view of matters, with the consequence that Hezekiah's "idealization" comes out looking more muted. Like Clements, Smelik ties the interpretation of material in 36–37 to the portrayal of Hezekiah, though with an emphasis on chapter 39. When he reaches historical conclusions, what is true for one part of the complex (36–39) is true for all others:

> [If 36–37] is a literary unity, we have to opt for the Persian period because some passages are rather similar to Second Isaiah. Also Isaiah xxxix cannot have been written earlier than the Persian period, because in its present form it predicts that the Davidic dynasty will not be restored to the Judaean throne. These chapters were probably written after the completion of Second Isaiah in order to create a bridge between the two parts of the book. ["Distortion," 85]

Several observations are to be made on the basis of these remarks. First, Smelik regards 36–39 as a single block of tradition, even though he fails to even mention chapter 38 in this particular context. Second, features in 36–37 and 39 give evidence, in his view, of a date in the Persian period. Yet ironically, far from presenting an idealized version of kingship based on Hezekiah, with the intent "to re-establish a rationale for restoring the Davidic kingship and for rebuilding the temple in the wake of what happened to both institutions in 587 B.C." (Clements), this unified complex is concerned to register precisely the opposite effect, viz., to "predict that the Davidic dynasty will not be restored to the Judaean throne" (Smelik). If idealization is going on, focused on Hezekiah or on the institution of the monarchy as such, and chapter 38 is to play a role in this tendency, then Smelik is right to wonder about the function of chapter 39 in such a portrayal. Obviously the problem is

---

12. "Central Passage," 261.

acute for him in his insistence at reading the entire complex (36–39) on one basic redactional level. This is another place where I prefer to keep the interpretation of these two chapters distinct. At the same time it must be acknowledged, against theories of unilateral Hezekiah idealization, that chapter 39 stands apart from such a move, if it is not in clear tension with it.

The strongest proponent of Hezekiah idealization has been Ackroyd, assisted in part by his reconstruction of three core narratives in Isa 36–39 whose original focus was wholly on Hezekiah, to the exclusion even of the prophet Isaiah.[13] Ackroyd plots the movement, in its earliest phases, in classic terms. The frank report of 2 Kgs 18:14–16 marks the beginning of the tradition process, before it moves ahead to B1 and then B2. The "elimination" of "Account A" in Isaiah marks a movement of idealization distinct to the Isaiah corpus. So too, one can detect specific movement toward idealization in chapters 38 and even 39. With respect to the former, Ackroyd sees a movement taking place within the chapter itself, as the theme of illness and recovery, complete in and of itself (38:1–6; 2 Kgs 20:1–7), has been joined by a more "miraculous motif" (in 38:7–8, 20–21; 2 Kgs 20:8–11) which "serves to underline the significance of Hezekiah's recovery."[14]

Even the divergences between Isaiah and Kings in chapter 38 point to an intentional movement toward idealization in the former. In Isa 38 "the departure of Isaiah from Hezekiah's presence is unmentioned (2 Kings 20:4–5a); the divine word is portrayed as coming as an immediate answer to the king's prayer and distress; the granting of a sign—as the text stands, and surely significantly—is not in response to a request for a sign (as in 2 Kings), but is offered as an immediate token of assurance."[15] It is somewhat surprising to find Wildberger acknowledge the "tendency often observed in these narratives, to increase the wonder and piety of the characters"—but to see it better represented in the Kings, not the Isaiah version.[16] This is another instance where the theory of idealization is maintained, even while discrepancies exist in the details of its proponents' reconstructions.[17] I will have occasion below to

13. "Babylonian Exile," 350. Ackroyd speaks of "the evolution of the figure of Hezekiah" (344), and "the scale towards idealisation" ("Death of Hezekiah," 22).
14. "Babylonian Exile," 344.
15. Ibid., 343, n. 3.
16. *Jesaja*, 1446.
17. Following the lead of Ackroyd, Sweeney also speaks of "the deliberate attempt not only to idealize Hezekiah as a faithful servant of God but to emphasize God's immediate response to Hezekiah's demonstrations of faith" (*Isaiah 1–4*, 13). Yet his proposal is far simpler. Even the most minor divergences between Isa 36–39 and 2 Kgs 18:13—20:19 are explicable on the basis of a theory of idealization, ruling out even commonly accepted text-critical and transmission explanations. 2 Kgs 18:14–16 (eliminated in Isa 36:17f.) "eliminates and modifies the text of 2 Reg 18,32," which had spoken of Hezekiah too disparagingly (13). Isa 38 stresses the immediacy of Isaiah's response by eliminating the fuller statement of 2 Kgs 18:4: "And Isaiah had not gone out from the middle court when the word of YHWH came to him" (14)—a text already fairly committed to immediacy!—in favor of the simpler "And the word of YHWH came to Isaiah" (following Ackroyd, "Babylonian Exile," 343, n. 3) and by "emending 'return' to 'go'" (14,

look at this specific section in chapter 38, in more detail and in comparison with Kings, to determine how it might function in a theory of idealization. Wildberger's exegesis of chapter 38 does raise questions about a consistent move toward idealization in the context of Isaiah, in contrast with that of Kings, or at least the general perspicacity of such a movement. The final stages of Ackroyd's idealization movement continue beyond Isaiah into Chronicles, Sirach, and even the later Jewish writings.

One would think that chapter 39—a text with the fewest divergences between Isaiah and Kings, and with no apparent evidence of idealization in either context—might create a problem in this scheme of unilateral movement. Naturally, one solution would be to view the composition of chapter 39 as serving a purpose quite distinct from idealization or nonidealization, in respect of Hezekiah, with its redactional interest in providing a setting for chapters 40ff. But Ackroyd does not take this tack. Instead, he posits the existence of "an older narrative in which Hezekiah comes under divine judgement through Isaiah because of his involvement with a foreign power."[18] Naturally with such an initial scenario, it is difficult to avoid an improvement in stature. But even granting such an unlikely original narrative, the final witness of chapter 39 is difficult to construe as positive in its portrayal of Hezekiah, much less as a move toward idealization. There is no avoiding the fact that a judgment oracle (39:5–7), and a severe one at that, follows upon Hezekiah's actions in respect of the Babylonian envoy (39:2).

Ackroyd's close analysis of this key passage, and especially of Hezekiah's final response (39:8), is quite impressive and a clear advance on earlier interpretations.[19] Rejecting more common *après moi le déluge* interpretations (so NEB) of Hezekiah's final words (*wayyōʾmer kî yihyeh šālôm weʾĕmet bĕyāmāy*), Ackroyd presses for a reading whereby the right conduct of Hezekiah is what is being held up for posterity. The king accepted the sentence of judgment with the proper response (*ṭôb dĕbar-YHWH ʾăšer dibbartā*), not with a response of smugness at having been personally exempted. Ackroyd rightly notes that it is in this spirit that the Chronicler interprets the notice, commending Hezekiah for having passed an important test. Ackroyd captures well the logic of the Chronicler:

contrary to Wildberger, *Jesaja*, 1446). Even the final response of Hezekiah in Isaiah "is intended to idealize the character of Hezekiah" (Isa 39:8), because the original wording of 2 Kgs 20:19 ("Is it not true there will be peace and security in my day?") implies conditionality and suggests doubt on the part of Hezekiah" (16). With its theory of unilateral redactional modification, Sweeney's study stands at the other end of a scale of complexity and subtlety from that of Wildberger (who in the account of Hezekiah's illness regards Isa 38 as preserving "die ursprünglichere Form der Erzählung" [1446], somewhat similar to his evaluation of the priority of Isa 36–37)—even while they both consider idealization a factor to be reckoned with in the tradition-history of Isa 36–39. More on the specifics of Sweeney's analysis below.

18. Isaiah has suddenly reappeared! ("Structure and Function," 13; compare "Babylonian Exile," 350, on the nonessential status of Isaiah in the tradition).

19. "Babylonian Exile," 332–43.

He assumes his readers' knowledge of the whole story and does not relate it himself, but simply comments on this as being an occasion when the divine protection and blessing attended Hezekiah: "So too it was in the incident of the emissaries of Babylon who were sent to find out about the sign that had occurred in the land, when God forsook him, testing him so as to know his true disposition." For the Chronicler, this was a moment in which the nature of Hezekiah's obedience was disclosed, and though tested he was found to be loyal. ["Babylonian Exile," 337–38]

In further support of Ackroyd's interpretation of Isa 38:8 with assistance from 2 Chron 32:31—a difficult passage in its own right—is the fact that the Chronicler is quite capable of rendering negative judgment over Hezekiah.[20] But he chooses as an example of disobedience the events of Hezekiah's illness, when according to the Chronicler Hezekiah received an answer to his prayer, "but did not make return according to the benefit done to him, for his heart was proud" (32:25). Only after humbling himself does the divine wrath, "which came upon him and Judah and Jerusalem" (2 Chron 32:25) "not come upon them" (32:26). The Chronicler seems to focus his attention on the sign that attended the healing—a sign that Hezekiah did not properly acknowledge. In the Chronicler's story, this same sign is the motivation for the visit of the Babylonian envoy (compare Isa 39:1 and 2 Kgs 20:12). What the Chronicler is apparently able to commend "in the matter of the envoys of the princes of Babylon" (32:31), in contrast to the matter of Hezekiah's sickness, is his proper response to the divine word. This is also evidence that the Chronicler was more interested in the tradition of Hezekiah's illness as found in Kings than in Isaiah, consistent with his utilization of that primary source.[21] For Kings has more potential for an interpretation that would emphasize Hezekiah's improper response (2 Kgs 20:10) than does Isaiah.

Ackroyd is correct to draw attention to the proper conduct of Hezekiah at the close of chapter 39, a feature that is often missed in pure *vaticinium ex eventu* readings that emphasize the redactional purpose of the chapter, accomplished by the negative prediction of Babylonian exile, if not the complete end of the monarchy (39:5–7). I agree that the chapter has an important redactional function, but in its depiction of Hezekiah it is far more subtle and

20. Ackroyd's rendering could be read as implying that God's forsaking of Hezekiah ('ăzābô, 2 Chron 32:31) occurred on the occasion of the sign—that is, with respect to events in Isa 38—not on the occasion of the Babylonian visitors. However the expression is to be understood, Ackroyd is correct that the Chronicler here commends Hezekiah for his obedient response.

21. Note the seemingly equivocal citation at 32:32: "Now the rest of the acts of Hezekiah, and his good deeds, behold they are written in *the vision of the prophet Isaiah* the son of Amoz, in *the Book of the Kings of Judah and Israel.*" In my view, the reference to "the vision of Isaiah," now the superscription for the entire Book of Isaiah (1:1), has been triggered in this context by the actual scene in which Isaiah "sees" the Babylonian days ahead (viz, 2 Kgs 20:16–18 = Isa 39:5–7). So while the Chronicler's reference to the vision of the prophet Isaiah might well refer to the Book of Isaiah and the narratives concerning Hezekiah found therein (36–39), the reference is finally predicated on there being a "Book of the Kings of Judah and Israel," which contains Hezekiah-Isaiah narratives, in which Isaiah has a "vision" of the exile.

nuanced than is often implied. By Hezekiah's actions, future Babylonian assault can be expected. But Ackroyd is finally correct that the focus does not fall on the impropriety of Hezekiah's conduct; he terms the king "an unwitting agent in bringing about the loss of the land."[22] The events of 39:1–4 unfold almost mechanically as the narrative proceeds ahead to make its essential point (39:5–7). Even the severe judgment oracle that follows, especially focused on the fate of the royal house (your house, your fathers, your sons), can only with difficulty be viewed as a kind of personal rebuke of Hezekiah. It may be incorrect to view Hezekiah as unwitting or as even inadvertently causing the exile—such a characterization seems too personal, given the terseness of the narrative.[23]

The point is this: the narrative treads a fine line between needing to establish the grounds for a severe sentence of judgment, while at the same time exempting from that judgment its agent—unwitting or otherwise. The contrast with 2 Kgs 18:14–16 is striking in this regard. And precisely as it treads that fine line it cannot serve any purpose in theories of alleged idealization or nonidealization. The terms are not apposite in this instance, and it is not clear in our view that they are apposite elsewhere. Precisely because of the subtlety and sophistication of Ackroyd's own interpretation of chapter 39, with which I largely agree, the theory of unilateral idealization is called into question. Other factors, unique to each literary context (Isa 36–37; Isa 38; Isa 39; 2 Kings 18:13—20:19; Chronicles, Sirach) must be considered more relevant.

As a classic example of this one need only consider the Chronicler— himself thought to be one stage further on a scale of idealization than either Isaiah or Kings. Yet he includes a clearly negative appraisal of Hezekiah (2 Chron 32:24–26). The greater irony is that he chooses as an example of disobedience a narrative some would argue is well on the way to idealization, relatively better seen in Isaiah 38 (Ackroyd, Sweeney) or 2 Kings 20:1–11 (Wildberger), but there in either case. The Chronicler chooses this episode over chapter 39's portrayal of Hezekiah in order to point up an instance of royal disobedience. Chapter 39 might have been thought to offer the better example of royal equivocation, but here the Chronicler goes his own way, refusing to conform to any simple pattern of idealization.

These observations on the alleged idealization of Hezekiah also serve to drive home the point that a variety of redactional influences can be detected in each of the sections represented by Isa 36–37, 38, and 39. There is not one single redactional hand at work on Isaiah 36–39, as is implied by Smelik's

---

22. "Babylonian Exile," 341.
23. Ackroyd captures well the real intent of the narrative (transfer of property) without undue focus on Hezekiah's disobedience—thus standing outside idealization or nonidealization schemes ("Babylonian Exile," 338–40).

literary and historical conclusions.[24] To its credit, Ackroyd's own deft analysis of Isa 39 has given the lie to any unidirectional model of idealization. Moreover, there is little evidence for a single redactional *tendenz* within the narrower context of Isa 38–39, as is implied when these chapters form the subject of a treatment on analogy with Isa 36–37. As such, the interpretation of chapter 39 should be kept distinct from that of Hezekiah's illness in Isa 38.

The aetiological character of chapter 39 is revealed by its interest not just in the future transfer of royal assets into Babylonian hands (39:6), but more specifically in the prediction that descendants of the royal house will be *sārîsîm* in the palace of the king of Babylon. Both statements conform too closely to events as they unfolded in 597–587 B.C.E., now recorded in the DtrH (2 Kgs 24:12–16; 25:7, 27–30), to be historically rooted in the Hezekiah period. 2 Kgs 24:13 has been explicitly linked to 2 Kgs 20:19 (= 39:8) with the expression *ka'ăšer dibber YHWH*.[25] The content and logic of Isa 39:8 (and 2 Kgs 20:19) have much in common with 2 Kgs 22:20, which predicts that Josiah will be spared seeing "all the evil which I will bring upon this place" having been "gathered to his grave in peace." Here we see themes that function within the redactional logic of the DtrH, and ones that appear to have very little influence on the report of Hezekiah's illness (Isa 38).

As such, chapter 39 must be treated on its own terms, quite apart from Isa 38. I wish to consider the possibility that the main linkage in Isa 36–39 exists between chapter 38 and the preceding narratives in 36–37. That linkage was forged early in the tradition process, close to the period of composition of the Hezekiah-Isaiah narratives (36–37), and well before Isa 39 (= 2 Kgs 20:12–19) took its place between 36–38 and Second Isaiah chapters. In this sense, I disagree with Smelik that Isa 39 has a position whose oddity is explicable only in the context of the Book of Isaiah, but not in the DtrH, even as I agree that it is essentially a narrative whose logic stands to the side of the narratives in 36–38. It serves the purpose nicely of introducing Second Isaiah chapters, and should properly be thought of in that context, as distinct from Isa 36–38.[26] But it is not the case that Isa 39's counterpart (2 Kgs 20:12–19) is blatantly more awkward in the context of the DtrH; in fact, it shows evidence of considerable redactional congruity with the final narratives in the DtrH. This point is somewhat lost on Smelik because he insists on interpreting all three narratives in Isaiah (chaps. 36–39) as though they formed one basic compositional and redactional effort ("an editorial bridge"), despite the obvious differences that

---

24. And from a different angle, by Sweeney's very simple view of the relationship between Kings and Isaiah.
25. Seitz, *Theology in Conflict*, 177–200. I hold for a redactional staging for chap. 24 separate from chap. 25, and for a series of redactions for each king after Hezekiah, built upon a major Hezekiah edition that ended at 2 Kgs 18:1—20:11*, and made with knowledge of the fate of Judah and the royal house in the last decade of their existence.
26. Melugin, *Formation*, 177.

exist between them.[27] These differences are most pronounced between Isa 36–37/38 and Isa 39.

What can be said then of a theory of idealization? First, the notion that there is a *scale* of idealization clearly overstates the evidence. It is not hard to place 2 Kgs 18:14–16 at one end of such a scale, to be sure. But the differences between all other portrayals—for example, between Isa 38 and 2 Kgs 20:1–12 (Sweeney and Ackroyd), or even between 2 Chron 29–32 (including 2 Chron 32:24–26) and Isaiah or 2 Kings—are so negligible as to render meaningless the notion of a scale. All of them offer positive depictions, and (1) the differences between them are not that pronounced, (2) there has hardly been monochromatic idealization that does not admit of nuance (Isa 39) or negative portrayal (2 Chron 32:24–26), and (3) it would be difficult to rule out a serious measure of positive depiction at the very root of the tradition. Again, the one text that stands outside such a depiction is 2 Kgs 18:14–16, and I would argue that without it Ackroyd could never have produced a concept like "scale of idealization" with respect to Hezekiah.[28]

Consistent with the conclusions reached above, and supported in an odd way by Hardmeier's analysis, 2 Kgs 18:14–16 is better seen as the intrusive element in the tradition process. It forms one part of redactional efforts at work in the DtrH, whatever its basis in historical fact. In some sense, it resembles the depiction of Isa 39 (= 2 Kgs 20:12–19) with its interest in Hezekiah's relationship to foreign powers. But it is far less subtle than that narrative. Working specifically within the context of the DtrH, Provan reaches a conclusion not far from the one being promoted here, both in respect of a Hezekiah redaction of Kings and of 2 Kgs 18:14–16. He also notes the possibility of a relationship between 2 Kgs 18:14–16 and 2 Kgs 20:12–19 (= Isa 39). The problem with the traditional "Account A" status of 2 Kgs 18:14–16 is addressed within the context of work on the editorial history of the DtrH:

> The possibility must be allowed that 18:14–16 represent a secondary insertion into the books [of Kings]. It must be admitted that the absence of these verses in the parallel Isa 36:1–3 cannot speak in favour of this possibility (Kaiser, "Verkündigung," 305–6), although this passage does at least demonstrate that 18:13 can introduce 18:17ff. quite as effectively as it does 18:14ff. At the same time, the apparent historical reliability of the verses (stressed by Clements, *Deliverance*, 9–13, for example) cannot speak against it. The fact that the material may come from an annalistic source and approximate what we are told in the Assyrian annals does not prove that it comprised part of the original books of Kings. It is simply a matter of judgement whether it is thought likely that the pre-exilic edition

27. "Distortion," 72–74, 85–86.
28. "Death of Hezekiah," 220. Is Sirach's glossary of ancient worthies best characterized as "idealization"? Hezekiah (48:17–22a) must share the stage with Isaiah (48:22b–25). The city is delivered "by the hand of Isaiah" (48:20) and by the intercession, not of Hezekiah, but of Jerusalem's citizenry (48:19–20). This hardly amounts to an idealization of Hezekiah.

of Kings as it has been described thus far contained this passage. In my judgement, it is more likely that it was added later, as part of an attempt, which may also be noted in 20:12–19, to tone down the rather exaggerated picture of Hezekiah which is given by the original account. [*Hezekiah and the Books of Kings*, 122, n. 82]

If one moves in the direction of Provan, and 2 Kgs 18:14–16 is construed in a different manner than traditionally proposed, it is not hard to see how quickly the theory of idealization falls to the side. Alternatively, the positive depiction has as much claim to being rooted in the sources, in which case 2 Kgs 18:14–16 serves "to tone down the rather exaggerated picture which is given by the original account."

A similar "toning down" or shift in emphasis can also be detected in the story of Hezekiah's illness, if it can be demonstrated that Kings has modified a better preserved account in Isa 38. Not only has the prayer of Hezekiah (38:9–20) not found its way into the tradition; it is also clear that the sign tradition (Isa 38:7–8) has been handled quite differently (2 Kgs 20:8–11). The effect of this is to have Hezekiah ask for a sign (cf. Isa 38:7), and then query the prophet about the sufficiency of its manifestation (20:10)—a move that has affected the Chronicler's evaluation of Hezekiah (2 Chron 32:24–26). Such a modification, if we are entitled to classify it as such, would match the tendency seen elsewhere in Kings, not to idealize Hezekiah but to modify the positive depiction of him rooted in the Isaiah traditions. I am not prepared to adopt the terminology of "idealization" or its opposite, however. It seems more likely that a different set of concerns has entered into the redactional history of Kings than that of Isaiah, not interested so much in "demoting" Hezekiah as in modulating his status in respect of other more important issues. These include the relative status of other kings, the subsequent history of the monarchy, and the fact of Jerusalem's defeat in 597–587 B.C.E.

Though it is impossible to determine, we also find it likely that 2 Kgs 18:14–16 took shape in conscious relationship to 2 Kgs 20:12–19. It might appear that they stand in some logical tension, since the former threatens to so deplete royal and temple treasures that there would be nothing for Merodach-baladan's ambassadors to view.[29] But the latter account works with a theologically significant notion of the Babylonian envoy "seeing" everything (esp. 20:13, 15), as pointed out by Ackroyd.[30] This "seeing" is intentionally depicted as so comprehensive as to go well beyond concern for consistency with 2 Kgs 18:14–16. Two different issues are at stake, though both suggest a concern with locating the initial stages of a foreign domination that would eventually result in the fall of Jerusalem in the reign of Hezekiah—the former quite directly, but with Assyria; the latter more proleptically, yet with a Babylon finally responsible for Judah's fall a century later.

---

29. See my remarks above, p. 57.
30. "Babylonian Exile," 338–41.

I have mentioned that a specific perspective on the question of Hezekiah's status is opened up when the relationship between Isa 38:1–22 and 2 Kgs 20:1–11 is properly understood. Several recent interpreters have argued that Hezekiah is more positively depicted in Isa 38, and that his status is the consequence of redactional modification of an original portrayal now found in the DtrH. Others see the Isaiah text as basically superior (with 38:9–20 as secondary), and view certain modifications in Kings as enhancing the wondrous and pious features of that earlier tradition.[31] In rejecting both alternatives, it is still crucial that the proper relationship be set forth. Our ultimate concern is not so much with the issue of Hezekiah's status as it is with the status of Isa 38 vis-à-vis the Hezekiah-Isaiah narratives of Isa 36–37. As such, an internal analysis of Isa 38 must be carried out. The divergences between the Isaiah and Kings traditions of Hezekiah's illness must also be accounted for.

ISAIAH 38: ANALYSIS

The problems associated with the exegesis of Isa 38 are well-known and need not be rehearsed in detail. First, there is the matter of divergence with 2 Kgs 20:1–11. Related to this is the reconstruction of the growth of tradition, in both accounts, and the general logic of each presentation. Finally there has been significant disagreement over the proper genre designation for the material found in Isa 38:9–20. Perhaps more important for our purposes is the rationale for the psalm's placement in the Isaiah tradition and the purpose achieved thereby.

Divergence

The most striking divergence between Isaiah and Kings is the Psalm of Hezekiah found in Isa 38:9–20, which is missing entirely in the latter. But when the problems associated with its interpetation and placement are bracketed out, there still remains a very different logic appropriate to each account, if one might call it that. Most striking is the different handling of the sign tradition and the notice of Isaiah's medical remedy. In Isaiah, a sign is offered by the prophet as confirmation of the divine promise to Hezekiah of extended life, and it occurs without any response from the king (38:8). Following the psalm, in what appears to be an isolated location (38:21–22), Isaiah gives a command regarding a medical procedure for Hezekiah, to which the king responds with a question about another sign, this time regarding when he should go up to the temple (*māh 'ôt kî 'e'ĕleh bêt YHWH*).

---

31. Speaking of the modification of 2 Kgs 20:5, Wildberger remarks: Kings "explicitly states that Yahweh heals him, and indeed so quickly, that already on the third day he can visit the temple again, which is certainly appropriate for a pious king" (*Jesaja*, 1446). This corresponds to the tendency of later traditions "to heighten the miraculous and augment the piety of the persons involved" (*Jesaja*, 1446).

In Kings, Hezekiah's going to the temple is no mystery, but is to occur "on the third day" (*bayyôm haššĕlîšî taʿăleh bêt YHWH*); this is mentioned before any promise of additional years is made (20:5). Following this promise (20:6), reference is made to the medical procedure (20:7). But then the king asks what the sign will be that he will be healed (20:8), as though the medical procedure had not occurred at all, and when he will go up to the temple, as though he had not already been told:

> What shall be the sign that YHWH will heal me,
>   and that I shall go up to the house of YHWH on the third day?

The prophet then does offer a sign, but in a way unique to such occasions. The sign is not the shadow going back ten steps, though this would be a sufficiently wondrous occurrence to function as a sign of confirmation (so Isa 38:8). Rather the sign in this case is the ability of God to do what Hezekiah requests:

> And Isaiah said: "This is the sign to you from YHWH,
>   that YHWH will do the thing that he has promised:
> Shall the sun go forward ten steps, or go back
>   ten steps?"

Hezekiah chooses the more difficult task, at least as he—revealingly—sees it, since whether it is in fact "easier" to make a shadow go forward or backward is not really at issue. It is important for the story that Hezekiah judges it that way ("it is an easy thing for the shadow to lengthen steps") and requests for the more difficult thing to be done. The prophet cries out to YHWH, and succeeds in getting God to do what the king had asked. With that the account ends.

Two features stand out in the Kings account. The first is the more central role of the prophet Isaiah. This is clearly seen in the affair of the "more difficult sign," where the sign's success (an issue of no importance in Isaiah where a test plays no role) is seen as dependent upon the prophet's cry (20:11). Less clearly is this evidenced by the position of the medical procedure immediately following the promise of additional years (20:7), before any mention is made of a sign. The effect is to have the prophet intervene with a medical procedure hard upon the divine word, in fulfillment of the promise of healing made in 20:5. Reference to healing (20:5) does not occur at the same juncture in the Isaiah tradition (compare the divine oracle in 38:5–6). One might argue that mention of the medical remedy at this point in the story (20:7), while enhancing the active role of the prophet, is nevertheless preemptive, since in the very next verse Hezekiah asks what the sign will be that YHWH will heal him.

The second feature unique to the Kings' depiction involves Hezekiah. Hezekiah asks for a sign, rather than simply receiving one from God (Isa 38:7), and then predicates how it is to be carried out, intentionally choosing the more difficult execution. The effect is to move Hezekiah in the direction of Ahaz

(7:11). Although he does not feign pious reserve, as his predecessor, his request could certainly be construed as a form of testing YHWH (as Ahaz had feared at Isa 7:12).[32] Isaiah's stature is enhanced through his ability to bring off the more difficult procedure; Hezekiah plays no role in the affair of the sign in 38:7–8, except to receive it as a confirmation of the promise of new life given in 38:6.

At first reading, priority would appear to go to the Isaiah account on the following grounds. By splicing into Kings mention of a visit to the temple in three days, associated with Hezekiah's healing (20:5), the effect is to make Hezekiah's request for a sign, associated in the Kings account with that same temple visit, unnecessary.[33] Hezekiah had been told he would be healed and that he would go up to the temple in three days (compare Hezekiah's final question in 38:22). In the Isaiah tradition, the sign functions as an appropriate confirmation, before any mention of healing had been made. The sign of confirmation (38:7) is distinct from the sign at 38:22, which has to do with not knowing when it would be appropriate to go to the temple.[34] But in Kings, these two signs have been conflated. The sign for visiting the temple has been associated with Hezekiah's healing and explicitly linked to the third day (20:5, 8). The effect is to make Hezekiah's request for a sign (20:8) unnecessary, though consistent with the picture at 20:10 of a king choosing to request more difficult things.

The odd way in which the tradition has been built up in Kings argues for the essential originality of the Isaiah tradition, at least in 38:1–8.[35] Smelik's judgment that "the theme of the sign is well integrated in the Isaiah-account and only added in the Kings version" is correct, but does not go far enough.[36] First, the tradition of the more difficult sign (2 Kgs 20:9–11) could never have existed without a prior tradition such as is found in Isa 38:7–8. That tradition is clearly presupposed in 20:9, where the phraseology of Isa 38:7 is employed

32. Ackroyd has done a good job noting the contrast between Hezekiah and Ahaz in Isa 36–39 and 6–8. Yet he fails to satisfactorily account for the different portrayals of Hezekiah in Isa 38 and 2 Kgs 20:1–12, in respect of this issue, because of the priority he gives to the Kings tradition. Thus he wonders: "Did the compiler responsible for the Isaiah form of this text modify the story to remove elements from its already familiar [? 2 Kings] form which he felt to be unsuited to its function in the book of Isaiah, to draw out this contrast between Ahaz and Hezekiah?" ("Structure and Function," 18).
33. There is no request in Isaiah (38:7), and no linkage of the sign with both temple visit and healing. Rather, the sign serves as a confirmation of a promise made to the king in 38:5–6.
34. RSV translates the Hebrew verbs in question (wayyō'mer in vv. 21, 22) with the pluperfect, thereby linking the sign of 38:22 with the sign of 2 Kgs 20:8 ("Hezekiah also had said, what is the sign that I shall go up to the house of the LORD?"). This implies a critical reconstruction. The NEB dispenses with this subtlety and simply transposes the two verses between vv. 6 and 7. But this ignores the fact that in the Kings tradition, we had already been told that Hezekiah would go up to the temple in three days. The further request for a sign, given the clearly stipulated three-day wait, is to be contrasted with the force of the question at 38:22. A simple transposition will not work, and use of the pluperfect is open to the same criticism.
35. So Wildberger, *Jesaja*, 1446.
36. "Distortion," 72.

almost exactly (*zeh-lĕkā hā'ôt mē'ēt YHWH kî ya'ăśeh YHWH 'et-haddābār 'ăśer dibbēr*), and yet in a manner that is inappropriate as an introduction to a question (*hālak haṣṣēl 'eśer ma'ălôt 'im-yāśûb 'eśer ma'ălôt*).

Moreover, the move to conflate two different signs from the Isaiah tradition (38:7 and 38:22) is explicable only from the direction of Isaiah to Kings, and not the reverse. Most regard Isa 38:21–22 as an attempt to preserve the tradition of a medical procedure and a trip to the temple, better integrated in Kings, once the Psalm of Hezekiah was brought into play.[37] That the account would end with a question is especially troubling to commentators.[38] Wildberger finds it puzzling that Hezekiah would ask for a sign at 38:22, as though the sign of the shadow had no effect on him at all.[39] But here Wildberger proceeds as though the tradition of a single sign (in Kings) were not a conflation. And yet he rightly regards the Isaiah tradition as original (in 38:1–8), lacking any mention of a sign associated with the temple visit. Isa 38:21–22 was added subsequent to the development of the parallel Kings account:

> A reader must have noted that the motif of Hezekiah's swift visit to the temple was missing in the Isaiah version and therefore supplied in a corresponding note in the margin, which then was inserted in the text at an inappropriate point. [*Jesaja*, 1447]

Variations of this "omission restored" theory to account for 38:21–22 are held by other interpreters. Still others speak of an original tradition below both Kings and Isaiah, comprised of just vv. 1 and 21, about "how the prophet Isaiah came to king Hezekiah, who was fatally ill, and healed him by application of figs to his body."[40] To this was then added a tradition of the miraculous sign, and finally the psalm was brought into play. Such a view of matters regards the sense of the material in its final form, in either Kings or Isaiah, as wholly controlled by the tradition process itself; one is not entitled to view the logic of the final form of the material as a matter of fundamental concern to that same tradition process.

In essential agreement with Wildberger, I regard the Isaiah tradition as the better preserved account (in 38:1–8), over against 2 Kgs 20:1–11. Yet I disagree with his assessment of Isa 38:21–22 as a mechanically introduced restoration of verses from Kings, essentially for reasons of preservation, for the

---

37. Isa 38:21–22 is "a later addition based on 2 Kgs xx 7,8" (Smelik, "Distortion," 88, n. 20). "It would appear that some later scribe, conscious that this element was missing, copied in here the relevant words from 2 Kings 20.7 and with them the opening of v. 8, in a slightly different and abbreviated form" (Ackroyd, "Babylonian Exile," 343, n. 3). Wildberger adopts a similar explanation (*Jesaja*, 1447).

38. Kaiser says: "Finally v. 22 must appear completely meaningless, unless we decide to translate it: 'Then Hezekiah said, What a sign for me to go up (once again) to the house of Yahweh'" (*Isaiah 13–39*, 400).

39. *Jesaja*, 1446.

40. Kaiser, *Isaiah 13–39*, 401; Würthwein, *Die Bücher der Könige. 1 Kön.17–2.Kön.25* (ATD 11,2; Göttingen: Vandenhoeck & Ruprecht, 1984) 433.

following reasons. First, I have noted the intrusive quality of both (1) the three-day temple visit notice (20:5), and (2) the medical remedy (20:7) in the Kings version. Their inclusion is explicable, however, on the grounds that the question of Hezekiah in 20:8 is thereby made to enhance the role of Isaiah. The prophet promises that he will heal Hezekiah and that he will be able to go to the temple in three days (20:5). The prophet then makes a medical prescription (20:6). Then the prophet brings off a difficult sign (20:11). In all these ways the focus shifts to a prophet who is able to heal, no matter what the odds.

While the story is explicable in its present form, it could not have achieved that form without the tradition of Isa 38:21–22, which it has utilized in its own intriguing way. Hezekiah's final question (38:22) is given an answer and converted into a statement from the prophet Isaiah, associated with his promise to heal. The medical procedure is moved to a location close to the promise of new life and delivery of the city, even though Hezekiah continues to press the prophet about the need for a sign—now involving both healing and the temple visit (about which he had already been informed at 20:5). Such transpositions and transformations are explicable from the direction of Isa 38:21–22, especially when the priority of Isa 38:1–8 is granted over 2 Kgs 20:1–11, but not from the direction of 2 Kgs 20:1–11 back to 38:21–22. Why did a reader zealous to preserve tradition not just insert it after the manner of 2 Kgs 20:1–11? Why was a statement converted into a question? Why was the medical procedure placed before the temple inquiry? These and other questions surround the theory of mechanical preservation at Isa 38:21–22. Naturally, then, the burden of proof lies with the establishment of a rationale for these verses in their present location in the Isaiah tradition.

Isaiah 38:21–22

These verses are commonly understood as having been inserted into Isaiah on the basis of the parallel Kings report. They should therefore either be transposed into the earlier Isaiah narrative, between vv. 6–7,[41] or treated as a retrospective, somewhat akin to the function of *'ănî 'āmartî* in the Psalm of Hezekiah (38:10).[42] They report what Isaiah *had* said, after the oracle at 38:6, and what Hezekiah *had* said, after the medical remedy had been prescribed. The problems with such a reconstruction were pointed out above. In either case, the verses are essentially regarded as not in their proper location. While the pluperfect translation may leave the verses in their present location, one should not regard the transposition solution as bolder or really different in kind. Both moves are an attempt to solve a problem that is conceded to exist.

Can the Isaiah tradition, including these verses, be meaningfully inter-

---

41. See for example Wildberger's synoptic Hebrew text (*Jesaja*, 1492).
42. So RSV translation. On the other hand, the annotation recommends transposition, so both options are available to the reader.

preted? I have already noted the tendency among some scholars to regard Isa 38:1–8 as an essentially unified and seamless narrative. Hezekiah is sick to the point of death; Isaiah's oracle confirms that he will not recover (38:1). Hezekiah responds in prayer and weeps bitterly (38:2–3). A fresh oracle confirms that Hezekiah's prayer has been heard, and that he and the city will be delivered (38:4–6). Then a sign is given to show that YHWH intends to do as he has promised (38:7–8). I noted above that a similar sequence can be seen in the previous chapter, in more extended form: royal prayer (37:16–20); positive prophetic response (37:21) and oracle promising deliverance (37:22–29); sign (37:30).[43] It is the Kings tradition that introduces the notion of Hezekiah *requesting* a sign, even after he had already been told he would go up to the temple in three days. The language of 38:7 (*wězeh-lěkā hā'ôt*) is clearly related to 37:30 (*wězeh-lěkā hā'ôt*), while it forms an odd introduction to a question in 2 Kgs 20:9.[44]

As in chapter 37, however, the recovery of the king-city does not take place simultaneously with the issuance of the oracle, or the provision of the sign. The sign is to confirm that YHWH will do the thing YHWH has promised he will do (38:7), *but has not yet done.* Only in the Kings' tradition, where the medical remedy is prescribed *before* the sign, might one be entitled to speak of a healing of the king—and even there the transpositions have created a sufficiently dense text so that this is not so clear.

But in the Isaiah tradition, no healing has taken place. There has only been a removal of the death sentence spoken by the prophet earlier (38:1). The reversal of the divine sentence of death is significant in and of itself. Sufficient light should be allowed to fall on the sentence of new life and the promise of fifteen extra years; these should not be preempted by assumptions of healing as such. Similarly, the city is not delivered in chapter 37 with the speaking of the taunt song or the delivery of the oracle promising deliverance (37:33–36)—an oracle whose language (*wěgannôtî 'al-hā'îr hazzō't*) again is closely connected with the promise made to an ill Hezekiah (*wěgannôtî 'al-hā'îr hazzō't*) at 38:6. The city is not actually delivered until after the prayer, the oracle, and the sign have been given, in the final verses of the chapter (37:36–38).

A problem is potentially created by the so-called superscription (38:9) to the Psalm of Hezekiah (38:10–34), which speaks of Hezekiah surviving his sickness (*miktāb lěḥizqiyyāhû melek-yěhûdāh baḥǎlōtô wayḥî mēḥolyô*). Yet this problem belongs to the wider problem of the psalm itself, and the rationale for its placement in Isaiah. That problem will be addressed shortly. On the other hand, the superscription does not necessarily frustrate a scenario

43. See p. 87.
44. See above, p. 181.

whereby Hezekiah had not yet been healed. Here too the distinction between thanksgiving for a death sentence being removed and actual healing should be maintained. The problems associated with genre designation for the psalm itself (thanksgiving; lament; petition; atoning poem) may have to do in part with a failure to adequately account for this distinction.[45] The psalm contains no explicit reference to healing, and in fact includes ardent request for the same (38:16).[46] Hezekiah's life has been held back from the pit of destruction (38:17), and for this he can give thanks (38:19). But the bulk of the psalm is a retrospective on severe illness (38:10–15), followed by thanksgiving for remaining among the living. It is not clear that actual healing from that illness has occurred by the psalm's end. In this the psalm stands in some contrast to other thanksgivings with which it is frequently compared, where the deliverance is more clearly and fully accomplished (Jo 2:1–9). In the case of several of the psalms, it is clear that a distinction exists between hearing God's verdict for life and full recovery from illness as such (esp. Pss 22, 31, 41).

If this is the case, then the insertion of the psalm does not upset the movement from oracle, to sign, to deliverance. Rather, it focuses on Hezekiah's memory of his near death state, and his thanksgiving for having had a death sentence removed. Isa 38:21–22 picks up where the narrative had left off in 38:8. Isaiah prescribes a remedy for the illness, termed *haššĕḥîn*, so that Hezekiah might recover. Hezekiah's final response is unrelated to the previous sign tradition (38:7–8). He asks what the sign will be that he might go up to the temple. In this, he is depicted as the consistently pious king, who inquires of the prophet when his state of uncleanness will be sufficiently gone, that he might again enter the temple—from which he was perforce absent during his death illness and his prayer ("he turned his face to the wall, and prayed to the LORD," 38:2). Failure to distinguish between the divine promise of new life (38:5–6) and Hezekiah's full recovery from illness has led to (1) confusion regarding the genre of the psalm (38:9–20) and (2) unnecessary transposition of the final verses, on the basis of a derivative Kings tradition. In fact, it is

---

45. Kaiser's translation and discussion point up the problems in the history of the discussion (*Isaiah 13–39*, 398; 403–7). He emends *miktāb* to *miktām* and translates "atoning poem" on the basis of headings to Ps 16 and Pss 56–60, and LXX (*proseuche*) (see also Duhm, *Jesaia*, 255; Wildberger, *Jesaja*, 1442). Then in his discussion he defines the category of the psalm "an individual psalm of thanksgiving" (404). At the same time he acknowledges that the opening *'ănî 'āmartî* does not require a past tense translation (as in "thanksgiving" classifications), and that the poem does not begin in a way typical for either a lamentation or a psalm of thanksgiving. Gesenius opted for *Danklied* (*Jesaia*, 978); Stade (*contra* Gesenius) "lediglich als Bittlied, als Hülfruf des Erkrankten" ("Miscellen," 185); Duhm for *Bittgebet* (*Jesaia*, 255); Begrich for *Danklied* (*Der Psalm des Hiskia: Ein Beitrag zum Verständnis von Jesaja 38,10–20* [FRLANT 25; Göttingen: Vandenhoeck & Ruprecht, 1926]). Westermann is most honest when he concludes that the psalm of Hezekiah, as with many of the psalms, is "on the way from petition or supplication and lament to praise" (*The Praise of God in the Psalms* [Richmond: John Knox, 1965] 80).

46. Stade, "Miscellen," 185.

difficult to imagine that any serious difficulty would have been seen in the Isaiah tradition—even ending with a question as it does—were it not for the existence of similar but slightly divergent material in 2 Kgs 20:1–11.

The Psalm of Hezekiah (38:9–20)

Mention has already been made of the problems associated with the interpretation of this psalm, and especially of its genre classification. It will not serve our purpose to enter that debate in any detail. I have made note of the fact that the classification "thanksgiving" is appropriate, so long as the fluidity of the genre is kept in mind,[47] and the peculiar shape of this particular psalm is not lost sight of. Interpreters have long made note of the fact that the descriptions of absolute release from distress are hardly overwhelming; at a minimum, the psalm makes sure to balance them with full description of the distress itself. The petition character of the psalm (38:16) is not lost even as thanksgiving breaks through (38:19). Whatever their diachronic relationship, the content of the psalm does not render the description of healing (38:21–22) obsolete, or force one to consider the final verses misplaced.

At the same time, two features can be spotted that raise the question more specifically about the precise relationship between the psalm and the final unit (vv. 21–22). There is no doubt that with 38:9 a new unit begins; similarly, 38:21–22 is properly understood as standing outside the psalm proper. Has the psalm been inserted into a continuous narrative running from 38:1–8 to 38:21–22? The two features that complicate the question are the similar phraseology in (1) 38:9 (*baḥălōtô wayḥî mēḥolyô*) and 38:21 (*wĕyeḥî*); and (2) 38:20 (*'al-bêt YHWH*) and 38:22 (*'e'ĕleh bêt YHWH*). Moreover, the translation of the superscription (38:9) and its relationship to the psalm proper figure into this question.

I have rejected the theory that the final verses (21–22) were simply added in order to preserve verses from the parallel Kings account. The logic of the theory is fairly strained. Isa 38:1–8 contains the core tradition; 2 Kgs 20:1–11 represents an expanded tradition; vv. 21–22 are added still later to Isa 38, once the tradition of 2 Kings was sufficiently fixed, so as to make their omission needful of remedy in the more "original" Isaiah tradition. The awkwardness of such a literary expansion ("Isaiah had said" . . . "Hezekiah also had said") stands in considerable contrast to similarly motivated redactional expansion in biblical narrative in general, and in Isa 36–39 in particular.[48] The transposition theory has some better claim to precedence (move vv. 21–22 between 38:6 and 38:7), though this sounds like a solution in search of a problem. It

---

47. See Westermann, *Praise of God*, 80.
48. One thinks of arguments for the secondary addition of the taunt song (Isa 37:22–29), or Hezekiah's prayer (37:16–20), or the report of the angel of death (37:36).

works better with the Kings tradition in a position of priority. Yet how did the verses get separated in Isaiah? And why are they in a slightly different form (compare 38:22 with 2 Kgs 20:5)?

I have argued above for a distinction between the reversal of a death sentence (so 38:5) and the promise of deliverance (so 38:6), on the one hand, and full recovery from illness, on the other. The distinction is important for appreciating the coherence of the Isaiah tradition of Hezekiah's illness, rooted in the narrative portions of text (38:1–8, 21–22). It is also important for understanding the genre of the psalm proper (38:10–20), over which there has been considerable debate. The psalm does offer thanksgiving for being held back from death (38:17–19). But it also contains a full description of the illness unto death (38:10–16) that was referred to in the opening of the narrative tradition (38:1). Full recovery from illness is a matter of grave concern in the psalm (38:16: *wĕtaḥălîmēnî wĕhaḥăyēnî*), even as the final verse looks forward to full life and participation in the temple community.[49]

At a minimum, then, it is incorrect to translate the superscription as though it sets the entire action of the psalm *after* healing has taken place.[50] RSV resolves all possible tension in the psalm by rendering 38:9: "A writing of Hezekiah king of Judah, after he was sick and had recovered from his sickness." Wildberger is unwilling to go this far.[51] By placing the action of the psalm completely in the past, no genre interpretation is possible except thanksgiving. The psalm is made to work as though it formed a precise parallel to Jo 2:2–9, where the *act* of deliverance is clearly set prior to the psalm (2:1), and where the content of the psalm immediately declares it to be a thanksgiving (2:2–3) for a rescue now past. The psalm of Hezekiah lacks both of these features. Significantly, neither does the psalm of Jonah have a superscription.

By rendering the explanatory phrase (*baḥălōtô wayḥî mēholyô*) in the manner of Duhm and Wildberger, 38:9 functions to describe the content of the psalm, not to rigidly fix its content temporally for means of determining its genre. The translation "when he was sick and lived beyond his sickness" describes the content of the psalm in its entirety, in its movement from

---

49. The first hemistich is unclear (*YHWH lĕhôšî'ēnî*). Begrich, followed by Duhm (399) and tentatively by Wildberger (*Jesaja*, 1445), inserts a finite verb (*hô'îl*) "was pleased"—not surprisingly with a past tense significance necessary for his thanksgiving genre (*Psalm des Hiskia*, 50). Targum also provides a verb (*YHWH lmprqn' 'mr*), producing a reading somewhat more consistent with our interpretation: "YHWH has spoken for healing." The Targum reading thus allows the final verse of the psalm to work in conjunction with the following two verses (38:21–22). YHWH has commanded healing; in v. 21, the prophet gives a command for the king's restitution.

50. In agreement with Duhm (*Jesaia*, 255), who adds with respect to 38:10: "'I said' does not mean that the poet has spoken and already the time has passed and he is once again healthy; he has spoken and made his complaint and he continues to do so even now."

51. "Als er krank war und von seiner Krankheit wieder genas" (*Jesaja*, 1440). Duhm renders: "als er krank war und wurde von seiner Krankheit gesund" (*Jesaia*, 255).

description of sickness (38:10–15), to petition for health (38:16), to thanksgiving for life out of death (38:17–19). The final verse, with its clear reference to future life (*kol yĕmê ḥayyênû*), circumscribes the movement at its final stage. Hezekiah was sick, and he has lived through that sickness. The superscription functions to describe the content of the psalm, not to fix it at one point in time.[52] In many respects it seems more closely connected to the content of the psalm than do many of the Psalter superscriptions. This argues against a more radical view of its secondary character, whereby a completely artificial setting is provided for a psalm whose origins lay elsewhere.

This moves us back to the question of 38:21–22. Has the psalm (and superscription) been spliced into a continuous narrative, or has 38:21–22 been added to the psalm? In my view, the question cannot be answered definitively. As in chapters 36–37, the tradition in chapter 38 appears to have developed gradually and incrementally. I shall put forward one likely scenario for that development, mindful of tendencies I have spotted elsewhere in the growth of the Hezekiah-Isaiah narrative traditions.

A narrative account of Hezekiah's illness was composed with a focus on new life out of death, for both king and city (38:1–8). The psalm provided further focus on the royal illness as such, as distinct from the fate of the city, and went on to speak of the king's full return to the life of praise in the temple (38:20). Yet that return to full health was not described in narrative form, as was the sickness itself (38:1–8). Isa 38:21 serves the purpose of directly narrating the prophet's prescription for healing. The deathly disease is specifically mentioned for the first time (*haššĕḥîn*). The remedy is to produce the health (*wĕyeḥî*) spoken of in the psalm's superscription. The final verse picks up on the last line of the psalm, which spoke of playing stringed instruments (*ûnĕginôtay nĕnaggēn*) at the house of YHWH "all the days of our life." Hezekiah obediently asks the prophet what the sign will be that he has sufficiently recovered to live out the promise made in the psalm, that he would spend his days praising God in the temple. Though the tradition process has come to an end in a way that strikes some as odd, it is not at all difficult to understand its development.

In sum, I lean toward viewing the final verses as occasioned by the content of the psalm (38:9–20) and the narrative itself (38:1–8). They speak of the direct healing of the king by the prophet, and of the king's obedient response. As such, the final verses, and the entire chapter, continue to give even attention to king and prophet, and to the necessity for their complementary functions. This is one more instance in which themes held in common by chapter 38 and chapters 36–37 are evidenced. It is to that commonality that we now turn.

---

52. Compare the superscription of Ps 34 with that of Ps 18.

TRADITION-HISTORY:
AN ALTERNATIVE RECONSTRUCTION

In agreement with tradition-historical reconstructions, I view chapter 38 in its present form as standing at the end of a gradual process of growth and literary accumulation. The psalm of Hezekiah is not an autograph from the king, and the stylized report of a death sentence reversed is more than a camera shot of dire medical circumstances in Hezekiah's fourteenth year. The same can be said of the narratives in chapters 36–37, whose point of origin is difficult to determine, and whose precise development is difficult to reconstruct.

In those Hezekiah-Isaiah narratives, I objected to the starting point frequently assigned for the tradition process: an objective, historically reliable three-verse account in 2 Kgs 18:14–16. Such a view of the tradition process believed that a point of origin could be recovered in historical events, to which portions (even minimal ones) of the present narrative gave testimony, in contrast to more subjective, theologically motivated portions. I questioned such a distinction, even as I argued for a closer connection to historical events than some would hold, and even as I saw that connection more evenly distributed throughout the present two-chapter account, without regard for the customary A/B1/B2 model of evolutionary growth (so recently Goncalves, Clements, Dion). The theory that 2 Kgs 18:14–16 provided a special glimpse at "what really happened in 701" was rejected (so also Provan, Hardmeier). Equally forcefully rejected was the notion that Isa 36–37 (or 2 Kgs 18:13—19:37) bore little or no connection with the events of 701—an increasingly popular view from a variety of proponents, for a wide variety of reasons (Smelik, Hardmeier, Kaiser, Clements).

A similar view of the tradition process is also seen to exist in the account of Hezekiah's illness (Isa 38:1–22; 2 Kgs 20:1–11). Kaiser's view is typical, in that he regards the starting point for the account of Hezekiah's illness, like the account of Jerusalem's deliverance, as tied to a small kernel of tradition, which referred to real events in history. From this small kernel (event-origin) the tradition developed. Speaking in the context of Isa 38, he says:

> For example, if we read v. 1, break off after "and said to him" and immediately go on to v. 21 without the introduction, we have a very short but coherent episode which lacks only an account of the success of the treatment. A glance at 2 Kgs 20.7 shows that this can easily be found in the received text. . . . Thus we conjecture that the story once told how the prophet came to king Hezekiah, who was fatally ill, and healed him by the application of figs to his body. [*Isaiah 13–39*, 401]

Incidentally, I would agree with Kaiser that the movement from v. 1 to v. 21 is quite logical (see the preceding section), even as I disagree that all intervening tradition needs to be stripped away, in order to get at the "very short but coherent" core episode that enshrines a story with roots in oral history. Such a reconstruction might be termed classic traditio-historical.[53]

I would argue that the origins of the story are at once simpler and more complex than Kaiser had imagined. About the historical roots of an actual Hezekiah illness it is difficult to conjecture, especially if this means extrapolating from the present narrative the precise contours of that original oral or literary story, in the manner of Kaiser (e.g., 38:1 + 21).[54] The present, coherent shape of the narrative account has obliterated all trace of any such original contours. Here the distinction between psalm (38:9–20) and narrative proper (38:1–8), for example, is of an altogether different order than between original oral story (38:1 + 21) and later narrative elaboration (38:1–8, 21–22). Moreover, Kaiser may be overly optimistic about his ability to discover where the narrative really touches down in terms of historical referentiality ("how the prophet Isaiah came to King Hezekiah, who was fatally ill, and healed him"). At issue here is whether the story of Hezekiah's illness ever circulated independently of the motif of the city's deliverance (38:5–6). Is this rather unusual feature an integral part of the tradition, or has it simply been tacked onto a more original, brief story about a sick Hezekiah—a story rooted in actual history?

The question is an important one because of the close connection that presently exists between chapter 38 and the preceding Hezekiah-Isaiah narratives (36–37). The connections are patent: (1) the opening temporal indicator; (2) the sequence threat/prayer/oracle/sign/deliverance, familiar from the 701 assault story; (3) the sustained interest in a balanced Hezekiah-Isaiah (king-prophet) portrayal; and (4) explicit language linkages (38:6 and 37:35). Viewed from this cumulative perspective, it is difficult to conceive of a narrative with these features stripped away, except as a purely hypothetical construct. They form the essential warp and woof of the story (38:1–8). Is there another way to view the origin of the Hezekiah illness tradition, not so much event-generated as text-generated? At this point another link with chapters 36–37 comes into view.

The final verses of chapter 37 speak of the death of Sennacherib in the house of his god (37:37–38) in fulfillment of the oracle at 37:7: "I will make him fall by the sword in his own land." Sennacherib appears to escape the death sentence that overtook his army (37:36), only to be killed by his own sons (37:38), in his own land, "as he worshiped in the house of his god." The

---

53. For a similar move in Kings, see also E. Würthwein: "Die Heilungslegende war ursprünglich sehr kurz; in sie eingearbeitet sind die leicht als dtr erkennbaren v.2b.3a.4–5" (*Bücher der Könige*, 433). Both Kaiser and Würthwein suggest an emendation of the final "that he may recover" (38:21; 2 Kgs 20:7) to "and he recovered" in order to make the original story end on a conclusive note. Emendations belong to the climate of classic traditio-historical reconstruction.
54. Requiring emendation of the final *wĕyeḥî* (38:21).

Hezekiah-Isaiah narratives have in central focus the victory of YHWH over the gods of the nations and their blasphemous representatives. A contrast is set up between the one God who delivers and those gods who are no gods, doomed to fail along with their worshipers (37:10–20).

That contrast is extended, in my view, into chapter 38, with its depiction of King Hezekiah. He too faces a death sentence, but unlike Sennacherib he is delivered. His prayer turns back the sentence of death, where Sennacherib is executed by his own sons while worshiping in the house of his god. The death sentence from which he appeared to be exempted was enforced by his own house. Hezekiah is charged to give command concerning his house (*ṣaw lĕbêtekā*), for he is soon to die (38:1). But his prayer—far from leading to death "in the house of his god"—leads finally to the promise of praise there, all the days of his life. The final question of the king points ahead to his final return to the temple, not for death but for life.

A close formal parallel to Isa 38:1–8 is found at Jer 45:1–5, in particular as they share a similar interest in temporal flexibility (45:1; 38:1) at the service of narrative depiction.[55] At the end of the prose tradition (Jer 37–44), after Baruch had followed Jeremiah into Egypt, a narrative appears that is temporally situated years earlier "when Baruch wrote these words in a book at the dictation of Jeremiah, in the fourth year of Jehoiakim" (45:1). Clearly the intent is to link this final narrative with one appearing much earlier (chap. 36) for important thematic reasons, even at the risk of upsetting the chronological movement of the prose tradition in its present configuration. So too, Isa 38:1–8 is situated as though the sickness of the king was coterminous with the "sickness of the city" (38:5–6), even as it uses for its literary point of departure the full narrative in its completed form, which has gone ahead to report the death of Sennacherib (37:36–38). This final report has provided the starting point for the development of the tradition regarding Hezekiah's illness. The opening "in those days" (38:1) functions in a similar manner to the rubric in Jer 45:1. Here, however, the narratives to which the author of 38:1–8 would direct our attention precede directly (chaps. 36–37), where in Jeremiah they are separated by extensive prose tradition (chaps. 37–44).

Both Jer 45 and Isa 38 have their point of origin not so much in events to which the narrative refers, nor in a small kernel of tradition that can be extrapolated from the present form of the narrative. Neither Jer 45:1–5 nor Isa 38:1–8 gives evidence at the literary level of that kind of multilayered quality. It is highly unlikely that lying below Jer 45:1–5 is an original, recoverable conversation that took place between Jeremiah and Baruch. Such an interpretation misreads the intent of the narrative within its present redactional framework, and misunderstands its real point of origin.[56] It is far more

---

55. See my discussion of Jer 45 in "The Prophet Moses," 18–24.
56. Representative of this form of approach is A. Weiser, "Das Gottewort für Baruch. Jer. 45 und die sogenannte Baruchbiographie," in *Glaube und Geschichte im Alten Testament* (Göttingen:

likely that Jer 45:1–5 was composed as a whole piece with a specific editorial function, and that it never had any other function.[57] Moreover, its composition took place with an eye toward other narratives in the Jeremiah prose tradition, especially Jer 36, but also the immediately preceding prose tradition (37–44) and the oracles concerning nations (MT: 46–51).

Here is where the analogy with Isa 38:1–8 is apt. The "tradition" of Hezekiah's illness originated in reference to and under the influence of the Hezekiah-Isaiah narratives, and especially the immediately preceding notice of Sennacherib's death (37:36–38). I have noted other formal correlations that have been structured into the brief narrative account. By far the most important for a continuous reading of Isa 36–38 is the temporal indicator "in those days." Like the reference to the famous fourth year of Jehoiakim in Jer 45:1, the opening *bayyāmîm hāhēm* functions to situate the narrative at the same point in time as events depicted in the preceding chapters, and to invite mutual influencing between the two stories. Both report situations of dire threat and near death sickness. Both hold king and prophet in equal focus. Both tell of a gracious deliverance prompted by the prayer of the king and confirmed by prophetic word and sign.

Clearly the second briefer account has been composed on the basis of the fuller Hezekiah-Isaiah narratives in 36–37, and not the reverse.[58] Here is another instance where the tradition-process, understood as text-generated, need not proceed from brief to full, or from kernel to "mature" growth. Of special interest to the derivative depiction of Isa 38:1–8 is the conflation of king and city (38:6). Interpreters are correct to see the oracle in 38:6 as based upon 37:35. The common language is a dead giveaway. But this is not an argument for its "secondary" nature within chapter 38, except insofar as *all* of 38:1–8 is secondary and based upon the preceding narratives. The language of the preceding chapter has been intentionally reused, and reused in precisely the same form (*wĕgannôtî ʿal-hāʿîr hazzōʾt*), in order that the dependence of chapter 38 on 36–37 not be missed and that the connection between king and city be underscored. Isa 38:1 and 38:6 mean to situate the narrative world (Hardmeier's *erzählte Situation*) "in those days"—the days of Assyrian assault—in order to emphasize the connection between Hezekiah and Zion.

Was Hezekiah ever fatally ill, as the narrative reports? In my judgment, the question can only be answered if one is prepared to strip away integral parts of the present narrative depiction. These make it clear that Hezekiah's

Vandenhoeck & Ruprecht, 1961) 326–29. Weiser does not posit tradition-critical layers in the text, even as he is confident about the text's origin in an oracle delivered by the prophet. Even attempts to strip away parts of the narrative are generally motivated by awareness of the temporal complexities in the account, more than by allegiance to a theory of comprehensive redaction (though see Thiel, *Redaktion*, 85).

57. See Seitz, "The Prophet Moses," 18–24.
58. The tradition of Hezekiah's illness never preceded the account of Jerusalem's deliverance, even hypothetically (cf. Smelik, "Distortion," 73).

sickness unto death is to be understood not in and of itself, as a separate historical datum, but only in relationship to the destiny of Zion. As such, the question of the historicity of Hezekiah's illness is misdirected. From its inception, the narrative understands the illness in relationship to the fate of the city, not in relationship to isolated *bruta facta*.

With respect to extensions of the base tradition within chapter 38 proper (38:9–22), I assume that a similar process of tradition building has taken place. As 38:1–8 has taken shape with reference to the Hezekiah-Isaiah narratives in 36–37, so too 38:9–20 and 38:21–22 have been composed with reference to the narrative of Hezekiah's illness, each addressing a separate facet of that illness (psalm of retrospection and thanksgiving; prescription for healing). In neither case is there strong evidence of great distance separating these two developments from the ground tradition. Similarly, there is no reason to date 38:1–8 or 38:1–22 much later than the Hezekiah-Isaiah narratives in 36–37. The Isaiah tradition had become sufficiently fixed, including the psalm and final report of healing, well before the rearrangements and modifications that characterize the Kings tradition at this point (2 Kgs 20:1–11). I regard those modifications as consistent with larger concerns in the DtrH at its final redactional stages, some of which have already been mentioned in the context of discussions of 2 Kgs 18:14–16 and 2 Kgs 20:12–19. More will be said about 2 Kgs 20:12–19 below, as conclusions are drawn concerning the function and placement of Isa 39:1–8 over against the Hezekiah-Isaiah material (36–38), and with respect to the Second Isaiah tradition that now follows in chapters 40–55.

A SICK CITY

I have argued that the linkage established within chapter 38 between Hezekiah and Jerusalem is intentional. Hezekiah receives a promise of fifteen additional years of life (38:5). God also promises to deliver him and the city from Assyrian threat, "and defend this city." The precise way in which these two promises are to be related is not spelled out. The first functions closely within the narrative logic: it comes as a response to Hezekiah's prayer (38:5), the content of which is provided in 38:3; it focuses on Hezekiah individually. If one had wished to mount the strongest case for the secondary quality of 38:6, based upon its interest in the fate of the city, it would have helped if 38:6 had made no reference to Hezekiah. Yet it opens with a promise directed to him, which links 38:6 to 38:5, before it proceeds to make reference (twice) to "this city":

> From the hand of the king of Assyria
> *mikkap melek-'aššûr*
> I will deliver you and this city
> *'aṣṣîlĕkā wĕ'ēt hā'îr hazzō't*

> And I will defend this city
> *wĕgannôtî 'al-hā'îr hazzō't*

The question facing the exegete is the degree to which Hezekiah's sickness is consciously linked to the "sickness" of the city. On the one hand, no explicit connection has been made. In 38:5 the text speaks to the issue of Hezekiah's prayer and Hezekiah's sickness unto death without reference to the city. At the same time, 38:6 immediately proceeds to speak of Hezekiah's deliverance from Assyrian threat, a deliverance that is of one piece with that of the city.

Similarly, in Hezekiah's psalm the focus rests on the king's individual state of wretchedness (38:9–15). At the same time, the first-plural reference at the psalm's conclusion ("we will play")—whatever its original function—indicates that the benefits of the king's recovery extend beyond himself.[59] The fate of the king is linked to the fate of the city and its citizenry. It is in this spirit that Sirach has interpreted chapters 36–38, when it reports the prayers of the wider population of Zion:

> Then their hearts were shaken and
>   their hands trembled,
> and they were in anguish, like
>   women in travail.
> But they called upon the LORD who
>   is merciful,
> spreading forth their hands
>   toward him;
> and the Holy One quickly heard
>   them from heaven,
> and delivered them by the hand
>   of Isaiah. [48:19–20]

The prayer that saved the city was not Hezekiah's alone, according to Sirach, even though this is the clear sense of the Hezekiah prayer tradition in 36–37 (37:16–20, 21). Similarly, it is Hezekiah's prayer that reverses a sentence of death in 38:2–5. Yet 38:6 envisions the deliverance of the king from sickness as having to do with the deliverance of the city "out of the hand of the king of Assyria." The linkage at 38:6 may be partly responsible for Sirach's working perspective. The fate of the king, sick unto death, was thought to be closely linked to the fate of the city.

It is here that the tradition of Hezekiah's illness reveals its central parabolic concern. In the Hezekiah-Isaiah narratives—which for obvious reasons must now be seen to extend into chapter 38—Judah's king has clearly been

---

59. The shift from singular to plural is not smooth in 38:20: *YHWH lĕhôšîʿēnî* ("me") *ûnĕginôtay nĕnaggen* ("we will play") *kol-yĕmê ḥayyênû* ("our lives"). But that a shift occurs is not to be disputed. See Wildberger for a thorough text-critical discussion (*Jesaja*, 1445–46).

portrayed in sharp contrast to Assyria's king: the prayer of one king saves a city; the "prayer" of another (37:38) finds its response in a sword of death. The contrast between YHWH and the other no-gods (37:17–20) has been sufficiently underscored in our prior discussion. A final contrast is to be seen at the level of the general populace, for whom the king is to stand as representative and defender. The Assyrian camp arose in the morning filled with dead bodies (37:36); but a near dead king received a sentence of new life—a sentence that finally involved not just himself, but the city as well. It is not surprising, then, that the plural reading appears at the conclusion of Hezekiah's psalm: "and we shall play (our) stringed instruments all the days of our life at the house of the LORD" (38:20).[60] Hezekiah looks forward to his new life in the temple in the company of other worshipers.

While the city shares in the recovery of the king, as a consequence of his prayer, what is to be said of the sickness motif—does it pertain to the city as well? The focus falls on royal sickness both in the narrative portions (38:1–5 and 38:21–22) and in the psalm itself (38:9–17). Yet ironically, Hezekiah's sickness is not depicted in such a way as to stress its relationship to sin or moral decay. In his prayer, Hezekiah reminds God "how I have walked before thee in faithfulness and a whole heart, and have done what is good in thy sight" (38:3). Nothing in the psalm would contradict such a portrayal. Even the reference to sins being cast behind the back (38:17) comes not in the context of confession or acknowledgment of past wrongs, but in the context of the thanksgiving for having been granted new life. The sickness itself (*haššĕḥîn*), referred to at 38:21, appears to have something of the same relationship to sin in Hezekiah's case as it does in the case of Job, smitten with the same affliction (see 2:7). It would not be overstating the evidence to say that Job is depicted in something of the same terms as Hezekiah. He is "blameless, upright, one who feared God and turned away from evil" (1:1). This is not a far remove from Hezekiah's self-description in the prayer, as one who walked before God faithfully, with a true heart, and did what was good in God's eyes. Both Hezekiah and Job are struck down with *haššĕḥîn*. In the latter case, Job's innocence is the explicit theme of the book. It is certainly an implicit theme in the case of Hezekiah.[61]

The irony is that while a sickness unto death appears unmerited in Hezekiah's case, the same could not be said of the wider populace delivered by that same king's intercession. At this point the relationship between the prose traditions under discussion (36–38) and the preceding poetic oracles

---

60. For consistent first-plural reference, read *nĕginôtēnû* instead of *nĕginôtay* (MT), in view of the following *nĕnaggēn* and *ḥayyênû* (so Wildberger, *Jesaja*, 1445). A simpler solution would be to drop the suffix altogether (*nĕginôt*).

61. See the interesting discussion of Ibn Ezra, in M. Friedländer, *The Commentary of Ibn Ezra on Isaiah* (New York: Philipp Feldheim, 1873) 167–68.

again comes to the fore. Consistent with the conclusions I reached in the context of evaluating 2 Kgs 18:14–16 over against Isa 36–37, I would argue that the portrayal of Hezekiah in 38:3 is not contradicted by the evidence of the poetic material. He is a king who according to the testimony of both prose and poetic tradition has "walked before thee in faithfulness and with a true heart, and done what is good in thy sight" (38:3).

But that sickness and moral decay infect all other levels of society is Isaiah's message in essence. The opening chapter, which has in clear view Zion's sparing (1:8–9), does not choose to view that deliverance except as a reminder of the judgment that fell elsewhere (1:7), and of the need for real repentance. The nation is sinful, laden with iniquity, full of evildoers (1:4)— and it continues to rebel and receive the proper punishment for it (1:5). The standing metaphor is sickness:

> The whole head is sick,
> > and the whole heart is faint.
> From the sole of the foot even to the head,
> > there is no soundness in it,
> but bruises and sores and
> > bleeding wounds;
> They are not pressed out, or bound up,
> > or softened with oil. [1:5b–6]

Debate about the proper diachronic reconstruction of chapter 1 is not likely to admit of resolution. Arguments have been put forward for a pre-701 date, a post-701 date, or a post-587 date—or some combination of all three— for the material in this key chapter (1:2–31).[62] The distinction made between Zion and the countryside at 1:7–9 does suggest a setting near 701; at the same time, there appears to be further movement in the chapter that takes into account the later 587 debacle, where such a distinction fell to the side (1:10–31). The faithful city became a harlot (1:21). The full redemption of Zion lies in the future (1:27).

Without moving to an analysis of the entire poetic tradition, or even one focused on chapter 1 as such, several conclusions can be reached with respect to the sickness motif in chapter 38. First, the focus remains on King Hezekiah, even as his recovery has an impact on the recovery of Jerusalem and its citizenry (38:6). The tradition has preserved brief reference to the wider effects of Hezekiah's new life (38:20). Second, Hezekiah's sickness has not been linked to prior sin in any explicit way. In my judgment, this is fully consistent with the view of Hezekiah preserved in the poetic tradition.[63] More-

---

62. For a recent attempt at reconstruction, see Sweeney, *Isaiah 1–4*, 101–33. Sweeney has 701 levels (1:2–9), pre-701 levels (1:10–18, 21–26), post-587 levels (1:19–20, 27–28), and "anonymous, late pre-exilic or exilic" (!) levels (1:29–31).
63. See above, chapter 3, 7th section.

over, Hezekiah's appeal to God based upon his past faithfulness (38:3), by its very synchronic location following the depiction of 36–37, invites an interpretation of the content of the appeal as related to his deportment in 36–37—even as the opening rubric of 38:1 locates the episode contemporaneous with those events. This is another instance where the temporal flexibility of Isa 38 resembles that of Jer 45.

Finally, while the city is not described in contrast to Hezekiah as meriting a death sentence and as afflicted by real sickness, the preceding poetic tradition invites such a comparison. This is true whatever the original scope of that tradition, so extensive is the prophetic theme of a nation diseased and awaiting judgment. Within the narrower scope of chapters 28–32, there is abundant evidence that the prophet addressed an Israel "sick unto death," and that as such "a decree of destruction from YHWH God of hosts" was to descend upon the whole land (28:22). In the midst of that cleansing judgment (28:15), the prophet also envisioned protection for those in Zion who believed (28:16) and returned in trust (30:15). Even those who erred in spirit would come to understanding, and those who murmured would accept instruction (29:24).

Hezekiah is depicted in chapter 38 as facing a death sentence, as *ḥālāh lāmût*. The psalm gives fuller expression to his anguish, cut off from the land of the living (38:11), consigned to the gates of Sheol (38:10). Yet Hezekiah is the faithful one (*hithallaktî lĕpānêkā be'ĕmet*), sound of heart (*bĕlēb šālēm*). His prayer here and in 37:16–20 has the power to divert a sentence of judgment—fully merited for the wider populace, unmerited in his own case, as one "who has done what is good in thy sight" (*haṭṭôb bĕ'ênêka 'āśîtî*). Hezekiah's weeping (38:3) is analogous to his behavior in 37:1–2. The psalm in 38:10–16 gives testimony to the actual content of his anguish. The prophet announces a sentence of new life for Hezekiah (38:5), whose consequence is deliverance for the city (38:6). The prophet sees to the king's final recovery (38:21). To the end, Hezekiah is portrayed as the obedient one, even to the extent of inquiring of Isaiah when he might return to the temple.[64] There he will praise God in the wider fellowship of an Israel delivered by his own prayer, and included by him when he says: "and we will play stringed instruments all the days of our life at the temple of YHWH" (38:20).

Although it stands to the side of our specific interest in the Hezekiah-Isaiah narratives (36–38), we would argue that the opening chapter of the Isaiah collection has been composed with an eye toward this prose material. The gracious sparing of Zion is cause for praise (38:20), but also for repentence

---

64. See the prescriptions of Lev 13. Sweeney (*Isaiah 1–4*, 15) sees the importance of the final question, but regards it as a redactional enhancement.

(1:2–20). The two are not in opposition, but are complementary. Zion's sparing (1:8–9) is itself an exhortation to:

> Wash yourselves; make yourselves clean;
>   remove the evil of your doings
>   from before my eyes;
> cease to do evil,
>   learn to do good. [1:18]

As the chapter proceeds to tell of the refusal to "be willing and obedient," as the conditioned promise had it (1:18), and of yet further sin and further judgment (1:21–31), one has the sense that the events of 701 have faded into the past, as the graceful deliverance and call for repentance went unheeded, leading to a correlation in the tradition process with later 587 judgment tradition. As such, Isa 1 gives evidence of the mature form of 701/587 correlation now permeating so-called First Isaiah chapters. In this role, Isa 1 serves as an introduction to the entire Isaiah collection. It shows an interest in Zion's final destiny, while the Hezekiah-Isaiah traditions (36–38) appropriately celebrate Zion's destiny at an earlier stage of resolution, calling for the kind of praise that should follow gracious deliverance and for a response of penitence and obedience, for which Hezekiah remains the supreme model.

In conclusion, chapter 38 does promote an identification between the king and the city, and in many respects this is its major contribution to the larger Hezekiah-Isaiah complex, whose foundation is to be seen in chapters 36–37. But the identification is not a flat one. The city's population is the beneficiary of an act of faith that is Hezekiah's alone. King and city share in the deliverance of 701 and in the opportunity for praise and thanksgiving. But Hezekiah's present and past faithfulness stand in contrast to that of Jerusalem's citizens, and of the wider population of Judah. The tradition has remembered Hezekiah as a unique figure, as a king truly reminiscent of David. Even the subsequent disobedience and sickness in Israel—and in the royal house— have not eradicated the tradition associated with King Hezekiah. By his prayer and obedience, he demonstrated what the prophet had in mind when he said:

> In returning and rest you shall be saved;
>   in quietness and in trust shall be your strength. [30:15]

In precisely this spirit, the Hezekiah-Isaiah narratives (Isa 36–38) have been constructed chiefly around the figure of Hezekiah. From the perspective of these narratives, Hezekiah was a king "who reigned in righteousness" (32:1).

With the psalm of Hezekiah, an early Proto-Isaiah collection was brought to a close, focusing on the piety (38:10–20) and obedience (38:22) of King Hezekiah. The frequent practice of placing poetic material toward the end of large tradition blocks (Gen 49; Deut 32–33) was adopted for the Proto-Isaiah material, by means of the psalm of the king (Isa 38:9–20). In this fashion, the analogy with King David—drawn explicitly by the Dtr Historian at 2 Kgs 18:3, 5—was formally structured into this early Isaiah collection (compare 2 Sam 22:1—23:7).

FINAL REMARKS: 2 KINGS 20:12–19 AND ISAIAH 39:1–8

In analyzing the wider complex 2 Kgs 18:13—20:19 (Isa 36–39), two tendencies have come into prominence in the history of exegesis. Most view the Isaiah material as secondarily developed on the basis of earlier tradition in Kings. In part because of the specific attention paid to the tradition complex in 2 Kgs 18:13—19:37 (cf. Isa 36–37) and the events of 701, the remaining material (2 Kgs 20:1–19; Isa 38–39) has been treated derivatively and as if it were essentially a single complex. It is clear that here too the priority given to Kings over Isaiah has influenced such a move, in a subtle but unmistakable way. After all, the episodes of Hezekiah's sickness (38:1–22) and the visit of ambassadors from Merodach-baladan (39:1–8) appear in a single chapter in Kings (20:1–19). The former is much reduced, thus allowing the "at that time" of 2 Kgs 20:12 to function in closer proximity to the "in those days" of 2 Kgs 20:1, which in turn permits two episodes with very little in common to unfold as though they were events occurring in sequence.

This suspicion is borne out by an examination of recent critical inquiry into Isa 38–39. The irony is that while the integrity of the Isaiah traditions as a collection (36–39) is vigorously defended, over against the comparable material in Kings, chapters 38–39 are basically treated as though they were composed as part of a single redactional effort and are understood to share an identical functional role in the larger Book of Isaiah. The context has shifted (Isaiah), but the reflex to treat the two episodes as one remains unaltered.

A major defender of Isaiah's special functional integrity has been Ackroyd. At one juncture he spelled out the practical limitations such a view of the priority of Kings has had:

> When writing a commentary on Isaiah for *The Interpreter's One-Volume Commentary*, I found myself put under restraint in writing on Isaiah 36–39, because, in the common view, these chapters belong in 2 Kings, and it is there that they will be fully handled. I was limited virtually entirely to points of difference, which meant little more than commenting on the psalm in 38. But this is to ignore what these chapters do to the book of Isaiah, how they function within it. ["Structure and Function," 15]

The contribution made to the study of Isaiah because of Ackroyd's call for a shift to a functional approach is beyond question. Yet with respect to chapters 38–39, the title and content of his earlier work are telling.[65] The bulk of the article is concerned with Isa 39, which is treated first and in detail.[66]

Several critical observations can be made about the design and intention of Ackroyd's approach. First of all, this chapter (39) is distinctive compared with Isa 36–37 and Isa 38, in that it is virtually identical to 2 Kgs 20:12–19. The divergences are quite minor and of an altogether different order than what was encountered at 2 Kgs 18:14–16 or Isa 38:9–22. So shifting the inquiry to Isaiah in the case of Isa 39 affects the larger contextual perspective, but that is all. Second, by treating Isa 38 and Isa 39 in the same article—and here the subtitle "A Study of 2 Kings 20" is significant—Ackroyd clearly means to stress that both chapters share a single redactional purpose, as though they formed one chapter (viz., 2 Kings 20). Yet quite unlike Isa 39, the story of Hezekiah's illness (38) goes its own way in Kings in contrast to Isaiah—due not just to the psalm, but for other reasons as well. Ackroyd judges the Kings tradition essentially superior.[67] It is in his analysis of the psalm—an addition made in Isaiah—that Ackroyd identifies the common redactional purpose spanning chapters 38 and 39:

> [The psalm's] climax is reached in a point which may be paralleled in other such psalms, the act of praise and worship in which the individual is joined by the community. Such a climax here provides a pointer to that longed-for restoration of the temple and its worship which is seen as the sequel to disaster in the fuller working out of that theme in the writings of the Chronicler. The illness of Hezekiah and the death sentence upon him thus become a type of judgement and exile, and in that measure they run parallel to the theme of judgement which is found in the ambassador story which follows.

Then Ackroyd also notes a contrast with chapter 39:

> But the theme of restored life and continuing rule which follows upon Hezekiah's strong appeal to the deity, is a pointer to the possibility of such a restoration for the community. ["Babylonian Exile," 345–46]

It is important to examine Ackroyd's conclusions in some detail, since his views on the common functional purpose of chapters 38–39 have been picked up and developed in more recent works. Clements has interpreted the inclusion of chapter 38° (that is, 2 Kgs 20:1–11) into the Isaiah complex (36–39) as part of a larger redactional concern "to re-establish a rationale for restoring the Davidic kingship and for rebuilding the Jerusalem temple in the wake of what happened to both institutions in 587 B.C.," also involving the B2 narra-

---

65. "An Interpretation of the Babylonian Exile: A Study of 2 Kings 20, Isaiah 38–39" (1974).
66. Isa 39: pp. 329–42; Isa 38: pp. 343–46.
67. "Babylonian Exile," 343, n. 3.

tive, Isa 14:24f. and 31:8.[68] Smelik agrees with the common function of Isa 38–39 within 36–39, even as he disagrees about what that function is, to the extent of arguing for the opposite *tendenz* from Clements.[69]

First, Ackroyd and Clements are in basic agreement that the redactional function of Isa 38 is revealed typologically. Ackroyd understands the sickness motif as related to exile, thus enabling him to locate the narrative diachronically after the events of 587. Note how obliquely the chapter makes its redactional point, in the final verse of the psalm (38:20). The return to the temple, interpreted above as having to do with Hezekiah's reversal of a death sentence involving the sickness of Israel, Ackroyd sees as "a pointer to that longed-for restoration of the temple and its worship." Yet how subtly the chapter reveals its redactional point of standing![70] Nothing in chapter 38 suggests the specific "death" of exile, nor is there any even oblique hint that the temple and its worship have come to an end. If anything, the opposite is true (see 38:20, 22). The problem, finally, is that Ackroyd's own reading is too subtle to be proved or disproved. That a later post-587 reading might have sensed something of "a longed-for restoration of the temple" at the conclusion of Hezekiah's prayer is not to be denied. But *relecture* is a different phenomenon than redactional composition.

Moreover, if Ackroyd's interpretation were granted, how different would be the redactional functions of chapters 38 and 39. Clements understands the purpose of the inclusion of chapter 38 as involving the fulfillment of the "proper spiritual conditions" necessary for YHWH's protection of Jerusalem "through the agency of a devout and obedient king of the Davidic royal house."[71] This is somewhat similar to Ackroyd's view. Yet Clements is certainly correct to avoid chapter 39 in the context of putting forward such a hypothesis, preferring to talk about the B2 narrative from Isa 36–37. For Ackroyd himself has rightly seen that chapter 39 has a very different final function in the Book of Isaiah than does Isa 38, especially in respect of Hezekiah.[72] While he may succeed in getting the sickness motif of chapter 38 to "run parallel to the theme of judgement found in the ambassador story which follows," chapter 39 does not end on a hopeful note even in his deft

68. "Central Passage," 261–62.
69. Isa 39 "predicts that the Davidic throne will not be restored to the Judaean throne" ("Distortion," 85); Isa 36–37 (38) tell of "the miraculous delivery of Jerusalem in contrast to the terrible fate Jerusalem met in Zedekiah's days" (86). Yet the narratives belong together as a group (36–39), serving as an "'editorial bridge' between the First and the Second Isaiah" (72).
70. Compare Hardmeier's carefully worked out argument for an *Erzählsituation* to be differentiated from the fictive *erzählte Situation* in Isa 36–37ᵃ.
71. "Central Passage," 261.
72. The most that can be said of Hezekiah in chapter 39 is that he is "an unwitting agent in bringing about the loss of the land" ("Babylonian Exile," 341). Ackroyd relies on the Chronicler for the final working out of Hezekiah's fate, as well as that of Manasseh. Chap. 39 is more centrally interested in "prophecy-fulfillment patterns" familiar from the DtrH. More on this below.

construal.[73] In the contributions of Ackroyd and Clements, chapter 38 is argued to have been composed with the purpose of pointing to restoration, after the events of 587 B.C.E. Chapter 39, whatever else is to be said about it, points to judgment, not restoration. It does so not metaphorically, nor in a veiled way, but by means of direct prophecy (39:5-7). Davidic kingship will come to an end, and Hezekiah's sons will be *sārîsîm* in the palace of the king of Babylon (39:7). In sum, it is difficult to see points of common redactional purpose spanning both of these chapters.[74]

The most obvious thing to be said about the relationship between Isa 38 and Isa 39—especially in an alleged redactional mode—is that Isa 39 is concerned with prophecy fulfillment in a direct sense, while no such function is to be identified in Isa 38. If Isa 38 is to be linked to the events of 587 B.C.E., Ackroyd and Clements are quite right to see that the linkage would have to be typological or symbolic. As such, Isa 38 reveals its internal logic as quite distinct over against that of Isa 39:1-8. For this and other reasons, Isa 39 belongs outside the tradition-historical orbit of the Hezekiah-Isaiah narratives (36-38). In Isa 39, the authority of the prophet over against the king comes into greater prominence than in 36-38. The pattern of prayer/oracle/sign/ deliverance familiar from 36-38 cannot be sustained, given the very different purpose of the chapter. And finally, it is surely no accident that in this episode no major divergences exist between Kings and Isaiah.[75] The significance of this can be explained with reference to the Hezekiah-Isaiah narratives in 36-38.

In an incisive piece of argumentation, Smelik promoted the priority of Isa 36-39 over the parallel Kings tradition by appeal to the logic of their arrangement—or better, their illogic.[76] In Smelik's estimation, a more appropriate order would have been sickness (38), Babylonian envoy (39), 701 deliverance (36-37). This order would have been consistent with the chronological principles of the DtrH. Departure from such principles is explicable in the context of Isaiah, where the Babylonian visit belongs last, before the following Second Isaiah material. Therefore, the "illogical" arrangement of Isa 36-39 is logical after a fashion, while the order of Kings is revealed to be essentially derivative and foreign to the larger principles of the DtrH.

How compelling is this argument for the priority of Isa 36-39? I noted above the danger of treating all three episodes as though they had a fixed sequence, confusing their respective histories of composition with their subsequent arrangement as a trilogy. Another objection must be lodged at this point. Smelik's argument suggests both that all three narratives require a

---

73. On this point see Smelik, "Distortion," 85.
74. In Kings this is somewhat easier, due to the more negative depiction of Hezekiah in 2 Kgs 20:1-11. As I shall show, such a move is explicable within the larger framwework of the DtrH, and is consistent with 2 Kgs 18:14-16.
75. Sweeney's evaluation of 2 Kgs 20:19 and Isa 39:8 is certainly oversubtle (*Isaiah 1-4*, 15-16).
76. "Distortion," 73-74.

common redactional explanation, and that as a group the logic of their placement is foreign to Kings. Here the proper understanding of the distinction
between Isa 38 and Isa 39 is critical.

There is every evidence that Isa 39 (= 2 Kgs 20:12–19) conforms quite
well to the larger logic and purpose of the DtrH. It is not to be denied that Isa
39 serves an important purpose in the Book of Isaiah, as a preface to 40–55; I
would argue that both in terms of composition and placement, here again it
shows itself to be distinctly different from 36–38.[77] But it would be wrong to
suggest that 2 Kgs 20:12–19 is not explicable as the final narrative in a three-
episode complex within the movement of the DtrH (so Smelik). The point is:
its position is completely logical in both contexts, and that is why alone among
the three narratives it gives no evidence of major divergences in either setting.
The two narratives (Isa 39:1–8 and 2 Kgs 20:12–19) are identical.[78] The same is
not true of Isa 36–37 and 2 Kgs 18:13—19:37, much less Isa 38:1–22 and 2 Kgs
20:1–11. This is another reason to make a distinction between the Hezekiah-
Isaiah narratives (36–38) and the final Merodach-baladan episode (Isa 39; 2
Kgs 20:12–19). In the context of the Book of Isaiah, the narrative belongs in
close proximity to the Second Isaiah material, in redaction and tradition-
critical terms. But this does not mean that 2 Kgs 20:12–19 is foreign to the
DtrH.

Before pursuing this last issue, our findings will be summarized with
respect to Isa 36–38. I would agree with Smelik that the order of Isa 36–37 and
38 is (1) somewhat peculiar within the movement of the DtrH, but (2) fully
explicable in the context of Isaiah. I have argued that the order in Isaiah (36–
37 + 38) has been intentionally structured so as to emphasize the relationship
of Hezekiah to the fate of the city. The order also reveals the direction of the
development of the traditions concerning the events of 701, Zion and Hezekiah. In my view, the Hezekiah-Isaiah narratives (36–38) were integrated into
Kings relatively soon after their composition.[79] In order to function in that
context—and here Smelik is right to view the Book of Isaiah as the primary
context, insofar as 36–38 are concerned—they were prefaced with an introduction (2 Kgs 18:1–8), familiar from other points in the DtrH. But this
introduction was also quite distinctive. That distinctiveness is traceable to the
core tradition (Isa 36–38), which portrayed a king who placed his trust in
YHWH, to the degree that his prayer diverted a sentence of judgment (37:14–
21; 38:2–3). The DtrH therefore judged Hezekiah a king "who did what was
right in the eyes of YHWH, according to all that David his father had done" (2

---

77. It is interesting to note that Melugin, one of the first to suggest that Second Isaiah was related to
   preceding tradition, focused his attention within 36–39 on chap. 39 (*Formation*, 177).
78. See Wildberger's synopsis (*Jesaja*, 1494–95). There are orthographic and other minor
   differences.
79. See our discussion above, chapter 3, 9th section.

Kgs 18:3) and went on to speak of his incomparability (2 Kgs 18:5). The Hezekiah-Isaiah narratives had depicted a king who would not serve other nations or other gods, and whose prayer wrought victory. The introduction in the DtrH corroborated this view: "YHWH was with him; wherever he went forth, he prospered. He rebelled against the King of Assyria and would not serve him" (2 Kgs 18:7). In this measure, we agree with Provan's final remarks concerning a first edition of Kings that ended with the reign of Hezekiah:

> The David theme . . . comes to a natural conclusion in the account of Hezekiah's reign in 2 Kgs 18–19, where Hezekiah is presented as a second David, and the Zion theology is portrayed as vindicated by the miraculous reversal of Assyria's fortunes recorded in 2 Kgs 18:17—19:37. [*Hezekiah and the Books of Kings*, 171]

Subsequent to this and with an eye toward larger concerns given the fall of Jerusalem in 597–587, the Hezekiah-Isaiah narratives were modifed in the context of Kings. Ample discussion has already been devoted to the addition at 2 Kgs 18:14–16 (which directly contradicts 18:7) and the modifications in 2 Kgs 20:1–11.[80] It is impossible to determine whether the psalm of Hezekiah was brought over from Isaiah as part of the original depiction of the DtrH. However, its omission is certainly consistent with the other modifications that have occurred in the story of Hezekiah's illness. In Kings the royal prayer may divert a sentence of judgment, but not without considerable assistance from the prophet Isaiah (2 Kgs 20:4, 7, 11). This is fully consistent with the significance granted to prophetic agency vis-à-vis the royal house in the final chapters of Kings (2 Kgs 21:10; 22:14–20; 24:3; 24:13). Moreover, Hezekiah's depiction in 2 Kgs 20:8–11 is difficult to square with the introductory notice at 2 Kgs 18:5, which had spoken of a trust never seen before in the royal house, and never to be equaled.

In the context of these modifications, the depiction of 2 Kgs 20:12–19 is hardly unusual.[81] On this score, Ackroyd's assessment is correct:

> Thus we have in this narrative an anticipation of exile which serves to make two points. In the first place, the experience of exile when it comes may be understood to have been foretold in prophetic judgment; and not merely that, its reality and legality are established by royal action and prophetic interpretation. The point is then part of other prophecy-fulfillment patterns to be found in the Deuteronomistic History. ["Babylonian Exile," 341]

The narrative relating the visit of an envoy from Merodach-baladan belongs fully within the logic and structure of the DtrH. In contrast to the Hezekiah-

---

80. See also Provan (*Hezekiah and the Books of Kings*, 122, n. 82).
81. "[2 Kgs 18:14–16] was added later, as part of an attempt, which may be also noted in 20:12–19, to tone down the rather exaggerated picture of Hezekiah which is given by the original account" (*Hezekiah and the Books of Kings*, 122).

Isaiah narratives (Isa 36–38), whose primary location was the Book of Isaiah, the Babylonian envoy episode (Isa 39) has its primary home in the DtrH. Yet, because of its suitability for prefacing the "Babylonian" material in Isa 40–55, and because of the connection that was made in Kings with the other Hezekiah-Isaiah traditions (2 Kgs 18:13—19:37, 20:1-11), 2 Kgs 20:12-19 also found its way into the Book of Isaiah, as the final episode in a trilogy whose main subject was Hezekiah, and as a preface to the following Second Isaiah material. As such, it would not be incorrect to say that it was composed for both contexts, about a century later than the composition of 36–38. At the same time, the modifications that are characteristic of the Kings tradition were introduced and were made to function in an integral way in that depiction.

Two other features argue for the full compatibility of 2 Kgs 20:12-19 with the final redactional levels of the DtrH. The motif of a prophetic oracle promising future (Babylonian) judgment (2 Kgs 20:16-18), addressed to a king who is spared its ill effects (2 Kgs 20:19), is recognizable at a later point in the DtrH, during the reign of Josiah. The prophetess Huldah delivers a similar oracle to an envoy from Josiah (2 Kgs 22:14-17), which also exempts the king, though in more fulsome terms than for Hezekiah (vv. 18–20). Second, in the description of the 597 siege, and in contrast to the Assyrian invader, the Babylonian King Nebuchadnezzar is depicted as fully successful (2 Kgs 24:10-17). The description of his hauling off the royal house and the treasures of palace and temple is clearly related to the earlier episode in Hezekiah's day, at which time the Babylonian ambassadors saw everything in the realm (2 Kgs 20:13), causing Isaiah to prophesy that everything would be carried off, including the royal house (20:17-18). In order that we not miss this connection, the Dtr. Historian makes it explicit at the conclusion of 24:12-13, with the phrase *ka'ăšer dibber YHWH*. In sum, Smelik may be right about the primary location of 36–38 in the Book of Isaiah; but the relatedness of 20:12-19 to its literary environment and to the final redactional stages of the DtrH is unmistakable.

One final note concerning Isaiah's prophecy of Babylonian exile, found now in two very different contexts (2 Kgs 20:12-19; Isa 39:1-8). One favorite theme of the final chapters of Kings is that YHWH had not failed to warn Israel and Judah through the prophets. The theme is prominent in the report of the fall of the northern kingdom ("Yet YHWH warned Israel and Judah by every prophet and every seer," 2 Kgs 17:13) and it extends to the fall of Judah, through the reigns of Manasseh (21:10), Josiah (22:15-17), and Jehoiakim (24:2). The situation is somewhat complicated in the case of Josiah, since like Hezekiah he was an exemplary king. The prophetic judgment oracle from Huldah therefore includes a rider for Josiah: "your eyes shall not see all the evil which I will bring upon this place" (22:20). A similar move was made in Hezekiah's case (20:19).

It must be said, however, that the report of Merodach-baladan's envoy to Hezekiah (2 Kgs 20:12–19) is distinctive within this prophecy-fulfillment scheme, if one might call it that. This is not general prophetic warning, replete with deuteronomistic rhetoric (2 Kgs 17:13–18; 21:10–15; 22:16–17), but rather a direct prophesy of future Babylonian exile, delivered from the mouth of the prophet Isaiah (20:16–18). Where did the Dtr. Historian get the notion that Isaiah was specifically responsible for prophesying Babylonian exile a full century before its occurrence? The question touches on matters of historicity, to be sure (Did Isaiah ever address Hezekiah in this fashion? Was there a visit to Jerusalem of ambassadors from the rebel Chaldean prince?). But of greater interest is the motivation for such a perspective on the fall of Jerusalem, apart from issues of historicity narrowly conceived. Why within a pattern of general prophetic warning, where the warnings of specific prophets are conspicuously underutilized (Micah, Jeremiah), does the prophet Isaiah suddenly put in an appearance, directly prophesying the exile and removal of the royal house to Babylon? Here we are talking not so much about an argument from silence,[82] but about an argument from silence broken.

The matter touches on the puzzle of the growth of the Book of Isaiah as well. There too Isaiah's judgment-tradition was subsequently linked to the events of 587 and the fall of Jerusalem, both within 1–39 and as a consequence of the expansion into 40–55. Yet within 1–39˚, the linkages are not usually so direct as in 20:12–19. The oracle concerning Babylon (13:1–22) heading the collection of nation oracles (13–23) might belong to such a tendency,[83] and the cosmic judgment scene in 24–27 has been convincingly set against the backdrop of 587 events as well.[84] Clements has argued persuasively for a comprehensive Babylonian redaction extending throughout Isa 1–39˚.[85] Yet one has the sense that the linkage between Assyria/Babylon has been made far more gradually, subtly, and certainly more indirectly, than what is evidenced in 2 Kgs 20:12–19. By the same token, it appears that the move to relate Isaiah's judgment-tradition beyond events of the eighth century to events involving Babylon and the fall of Jerusalem did not occur by application of unreasonable force or external manipulation; rather, it grew out of a process of *relecture* and of careful listening for the word of God in the word of his servant Isaiah. A potential for dissonance existed in the material in chapters 36–38, which spoke of Zion's deliverance from Assyrian threat and prophetic judgment, due to the trust and obedience of its king.

I offer the following reconstruction. The move to link Isaiah's prophecies involving Assyria as agent of divine judgment to the events of 597–587 and

---

82. As in the subtitle of Pohlmann's essay: "Erwägungen zum Schlusskapitel des deuteronomistischen Geschichtswerkes. Oder: Warum wird der Prophet Jeremia in 2.Kön.22–25 nicht erwähnt?" (1979); also Seitz (*Theology in Conflict*, 215–21).
83. Clements (*Isaiah 1–39*, 132).
84. D. Johnson, *From Chaos to Restoration* (JSOTSup 61; Sheffield: JSOT Press, 1989).
85. Clements ("Fall of Jerusalem").

final Babylonian assault had already begun within the context of the developing Book of Isaiah. This gradual, subtle, yet unmistakable process of reapplication led to the conviction within the developing DtrH that Isaiah had directly prophesied Babylonian exile and the removal of royal house and the treasures of temple and palace (2 Kgs 20:12–19). There was no reason why such a conviction needed to be expressed in similarly direct form in the Book of Isaiah, where the movement toward reapplication originated—except for one fact. That was the existence of the Hezekiah-Isaiah narratives (36–38), which spoke of Zion's deliverance and the reversal of a sentence of death based upon the prayer of the king. The motivation for (1) the inclusion of 2 Kgs 20:12–19 (= Isa 39) in Isaiah as well as (2) its placement following the Hezekiah-Isaiah narratives and preceding Second Isaiah chapters can be explained as follows.

Isa 39 serves the purpose of reminding the reader of Isa 36–38 that the final word of the prophet Isaiah involved not recovery (38:21), but an unavoidable journey into exile (39:5–7). Hezekiah is granted "peace and security in his days" (39:8), and thus the traditions of 36–38 are allowed to stand unaltered in their Isaianic context. Hezekiah is an "unwitting agent in bringing about the loss of the land"[86] in a strict sense only from the perspective of and in the context of the DtrH, enhanced by the modifications at 2 Kgs 18:14–16 and within 2 Kgs 20:1–11. In the context of the Book of Isaiah, it is the judgment tradition from the prophet Isaiah, spoken in respect of an eighth-century Judah and an Assyrian instrument of wrath (10:5), that is finally judged too strong to be reversed by the events of 701 and a singular case of royal obedience. Zion's destiny in 701 would ultimately be overshadowed by the events of 587 B.C.E.

Celebration of Zion's near destiny in the Hezekiah-Isaiah narratives (36–38) would ultimately give rise to questions about Zion's final destiny. Those questions are ultimately addressed not so much within the context of the Deuteronomistic history (though see 2 Kgs 25:27–30) as within the larger Book of Isaiah. In my judgment, Second Isaiah chapters were composed with one eye trained on the preceding material (the "former things") and the other on God's plans for the future, given the dramatic execution of a sentence of judgment, not in 701, but in 597–587. Seen from that perspective, the final word of the prophet is not heard at 39:5–7, but only as God spoke again from the divine council, "to the heart of Jerusalem" (40:2).[87] The sentence of judgment diverted in Hezekiah's day was finally carried out. On the other side of that judgment, it could be said that Zion's term of service was over. Now a highway would be built for God (40:3) that the full "glory of YHWH might be

86. Ackroyd, "Babylonian Exile," 341.
87. Seitz, "New Prophecy," 245.

revealed." For the mouth of YHWH had spoken (40:5). Now God would do a new thing, involving Zion's final destiny.

In Isaiah 38 the fate of Zion is linked to King Hezekiah. His obedient trust saves a city and leaves open the possibility of health and repentance for its citizens. But from the larger perspective of the Book of Isaiah and the events of 597–587, the royal house finally proves untrustworthy, joining Israel in its disobedience and sharing its sentence of judgment (Isa 39:7). Alone with no comforter is Zion (Lam 1:2). What of its final destiny? Shall one speak of a bill of divorce from YHWH (Isa 50:1a)? Is it right to talk of Zion's own transgressions and iniquities, as well as those of its citizens and its king (50:1b)? Precisely these sorts of questions have given rise to the prophetic word now found in Isa 40–55. As the former things had their final outcome (41:22), so too God would do a new thing "created now, not long ago" (48:7). It is about Zion—and not just Israel or even an exiled Israel—that that new thing had to do. In order to see this in proper perspective, our analysis must move to Second Isaiah chapters. But the groundwork has been laid within the context of First Isaiah and especially the Hezekiah-Isaiah narratives of Isa 36–38.

The Hezekiah-Isaiah Narratives and the Growth of the Book of Isaiah

RETROSPECT

A venerable history of inquiry precedes the analysis of Isaiah 36–39 set forth in this study. It is hoped that the present treatment has made a contribution to this inquiry, with which it holds much in common, in terms of both exegetical interest and broader interpretive goals.

At the same time, this study has participated in the history of inquiry with a different set of final concerns, involving the redactional development of the Book of Isaiah as a whole. While this perspective has been a factor in recent studies, it has been granted a more sustained and substantive role in the preceding analysis. Concern both with the reverse and the forward relationship of these four chapters to the larger context of the Book of Isaiah has marked even the more minute aspects of exegesis in Isa 36–39. This can be seen in the concern to link the evaluation of Hezekiah's status in 36–38 with the presentation of him in 1–35˚. The same holds true for Zion theology, as expressed both in Isaiah's proclamation and in the example of "narrative theology" represented by the Hezekiah-Isaiah narratives.

In both of these cases, I have consistently urged that Isaiah 36–38 be interpreted in proximity to the traditions of Isaiah appearing earlier in the book. As such, the arguments of both type A and type B redaction-critics have been rejected, though for different reasons. The former had excluded 36–39 from consideration altogether, because of a prior commitment to interpreting these chapters in the context of Kings. For those in this group interested in final redactional shape, Isa 36–39 was allegedly drafted from Kings in order to help the "book" of First Isaiah conform to some larger structural pattern, tripartite (Duhm, Barth, Vermeylen, Bogaert) or otherwise (Steck), on supposed analogy with a Jeremiah (LXX), also concluding with a historical appendix from Kings. Alternatively, the latter group urged greater recognition of the place and function of Isa 36–39 within the specific context of the Book of Isaiah, even going so far as to argue for the original location of this material in Isaiah (Smelik). Yet ironically, with the plea for interpretation in the context of Isaiah, especially in relationship to Second Isaiah, came also an increasing tendency to date all or part of chapters 36–39 *later than* 40–55 and to understand the function of these chapters as related to the theological and political concerns of the exilic or postexilic community. The redactional relationship between 36–39 and 40–55 was for the most part to be conceived as running from the latter to the former.

The analysis of chapters 36–38 set forth above has called for a fresh appreciation of the pivotal role of these chapters in the tradition-historical and editorial development of the Book of Isaiah. In the course of this investigation I came to speak of a complexity and ambiguity characterizing the Isaiah traditions' exposition of Zion theology, spanning prose and poetic formats, and of the possibility that just such an ambiguity played a key role in the growth of the Book of Isaiah, and in the final attempt to understand God's word to Zion in 701 from the perspective of 587 events and their aftermath.

Just as it is appropriate to emphasize the relationship of 36–38 to 1–35° on matters of Zion and king, so too I have argued for a forward direction of influence, from the Hezekiah-Isaiah narratives to Second Isaiah. This influence is to be understood both at the specific, exegetical level, and in a broader conceptual sense, involving the puzzle of Isaiah's growth, governed by a profound concern with Zion's final destiny. One example of a specific exegetical form of influence was identified in the reference to the plan of old at Isa 37:26. The possibility that other such forms of influence might also be identified within chapters 36–38 was kept open. I will return to this possibility shortly.

The larger conceptual question has been treated on virtually equal footing with the exegetical task as such. As chapters 3 and 5 have examined the Hezekiah-Isaiah narratives in detail, addressing the wide range of exegetical, historical, and interpretive problems characteristic of them, so chapters 1, 2, and 4 have set this examination within the context of redactional inquiry into the larger Book of Isaiah, characteristic of recent and also older (Duhm) studies. Especially in chapter 4, it was insisted that the cogency of my argument for the preexilic origin of Isa 36–37 would finally call for support from the side of Second Isaiah chapters and the concerns addressed there. Here the interlocking nature of the argument for the pivotal role of the Hezekiah-Isaiah narratives in the tradition-historical and editorial growth of the Book of Isaiah is revealed. In order for there to be a forward exegetical influence, confirming the preexilic origin of chapters 36–38 and the essential rootedness of these chapters within the Proto-Isaiah traditions, there should be evidence of its effect within chapters 40–55, given the parameters within which my argument has been set. The forward influence of the Hezekiah-Isaiah narratives on chapters 40–55 forms a critical part of a larger thesis regarding the place of these narratives within First Isaiah proper.

IMPLICATIONS: FIRST ISAIAH

Given the specific attention paid to Isa 36–39, it has not been possible to treat all the many problems associated with the fuller witness of Isa 1–39˚. At points in the discussion, reference has been made to the exegesis of Isa 1, 6–8, 13, 22, and 28–32, as related to the Hezekiah-Isaiah narratives. I have also suggested that Barth's Assyria-redaction might profitably be adjusted, (1) by moving its date of composition closer to the period of Isaiah's actual prophetic activity and (2) by shifting the editorial interest away from the figure of Josiah, who is never mentioned in the book, even in an oblique editorial manner, to Hezekiah. Whether this adjustment can be made easily will depend in large measure on the success of my reconstruction of the role of Isa 36–38 within the development of Isaiah traditions. My own view is that the salient points in Barth's treatment are registered on the side of literary and redactional analysis. His historical and sociological conclusions are not so central as to necessitate a date for this first Isaiah edition in the period of Josiah.

In the light of this analysis of the Hezekiah-Isaiah narratives, two implications for the exegesis of First Isaiah are suggested. First, the traditions have grown up in such a way as to make clear the contrast between the responses of the royal house represented by the figures of Ahaz and Hezekiah. Two key prose sections (7–8, 36–37) of the Book of Isaiah offer contrasting pictures, both of them set at the fateful "conduit of the upper pool on the highway to the Fuller's Field" (7:3; 36:2). Both relate situations of military threat in which the faith of the royal house is put to the test (7:4; 37:6–7). Isaiah puts it bluntly: if Ahaz does not believe, he will not be established (7:9b). The refusal to ask for a sign, as urged by the prophet himself, is interpreted in the tradition as a sign of Ahaz's unbelief (7:10–13); as such it stands in contrast to the portrayal of Hezekiah, whose prayer effectively stays the Assyrian assault (37:21; 38:5–6), and who accepts the sign given by the prophet (37:30–32; 38:7–8). In the place of prophetic confrontation (7:3–13), the tradition tells of Isaiah's cooperation with a king to whose prayer and trust he adds his own prophetic endorsement. The weak heart of the house of David (7:2) may even be responsible for the coming Assyrian threat, though the tradition is complex and multivalent at this juncture (7:16–25). Yet even with all the power and terror the Assyrian king will muster (8:6–7), the threat will reach only to the neck (8:8). Finally, it will not stand (8:10).

Precisely because the contrast is so thoroughly woven into the literary presentations of both prose sections (7–8, 36–38), it is not always possible to detect the direction of influence. At some points it appears that Hezekiah has been portrayed in contrast to Ahaz (the sign motif); at other points, the traditions of Syro-Ephraimitic threat in the days of Ahaz appear to have been back-influenced by the record of Jerusalem's deliverance in 701, and in the light of a later and more awesome Assyrian display of force. Yet in the final depiction of 7–8 and 36–38, we come to learn: the greater the threat, the greater the faith. Hezekiah reestablishes a house of David weakened by Ahaz, and in so doing delivers a city and its people, as, according to the tradition, God had promised (8:9–10).

The second implication of this analysis is a more general one. Appreciation of the central role the figure of Hezekiah plays in the narratives of 36–38 serves to remind us what a special interest the Isaiah traditions have in the royal house as such. The royal house literally has the potential to save the nation—but also to expose it to mortal danger. Isaiah asserts the unique prerogative of the house of David, at the same time reminding the king of the larger responsibility that attends his divine charge (7:9b). The actions and deportment of the king involve not just himself, but "you and your people and your father's house" (7:17). Lack of faith on the king's part exposes an entire people to Assyrian threat. Only proper faith and obedience, as exhibited by King Hezekiah in the later 701 crisis, is capable of delivering that same people from a sentence of death. The analysis of Isa 36–38 set forth above has led to the conclusion that First Isaiah chapters have fundamentally to do with God's anointed one—God's rights, but above all God's responsibility for the nation and God's power to effect change by dint of obedience and trust.

IMPLICATIONS: SECOND ISAIAH

It is not possible to set forth in any detailed way all the implications of the proposed thesis regarding chapters 36–39 for the interpretation of Second Isaiah. This calls for a separate treatment, though one that would clearly build on the conclusions drawn here and would operate with a similar set of broader redactional concerns. As such, the contribution the present study makes will have to be evaluated on its own merits within the context of First Isaiah analysis, and especially those more recent studies that have set such analysis within a larger framework interested in the redactional integrity of the Book of Isaiah as a whole.

By the same token, the present study has raised a sufficient number of questions concerning the relationship between the Hezekiah-Isaiah narratives and Second Isaiah chapters to warrant at least a brief overview in the context of the present work. Consequently, I will work through several of the more prominent examples of that relationship within this concluding chapter, thereby setting the analysis of the Hezekiah-Isaiah narratives undertaken here within the larger and more appropriate context of the Book of Isaiah as a whole. This will be done in an intentionally cursory manner so as to respect the integrity of the present work, as well as a possible future study. Such a work would seek to understand the sociological origins, literary structure, and theological content of Second Isaiah from the perspective of a form of redactional analysis termed in chapter 1 "type C." Such analysis would investigate Second Isaiah chapters with a view toward determining whether this material was composed, from its inception, in response to First Isaiah prophecies. On the basis of this study, it should be clear that I regard the Hezekiah-Isaiah narratives as occupying a pivotal position within these "former prophecies."

Return to the Divine Council

Earlier studies of Cross and Rowley urged that Isa 40:1–8(9–11) be interpreted against the backdrop of the language and setting of the divine council, familiar from other parts of the OT, especially Psalms, Job, and Zechariah.[1] More recently the redaction-critical significance of this observation has been explored, under the possible condition that Second Isaiah's introduction has intentionally evoked the divine council scene of First Isaiah (6:1–13).[2] As has been rightly noted in these redaction-critical studies, the movement toward identifying such "reciprocal relationships" between First and Second Isaiah calls into question the strict independence of the latter as traditionally brokered in prophet of the exile models. In my contribution to this line of approach, I argued that the purpose of the utilization of an older scene of prophetic commissioning at the opening of Second Isaiah was to ground this new form of prophetic discourse in the same divine council responsible for Isaiah's proclamation, thereby maintaining a degree of continuity with the "former things" yet allowing a new word from God to go forth.

In the context of these remarks, it was suggested that the imagery of "grass of the field" (40:6), to which an objecting voice has compared "all flesh" (40:6), was not drawn arbitrarily, nor as a reflection on the state of exilic hardship, but in conscious reference to earlier prophecies of Isaiah. A key text in this regard is, not surprisingly, the earlier divine council scene, where Isaiah's message of judgment is linked temporally to the utter desolation of the land (6:12). In a later scene of judgment, the glorious beauty of the proud crown of Ephraim (28:4) is likened to a fading flower (*ṣîṣat nōbēl*)—an image strikingly similar to that found in 40:6 (*ṣîṣ haśśādeh*).

More relevant in the context of this study is the reference in the Hezekiah-Isaiah narratives to God's plan of old, involving Assyria as agent of judgment (37:26). Those who must endure the Assyrian onslaught are "shorn of strength," "dismayed and confounded" (37:27a). Their fortified cities have crashed into heaps of ruin. They have become "like plants of the field" (*'ēśeb*

---

1. F.M. Cross, "The Council of Yahweh in Second Isaiah," *JNES* 12 (1953) 274–77; H.H. Rowley, "The Council of Yahweh," *JTS* 45 (1944) 151–57.
2. Melugin, *Formation*, 83, 176; Ackroyd, "Structure and Function," 5–7; Rendtorff, "Jesaja 6 im Rahmen der Komposition des Jesajabuches" (1989) 73–83; Seitz, "New Prophecy," 229–47.

śādeh), "like tender grass" (*wîraq deše'*), "like grass on the housetops" (*ḥăṣîr gaggôt*). In my view, the reference in 40:6 to "all flesh as grass, its beauty as a flower of the field" is not a case of prophetic despondency (Westermann) or a piece of sententious wisdom (McKenzie). Rather, a voice from the divine council simply declares what is a fact: the people are as grass that withers when the Lord blows on it. And so God has. The voice tells of the fulfillment of God's plan of old, a plan that would lead finally to utter destruction (6:11b–12), to people becoming "like plants of the field, like tender grass, like grass on the housetops" (37:27). In the context of the Hezekiah-Isaiah narratives, Jerusalem is spared a desolation at the hands of Assyria that is meted out to other nations and peoples—including the "fortified cities" of Judah (36:1). The voice from the divine council announces that no one was finally exempt. *All* flesh is grass. Only the word of God—the same word that called for judgment—stands forever (40:8; 55:11), capable of creating life out of death, replacing brier and thorn with cypress and myrtle (55:13).

The divine council scene of 40:1–11 deliberately evokes the earlier council, where a word of deafness and judgment had gone forth (6:1–13). Only a tenth was to remain, themselves to be burned again (6:13). The plan of old, referred to at 37:26, has to do with the agent of judgment commissioned by God. The Hezekiah-Isaiah narratives tell of God's gracious sparing of Jerusalem in 701, brought about by Hezekiah's prayer and obedience, "for my own sake and for the sake of my servant David" (37:35). But even this "tenth" will be burned again.[3] A return to the divine council confirms that such a burning has been carried out. It is time for a fresh word from the divine council.

The reference to all flesh as grass in 40:6–7 could not itself establish that a conscious relationship exists between the Hezekiah-Isaiah narratives and Second Isaiah chapters. More important is the reutilization of the divine council scene to ground a new prophetic word and provide the proper temporal perspective for the chapters that follow.[4] It is in reference to this latter function that the relationship with the Hezekiah-Isaiah narratives is more likely.

The key opening unit of Second Isaiah (40:1–11) is concerned not with the fate of exiles or some other special group within Israel, but with Zion/Jerusalem. Only in the context of the charge to comfort Jerusalem is reference made to "my people." It is Zion's warfare, its pardoned iniquity, and its full recompense (*kiplayim*) about which God speaks. In my judgment, Zion has become the wilderness that God is about to redeem—or, to use the language of Isa 37:26, a fortified city has become a heap of ruin. It is to Zion, Jerusalem,

---

3. It is possible that Isa 6:13 is a secondary addition, made on the basis of 587 events. See Clements, "Fall of Jerusalem," 426; Wildberger, *Jesaja*, 241, 257; Barth, *Jesaja-Worte*, 195–96.
4. Seitz, "New Prophecy," 245.

and the cities of Judah that the *mĕbaśśeret* is to say "Behold your God!"[5]
Heralds are dispatched from the divine council to announce God's return to
Zion. They and the anonymous voices of vv. 3–8 comprise the divine retinue;
they resemble the angelic figures of Zech 1:8–17, who express their concern to
God about the destiny of Zion (1:12). In Isa 40, God speaks directly of the need
for Zion's comforting. God does not learn of Zion's state from a unit patrolling
the earth (Zech 1:8–11) or an angelic messenger (Zech 1:12–13); rather, God
gives charge directly to attendants and heralds who do God's bidding.

It is above all the focus on Zion/Jerusalem in 40:1–11 that points to an
awareness of the Hezekiah-Isaiah narrative portrayal. No other section of Isa
1–39 shows the same steady interest in Zion's fate during times of threat (esp.
37:35; 38:6). But as Zion was delivered in 701, so later it was to endure a term
of service (*ṣĕbā'āh*). The plan of old, involving fortified cities crashing into
ruin, was extended to include Zion. Upon seeing the extent of the desolation
wrought by a later agent of judgment (not Assyria but another foe from the
north) a voice from the heavenly council cannot at first cry, as commanded
(40:6), but only acknowledge that all flesh is grass "when the breath of the
LORD blows upon it" (40:7). A new word of God must go forth, as it does,
dispatching heralds to announce the return of God to Zion (40:9–11).

Appeal to Former Things

In order to confirm that the divine council introduction (40:1–11) has
been composed with one eye on the Hezekiah-Isaiah narrative portrayal, it is
necessary to examine in more detail the appeal to former things as it appears
in chapters 40—48, as well as in 37:26.

Such appeal does not occur in one stereotyped formula in Second Isaiah,
nor is its distribution clearly motivated. Explicit use of the term "former
things" (*hāri'šōnôt*) occurs at 41:22, 43:18, 46:9, 48:3. Similar expressions also
appear: at 40:21 "from the first" (*mērō'š*); 44:7 (emended) "from eternity"
(*mē'ôlām*); 45:21 "long ago, of old" (*miqqedem, mē'āz*); 46:9 "from eternity"
(*mē'ôlām*); 46:10 "from the first, from before" (*mērē'šît, miqqedem*); 48:3, 7
"of old" (*mē'āz*). They are occasionally used together, as in "the former things
of old" (46:9) or "the former things I declared of old" (48:3). Former things are
sometimes set in contrast to new things (42:9, 43:18, 48:6). In the last two cases,
one is not to recall the former things; in another context, one is to remember
them (46:9). Finally, the former things are frequently linked to their outcome
(*'aḥărîtān*, 41:22), which now stands in the past ("behold they have come,"
42:9; 45:21—if the reference is to the calling of Cyrus at 45:1, 48:3).

Is there one frame of reference into which this wide variety of usage can

---

5. The appositional reading "Zion, herald" runs into complications at 41:27 ("to Jerusalem I give a
herald of good tidings") and 52:7 ("How beautiful on the mountains are the feet of the *mĕbaśśēr*
. . . who says to Zion 'Your God reigns'"). See Seitz, "New Prophecy," 243.

fit? Is there one fixed referent for the "former things" or the "things to come" or the "new thing"? How do the references function in the context of challenges to other deities and their representatives (43:8–13), or the futility of idols (41:5–9), or both (41:21–29; 45:20–21; 46:8–11)? Do the references to God as eternal (40:21–31; 48:12–13) or incomparable (44:6–8) belong within this same context?

In my view, Isa 40–48, with all its evidence of seams and breaks and patent discontinuities, maintains a consistent rootage in the setting of the divine council. The variety of speeches contained in these chapters all have God as their speaker, with no evidence of a separate prophetic voice or persona. God's speech is directed initially to God's own attendants (40:1–11). But from this same divine council backdrop God addresses Israel in the context of a challenge put to God by other deities, their idols, and their manufacturers and worshipers. This explains the pervasive use of courtroom language and the frequent call to assemble or bring testimony (41:1; 41:21; 43:8; 44:20; 48:14) as well as the persistent rhetorical questioning (40:12–31; 41:26; 42:18–25; 43:19; 44:7; 45:21; 46:5; 48:14). Israel is caught up within the web of this challenge to YHWH. YHWH defends his own cause, constantly asking other "gods" to put forth their testimony, in a manner similar to the divine council setting in Ps 82. The strongest piece of evidence YHWH presents involves the ability to speak reliably—and uniquely—from the divine council of the fate of Israel and the nations (cf. Ps 82:5).

The appeal to former things as things of great antiquity (43:18; 46:9; 48:3), together with YHWH's self-declaration as first and last (41:4; 44:6), without peer (40:18; 40:25; 41:26–29; 43:10–13; 44:8; 46:5), and all knowing (41:26; 44:7; 45:20–21; 46:10), suggests that YHWH conceives of the former things as eternal decrees known by YHWH alone, and shared only with Israel, YHWH's witnesses (41:27; 43:10; 44:8; 44:26). As such other gods and their peoples cannot declare them when challenged to do so (41:28–29; 43:9; 45:20–21). The root of this conception can be found in Isa 37:26, where YHWH describes the plan of old, determined "long ago" (*lĕmērāḥôq*). At 37:26 the plan involves the destructive agenda of Assyria. As in 10:13–18, it is clear that Assyria regards the plan as its own when in fact it belongs to YHWH. YHWH has dispatched Assyria as instrument of judgment (10:5; 5:26), and can recall Assyria at will (37:29), which YHWH chooses to do during the events of 701, so far has Assyria's arrogance and blasphemy extended.

Rooted in Isa 36–38 is also the concept of challenge by foreign nations and especially their gods (36:18–20; 37:10–13; 37:16–20). Second Isaiah works from a similar perspective at a later point in time. In the context of the taunt song (37:22–29), however, God speaks of the "plan of old" in order to squelch Assyria in its arrogant claim to self-determination vis-à-vis Israel. This works in conjunction with the "rod of my anger" conception earlier in the tradition

(10:5–19; also 5:26; 14:26–27). Latent within the appeal is a related conception of YHWH's plan of great antiquity, and of the continuity of God's word across time.

It is this aspect that Second Isaiah has chosen to develop, thus explaining the appearance in YHWH's appeal of the term "former thing" as a past thing already come about. Assyria as agent of destruction has been exchanged for Babylon. From the perspective of Second Isaiah, the "former things" are things of old, insofar as they involve YHWH's "plan of old" from Isaiah's day. This plan involved destruction through the agency of foreign powers as chastisement for Israel's sins, summarized in the motif of YHWH's outstretched hand (5:25; 9:12, 17, 21; 10:4; 14:26). Other nations might try to claim they were called by YHWH for a task of destruction directed at Israel—a notion to be found, not surprisingly, in the Hezekiah-Isaiah narratives in the speech of the Rabshakeh (36:10). But in Second Isaiah the emphasis falls on YHWH's unique ability to fulfill what YHWH had earlier, in the divine council, planned and then revealed to Israel, YHWH's servant (41:27; 43:10; 44:8). No one can tell what God told "first to Zion" (41:27). Idols cannot speak; the gods they presume to represent are mute as well when it comes to telling the former things and their outcome (41:21–22; 43:9; 44:7; 45:21). So much less can they say what will happen in the future, what YHWH is planning as a new thing (41:23). Even for Israel the new thing cannot be determined by an appeal to past revelation, such is its unique force in the present (48:6–8).

In sum, the "former things" as employed in Isa 40–48 have no one fixed referent. They refer to plans executed in the divine council, revealed to Israel. In this they serve as a unique defense in YHWH's cause. In terms of content, they refer to Isaiah's proclamation involving YHWH's dispatching of nations for a task vis-à-vis Israel. Within Isa 1–39° this dispatching is itself referred to as a "plan of old" (14:24–27; 22:11; 37:26–27). The motif is employed in Second Isaiah in combination with a related temporal emphasis, which speaks of the plan of old in a new context as "former things" or "former things of old." The "former things" are primarily Isaiah's judgment proclamation—in his own day involving Assyria, seen in a later day as replaced by Babylon (so the gloss at 23:13).[6] But seen from the perspective of the plan of YHWH in the divine council involving the nations, the "former things" can also refer to the call of Cyrus (45:21), as instrument of judgment, not against, but on behalf of Israel.

The fuller implications of such an interpretation of the "former things" in Second Isaiah would have to be worked out in a separate study. My remarks are intended as provisional observations only. In my view, the motif has been developed on the basis of the Hezekiah-Isaiah narratives, with their larger

---

6. Clements, "Fall of Jerusalem," 429.

portrayal of a contest between YHWH and the gods of Assyria and the nations. The "former things" are not specific isolated prophecies in First Isaiah to which Second Isaiah refers.[7] The motif itself is rooted in First Isaiah, in the conception of YHWH's plan of old. As indicated above, the question of the former things is best answered within the larger context of the divine council setting, where the nations and their gods are brought forward, questioned, and judged. The juridical aspects of the divine council come to the fore in Second Isaiah, on analogy with uses of the divine council in the Psalter. In Isaiah 6 (cf. 1 Kgs 22) the divine council setting was adapted for a prophetic context, in which the prophet was taken up into the divine council, cleansed, and commissioned for a task vis-à-vis Israel. This prophetic commissioning function has been held back in Isa 40–48 so that YHWH's direct speech and challenge to the nations, using the evidence of the former things of old, might come to the fore.

Related to this, it is not clear in Second Isaiah who is to take up the prophetic task on analogy with Isaiah, so in need of cleansing and emboldening is the downtrodden Israel. In my view the prophetic commissioning element does not emerge clearly until 48:16 and 49:1–6—one of the so-called servant songs.[8] Here for the first time one encounters first-person speech differentiated from direct YHWH speech. The call to comfort, issued in 40:1, is not taken up until after YHWH's extended defense in 40–48; then at last a prophetic figure steps forward in 49:1–6 and tells of God's call, like that of Jeremiah, in the womb (49:5). At this juncture, the focus shifts back to Zion as recipient of the comfort proclamation called for from the divine council at 40:1–11. Zion occupies center stage in this second half of the Second Isaiah material (50:14—55:13), as the one addressed by a fresh prophetic word.

Zion's Final Destiny

I have spoken at length about the role Zion's destiny has played in the Hezekiah-Isaiah narratives and in the extension of Isaiah tradition beyond so-called First Isaiah material. Concern with Zion's destiny also clearly marks the introduction to Second Isaiah chapters (40:1–11), as pointed out above. Not until God has concluded an extended defense from the divine council, aided by the testimony of the "former things," do Second Isaiah chapters resume their specific interest in Zion (49:7—55:13). Much could be said about the role Zion plays in Second Isaiah,[9] but I will restrict my remarks to the possible relevance Zion may have for the interpretation of the Hezekiah-Isaiah narratives.

---

7. If they were, one might have expected a more direct cross-referencing term, like "the words of Isaiah," or "as Isaiah said," "as it is written in the prophecies of . . . " (so Chronicles, for example).
8. Seitz, "New Prophecy," 245–46.
9. See most recently, J. Sawyer, "Daughter Zion and Servant of the Lord in Isaiah: A Comparison," *JSOT* 44 (1989).

Zion is depicted as afflicted (49:13; 51:21; 54:11), wasted and desolate (49:19; 51:3; 51:19), exiled (49:21), a wilderness (51:3), staggered (51:22), barren (54:1), like a wife forsaken (54:6), storm tossed, not comforted (54:11). The metaphors swim into one another, so that Zion is wife (54:5–6) and young bride (49:18; 54:6), mother of children (50:1; 51:20; 54:13) and barren one (49:21; 54:1). Zion is also like a son of God's womb (49:15) and a nursing child (49:15). Zion is one not comforted (54:11), yet now to be comforted by God (51:3; 52:9; 54:10).

Zion's personification in 49:7—55:11 resembles Jacob/Israel's personification as God's servant in the first half of the material (41:8, 9; 43:10; 44:1, 2, 21; 49:3), though obviously this is not Zion's "ideal" but rather its real state. God is concerned to register that Zion's condition of bereavement and desolation has come to an end, and that it is now to be comforted. At several junctures the wider Israel is either directly addressed as Zion's "children" (50:1–3) or referred to as such (51:18–20; 54:1). At 50:1–3 God speaks of Israel's having been sold "on account of your iniquities" and "for your transgressions," consistent with the images of just judgment to be found in 40–48. By contrast, the sinfulness of Zion is not a major theme in the second half of the book, but rather its state of wretchedness. This is to be contrasted with the presentation of Zion in Lamentations, which is likewise concerned to describe Zion as wretched and without comforter, and Ezekiel; in both cases, sinfulness is clearly attributed to the personified Zion (Lam 1:8–9, 14; Ez 16). The sole reference to Zion's sin comes in the opening unit (40:1–2), where the sin and iniquity of Jerusalem are said to be pardoned.

By contrast, within the metaphorical setting of mother/children found in 50:1–3, the children are sold for their iniquities, and it is on account of *their* transgressions that mother Zion was put away. That is: there was no bill of divorce from God's side, based upon a breach of faith on the part of Zion (50:1). Zion was put away not for its own sins, but for the sins of its children (50:1b). A similar kind of distinction—between the sinfulness of one group and the innocence of another—obtains in the so-called fourth servant song (52:13—53:12). The images of affliction found there are certainly consistent with those of the surrounding context, where they are applied to Zion (see above). Because context has not been regarded as a reliable exegetical guide in strict form-critical treatments,[10] and because of the masculine language of the song—not to mention a lengthy history of interpretation in Christian and Jewish circles—an interpretation of the servant of 52:13—53:12 as Zion has found no following.[11] Yet Zion can be depicted as "son of her womb" (*ben-biṭnāh*) in 49:15, without causing undue strain on the other images of wife and

10. See the recent essays of Wilcox and Paton-Williams ("The Servant Songs in Deutero-Isaiah," *JSOT* 42 [1988] 81–102) and J. Sawyer ("Daughter Zion" [1989]).
11. Though see L. Wilshire, "The Servant-City: A New Interpretation of the 'Servant of the Lord' in the Servant Songs of Deutero-Isaiah," *JBL* 94 (1975) 356–67.

mother. Lamentations 3 is frequently regarded as an individual lament from the personified Zion, and the language of the lament is masculine (3:1, *'ănî haggeber rā'āh 'ŏnî*).[12] Presumably the formal nature of the lament has over-ridden concerns over clean masculine/feminine distinctions.[13]

Obviously much more work would have to be done in order to ground such an interpretation, and this is not the place to pursue the details of such a proposal. Yet an interpretation of the servant in 52:13—53:12 as Zion would not only be consistent in the Second Isaiah context; it is also in continuity with the depiction of Zion-King in Isa 38. Hezekiah is sick and at the point of death. The emphasis is not on his sinfulness (38:17), but on his state of illness (38:9–20) and his prior faithfulness (38:3). The psalm narrates the movement from sickness, to near death, to new life, to awaiting full health.

Has the final servant poem been composed for Zion on analogy with the psalm for Hezekiah? The poem looks forward to Zion's future exalted state (52:13) as a return to the position Zion is intended to have: "exalted, lifted up, very high" (cf. Isa 2:2). It tells of Zion's humble origins (53:1–2) in language somewhat similar to Ez 16:1–7 ("no eye pitied you . . . I said, Live, grow up like a plant of the field"), before it goes on to tell of Zion's sickness and desolation. The confession is made that Zion was wounded not for its own transgressions (so 50:1–3), but for the iniquities of others (53:5). Zion is finally "cut off from the land of the living" (53:8) and set in its grave (53:9)—in this, moving beyond Hezekiah before him (38:11). Yet the final word to Zion, as to Hezekiah, is for life, not death. Straining the metaphorical personification of Zion to its limit, Zion is even depicted, like Hezekiah, as making intercession on behalf of others whose death sentence was merited (53:12). Hard upon this description of Zion's desolation and sacrifice, the charge is given for the barren one to enlarge the place of its tent, that the descendants might have room to dwell under its protection (54:3). The celebrative force of this long poem (54:1–17) comes as a fulfillment of Zion's destiny as set forth within the poem. Zion sees its offspring (53:10—54:1), the other side of its travail (53:11—54:2), and it divides the spoil with the strong (53:12—54:3).

This controversial and unusual interpretation of Zion as servant requires further support and greater attention to detail than is possible here. I have raised the possibility both that Zion is the innocent servant depicted in the song, and that the song has been composed on loose analogy with the psalm of Hezekiah. But whereas Hezekiah and the city only approach "death" (*hālāh lāmût*, 38:1) in the events of 701 B.C.E., Zion must finally "make his grave with the wicked" and "pour out his soul to death" (*he'ĕrāh lammāwet napšô*,

---

12. On the relationship of Second Isaiah and Lamentations, see N. Gottwald, *Studies in the Book of Lamentations* (SBT 14; Chicago: Allenson, 1954) 42–46.

13. Kraus states: "גבר stands here without stress on the specific masculine meaning in the sense of איש (so also in 27.35.39)" (*Klagelieder* [BKAT 20; Neukirchen, 1956] 54).

53:12). By that act the full sentence of judgment is served, for all Israel, and God can begin again and speak a new word—to Zion servant, as well as Israel servant. Zion's final destiny is the final concern of the Book of Isaiah, as it moves beyond Second Isaiah chapters and into Third Isaiah (56–66).

Whether or not it is possible to sustain this interpretation of Zion in the fourth servant poem, it should be clear that concern over Zion's final destiny stands in the foreground in chapters 49–55 of Second Isaiah. The Zion who was delivered in 701 was ultimately handed over to desolation and destruction in 587 B.C.E. From the very beginning of Second Isaiah chapters, the concern is with the need to comfort Zion, as though in response to the Lamentations' plaintive refrain: "she has no comforter" (1:2, 9, 16, 17, 21; 2:13). Unlike Lamentations, however, which is similarly concerned to personify Zion and describe its suffering, Second Isaiah does not focus on Zion's sinfulness (Lam 1:8, 9, 14, 17, 20; cf. 5:7). Rather, the focus falls on Zion's final restoration, brought about by God, which in turn produces bounty and richness in God's wider creation (55:1–13).

Exilic Provenance?

The question was raised in chapter 1 whether the exilic provenance played a prominent role in Duhm's reconstruction, or if the strict separation of Second (and Third) Isaiah chapters was achieved by Duhm more on the grounds of literary and editorial reconstruction. Duhm's close reading of chapters 40–55 led to the conviction that Deutero-Isaiah "certainly did not live in Babylon." Not a few other interpreters, some dramatically (C.C. Torrey), others more subtly (Mowinckel, Bunsen, Ewald, Smart, Barstad, and Vincent), have concurred with Duhm's view. Pivotal in their arguments was (1) the depiction of exiles not from the standpoint of Babylon, but north, south, east, and west (43:5–6; also 49:12), and at the ends of the earth (43:6); (2) Cyrus as coming from the "north, from the rising of the sun" (41:25; cf. 41:2) and "from a far country" (46:11); (3) the complaint about Jacob/Israel's failure to offer sacrifice (43:22–24)—gratuitous if in exile; (4) the focus on Zion/Jerusalem; also Judah (40:9; 44:26) and the rebuilding of the temple (44:28); (5) the depiction of Babylon as "out there" ("for your sake I will send to Babylon," 43:14); so too the exiles (49:22); and (6) the depiction of Israel as "robbed and plundered, trapped in holes" (42:22).[14]

Interesting in this regard is the depiction of Zion as itself "exiled" (*gōlāh*, 49:21), yet without a suggestion of actual physical deportation. One wonders if too great an emphasis has been placed on "exile" as a specific place of deportation. In my judgment, the same is true of "wilderness" in Second

---

14. Mowinckel, "Die Komposition des deuterojesajanischen Buches," *ZAW* 49 [n.s. 8] (1931) 244 (full quote in note 25, chapter 1).

Isaiah. Zion is depicted as a *midbār* at 51:3, and is frequently spoken of as devastated, wasted, ruined. This is not to say that Second Isaiah has only Zion in mind when he talks of wilderness or exiles. The exiles are, however, "out there"—and their place of exile is by no means restricted to Babylon. Rather, they are "the dispersed" of Israel and as such can be found north, south, east, and west.[15] The point is: Second Isaiah addresses the topic of the fate of Israel's dispersed, together with a concern over Zion's destiny. But this is an altogether different matter than arguments for Second Isaiah as a prophet *in exile* would have it. The perspective of Second Isaiah is Zion-centered, in geographical and theological terms, even as the material shows great concern with the fate of the dispersed and of their return to Zion. By the same token, the introduction speaks of *God's* return to Zion—a return that will transform Zion as wilderness into Zion as fertile land.[16] It is on this note that Second Isaiah concludes (55:13).

Separation of Second Isaiah chapters from their Isaianic context has led to an overemphasis on exilic provenance, and the historical circumstances associated with deportation, with a consequent underemphasizing of the significance of Zion. Attention to the wider Isaiah traditions, and especially the Hezekiah-Isaiah narratives, helps to refocus the pivotal role Zion was meant to have in Second Isaiah. The same could be said of the overemphasis on Second Isaiah as biographical-theological entity, especially in form and tradition-critical treatments of this century. We know nothing of Second Isaiah the prophet. The literature functions suprisingly well without an originating prophetic voice, first-person "speaker" behind the literature, on analogy with preexilic prophecy.[17] In Second Isaiah, the "prophet" becomes a figure depicted in the literature (49:1–6; 50:3–9) alongside Zion and Jacob/Israel servant. In this manner the single identifiable prophetic voice in the wider book—the prophet Isaiah—is respected and allowed to stand alone.

The theological "provenance" of the literature is the divine council (40–48) and Zion-Jerusalem (49–55). God will gather the dispersed like "lambs in his arms" (40:11). God will bring them to Zion, as God returns. Second Isaiah is concerned with the return of exiles, from all compass points, to a restored Zion. As such, Second Isaiah chapters operate from the same working perspective as chapters 1–39 and 56–66: that of Zion. Arguments for an exilic provenance for Second Isaiah (1) ignore the Zion orientation of the literature; (2)

---

15. Consistent with the portrayal of Israel's gradual dispersion in Isa 1–39. See Torrey, *Second Isaiah*, 30–32.

16. Emphasis on the second exodus in Second Isaiah derives from a faulty identification of wilderness as a *terra intermedia* between Babylon and Palestine, on strict analogy with the *midbār* in the exodus narratives. It is little wonder that Zion receives scant attention in this scenario.

17. See Seitz, *Reading and Preaching*, 116–21; "New Prophecy," 246.

place undue emphasis on Second Isaiah as prophetic individual among exiles; (3) generally regard the juxtaposing of 40–55 and 1–39 as accidental or externally imposed, rather than organically and exegetically significant.

Second Isaiah as Prophecy

The debate over how to characterize chapters 40–55 in precise form and literary-critical terms is as old as the theory of Second Isaiah itself. The determination of individual units, the tracing of these units to convincing and appropriate *Sitz im Leben*, the accounting for their present arrangement (if even possible), and the reconstruction of their originating circumstances (oral; written; literary imitation of oral forms; rhetorically composed for oral delivery) have occupied the labors of scholars over the past hundred years. The shift to rhetorical analysis may signal a general weariness with the traditional sociological/biographical dimension of form-critical analysis (Muilenberg, Gitay), yet it is not clear that this dimension ought to be bracketed out entirely.[18]

The analysis of the Hezekiah-Isaiah narratives set forth above makes a contribution to this issue, in general terms. I have argued that Second Isaiah chapters were composed from their inception to be included along with developing Isaiah traditions (so Clements). The analysis of Isa 36–39 was undertaken in part to get a better purchase on the question of the scope and rationale of this developing Isaiah core. I concluded that chapters 36–38 formed an essential part of this Isaiah core, with their portrayal of Hezekiah as obedient king who by dint of prayer and trust diverted a sentence of death, in contrast to his predecessor Ahaz (Isa 7–8°). I have further argued that these chapters play a pivotal role in the extension of Isaiah tradition, as the deliverance of 701 was later overshadowed by the overrunning of Zion in 597–587 B.C.E. That role is understood in part as exercising an exegetical influence over the composition of chapters 40–55. I have seen evidence of influence in the divine council depiction of 40:1–11 and following; in the motif of "the former things of old" as a subtle transformation of Isaiah's plan of old; in the challenge of the nations and their idols; and in the concern over Zion's final destiny.

By the same token, chapters 40–55 do not take their compositional bearings from the exegesis of Isa 36–38 alone. These chapters represent a vigorous, provocative, sustained, fresh prophetic word from the divine council. In claiming that Second Isaiah has been composed "with an eye" on the Hezekiah-Isaiah narratives, I mean no more and no less than that. No more, in that the chapters have their own integrity and independent life. No less, in that they give evidence of a conscious relationship to chapters 36–38 one

---

18. See the quote of Westermann above, chapter 1 (note 36).

might term exegetical, if by that is implied the sort of relatedness isolated above, involving Zion, the nations, the divine council, and the former things of old. This relatedness is itself differently expressed, from more direct literary affiliation (in the case of the former things motif), to a more conceptual and theological association (in the case of Zion and the divine council).

On the basis of my findings, I reject the "oral prophecy in exile" model for understanding the origins of chapters 40–55 as literature. Imitation of older formal types is far closer to the mark (Begrich) as a description of the technique employed in the composition of these chapters. "Imitation" as a classification respects the mature, almost stylized, form of composition at work in Second Isaiah, making these chapters distinctive over against preexilic prophetic witness. Moreover, such a designation is fully consistent with my thesis that Isa 40–55 has been composed in relationship—not just to older forms—but to an actual developing body of Isaiah tradition, most notably the Hezekiah-Isaiah narratives.

CONCLUSION

Sufficient are these remarks concerning Second Isaiah to indicate the nature of the relationship that exists, in my judgment, between these chapters and the preceding material in Isa 36–38, termed here the Hezekiah-Isaiah narratives. It is tempting to say more as a hedge against the provisional character of my observations—to say nothing of their radical departure from the standard approach. But that fuller treatment belongs to another work. It is hoped that enough has been said to expose the forward influence of these chapters on Second Isaiah, in support of the argument for the integral place of the Hezekiah-Isaiah narratives within developing First Isaiah traditions. In my view, the Hezekiah-Isaiah narratives are the pivot on which the entire tradition process turns, explaining the puzzle of Isaiah's growth, on the one hand, and much of the shape and character of Second Isaiah, on the other.

The contribution this work makes lies chiefly in the area of method and exegesis, as this affects the interpretation of Isa 36–39. At the same time, my conclusions regarding the Hezekiah-Isaiah narratives have a decided impact on the larger conception of the Book of Isaiah as a whole. It is hoped that my fresh proposal for the interpretation of Isa 36–38 has opened up new possibilities for conceiving of the relationship between the first two sections of the Book of Isaiah, traditionally handled as two discrete areas of inquiry. I have tried to demonstrate the pivotal role the Hezekiah-Isaiah narratives play in the growth of the Book of Isaiah, bringing First Isaiah traditions to their culmination, while at the same time raising theological issues only subsequently worked through in the context of Second Isaiah chapters. A fuller treatment of this second topic belongs to a future study.

BIBLIOGRAPHY

Ackroyd, Peter R. "Historians and Prophets." *SEA* 33 (1968) 18–54.

———. "An Interpretation of the Babylonian Exile." *SJT* 27 (1974) 328–352.

———. "Isaiah I-XII: Presentation of a Prophet." *VTSup* 29 (1978) 19–21.

———. "Isaiah 36–39: Structure and Function." In *Von Kanaan bis Kerala. Festschrift für Prof. Mag. Dr. Dr. J.P.M. van der Ploeg, O. P. zur Vollendung des siebzigsten Lebensjahres am 4. Juli 1979*, ed. by W.C. Delsman, J.T. Nelis, J.R.T.M. Peters, W.H.Ph. Romer, and A.S. van der Woude, 3–21. AOAT 211. Neukirchen-Vluyn: Neukirchener, 1982.

Barrick, W. Boyd. "On the 'Removal of the "High-Places"' in 1-2 Kings." *Bib* 55 (1974) 257–59.

Barstad, Hans W. "Lebte Deuterojesaja in Judaa?" *NorTT* 83 (1982) 77–87.

Barth, Hermann. *Die Jesaja-Worte in der Josiazeit: Israel und Assur als Thema einer produktiven Neuinterpretation der Jesajasüberlieeferung.* WMANT 48. Neukirchen-Vluyn: Neukirchener, 1977.

Becker, Joachim. *Isaias—der Prophet und sein Buch.* SBS 30. Stuttgart: Katholisches Bibelwerk, 1968.

Beebe, H. Keith. *The Old Testament; An Introduction to Its Literary, Historical and Religious Traditions.* Belmont, Calif.: Dickenson Publishing Co., 1970.

Begrich, Joachim. *Der Psalm des Hiskia: Ein Beitrage zum Verständnis von Jesaja 38, 10–20.* FRLANT 25. Göttingen: Vandenhoeck & Ruprecht, 1926.

———. "Das priesterliche Heilsorakel." *ZAW* 11 (1934) 81–92.

Bogaert, Pierre-Maurice. "L'organisation des grands receuils prophétiques." In *The Book of Isaiah*, ed. by Jacques Vermeylen, 147–53. BETL 81. Leuven: University Press, 1989.

Bright, John. *A History of Israel*, 3d edition. Philadelphia: Westminster, 1981.

Brinkman, J.A. "Elamite Military Aid to Merodach-Baladan." *JNES* 24 (1965) 161–66.

———. "Sennacherib's Babylonian Problem: An Interpretation." *JCS* 25 (1973) 89–95.

Brueggemann, Walter. "Unity and Dynamic in the Isaiah Tradition." *JSOT* 29 (1984) 89–107.

Budde, Karl Ferdinand Reinhard. *Isaiah.* Die Heilige Schrift des Alten Testaments. Fourth Edition, Tübingen, 1922.

Burney, Charles Fox. *Notes on the Hebrew Text of the Books of Kings*. Oxford: Clarendon, 1903.

Childs, Brevard S. *Isaiah and the Assyrian Crisis*. SBT 3. Naperville, Ill.: Alec R. Allenson, 1967.

_____. "The Canonical Shape of the Prophetic Literature." *Int* 32 (1978) 46–55.

_____. "Isaiah." Chap. 17 in *Introduction to the Old Testament as Scripture*. Philadelphia: Fortress, 1979.

Clements, Ronald. *Isaiah 1–39*. NCB. Grand Rapids/London: Eerdmanns/Marshall, Morgan & Scott, 1980.

_____. *Isaiah and the Deliverance of Jerusalem*. JSOTSup 13. Sheffield: JSOT Press, 1980.

_____. "The Prophecies of Isaiah and the Fall of Jerusalem in 587 B.C." *VT* 30 (1980) 421–36.

_____. "The Unity of the Book of Isaiah." *Int* 36 (1982) 117–29.

_____. "Beyond Tradition-History: Deutero-Isaianic Development of First Isaiah's Themes." *JSOT* 31 (1985) 95–113.

_____. "Isaiah 14,22–27: A Central Passage Reconsidered." In *The Book of Isaiah*, ed. by Jacques Vermeylen, 253–62. BETL 81. Leuven: University Press, 1989.

Clifford, Richard J. *Fair Spoken and Persuading: An Interpretation of Second Isaiah*. New York: Paulist, 1984.

Cohen, Chaim. "Neo-Assyrian Elements in the First Speech of the Biblical Rabshaqe." *IOS* 9 (1979) 32–48.

Cross, Frank. "The Council of Yahweh in Second Isaiah." *JNES* 12 (1953) 274–77.

Dietrich, Walter. *Jesaja und die Politik*. BEvT 74. München: Kaiser, 1976.

Dion, Paul E. "Sennacherib's Expedition to Palestine." *Eglise et Theologie* 20 (1989) 5–25.

Donner, H., *Israel unter den Völkern: Die Stellung der klassischen Propheten des 8. Jh. v. Chr. zur Aussenpolitik der Könige von Israel und Juda*. Leiden: E.J. Brill, 1964.

Driver, Samuel Rolles. *An Introduction to the Literature of the Old Testament*. New York: Charles Scribner's Sons, 1891.

Duhm, Bernhard. *Die Theologie der Propheten als Grundlage für die innere Entwicklungsgeschichte der israelitischen Religion*. Bonn: Adolph Marcus, 1875.

_____. *Das Buch Jesaia*. HKAT 3.1. Göttingen: Vandenhoeck & Ruprecht, 1892.

Eaton, John H. "The Origin of the Book of Isaiah." *VT* 9 (1959) 138–57.

Eichhorn, J.G. *Einleitung in das Alte Testament*. (3 vols., 1980–83).

Elliger, Karl. *Die Einheit des Tritojesaia (Jesaia 56–66)*. BWANT 45. Stuttgart: W. Kohlhammer, 1933.

_____. *Deuterojesaja in seinem Verhältnis zu Tritojesaia*. BWANT 63. Stuttgart: W. Kohlhammer, 1933.

Ewald, Georg Heinrich. *Die Propheten des alten Bundes*. 1. Bd. Jesaja mit den ubrigen alteren Propheten. Gottingen: Vandenhoeck & Ruprecht, 1867.

Fohrer, Georg. *Das Buch Jesaja*. Three Volumes. Zürcher Bibelkommentare. Zürich/ Stuttgart: Zwingli, 1960–1964.

_____. *Introduction to the Old Testament*. Nashville: Abingdon, 1968.

_____. *Einleitung in das Alte Testament*. Begrundet von Ernst Sellin. Heidelberg: Quelle & Meyer, 1969.

Friedländer, Michael, ed. and trans. *The Commentary of Ibn Ezra on Isaiah*. New York: Philipp Feldheim, 1873.

Gammie, John G. *Holiness in Israel*. OBT. Minneapolis: Fortress, 1989.

Gesenius, Friedrich Heinrich Wilhelm. *Philologisch-kritischer und historischer Commentar über den Jesaia.* Leipzig: F.C.W. Vogel, 1821.

Geyer, John B. "2 Kings XVIII 14–16 and the Annals of Sennacherib." *VT* 21 (1971) 604–6.

Gitay, Yehoshua. "Deutero-Isaiah: Oral or Written?" *JBL* 99 (1980) 185–97.

Goncalves, Francolino J. *L'expédition de Sennachérib en Palestine dans la littérature hébraïque ancienne.* Paris: Gabalda, 1986.

Gottwald, Norman Karol. *Studies in the Book of Lamentations.* SBT 14. Chicago: A. R. Allenson, 1954.

Gray, John. *I & II Kings: A Commentary.* OTL. Philadelphia: Westminster, 1964.

Gressmann, Hugo. "Die literarische Analyse Deuterojesajas." *ZAW* 34 (1914) 254–97.

Hanson, Paul D. *The Dawn of Apocalyptic: The Historical and Sociological Roots of Jewish Apocalyptic Eschatology.* Revised edition. Philadelphia: Fortress, 1979.

Hardmeier, Christof. *Prophetie im Streit vor dem Untergang Judas. Erzählkommunikative Studien zur Entstehungssituation der Jesaja- und Jeremiaerzählungen in II Reg 18–20 und Jer 37–40.* BZAW 187. Berlin: Walter de Gruyter, 1990.

Hayes, John Haralson, and Irvine, Stuart A. *Isaiah, the Eighth-Century Prophet: His Times and His Preaching.* Nashville: Abingdon, 1987.

Hessler, Eva. *Gott der Schöpfer: Ein Beitrag zur Komposition und Theologie Deuterojesajas.* Ph.D. diss., Greifswald, 1961.

Honor, Leo Lazarus. *Sennacherib's Invasion of Palestine. A Critical Source Study.* New York: Columbia University Press, 1926.

Huber, Friedrich. *Jahwe, Juda und die andern Völker beim Propheten Jesaja.* BZAW 137. Berlin: Walter de Gruyter, 1976.

Hutter, Manfred. *Hiskija König von Juda: Ein Beitrag zur judäischen Geschichte in assyrischer Zeit.* Grazer Theologische Studien, Bd. 6. Graz: Im Eigenverlag des Instituts für ökumenische Theologie und Patrologie an der Universität Graz, 1982.

Jenkins, A.K. "Hezekiah's Fourteenth Year: A New Interpretation of 2 Kings XVIII 13–XIX 37." *VT* 26 (1976) 284–98.

Jepsen, Alfred. *Die Quellen des Königbuches.* Halle: M. Niemeyer, 1953.

Johnson, Dan G. *From Chaos to Restoration: An Integrative Reading of Isaiah 24–27.* JSOTSup 61. Sheffield: JSOT Press, 1988.

Jones, Douglas R. "The Traditio of the Oracles of Isaiah of Jerusalem." *ZAW* 26 (1955) 226–46.

Kaiser, Otto. "Die Verkündigung des Propheten Jesaja im Jahre 701. I. Von der Menschen Vertrauen und Gottes Hilfe. Eine Studie über II Reg 18,17ff. par. Jes 36,1ff. 1. Das literar- und textkritische Problem." *ZAW* 81 (1969) 304–15.

————. *Isaiah 13–39: A Commentary.* Translated by R. A. Wilson. OTL. London: SCM, 1974.

————. *Isaiah 1–12: A Commentary.* Translated by John Bowden. OTL. Second Edition. Philadelphia: Westminster, 1983.

————. *Einleitung in das Alte Testament.* Fifth edition. Gütersloh: Gütersloher Verlagshaus Gerd Mohn, 1984.

Katzenstein, H. Jacob. "The Royal Steward (Asher 'al ha-Bayith)." *IEJ* 10 (1960) 149–54.

Kessler, Werner. *Gott geht es um das Ganze: Jesaja 56–66 und Jesaja 24–27 übersetzt und ausgelegt.* Die Botschaft des Alten Testaments 19. Stuttgart: Calwer, 1960.

Knight, G.A.F. *Isaiah.* 1965.

Köhler, Ludwig. *Deuterojesaja (Jesaja 40–55) stilkritisch untersucht.* BZAW 37. Berlin: Walter de Gruyter, 1923.

van der Kooij, Arie. "Das assyrische Heer vor den Mauern Jerusalems im Jahr 701 v. Chr." *ZDPV* 102 (1986) 93–109.

Kraus, Hans-Joachim. *Klagelieder (Threni).* BKAT 20. Neukirchen-Vluyn: Neukirchener, 1956.

Kuenen, Abraham. *Historisch-kritische Einleitung in die Bücher des Alten Testaments hinsichtlich ihrer Entstehung und Sammlung. Zweiter Teil.* Leipzig: O. R. Reisland, 1892.

Laato, Antti. "Hezekiah and the Assyrian Crisis in 701 B.C." *SJOT* 2 (1987) 49–68.

————. *Who is Immanuel? The Rise and the Foundering of Isaiah's Messianic Expectations.* Abo: Abo Akademis Forlag—Abo Academy Press, 1988.

Lack, Remi. *La symbolique du livre d'Isaïe: Essai sur l'image littéraire comme élément de structuration.* AnBib 59. Rome: Biblical Institute, 1973.

de Lagarde, Paul Anton. *Symmicta.* 2 volumes in 1. Gottingen: Dietrich, 1877–80.

van Leeuwen, Cornelius. "Sencherib devant Jerusalem." *OTS* 14 (1965) 245–72.

Liwak, Rüdiger. "Die Rettung Jerusalems im Jahr 701 v. Chr.: Zum Verhältnis und Verständnis historischer und theologischer Aussagen." *ZTK* 83 (1986) 137–66.

Lohfink, Norbert. "Die Gattung der 'Historischen Kurzgeschichte' in den letzten Jahren von Juda und in der Zeit des Babylonischen Exils." *ZAW* 90 (1978) 319–47.

Maass, Fritz. "Tritojesaja?" In *Das Ferne und Nahe Wort. Festschrift Leonhard Rost zur Vollendung seines 70. Lebensjahres am 30. November 1966 gewidmet,* ed. by Fritz Maass, 153–63. BZAW 105. Berlin: Walter de Gruyter, 1967.

Marti, K., *Das Buch Jesaja* (Kurzer Hand-Commentar zum Alten Testament, 10), Tübingen 1900

Mayes, Andrew David Hastings. *The Story of Israel between Settlement and Exile: A Redactional Study of the Deuteronomistic History.* London: SCM, 1983.

McKenzie, John L. *Second Isaiah. Introduction, Translation and Notes.* AB 20. Garden City: Doubleday, 1968.

Meade, David G. *Pseudonymity and Canon: An Investigation into the Relationship of Authorship and Authority in Jewish and Earliest Christian Tradition.* WUNT 39. Tubingen: J. C. B. Mohr (Paul Siebeck), 1986.

Melugin, Roy F. *The Formation of Isaiah 40–55.* BZAW 141. Berlin: Walter de Gruyter, 1976.

Mettinger, Tryggve N.D. "Die Ebed-Jahwe-Lieder: Ein fragwürdiges Axiom." *ASTI* 11 (1977/8) 68–76.

————. *A Farewell to the Servant Songs: A Critical Examination of an Exegetical Axiom.* Translated by Frederick H. Cryer. Lund: C. W. K. Gleerup, 1983.

Millard, Alan Ralph. "Sennacherib's Attack on Hezekiah." *TynBul* 36 (1985) 61–77.

Mowinckel, Sigmund. "Die Komposition des deuterojesajanischen Buches." *ZAW* 8 (1931) 87–112, 242–60.

————. *Prophecy and Tradition: The Prophetic Books in the Light of the Study of the Growth and History of the Tradition.* Oslo: I Kommisjon hos J. Dybwad, 1946.

Muilenburg, James. *Isaiah 40–66: Introduction and Exegesis.* (IB, 5) Nashville: Abingdon, 1956.

Norin, Stig. "An Important Kennicott Reading in 2 Kings XVIII 13." *VT* 32 (1982).

North, Christopher Richard. "The 'Former Things' and the 'New Things' in Deutero-Isaiah." In *Studies in Old Testament Prophecy: Presented to Professor Theodore H. Robinson by the Society for Old Testament Study on His Sixty-fifth Birthday,*

August 9, 1946, ed. by Harold Henry Rowley, 111–26. Edinburgh: T. & T. Clark, 1950.

Parpola, Simo. "The Murderer of Sennacherib." In *Death in Mesopotamia* (Rencontre assyriologique internationale, 26th: 1979: Copenhagen) ed. by Bendt Alster, 171–82. Mesopotamia, Copenhagen Studies in Assyriology 8. Copenhagen: Akademisk Forlag, 1980.

Pauritsch, Karl. *Die neue Gemeinde: Gott sammelt Ausgestossene und Arme (Jesaia 56–66): Die Botschaft des Tritojesaia-Buches literar-, form-, gattungskritisch und redaktionsgeschichtlich untersucht.* AnBib 47. Rome: Biblical Institute, 1971.

Pohlmann, Karl-Friedrich. *Studien zum Jeremiabuch. Ein Beitrag zur Frage nach der Entstehung des Jeremiabuches.* FRLANT 118. Göttingen: Vandenhoeck & Ruprecht, 1978.

———. "Erwägungen zum Schlusskapitel des deuteronomistischen Geschichtswerkes. Oder: Warum wird der Prophet Jeremia in 2. Kön. 22–25 nicht erwähnt?" In *Textgemäss. Aufsätze und Beiträge zur Hermeneutik des Alten Testaments. Festschrift für Ernst Würthwein in zum 70. Geburtstag*, ed. by Antonius H. J. Gunneweg and Otto Kaiser, 94–109. Göttingen: Vandenhoeck & Ruprecht, 1979.

Polan, Gregory J. *In the Ways of Justice Toward Salvation. A Rhetorical Analysis of Isaiah 56–59.* American University Studies VII.13. New York: Peter Lang, 1986.

Pope, Marvin. "Isaiah 34 in Relation to Isaiah 35, 40–66." *JBL* 71 (1952) 235–43.

Provan, Iain W. *Hezekiah and the Book of Kings: A Contribution to the Debate about the Composition of the Deuteronomistic History.* BZAW 172. Berlin: Walter de Gruyter, 1988.

Rad, Gerhard von. *Old Testament Theology II.* Translated by D.M.G. Stalker. New York: Harper & Row, 1965.

Rendtorff, Rolf. "Zur Komposition des Buches Jesaja." *VT* 34 (1984) 295–320.

———. *The Old Testament: An Introduction.* Philadelphia: Fortress, 1986.

———. "Jesaja 6 im Rahmen der Komposition des Jesajabuches." In *The Book of Isaiah*, ed. by Jacques Vermeylen, 73–82. BETL 81. Leuven: University Press, 1989.

Roberts, J.J.M. "Isaiah in Old Testament Theology." *Int* 36 (1982) 130–43.

Rowley, H.H. "The Council of Yahweh." *JTS* 45 (1944) 151–57.

Sawyer, John F.A. "Daughter of Zion and Servant of the Lord in Isaiah: A Comparison." *JSOT* 44 (1989) 89–107.

Sehmsdorf, Eberhard. "Studien zur Redaktionsgeschichte von Jesaja 56–66 (I): (Jes 65, 16b–25; 66, 1–4; 56, 1–8)." *ZAW* 84 (1972) 517–76.

Seitz, Christopher R. "The Crisis of Interpretation over the Meaning and Purpose of the Exile: A Redactional Study of Jeremiah xxi–xliii." *VT* 35 (1985) 78–97.

———. "The One Isaiah // The Three Isaiahs." In *Reading and Preaching the Book of Isaiah*, ed. by Christopher R. Seitz, 13–22. Philadelphia: Fortress, 1988.

———. "Isaiah 1–66: Making Sense of the Whole." In *Reading and Preaching the Book of Isaiah*, ed. by Christopher Seitz, 105–26. Philadelphia: Fortress, 1988.

———. "The Prophet Moses and the Canonical Shape of Jeremiah." *ZAW* 101 (1989) 3–27.

———. *Theology and Conflict: Reactions to the Exile in the Book of Jeremiah.* BZAW 176. Berlin: Walter de Gruyter, 1989.

———. "The Divine Council: Temporal Transition and New Prophecy in the Book of Isaiah." *JBL* 109 (1990) 229–46.

———. "Isaiah (First)." *AB Dictionary*, forthcoming.

Sekine, Seizo. *Die tritojesajanische Sammlung (Jes 56–66) redaktionsgeschichtlich untersucht.* BZAW 175. Berlin: Walter de Gruyter, 1989.

Shea, William H. "Sennacherib's Second Palestinian Campaign." *JBL* 104 (1985) 401–18.

Smart, James Dick. *History and Theology in Second Isaiah: A Commentary on Isaiah 35, 40–66.* Philadelphia: Westminster, 1965.

Smelik, Klaas A.D. "Distortion of Old Testament Prophecy: The Purpose of Isaiah xxvi and xxvii." *OTS* 24 (1989) 70–93.

Smend, Rudolf. *Die Entstehung des Alten Testaments.* Stuttgart: W. Kohlhammer, 1978.

Stade, Bernhard. "Miscellen. Anmerkungen zu 2 Kö. 15–21." *ZAW* 6 (1886) 156–92.

Steck, Odil Hannes. *Bereitete Heimkehr: Jesaja 35 als redactionelle Brücke zwischen dem Ersten und dem Zweiten Jesaja.* SBS 121. Stuttgart: Katholisches Bibelwerk, 1985.

———. "Tritojesaja im Jesajabuch." In *The Book of Isaiah*, ed. by Jacques Vermeylen, 361–406. BETL 81. Leuven: University Press, 1989.

Stohlmann, Stephen. "The Judean Exile after 701 B.C.E." In *Scripture in Context II: More Essays on the Comparative Method*, ed. by William W. Hallo, James C. Moyer, and Leo G. Perdue, 147–75. Winona Lake, Ind.: Eisenbrauns, 1983.

Sweeney, Marvin A. *Isaiah 1–4 and the Post-Exilic Understanding of the Isaianic Tradition* BZAW 171. Berlin: Walter de Gruyter, 1988.

Tadmor, Hayim. "Sennacherib's Campaign to Judah: Historical and Historiographical Considerations." *Zion* 50 (1985) 65–80 (Hebrew).

Talmon, Shmarjahu. "Aspects of the Textual Transmission of the Bible in the Light of Qumran Manuscripts." *Textus* 4 (1964) 107.

Torrey, Charles Cutler. *The Second Isaiah: A New Interpretation.* New York: Charles Scribner's Sons, 1928.

Vermeylen, Jacques. *Du prophète Isaïe à l'apocalyptic.* 2 vols. Paris: Gabalda, 1977–78.

———. "L'unité du livre d'Isaïe." In *The Book of Isaiah*, ed. by J. Vermeylen, 11–53. BETL 81. Leuven: University Press, 1989.

Vincent, Jean Marcel. *Studien zur literarischen Eigenart und zur geistigen Heimat von Jesaja, Kap. 40–55.* BEvT 5. Frankfurt/Bern/Las Vegas: Peter Lang, 1977.

Vuk, T. *Wiedererkaufte Freiheit. Der Feldzug Sanheribs gegen Juda nach dem Invasionsbericht 2 Kö 18.13–16.* Thesis, Pontificium Athenaeum Antonianum. Facultas Hierosolymitana Theologiae Biblicae, 1979.

von Waldow, E., *Anlass und Hintergrund der Verkündigung des Deuterojesaja,* Diss. Bonn, 1953

Wallis, Gerhard. "Gott und seine Gemeinde: Eine Betrachtung zum Tritojesaja-Buch." *TZ* 27 (1971) 182–200.

Watts, John D.W. *Isaiah 1–33.* WBC 24. Waco, Tex.: Word Books, 1985.

Weippert, Helga. "Die 'deuteronomistischen' Beurteilungen der Könige von Israel und Juda und das Problem der Redaktion der Königsbücher." *Bib* 53 (1972) 301–39.

Weiser, Artur. "Das Gotteswort für Baruch. Jer. 45 und die sogenannte Baruchbiographie." In *Glaube und Geschichte im Alten Testament und andere ausgewählte Schriften*, 321–29. Göttingen: Vandenhoeck & Ruprecht, 1961.

Wellhausen, Julius. *Die Composition des Hexateuchs und der historischen Bücher des Alten Testaments.* 4th ed. Berlin: Walter de Gruyter, 1963.

Werner, Wolfgang. *Eschatologische Texte in Jesaja 1–39. Messias, heiliger Rest, Völker.* FB 46. Wurzburg: Echter, 1982.

Westermann, Claus. *Sprache und Struktur der Prophetie Deuterojesajas.* München: Kaiser, 1964.

————. *The Praise of God in the Psalms.* Translated by Keith R. Crim. Richmond: John Knox, 1965.

Wilcox, Peter, and David Paton-Williams. "The Servant Songs in Deutero-Isaiah." *JSOT* 42 (1988) 79–102.

Wildberger, Hans. "Die Rede des Rabsake vor Jerusalem." *TZ* 35 (1979) 35–47.

Wilshire, Leland Edward. "The Servant-City: A New Interpretation of the 'Servant of the Lord' in the Servant Songs of Deutero- Isaiah." *JBL* 94 (1975) 356–67.

Würthwein, Ernst. *Die Bücher der Könige. 1 Kön. 17—2 Kön. 25.* ATD 11, 2. Göttingen: Vandenhoeck & Ruprecht, 1984.

Zimmerli, Walther. "Zur Sprache Tritojesajas." In *Gottes Offenbarung. Gesammelte Aufsätze zum Alten Testament,* 217–33. München: Chr. Kaiser, 1963.

SCRIPTURE INDEX

HEBREW BIBLE

Genesis
49   182

Exodus
3:12   94 n.135

Leviticus
13   180 n.64

Deuteronomy
32–33   182

2 Samuel
8:18   86
22:1—23:7   182

1 Kings
1:11–40   101
8:14ff.   86
11:26–40   105
17—19   105
21   105

2 Kings
8:13–16   104 n.163, 139 n.56
16   97 n.143
16:2–4   72
16:5   58, 59, 66
16:5–9   56–57, 59, 61
16:5–20   59
16:7   59, 72
16:7–8   59
16:7–9   58, 66
16:10–16   59
16:18   59
17   59, 103
17:13   188
17:13–18   189

18   70, 103
18—19   187
18—20   3 n.7, 19, 20, 26, 29, 29
                   n.85, 58, 100 n.151, 104,
                   105
18:1–2   56
18:1–7   72, 76
18:1–8   59, 60 n.45, 141, 186
18:1–12   132
18:1—20:11   159 n.25
18:1—20:17   66
18:2   53, 152
18:3   87, 182, 187
18:3–8   72
18:4   155 n.17
18:5   59, 72, 87, 88, 116, 141,
                   144, 182, 187
18:7   59, 72, 187
18:8   72
18:9   132
18:9–10   141 n.59
18:9–12   131
18:9—19:37   104, 131
18:10   141
18:10–12   141
18:13   50, 51, 52, 53, 54, 56, 57,
                   58, 59, 62, 76, 104, 132,
                   132 n.34, 141, 141 n.59,
                   144, 160
18:13–16   51, 52, 58 n.36, 59, 61,
                   62, 80 n.94, 100 n.151,
                   118, 131 n.32, 132, 132
                   n.34, 141, 143, 143 n.64,
                   144, 145
18:13–17   53, 100 n.151
18:13–18   124
18:13—19:17   49
18:13—19:37   47, 48, 51, 56, 58, 59, 60,
                   66, 102, 117, 172, 182,
                   186, 188

217

2 Kings, *cont.*,

18:13—20:19	3, 34, 97, 104, 155 n.17, 158, 182
18:14	51, 64
18:14ff.	160
18:14–16	45, 49, 50, 51–66, 80, 98, 100 n.151, 104, 105, 141, 142, 143, 144, 145, 146, 155, 155 n.17, 158, 160 161, 172, 176, 179, 183, 185 n.74, 187, 187 n.81, 190
18:14—19:7	69
18:17	50, 51, 52, 53, 54, 56, 60 n.44, 142
18:17ff.	143, 144, 160
18:17—19:9	50, 66, 67, 132
18:17—19:17	144
18:17—19:37	50, 57, 58, 59, 76, 77, 104, 128, 143 n.64, 187
18:18	124
18:19	54, 74
18:19–20	59
18:19–25	53, 72
18:20	74, 78
18:20–21	72 n.76
18:21	70, 72
18:22	54, 73
18:22ff.	72
18:25	73
18:26	73
18:27	73
18:28–35	73
18:29	54, 81 n.97
18:30	54, 73, 81 n.97
18:31	54
18:32	74, 155 n.17
18:37	54
19	68
19:1	54, 56
19:1–4	74
19:2	78
19:3	54
19:5	54, 56
19:6–7	78
19:7	50, 69, 70, 71, 74, 81, 137
19:8	69
19:8–13	56
19:9	50, 53, 54, 62, 68, 69, 70, 71, 73, 74, 78, 132, 135 n.47
19:9b–13	70
19:9–20	66
19:9b–35	66, 67
19:9–36	132 n.33
19:10	54, 56, 81 n.97
19:11	56
19:14	54, 86 n.109
19:14–19	70, 72, 74, 81

19:14–20	78
19:15	54, 74, 84 n.107, 85 n.107
19:19	85 n.107
19:20	54
19:20–21	74
19:20–37	88–94
19:21–28	68, 103
19:28b	50, 69, 70, 71, 137
19:29–31	68
19:32	66
19:32–34	71
19:32–37	70
19:33	50, 69, 70, 137
19:34–35	66
19:35	69, 70, 71, 95 n.137
19:36	66, 67
19:36–37	66, 68, 69, 70, 71
19:37	59, 62, 142
20	87
20:1	182
20:1–7	74, 155
20:1–11	45, 97, 104 n.164, 154, 158, 162, 165, 166, 169, 172, 176, 183, 185 n.74, 186, 187, 188, 190
20:1–12	160, 164 n.32
20:1–19	98, 131, 182
20:2	173 n.53
20:3	173 n.53
20:4	187
20:4–5	155, 173 n.53
20:5	162 n.31, 163, 164, 166, 170
20:6	52, 74, 163, 166
20:7	163, 165 n.37, 166, 172, 173 n.53, 187
20:8	163, 164, 164 n.34, 165 n.37, 166
20:8–11	155, 161, 187
20:9	164, 167
20:9–11	164
20:10	157, 161, 164
20:11	163, 166, 187
20:12	157
20:12–19	57, 58, 98, 100 n.151, 159, 160, 161, 176, 182–91
20:13	161
20:15	161
20:16–18	157 n.21
20:19	156 n.17, 159
21:1	100
21:1–9	59
21:1–18	101
21:3	102
21:10	187, 188
21:10–15	189
21:12–15	59
21:23–24	100 n.153, 101

22	109, 111, 202
22:3	109
22:8–10	109
22:9–10	109
22:11–13	109
22:14–17	188
22:14–20	187
22:15	109, 109 n.179
22:15–17	188
22:16–17	189
22:18–20	188
22:20	188
23:26–27	60
24	159 n.25
24–25	103 n.161
24:2	188
24:3	187
24:10–17	188
24:12–16	159
24:13	159, 187
24:20b	100 n.151
25	3 n.7, 25, 159 n.25
25:7	159
25:27–30	159, 190
Isaiah	
1	37, 77, 179, 181, 195
1—11	23, 24
1—12	3, 19, 20, 21, 27, 41
1—32	128
1—35	3, 5, 19, 24, 34, 35, 37, 38 n.3, 44, 75, 76, 77, 80, 90, 101, 129 n.26, 146, 147, 193, 194
1—39	1–22, 25, 26, 27, 28, 29, 31, 33, 34, 35, 37, 38, 39, 41, 92, 107 n.172, 119, 120, 122, 124, 129, 148, 189, 195, 199, 201, 206 n.15, 207
1—55	31
1:1	90, 90 n.125, 157 n.21
1:2–9	179 n.62
1:2–20	181
1:2–31	179
1:4	75, 179
1:4–8	60 n.44, 78
1:4–10	24
1:5	179
1:5–6	179
1:7	179
1:7–9	179
1:8	125
1:8–9	179, 181
1:9	121
1:10–18	179 n.62
1:10–31	179
1:11—2:3	24
1:18	181
1:19–20	179 n.62
1:21	179
1:21–26	179 n.62
1:21–31	181
1:27	179
1:27–28	179 n.62
1:29–31	179 n.62
2:1	90, 90 n.125
2:2	204
2:18	121
2:20	121
4:2–6	90 n.125, 91 n.126
5	92
5:7	205
5:25	201
5:26	91, 200, 201
6	27, 85, 202
6—8	60 n.42, 61, 79, 96, 164 n.32, 195
6—9	26, 90 n.122
6:1–2	85
6:1–13	197, 198
6:6	85
6:11–12	198
6:12	196
6:12–13	121
6:13	198, 198 n.3
7	97 n.143
7—8	105, 195, 196, 207
7:2	57, 195
7:3	55, 89, 90 n.121, 108, 195
7:3–13	195
7:4	195
7:9	75, 195, 196
7:10–13	195
7:11	164
7:12	57, 89, 164
7:13	89
7:14–17	89
7:16–25	195
7:17	196
8:6–7	195
8:8	125, 195
8:9–10	196
8:10	195
8:16	41, 90 n.121
8:21–22	121
8:23—9:6	40, 61
9:1–6	89, 113
9:5	112
9:6	90, 112
9:7	90
9:12	201
9:17	201
9:21	201
10—14	92
10:4	201
10:5	40, 91, 107 n.172, 125, 190, 200
10:5–11	91

Isaiah, *cont.*,

10:5–15	38 n.5
10:5–19	201
10:13–18	200
10:15	95
10:15–19	125
10:16	95, 95 n.137
10:16–19	91
10:20	75
10:20–27	90 n.125
10:32	125
10:33–34	91
11:1–10	61, 61 n.47
11:5	112
11:13	100
13	6, 195
13—23	3, 20, 189
13—27	20, 21
13—34	23, 24
13—35	19
13:1–22	189
13:1—14:22	5–6
13:17	43 n.27
14:22–27	38 n.4
14:24	91
14:24ff.	128, 184
14:24–25	43
14:24–27	38, 42 n.23, 201
14:26	201
14:26–27	201
14:32	154
17:4	95 n.137
17:12–14	38
18	77
18:1–2	76
18:1–7	75
18:4	76
20	60 n.43
20—32	60
21	6
21:1–15	6
22	77, 115 n.187, 124, 125, 195
22:1–4	60 n.44, 78, 80, 124
22:3	75
22:8	80, 110, 125
22:8b–13	60 n.43
22:11	75, 125, 201
22:12–14	124
22:15	110, 111
22:15–18	110 n.182
22:15–19	110, 111
22:15–25	60 n.43, 110, 114
22:16	110
22:18	110
22:19	111
22:20	109, 110, 112
22:20–21	112
22:20–23	110, 111, 112, 113, 114
22:20–25	109
22:21	112
22:22	112, 113, 114
22:23	112, 113
22:24	112
22:24–25	109 n.178, 110, 112
22:25	113, 121
23:13	121, 201
24—27	5, 189
24—35	3, 3 n.4, 20, 22, 48
26:1	108
27:1	108
28—31	37, 79, 129
28—32	180, 195
28—33	79
28—35	20, 21
28:1	79, 108
28:4	197
28:11–13	75
28:14	78
28:15	180
28:16	79, 80, 125, 180
28:22	180
29	77
29:1	78, 79
29:1–4	60 n.44, 77, 78
29:1–8	125 n.19
29:2	125
29:5–8	38
29:8	125
29:15	79
29:18	79
29:24	180
30—31	77
30:1	78, 79
30:1–5	60 n.44, 76, 77, 78
30:1–7	75, 76
30:2	78
30:6–8	76
30:8–14	75
30:9	79
30:15	80, 180, 181
30:15–17	76
30:16	75, 79
31:1	75, 78, 79, 88
31:1–3	60 n.44, 75, 76, 77, 78
31:3	78
31:4	60 n.44
31:5	38, 125
31:8	42 n.23, 43, 128, 184
32	79
32:1	79, 80, 108, 182
32:1–5	40, 61 n.47
32:1–8	61
32:3	79
32:5	79
32:10	79
32:15–20	79
33	23
33—35	5
33:1	79

34	23, 23 n.61, 24
34—35	15 n.32
35	18, 23, 23 nn.58, 61; 24 n.62, 103
36	51, 103, 110 n.182, 143, 174
36—37	34, 37, 38 nn.5, 8; 47–48, 57, 60 n.45, 61, 66–72, 75, 76, 77, 79, 80, 81, 87, 88, 90, 94, 97–118, 119–48, 149, 150, 151, 152, 153, 154, 156 n.17, 158, 159, 162, 171, 172–82, 183, 184, 184, nn.69,70; 185, 186
36—38	129, 151, 159, 175, 176, 177, 179, 181, 185, 186, 188, 189, 190, 191, 200, 207, 208
36—39	3, 3 n.7, 5, 18–29, 34, 35, 37–39, 42 n.23, 43–46, 48, 49, 51, 58, 60, 61, 61 n.47, 66, 68, 71, 75, 90 n.120, 97, 101, 102 n.158, 103, 104, 105, 106, 117, 127, 128, 129 n.26, 149, 151 n.7, 153, 154, 155, 155–56 n.17, 157 n.21, 158, 159, 164 n.32, 169, 182, 183, 184, 184 n.69, 185, 186 n.77, 193–96, 207, 208
36:1	52, 53, 54, 55, 79, 89, 91, 93, 108, 141, 149, 150, 152, 198
36:1–3	94, 160
36:1—37:7	69
36:1—37:38	143 n.64
36:2	52, 53, 54, 55, 57, 89, 195
36:3	108, 109, 110, 111
36:4–10	89, 94, 115
36:6	82, 135
36:7	82
36:9	135
36:10	108, 201
36:11	108, 109, 115
36:11–12	94
36:12	108
36:13–20	81, 89, 94
36:13–21	115
36:15	82
36:16	108
36:17ff.	155 n.17
36:18	86
36:18–20	55, 81, 82, 86, 87, 200
36:19	82, 82 n.100, 86, 108
36:20	108
36:21	108, 115
36:21–22	94
36:22	108, 109, 110, 111, 115
36:24	108
36:26	108
37	94, 167, 173
37—41	108
37:1	111
37:1–2	180
37:1–4	94, 108
37:1–5	115
37:1–7	111, 112
37:2	111
37:3	87, 111, 112
37:3–4	109 n.177
37:4	87, 89
37:5	111, 112, 149
37:5–7	94
37:6	149
37:6–7	87, 195
37:7	81, 81 n.95, 87, 89, 90 n.122, 94, 95, 99, 100, 135, 137, 173
37:8	69, 93, 108
37:8–9	94, 135
37:9	69, 81, 86 n.109, 87, 94, 99, 100 n.151, 114, 135, 135 n.47
37:10	81
37:10–12	87
37:10–13	81, 86, 86 n.109, 94, 200
37:10–20	174
37:11	86
37:11–13	82
37:12	86
37:12–13	81, 108
37:13	82, 82 n.100
37:14	85
37:14–20	55, 81, 83, 87, 88, 94, 117
37:14–21	72, 186
37:15	83, 85 n.107
37:16	84 n.107, 85, 86
37:16–20	82, 84, 93, 153, 167, 169 n.48, 177, 180, 200
37:17	92
37:17–20	178
37:18	83, 85, 86
37:18–19	86
37:19	83, 85, 85 n.107, 86, 94
37:20	84 n.107, 85 n.107
37:21	55, 87, 167, 177, 195
37:21–29	117
37:21–38	88–94, 117
37:22–29	81, 84, 95, 117, 167, 169 n.48, 200
37:26	68 n.70, 84, 194, 197, 198, 199, 200
37:26–27	201
37:27	197, 198
37:29	95, 100, 200
37:30	57, 167

Isaiah, *cont.*,

37:30–32   117, 195

37:31–32   44, 112

37:33–35   95, 117

37:33–36   167

37:34   95

37:35   44, 45, 80, 88, 149, 149 n.1, 173, 175, 198, 199

37:36   69, 95 n.137, 173, 178

37:36–38   55, 81, 95, 117, 167, 174, 175

37:37   95, 99, 100

37:37–38   69, 95, 173

37:38   81, 81 n.95, 99, 100, 114, 173, 178

38   61, 68, 75, 87, 88, 90, 96, 97, 100 n.150, 103, 104, 104 n.164, 118, 121, 122, 123, 127, 129 n.24, 148, 149–66, 171, 172–82, 183, 184, 184 n.69, 185, 186, 191, 204

38—39   97, 101 n.154, 159, 182, 183, 184

38:1   87, 88, 167, 170, 205

38:1–8   53 n.26, 87, 123, 167, 169, 170, 171

38:1–22   45, 186

38:2   168

38:2–3   88, 167, 186

38:3   87, 204

38:4   87

38:4–6   88, 167

38:5   87, 88, 170

38:5–6   168, 195

38:6   87, 167, 169, 170, 199

38:7   167, 169

38:7–8   87, 88, 167, 168, 195

38:8   168

38:9   135, 167

38:9–20   168, 169–71, 204

38:9–22   123, 183

38:10–15   168

38:10–34   167

38:11   204

38:16   168

38:17   168, 204

38:19   168

38:20   184

38:21   170 n.49, 171, 190

38:21–22   49, 166–69, 170, 170 n.49, 171

38:22   170, 184

39   27, 61, 68, 90, 96, 97, 98, 100 n.150, 103, 104, 118, 121, 122, 122 n.13, 123, 127, 129, 129 n.24, 146, 148, 149, 151 n.5, 152, 153, 154, 156, 157, 158, 159, 160, 183, 184, 184

    nn.69, 70; 185, 186, 186 n.77, 188, 190

39:1   149, 151, 157

39:1–4   158

39:1–8   57, 176, 182–91

39:2   156

39:5–7   44, 45, 151, 156, 157, 157 n.21, 158, 190

39:5–8   152

39:6   159

39:7   97, 122, 122 n.13

39:8   20, 105 n.167, 151, 156, 156 n.17, 159

39:9   135

40   23, 23 n.61, 27, 27 n.75, 38 n.7, 121, 151, 199

40—48   42, 199, 200, 201, 202, 203, 206

40—55   1–22, 24, 26, 26 nn.70, 71; 27, 28, 28 n.84, 30–35, 37, 38, 39, 39 n.10, 42, 43, 44, 68, 75, 84, 86, 91, 92, 104, 117, 120, 121, 122, 123, 126, 129, 156, 176, 186, 188, 189, 191, 194, 195, 205, 207, 208

40—62   18

40—66   1–22, 24 n.62, 27 n.73, 29, 38, 41, 43

40:1   202

40:1–2   203

40:1–8   197

40:1–11   198, 199, 200, 202, 207

40:2   45, 190

40:3   190

40:3–8   199

40:5   191

40:6   197, 198, 199

40:6–7   198

40:7   199

40:8   42 n.24, 198

40:9   147, 205

40:9–11   197, 199

40:11   206

40:18   200

40:18–20   85

40:20   84

40:21   199

40:21–31   200

40:22   85

40:25   200

40:28   84

40:27—41:4   42

41:1   200

41:2   42, 205

41:4   200

41:5–7   85

41:5–9   200

41:8   203

41:9	203
41:21	200
41:21–22	201
41:21–29	42, 200
41:22	42, 91, 191, 199
41:22–23	84
41:23	201
41:24	85
41:25	42, 43 n.27, 205
41:26	91 n.128, 200
41:26–29	200
41:27	199 n.5, 200, 201
41:28–29	200
41:29	85
42:9	91, 199
42:16	31
42:17	85
42:18–19	31
42:22	205
43:5–6	205
43:6	205
43:8	31, 200
43:8ff.	83 n.102
43:8–13	200
43:9	200, 201
43:10	200, 201, 203
43:10–13	200
43:11	84
43:14	205
43:15–21	42
43:18	43, 91, 91 n.128, 199, 200
43:22–24	205
44:1	203
44:2	203
44:6	84, 200
44:6–8	42, 200
44:7	84, 199, 200, 201
44:8	84, 91 n.128, 200, 201
44:9–20	85
44:18	31
44:20	200
44:21	203
44:24	85
44:26	45, 200, 205
44:28	5 n.10, 205
45:1	199
45:1–7	42
45:5	84
45:5ff.	83 n.102
45:6	84
45:20	85
45:20–21	200
45:21	84, 91 n.128, 199, 201
45:22	84
46:5	200
46:5–7	85
46:8–11	200
46:9	91, 91 n.128, 199, 200
46:10	199, 200
46:11	205
48:3	43, 199, 200
48:6	91, 199
48:6–8	201
48:7	91 n.128, 191, 199
48:12–13	200
48:14	200
48:16	202
49—55	127, 147, 205, 206
49:1–6	202, 206
49:3	203
49:5	202
49:7—55:11	203
49:7—55:13	202
49:12	205
49:13	203
49:14–26	147
49:15	203, 204
49:18	203
49:19	203
49:21	203, 206
49:22	205
50:1	191, 203
50:1–3	147, 203, 204
50:3–9	206
50:14—55:13	202
51:1—52:10	147
51:3	203, 206
51:18–20	203
51:19	203
51:20	203
51:21	203
51:22	203
52:7	199 n.5
52:9	203
52:13	204
52:13—53:12	203, 204
53:1–2	204
53:5	204
53:8	204
53:9	204
53:10—54:1	204
53:11—54:2	204
53:12	204, 205
53:12—54:3	204
54	147
54:1	203
54:1–17	204
54:3	204
54:5–6	203
54:6	203
54:10	203
54:11	203
54:13	203
55	147
55:1–13	205
55:11	42 n.24, 198
55:13	198, 206
56—66	1–22, 27, 39, 205, 207

Jeremiah

MT

1—6	145
1:1—25:13a	21
2:4–45	24
4:5–8	125
7:16	108
7:16–20	145
11:14	108
15:1	108
19:1–15	105
21—24	105
25:11	5 n.10
25:12	5 n.10
25:13–38	21
26	105, 106, 106 n.169
26—35	21
26—45	25, 26
26:10	105
26:16–19	106, 120
26:17	105
26:18	105, 106
26:19	105, 106 n.169, 109 n.175, 114
26:20–23	102 n.156
26:20–24	105
27:1–11	107 n.172
29:7	133 n.39
29:10	5 n.10
36	105, 109, 111, 113, 175
36—45	20
36:10	109
36:12	109
36:14–19	109 n.176
36:16	109
36:20	109
36:21	109
36:24	108
36:25	109
36:26	109
37—39	105
37—40	99 n.148, 106 n.169, 132
37—43	106, 116
37—44	174, 175
37—45	102 n.156
37:2	133 n.39
37:5	100 n.151, 132
37:8	133
37:13	133 n.39
38:2	133
38:17	133 n.39
38:17–23	133
41:1–3	133 n.39
45	174, 174 n.55, 175 n.56, 180
45:1	174, 175
45:1–5	113, 174, 175
46—51	21, 24, 175
52	3, 3 n.7, 20, 22, 25, 25 n.66, 26, 29, 48, 101, 104, 117
52:31–34	20

LXX

1:1—25:13	21, 23
25:13—32:38	21
25:14—32:38	23
33—42	21
33—51	23, 25
43—51	20

Ezekiel

1—24	21
16	203
16:1–7	204
17:15	100 n.151, 133 n.37
17:16	133 n.37
25—32	21
33—48	21
40—48	22, 24 n.62

Hosea

14	126

Amos

1—2	22 n.56
7	105
9:11–15	126

Jonah

2:1	170
2:1–9	168
2:2–3	170
2:2–9	170

Micah

3:1	105
3:5	105
3:7	105
3:9	105
3:12	105, 120
4—5	22 n.56
4:1—5:15	126

Zephaniah

3:9–20	24

Zechariah

1:8–11	199
1:8–17	199
1:12	199
8:12–13	199

Psalms

16	168 n.45
18	171 n.52
22	168
31	168
34	171 n.52

41   168
56—60   168 n.45
82   200
82:5   200

Job
1:1   178
2:7   178

Proverbs
25:1   115 n.186

Lamentations
1:1–9   203
1:2   191, 205
1:8   205
1:9   205
1:14   203, 205
1:16   205
1:17   205
1:20   205
1:21   205
2:13   205
3   204
3:1   204

Daniel
2—6   96 n.139
5   96 n.139

Ezra
1:1   4, 5 n.10

2 Chronicles
28   97 n.143
29—32   97 n.143, 160
32   98
32:24–26   158, 160, 161
32:25   157
32:26   157
32:31   157, 157 n.20
32:32   5, 5 n.11, 18 n.44, 23
                   n.61, 157 n.21
36:12   4, 5 n.10
36:22   5 n.10

APOCRYPHA
Sirach
48   97 n.143, 98
48:17–22   160 n.28
48:17–25   5 n.11
48:19–20   160 n.28, 177
48:20   160 n.28
48:22–25   160 n.28
48:23   119

MISHNA
Baba Batra
14   115
15   25 n.64, 115

A U T H O R   I N D E X

Ackroyd, P.R., 3 nn. 5, 7; 7 n.18, 15 n.31, 19, 21, 25–30, 34, 39, 40, 41, 43, 44, 55 n.30, 57, 58 n.39, 60 nn.43, 45; 61 nn.46, 47; 68, 71 n.75, 89, 91, 96 n.141, 97, 103, 104, 106 n.168, 119, 120, 121, 123, 129 n.26, 149 n.2, 150, 151, 153, 155, 156, 157, 158, 160, 161, 164 n.32, 165 n.37, 182, 183, 184, 185, 187, 190 n.86, 197 n.2, 209

Barrick, W.B., 60 n.42, 209
Barstad, H.W., 9 n.,25, 205, 209
Barth, H., 3 n.3, 6 nn.14, 15; 17 n.41, 19, 23, 24, 25, 28, 31, 35, 38, 40, 41, 49, 61, 67 n.66, 101, 102, 120 n.6, 131, 134 n.40, 193, 195, 198 n.3, 209
Becker, J., 26, 27 n.72, 209
Beebe, H.K., 32 n.93, 209
Begrich, J., 8 n.21, 16 n.36, 170 n.49, 208, 209
Bogaert, P.-M., 3 n.3, 6 nn.14, 15; 22, 23 n.60, 24, 25 n.64, 41, 193, 209
Bright, J., 62 nn.51, 52; 63 n.56, 66 n.63, 75 nn.82, 83; 209
Brinkman, J.A., 150 n.4, 209
Brueggeman, W., 26, 29, 41 n.20, 209
Budde, K.F.R., 16 n.35
Bunsen, C., 9 n,25, 205
Burney, C.F., 54, 209

Childs, B.S., 3 n.7, 7 n.18, 27, 29, 30, 32, 34, 35, 38 n.5, 41 n.20, 42, 43 n.27, 45, 47 n.2, 50, 52 n.20, 53 n.23, 54, 55, 56, 60 n.43, 62, 66, 67 n.67, 68, 70 n.74, 71 n.75, 78, 81 n.96, 83 nn.102, 103; 86, 87 n.112, 88 n.114, 89 n.119, 96 n.141, 124 n.17, 125 nn.18, 19, 20; 135, 138, 143 n.64, 210
Clements, R., 2 n.2, 3 n.7, 7 n.18, 15 n.31, 27–35, 38, 39, 40 n.13, 41–44, 45, 47 n.2, 50, 53 n.23, 58 n.38, 60 nn.44, 45; 61, 62,

65, 67 nn.66, 67; 68, 71, 72 n.77, 75 n.81, 76, 77, 78, 80, 83, 89, 96 n.141, 98, 101, 109 n.178, 119, 120, 121, 122, 124 n.16, 127–29, 133, 134 n.40, 135, 138, 140, 147 n.66, 153, 154, 160, 172, 183, 184, 185, 189, 198 n.3, 201 n.6, 207, 210
Clifford, R.J., 6 n.16, 210
Cohen, C., 47 n.2, 210
Cross, F., 197, 210

Dietrich, W., 75 n.82, 210
Dion, P.E., 45, 46, 47 n.2, 48 n.4, 50 nn.13,15; 51, 53 n.23, 55, 60 n.42, 62 nn.51, 54; 67 nn.66, 67; 68, 71, 80 n.94, 81, 82, 83, 83 n.109, 88, 89 n.119, 90 n.124, 93, 96 nn.140, 141; 98, 99 n.147, 101, 172, 210
Döderlein, 2
Donner, H., 75 n.82
Driver, S.R., 8 n.22, 11 n.28, 16 n.36, 210
Duhm, B., 1–29, 33, 34, 38, 39, 41, 44, 48, 168 n.45, 170, 193, 194, 205, 210

Eaton, J.H., 31 n.92, 210
Eichhorn, J.G., 2, 25 n.64
Elliger, K., 10 n.26, 210
Ewald, G.H., 9 n.25, 16 n.35, 205

Fohrer, G., 15 n.32, 20 n.49, 40 n.14, 210
Friedlander, M., 179 n.61, 210

Gammie, J.G., 32 n.93, 210
Gesenius. F.H.W., 2, 3 n.6, 25, 45, 48, 49, 50, 51, 53, 54, 58, 61, 102, 103, 106, 144, 168 n.45, 210
Geyer, J.B., 53 n.25, 63, 210
Gitay, Y., 16 n.36, 207, 210
Goncalves, F.J., 38 n.8, 45, 46, 47 n.2, 50, 52 n.20, 53 n.23, 54, 55 n.31, 56 n.33, 61, 62,

65 n.61, 66, 67 n.66, 71, 75 nn.81, 82; 76, 77, 80, 81 nn.95, 97; 84 n.106, 93, 96 n.141, 98, 118, 128, 172, 210
Gottwald, N.K., 204 n.12, 210
Gray, J., 152 n.8, 211
Gressmann, H., 8 n.21, 16 n.36, 211

Hanson, P.D., 6 n.16, 10 n.26, 17 n.39, 211
Hardmeier, C., 45, 46, 51 n.17, 58 n.36, 59 n.41, 61, 99 n.148, 100 n.151, 104, 105, 106 nn.169, 170; 107 n.172, 109 n.175, 115 n.187, 116 n.189, 118, 120 n.6, 131–46, 160, 172, 176, 184 n.70, 211
Hayes, J.H., 17 n.40, 37 n.1, 75 n.82, 211
Hessler, E., 8 n.20, 211
Hölscher, G., 9 n.25
Honor, L.L., 47 n.2, 211
Huber, F., 75 n.82, 211
Hutter, M., 75 n.82, 211

Irvine, S.A., 17 n.40, 37 n.1, 211

Jenkins, A.K., 47 n.2, 52 n.21, 211
Jepsen, A., 54, 58, 211
Johnson, D.G., 189 n.84, 211
Jones, D.R., 7 n.18, 27 n.72, 29 n.87, 31 n.92, 90 n.125, 211

Kaiser, O., 3 n.3, 5 n.12, 6 n.14, 13 n.30, 19, 20, 35, 37 n.1, 47 n.2, 50 n.15, 77, 80, 90 n.125, 109 n.178, 120 n.6, 129–31, 134, 135, 140, 160, 165 nn.38, 40; 168 n.45, 172, 173, 211
Katzenstein, H.J., 110 nn.180, 181; 211
Kessler, W., 17 n.39, 211
Knight, G.A.F., 6 n.16
Köhler, L., 8 n.21, 16 n.36, 211
Kooij, A. van de, 47 n.2, 211
Kraus, H.-J., 204 n.13, 211
Kuenen, A., 54, 211

Laato, A., 47 n.2, 52 n.19, 53 n.26, 55, 67 n.67, 68, 69, 71, 76, 77, 89 n.120, 96 n.141, 98 n.144, 212
Lack, R., 7 n.18, 16, 19, 212
Lagarde, P.A.de, 27 n.72, 212
Leeuwen, C.van. 47 n.2, 212
Liwak, R., 47 n.2, 212
Lohfink, N., 116 n.189, 212

Maass, F., 17 n.39, 212
Marti, K., 9, 25
Mayes, A.D.H., 102 n.158, 212
McKenzie, J.L., 15 n.32, 198, 212
Meade, D.G., 7 n.18, 27, 28, 29, 41, 42 nn.24, 25; 119, 121 n.8, 124, 125, 212
Melugin, R.F., 7 n.18, 8 n.20, 15, 16 nn.36, 37; 27, 29, 30, 32, 34, 35, 39, 43, 44, 68, 89 n.116, 103, 121 n.8, 122 n.13, 125, 126, 159 n.26, 186 n.77, 197 n.2, 212

Mettinger, T.N.D., 8 n.20, 16 n.37, 212
Millard, A.R., 65 n.60, 76 n.84, 212
Miller, J.M., 75 n.82
Mowinckel, S., 8, 9 n.25, 16 n.36, 31, 205, 212
Muilenburg, J., 6 n.16, 16 n.36, 207

Norin, S., 52 nn.18, 19; 54, 121
North, C.R., 6 n.16, 29 n.87, 212
Noth, M., 75 n.82

Parpola, S., 81 n.95, 99 n.149, 212
Paton-Williams, D., 16 n.37, 203 n.10, 214
Pauritsch, K., 10 n.26, 17n.39, 212
Pohlmann, K.-F., 26 n.66, 135 n.43, 189 n.82, 212
Polan, G.J., 17 n.39, 213
Pope, M., 15 n.32, 213
Provan, I.W., 51 n.17, 57, 58 n.35, 60 n.42, 102 n.158, 118, 160, 161, 172, 187, 213

Rad, G. von, 31, 88 n.113, 213
Rendtdorff, R., 2 n.2, 7 n.18, 8 n.20, 16, 27, 28, 29, 197 n.2, 213
Roberts, J.J.M., 42 n.26, 213
Rowley, H.H., 197, 213

Sawyer, J.F.A., 202 n.9, 213
Sehmsdorf, E., 17 n.39, 213
Seitz, C.R., 2 n.2, 3 nn.5, 6, 7; 7 n.18, 10 n.26, 24 n.62, 26 n.66, 27, 35 n.94, 43 n.27, 45 n.37, 46 n.40, 63 nn.57, 58; 74 n.80, 79 n.93, 100 n.153, 106 n.170, 107 n.171, 108 nn.173, 174; 113 n.185, 127 n.21, 133 n.39, 135 n.43, 159 n.25, 174 n.55, 175 n.57, 189 n.82, 190 n.87, 197 n.2, 198 n.4, 199 n.5, 202 n.8, 206 n.17, 213
Sekine, S., 10 n.26, 17 n.39, 213
Shea, W.H., 47 n.2, 62 n.51, 213
Smart, J.D., 15 n.32, 205, 213
Smelik, K.A.D., 3 nn.6, 7; 5 n.11, 26, 29 n.85, 39, 45, 46, 48, 53 n.24, 55, 57, 58 n.40, 60, 61, 66–71, 80, 81, 83, 86 n.110, 89 n.116, 90, 94, 96, 97, 98, 103, 104, 117, 121 nn.8, 9; 129, 133 n.40, 136–40, 149 n.2, 150, 151 nn.5, 7; 153 n.11, 154, 158, 159, 164, 165 n.37, 172, 175 n.58, 184, 185, 188, 194, 213
Smend, R., 3 n.5, 5 n.10, 24 n.62, 213
Stade, B., 45, 50, 51, 53, 54, 55, 58, 62, 66, 67, 69, 70, 71, 81, 135, 136, 137, 168 nn.45, 46; 213
Steck, O.H., 2 n.2, 3 nn.3, 5; 5 nn.11, 12; 6 nn.14, 15; 7 n.18, 15 n.32, 16, 18, 19, 23, 24, 25, 41, 193, 213
Stohlmann, S., 63 n.58, 214
Sweeney, M.A., 7 n.18, 27, 28, 29, 34, 121 n.8, 155 n.17, 158, 160, 179 n.62, 180 n.64, 185 n.75, 186, 214

Tadmor, H., 47 n.2, 214
Talmon, S., 136 n.47, 214
Thiel, 175 n.56
Torrey, C.C., 7 n.17, 8 n.21, 15 n.32, 43, 205, 206 n.15, 214

Vermeylen, J., 2 n.2, 3 n.3, 6 nn.14, 15; 7 n.18, 20, 21, 22, 23 n.60, 24, 26, 29 n.85, 35, 41, 131, 193, 214
Vincent, J.M., 16 n.37, 205, 214
Vuk, T., 65 n.61, 214

Waldow, E. von, 16 n.36
Wallis, G., 17 n.39, 214
Watts, J.D.W., 140 n.58, 214
Weippert, H., 60 n.42, 214

Weiser, A., 175 n.56, 214
Wellhausen, J., 54, 67 n.67, 68, 214
Werner, W., 120 n.6, 214
Westermann, C., 6 n.16, 8 n.20, 10 n.26, 16 n.36, 168 n.45, 169 n.47, 198, 207 n.18, 214
Wilcox, P., 16 n.37, 203 n.10, 214
Wildberger, H., 45, 47 n.2, 48 n.6, 52 n.20, 53, 60, 93 nn.132, 133; 96 n.141, 105, 109 n.178, 110 nn.179, 182; 155, 156, 158, 162 n.31, 164 n.35, 165, 166, 170, 177 n.59, 178 n.60, 186 n.78, 198 n.3, 214
Wilshire, L.E., 204 n.11, 214
Würthwein, E., 165 n.40, 173 n.53, 214

Zimmerli, W., 17 n.39, 214